The Lord shall preserve

thy going out and

thy coming in

from this time forth,

and even for evermore.

Psalm 121:8

Design: Paula J. Bogert, David Ashton and Associates

Printing: Schneidereith and Sons Printing

Paper: Potlatch Northwest Dull

Typeface: Bembo and Trajan

Executive Editors:

George C. O'Connell '35

Penelope Partlow

Copy Editor:

Sarah D. Bunting

St. Paul's School

Brooklandville, Maryland 21022

St. Paul's School is a college-preparatory school with an Episcopal tradition for boys and girls in pre-first through fourth grades, and all boys in fifth through twelfth grades. St. Paul's welcomes and encourages applications from students without regard of race, color, religion, or national origin, and does not discriminate in its educational policies, financial aid programs, or school-administered extracurricular programs.

In preparing this history, the author collected and compiled the names, dates, and historical notes to the best of his ability. On behalf of the School, the author apologizes in advance for any factual inaccuracies, misspellings, or typographical errors. Please send any corrections to:

Publications Office

St. Paul's School

P.O. Box 8100

Brooklandville, MD 21022

WE HAVE KEPT THE FAITH

the first

150 YEARS

of the BOYS' SCHOOL

of ST. PAUL'S PARISH

1849
1999

by

ANGELO OTTERBEIN '91

St. Paul's School
Brooklandville, Maryland

ACKNOWLEDGMENTS

For the early history, the editors who provided shape and direction to what began as a mess: Charlie Mitchell '73, trustee Dr. David Hein '72, the Very Reverend William McKeachie, Dr. Garner Ranney of the Episcopal Diocese, who is no less than a blessing to the archives and to church and parish history, and the Reverend Frank Strasburger, who actually was the very first to suggest the title (followed by Robert Hallett).

Welby Loane and Diane Boynton: thank you for bringing your father Mr. Hamilton so close. To Dorsey Myers Donnelly for helping me to understand her father, Howdy. To Emily Durham and Carter Bond for sharing stories of their father Appy Middleton. To Donald McDorman '33 for his incredible stories and passion for the School. To Jack Ordeman for your reading and re-reading, and for the pictures; thanks to Mary Ordeman for her art, to their daughter, Jessica, for the picture of her dad.

And so many advisors and readers: Kirk Evans, Jeanne Shreeve, Ann Stellmann, Mona Miller, Winnie Flattery, W. James Price IV '42, Geordie Mitchell '78, Rick Collins, George Mitchell '44, John Thorpe, Bill Bassett, Chris Dorrance, Mitch Tullai, Lynn Rauch, Tom Longstreth, John and Anne Patterson, Derek Stikeleather, Mitch Whiteley, John Morton '68, Michael Schuler '76, Penny Witter, Rick Brocato, Jamie Andrew, Cliff Low '65, Elke and William Durden, Steven Stenersen '78, Kevin Cronin, Brian Abbott '85, Skip Darrell '60, Howard Schindler, Desi McNelis, and Carolynn Bell. Special thanks to Barbara Mills, who read this about 100 times.

Cathy McAuliffe is the most organized hero around; Betty Jean Tyler, an archivist who in her spare time makes an Upper School run, along with Robin Webster; Linda Knox, for reading so much and throwing parties all year long; wonderwoman Judi Meigs; Kit Slafkosky; Ellen Spicer; Jennifer Peterson; Claire Acey; others in the mansion who took an interest in what (and whatever it was) I was doing: Susan Lang, Barbara Hoey, Donna Reid. At the Parish office, Maisie Heil could strong-arm a copier faster I could hit start. The Reverend David Cobb and Richard Tomlinson were a tremendous help at the Church.

Others who were supportive and who helped in important ways were James Tuvin '52; the Reverend Michael Wallens; Pete O'Connell; Wade Chilcoat '91; Clifford Lull '78; Douglass Forsyth '56; Carol Pieper and her children; Laurie Lijoi; Malcolm Parker '49; Thom Hook '41; Rodney Rice; Lee Mueller; Karen Levin; Kirk Unruh '66; Florian Svitak; the extraordinary author Ann Tracy; and Iris and Nancy at Cafe Hon, who know how best to keep mugs full of tea and coffee. I'd thank loyal friend Brendon Hunt '92, but I'm still busy interpreting the epilogue. Sarah D. Bunting, my colleague: this (pen) cap's off to you; she found the dot where there should be a semicolon. Special thanks to Edward Brown for many of the photos.

To Paula Bogert, the designer, who is why this book is so beautiful. Many thanks to Scott '81 and Wilbur Schneidereith '83 at Schneidereith and Sons for printing and assembling this book—his shop also turns 150 in 1999. Gratitude to James Silvan, the patient and diligent gardener who put this index together.

And George. And Penny. And Michal. O'Connell, Partlow, and Makarovich. Memory, Style, and Character. Fastidious and bold. Earnest, hard-working, and honest. Food and drink. Dinner at my house. You have been my right arm.

Sincere gratitude to headmaster Robert Hallett for his complete faith in me to tackle this project and for letting me run with it.

To my parents who have been and are always with me every step of the way.

TABLE OF CONTENTS

Forward

W hile I was a student at the Episcopal Academy, sacred studies was required fare. I was a dim student but recall an observation of Jesus, found in St. Matthew, chapter nine, about how unwise it was to pour new wine into old bottles. Jesus observes for his disciples that men do not put new wine into old bottles (really wineskins) lest the skin break; instead they put new wine into new bottles and so preserve both. These comments from Jesus, while confusing to the disciples, were preparation for a new covenant between man and God.

Headmaster Robert W. Hallett

In 1849, Dr. William E. Wyatt created a new bottle, a covenant if you will, for Baltimore's educational consideration—namely, The Boys' School of St. Paul's Parish—pouring into it the vintage that sustains us even now. Of the numerous examples of schooling extant in the country, few can lay claim to such a rich and variegated story as that of St. Paul's School, whose humble genesis, steeped for noble purpose, could not have foreseen the multifaceted, vigorous school we know today.

The Gospel reference may seem a strange beginning for the introduction of our history. For me it gives foundation for an obvious question: has the vintage sustained its integrity? It is clear that Dr. Wyatt began his vineyard with a strong and mighty root that nourishes us even today. Annually, for 150 years, it has produced vintage wine aged within the oaken crucible of School and Church. True, each year has yielded a different flavor, befitting nature's whims and the vintner's expertise. Yet, there has been quality, consistent with the first harvest.

Imbedded in Dr. Wyatt's vision and alchemy was the fundamental recognition that in addition to classical academic training, spiritual life would see an equal, if not greater measure of attention. Rectors, vestrymen, headmasters, trustees, and faculty were resolute in the preservation of a vision—keeping faith with the expressed mission of the School.

This remains the eternal challenge for the School, beset by the insatiable secularism of today. Our wineskin has traveled (thankfully intact!), but our roots are still firmly grounded. Like St. Paul's Second Letter to Timothy, we continue to fight the good fight, our course is not finished, we are keeping the faith.

We offer our history for all to see, unvarnished and proud. Our debt to Angelo Otterbein '91 cannot be measured.

Robert W. Hallett
Headmaster

Preface

George S. Hamilton (headmaster, 1932-1944)
with his wife, Vyvyanna Sanz, in 1932.

Here is a picture of headmaster George Hamilton and his wife Vyvyanna just after they were secretly married in 1932. They are on their way to begin the first of 12 years at The Boys' School of St. Paul's Parish in Mt. Washington, Maryland; they had not heard of St. Paul's before.

Of the thousands of pictures I have looked at over two years—in the archives, in dog-eared scrapbooks, in laminated newspaper clippings—this one is my favorite. Which might seem odd. It's a faded snapshot. There are no students cheering or campus buildings in the background. Nor had George even become headmaster.

I graduated from St. Paul's School, but this entire history is of a school I never knew existed. Even the years when I was there. Even now. The shapes and lines of its story have only become clearer after a lot of listening, looking, interviews and newsletters and minute books, semi-consequential stories told semi-recklessly over an empty cocktail glass. This 150-year history—seemingly finite—is, to be sure, endless.

This history is people. Who worry and plan, love and fight, plan and grow wiser and more wary, thoughtful, hopeful or concerned. Here is a rector, the Reverend William McKeachie, who writes in this book about the Church; there Jack Ordeman, a former headmaster, who considers a Christian education. See Mitch Tullai, who has found truth and education in history, helmets and fields, Tom Longstreth, who has found truth in books and basketball courts, and both who have found truth in the discovery—and re-discovery—of teaching, learning, and opening minds. They are heroes. Michael Schuler '76 will tell you about Middle Schoolers most of us mortals will never understand. Barbara Mills revels in the Lower School. There's Michal Makarovich who will describe and defend long hair, the arts, ideas, and who helps us see life more clearly. Brendon Hunt '92 offers enlightenment in a mission statement. And students: Emily Fusting '09, Harrison Davis '03, Bill Launder '99. They are in here. They will give you a hint. And yes, there is a history in these pages, organized thematically in an expected triad—spirit, body, and mind—which mapped well to the School's focus over 150 years. You will find lacrosse and choir, film and theater, classroom and buildings, victories, change, and people, and people, and people.

So. How to title it. *We have kept the faith*. Hopeful. Recognizable. Resolute. Of Saint Paul. But that doesn't cut it really.

It rang true, for one, because in our relentlessly secular world, faith is an even more critical idea than it has been in the past. But I personally never understood what faith meant. I'm not saying I do now. Here, teetering on the millennial pirate's plank in 1999, we should and can have faith. But, (gasp) so what? And, (gasp, gasp) *in* what?

There arose another potential shortfall with the title. In the 1872 Parochial Charities report of St. Paul's Parish are the words: "Faith, if it hath not works, is dead." For to believe is one thing, but to *act*—earnestly and decisively—upon one's faith is something quite different. Sure, we have kept the faith—all great efforts require it—but that's not all we should do.

Meanwhile, this book has had me thinking about the relationships among faith, God, and patterns. Patterns like mountaintops, trees, crowds, cities, and the stock market. We all see and are a part of these patterns—beautiful, clearly ordered, infinite. This history has a pattern—an intricate and wonderfully unpredictable result of success, error, and uncertainty. In an earlier preface, I claimed that if you believe in, and if you see these patterns, then you must believe in the divine, and that *if* you believe in the divine, then you must believe in God, in whatever shape, form, and gender you like. It occurred to me that perhaps, just perhaps, we can have faith in God because for the first time in the history of mankind, there is evidence—*clear* evidence for the common wayward soul like myself, who looks out from the doorstep of the twenty-first century overwhelmed by too much of everything. God has given us a way to see these patterns, a doorway to the divine. This history of St. Paul's may just be door number one.

So why this picture? Because it is the best image I can find of someone who so clearly looks with faith to a future that cannot be directed, but in which we can certainly play a part. I also chose it because Hamilton here epitomizes a spirit that so many have tried to articulate about St. Paul's over the years. And there they stand, articulating it so gracefully and easily. Lastly, I chose this picture, well … I must be honest. I chose it simply because it makes me happy.

Please enjoy this ride.

Angelo F. Otterbein '91
May 1, 1999

"...hool is no longer
...eriment. It has proved
...ulness ... It has
...the confidence of our
...ople. It has a name
...them, and its privileges
...ght after from afar.
...y of its weakness seems
...d it is now in a fair
...on to carry on its work
...re effectively than in
...t ... The School as
...h school is unique.
...ot its counterpart
...country."

...erend John S. B. Hodges, 1905

by Emily Fusting, Class of 2009

I am in the fourth grade at the St. Paul's Lower School, and I go to chapel twice a week. In chapel, we don't just say prayers and hear stories. We have demonstrations which help us to understand what these stories are trying to teach us.

There are seats on both sides of the Chapel that face each other. The seats are higher up in the back so everyone can see. I like it this way, because you aren't looking at someone's back. Sometimes the chaplain picks volunteers, and they act out the story. This gives us a chance to learn, have fun, and experience God's message all at the same time.

Students in the fourth grade can sign up to be on the vestry. The vestry lights the candles, carries the cross, and helps out during the service.

There is a stained glass window at the front and at the back of the Chapel. When I sit in Chapel and look up at these windows, they make me feel small but important in God's eyes.

The Chapel seems to be the heart of St. Paul's.

OPPOSITE: Choristers and brothers T. Benson Musgrave '29 (left) and Arthur Musgrave '27.

PREVIOUS SPREAD: The earliest graduation photo of The Boys' School of St. Paul's Parish, taken in the late 1800s. The students and their master were not identified.

NOTE TO READER: *This Lower School piece is the first of three student contributions which supplement essays at the beginning and end of each chapter. These essays try to articulate in a more personal and reflective way the essence and character of St. Paul's School and use multiple approaches to address the often-stated—but less often considered—educational paradigm built around central tenets of cultivating the mind, the body, and the spirit. Ultimately, their words also speak to what has transpired over the course of 150 years. The history of the School runs in between these essays.*

The Good and the Clever at St. Paul's

by the Very Reverend William N. McKeachie

Many holy men are altogether ignorant of the liberal arts,
and some who know the liberal arts are not holy.

St. Augustine of Hippo

Morals have no basis but religion.

The Reverend Dr. William E. Wyatt,

VIII Rector of St. Paul's Parish

Founder of The Boys' School of St. Paul's Parish

Already in the fourth century St. Augustine understood the dilemma. Dr. Wyatt, in the early nineteenth century, proposed the plan. Now, at the turn of the twenty-first century and a new millennium, St. Paul's bears witness to the fruition, but also to the continuing crusade.

The thesis of this essay is that the best basis of secondary education in the liberal arts, whatever the century, is "holiness," or at least what *The Book of Common Prayer* calls "true religion and virtue."

It is perhaps also the case that the best basis of "history" is "stories," and I only wish there were more old-timers left to tell stories of the days when students were bused to Old St. Paul's Church downtown, and the lacrosse team (famous for its sportsmanship) marched to Gilman across the Jones Falls from Rogers Avenue, and day students were the exception to the regimen. In those days, or so I have been told, there were giants, and they all knew the Apostles' Creed by heart.

There are surely many "stories," and indeed more than one "history," that could be offered about St. Paul's School and its evolution from a small urban mission (of a Church with a social conscience) into a major Middle Atlantic college-preparatory institution (still claiming its Church affiliation) 150 years later.

My own fifteen-year perspective reflects one of the continuities (albeit waxing and waning and waxing again) of that evolution: the Church. Specifically, the Episcopal Church. More generally, Anglican educational heritage. More precisely, the self-conscious mission of the Mother Parish of Baltimore and its School, reclaimed and renewed toward the end of the twentieth century.

My conviction is this: The Boys' School of St. Paul's Parish reaffirmed its distinctive identity in the 1980s and '90s against all odds, bucking the educational and ecclesiastical trends of the times.

The distinguished historian Dr. David Hein '72 has elsewhere suggested that many nominally Episcopal schools have enjoyed marked success in recent years because of their "somewhat nebulous identification with the church" and their "fondness for everything in moderation." Yet St. Paul's during the same period put more (and more vivid) emphasis on its stand-apart distinctiveness, within the independent school market, as Church-rooted and grounded. So successful was St. Paul's in this endeavor that the president of the board of a rival Baltimore institution often publicly averred that the Church connection was what he most envied about St. Paul's.

When the vestry of St. Paul's Parish called me as rector in 1981, the Church's relationship with The Boys' School ("of St. Paul's Parish") was for me an added value and an irresistible incentive. I knew little of the School's beginnings. I did know, however, that I believed in the Anglican heritage of commitment to liberal education in a spiritual context, and I was intrigued to find it alive and relatively well at St. Paul's. But I also knew how peculiar and precarious such a heritage had become in late twentieth-century America. Many schools with histories similar to St. Paul's were gradually but inexorably shedding their churchly character; the species had become endangered.

There was a story often told me—as I began to fathom the Byzantine depths, complexities, and ambiguities of the Church-School relationship—about a decades' earlier candidate for rectorship of St. Paul's who had declined the post because, believing his vocation to be primarily pastoral, he did not feel "called" to preside over an "empire."

Would that history had known more truly pastoral emperors! It seemed to me, anyway, that if the Church-School relationship connoted "imperialism," then it was simply and distinctly a proper "burden" of Anglican educational heritage and, indeed, an honorable one. My role as chairman of the board was to a great degree, in fact, pastoral; to no degree, dictatorial; to some degree, importantly, theological.

Had I known more of the School's beginnings in 1981, I surely would have quoted in my first address to the trustees the School's founder, the Reverend William Wyatt. In his *Discourse on Christian Education* (1833), he characterized the purpose of a program such as he eventually set forth for St. Paul's as "education for eternity, in contradistinction to education for the world." Not to denigrate the latter, but to correct it, complement it, and make it complete—in the spirit (it could be said) of St. Augustine's admonition about holiness and knowledge. Moral virtue and liberal education would go hand-in-hand under Church auspices. Thus, there would be provided whatever might be lacking in parental or societal commitment to "spiritual things" over merely worldly and material "passions."

As I delved into the history of St. Paul's and learned of Wyatt's motivation in founding this church school, his concerns seemed strikingly relevant almost a hundred and fifty years later. A school true to his proposal would stand over and against the secular materialism of so many institutions on the one hand, but also over and against religious fundamentalism on the other. It seemed to me a worthy witness and a worthy vocational, and indeed pastoral, dimension of ministry for a rector who also served *ex officio* as chairman of the school board. But would it be an uphill struggle? Would I be "the last emperor"?

On the contrary, in our own most "worldly" and "material" *fin de siècle*, St. Paul's School seemed increasingly and wondrously out of step with its institutional peers in reclaiming its churchly heritage. And it all came together at the outset of the 1990s.

First, the School adopted a mission statement that put its church affiliation at the top of the list.

Second, the School committed itself, on the motion of a Jewish board member, to raise the capital funds necessary to build a new chapel on the brow of its most prominent undeveloped site. Moreover, one of the most venerable aspects of the Church-School relationship, the St. Paul's Choir of Men and Boys, would thus again have a room of its own for regular weekday practice in the

Chapel building itself.

Third, the School committed its students to a requirement of community service that reflected its original identity as a "mission" to the least advantaged citizens of urban Baltimore.

Fourth, in 1992 St. Paul's sponsored and hosted a national conference on the future of Episcopal schools. Subsequently, the School invited two of Maryland's most eminent apologists for Christian moral education to assume positions of advocacy in its institutional councils: Dr. David Hein of Hood College and Dr. Vigen Guroian of Loyola College.

Is the struggle really any different or any less imperative (pun intended!) than it was for St. Augustine 1,500 years ago, or Wyatt 150 years ago, or the anonymous author of an ironic ditty, also long associated with the Anglican heritage in education? The ditty runs:

> *If only the good were clever*
> *And the clever were only good*
> *This world would be so much better*
> *Than ever we thought it could.*
> *But the good are seldom clever*
> *And the clever are hardly good:*
> *The good are so harsh to the clever*
> *And the clever so rude to the good.*

St. Paul's School was founded as a place of both sanctity and scholarship. Our forebears considered the two to be mutually necessary and complementary, and the quality of goodness or morals dependent on the knowledge (and more than knowledge) of religion. Many schools other than St. Paul's have in recent years undermined, if not driven a wedge between, liberal education and faith tradition. On the contrary, and perhaps somewhat miraculously, St. Paul's has sought the renewal of their mutuality, to keep them yoked together as together befitting a life worth living, a life fully human and potentially divine.

At the same time, we suffered losses along the way. In fact, during my tenure, while bucking the trend of church disaffiliation elsewhere, St. Paul's Parish and School had to contend with two kinds of loss. First, by natural attrition, the School lost innumerable faculty and alumni who, well into the '80s, had embodied a certain corporate memory of the way things had once been. When I became rector in 1981, there were even a few living alumni who had been pupils at the Franklin Street location before 1922; many others had attended the School at its Mt. Washington site before 1952 and represented a certain continuity with the School's origins. Likewise, it was my sad privilege to officiate at the funerals of the living legends, among others, of Frank Mead '21, George Hamilton, Farnham Warriner, and Louis Dorsey Clark. What they and their ilk had taken as "givens" in the Church-School relationship now had to be self-consciously recovered and cultivated.

The second serious loss during the 1980s and '90s was not personal but ecclesiastical. The Episcopal Church increasingly experienced what might be called radical "deconstruction" of its own doctrinal heritage and identity. What once constituted virtually unquestioned orthodoxy of basic belief was not only now called into question but sometimes unequivocally denied, even within the denomination's putative leadership. So how does one affirm a School's church-affiliated identity if the Church's denomination itself has become uncertain of its own identity?

Together, these two losses will not soon or easily be overcome. The uphill struggle, or rather the crusade, is never finished. In the next century, the imperative and the obstacles will not diminish.

So the questions are several. Will the St. Paul's experience continue to bring students to grips with the relationship between scholarship and sanctity, between faith and reason, between science, morality and religion? Will future trustees and faculty members share any real commonality of understanding about the mission of this church-affiliated School? What are the proper criteria and strategic priorities for ensuring the continued rootedness of St. Paul's School in its heritage of unfettered intellect but also revealed religion, where devout worship and scholarly pursuit of knowledge go hand in hand; where God is acknowledged, as *The Book of Common Prayer* expresses it, "to be the source of all truth"; and where leadership is entrusted to those who hold in common a commitment to education not for labor only, but for life, not for temporal aspiration only, but for eternal destiny? Such are questions of institutional identity that must be perennially revisited, and the answers perseveringly reclaimed.

When all the spiritual, institutional, curricular and extra-curricular aspects of the mission of St. Paul's as a church-affiliated school are set in perspective, there comes a bottom line—two basic issues remain to be faced.

First, there is the issue of *coherence of spiritual commitment by the corporate body which is St. Paul's*, embodied in particular in its board of trustees. This concerns the context within which every other aspect of the School's program is intended to be conducted. St. Paul's does not demand of its students or faculty, as individuals, that they profess Christian faith; St. Paul's does not intend to be sectarian, to indoctrinate, or to proselytize. But St. Paul's is rooted in the Anglican heritage of setting the liberal education it offers in the Judaeo-Christian context of revealed religion, institutionally affirmed.

Second, there is the issue of *the coherence of curricular commitment by the corporate leadership of headmaster and faculty*. Without such coherence and integration of academic and religious study, no variety or sophistication of individual course requirements can ensure "education for eternity" or even education of the whole person, intellectually and morally.

The question of coherence at these two levels (ideological at the board level, curricular at the faculty level) will be the 21st century's *sine qua non* issues of institutional faithfulness at The Boys' School of St. Paul's Parish in the City and County of Baltimore. The crusade continues.

The Very Reverend William N. McKeachie was rector of St. Paul's Parish and chairman of the board of trustees of St. Paul's School from 1981 to 1996.

1849-1923

BEGINNING

OPPOSITE: This picture appeared in the boys' literary magazine, *Triakonta*, in 1912, but unfortunately there is no other information about it. The earliest documented student club was the Boys' Friendly Society in 1889, with 26 members and meetings every two weeks at St. Paul's House, but the short passage about it in the *Parish Notes* does not describe its purpose. The members (and the earliest documented students): Harry Berlin, Howell Coryell, Harold Covington, John Fairfax, Condit Groome, Carey Johnson, Frank Mellier, George Prothero, Edward Olmstead, Vernon M. Smith, William Stone, Loring Stone, Clarence Stelle, and Frank Whittaker.

At the time that Dr. William Edward Wyatt founded The Boys' School of St. Paul's Parish in 1849, the word buzzing on the street was "steam." Only a few were beginning to imagine what hot water could do. Things were strong, but here was industrial strength. Things were fast, but here were machines. The marvels of mechanical efficiency and engineering geared cities like Baltimore, and people like Wyatt, for a future that was faster and more complex, certainly; more dangerous, likely; and better no less, with strong prayer and hard work.

But as the industrial age hurried closer, Wyatt had one "gadget" that his business and legal counterparts could not blueprint. He had an institution, St. Paul's Parish and its Mother Church, which began long before the city of Baltimore, and which would continue, situated in the Kingdom of God, long after. In short, Wyatt had faith. Metal rusts. The well runs dry. But he and his new School had a divine machine that they could, and would, depend on for the next 150 years, and for that matter, eternity. It was a creation which would counteract, as he put it, the "vast and most complicated machinery constantly in operation to supply the wants of *the body*."[1]

Wyatt, however, was a pragmatic man of faith. "The distinguished men of the country are all practical men," he once preached. He could implement his vision, which was not so much for distance, necessarily, as for clarity and timing. And in the highly social and upper-class atmosphere of downtown Baltimore, right near his church with its same 1692 footings on Charles Street and Saratoga, and among an affluent congregation that included the famous and the prestigious, Wyatt found the energy as well as the people influential enough to help him execute his ideas. After 35 years in the Parish, this was a time of opportunity for him, as for Baltimore in 1849—a time to appreciate the city's reputation for its chewing tobacco, its southern breed of northern mercantilism, its beautiful women, its cheer rallies for competing fire companies, its horse races and rowing clubs, its elaborate outdoor picnics for 40 people, and its hotels serving terrapin, oysters and canvasback.[2]

This was also a time of new threats and challenges. Between 1837 and 1860, Baltimore had tripled its number of churches and chapels, as well as its number of houses

"Education is a matter to be carefully weighed, whether

such a community should bind their offspring,

almost exclusively for a long and important period,

when so many other departments of knowledge, equally

fascinating, and to us, as a nation, much more directly

useful, might be slightly attained."

The Reverend William E. Wyatt, *A Discourse on Christian Education*, 1833

erected; had built 40 Episcopal churches within the original limits of St. Paul's Parish by 1855; and had doubled its population in the span of a single generation. Here was a city just shy in size only of New York and Philadelphia, a city strongly rebounding from a dismal decade economically in the mid-1830s and early 1840s to attain a level of confidence some historians call "euphoric." Yet here was a city also riddled with significant issues of sewage disposal, violence, heavy debts, epidemics and, of course, segregation and slavery. The rise of the "poor and helpless" during this time was just one of the complex and inevitable outcomes of urban prosperity (by one account of that time, half of the city's population was described as a "nuisance" or a "threat").[3] The poor were, according to Wyatt, "irreversibly doomed to all that is groveling and menial in life. And except in regard to the single modification of labor to which the necessity of their wretched sustenance drives them, they attach no value to the hours and years which pass over them, no sense of their having a bearing upon eternity."[4]

Thus Wyatt, known for his own "magnificent" pastoral ministry which "endeared him to the poor, the orphans and prisoners in the city," had to respond to a city in need.[5] Fortunately, his Parish had been helping the poor and homeless through outreach efforts long before he arrived. "As St. Paul's moved in the nineteenth century, it began to devote more attention to community problems. The Reverend Joseph Grove John Bend [rector 1790-1812] kept a large pot of soup on his kitchen stove, always ready to feed the hungry."[6] Yet, amidst the current optimism of his wealthy congregation, he also had to awaken in them a new level of social responsibility "for ameliorating human wants and perils."[7] In his rhetoric, he entreated them to help not only out of altruistic motives but also out of fear. "Much of the value of all the privileges of wealth and station depend upon the condition of character of the community amidst which you are placed," he later wrote in a fund-raising effort for the boys' school orphanage he started in 1849. "No man toils for wealth with the view of enjoying its fruits in a wilderness. Is there any security to an estate, to comfort, to life, in the midst of an ignorant, daring, licentious, rebellious populace?"[8]

Wyatt had a practical idea to address this question and allay his congregation's fear.

OPPOSITE: 1921 basketball team, with the first sweaters with a monogram. These boys played at the nearby YMCA or at the St. Paul's Guild House, and were instructed by master Ernest B. Marx. Their only recorded game was a 10-9 loss against the YMCA Juniors. Though not every boy in this picture was identified, that year's team included: William H. Purnell, Beverly R. L. Rhett '21 (first row, left), Robert L. Bull, Jr. '21, Robert V. Elliott '23 James W. Chapman III '24, and team captain Frank D. Mead '21, the School's first athletic director (first row, center).

He had faith that they would listen and he had faith in the city. And he had experience: he had an enormous and successful Sunday School enterprise thirty years in the making, and an orphanage for girls through his Benevolent Society for half a century.[9] He also had a larger mandate to consider: the Episcopal Diocese at this time was appealing to its parishes that Baltimore needed more parochial schools to train and guide children, "securing," as he put it, "an inheritance in God's blissful and everlasting presence." Wyatt hoped to help children who would otherwise have access to a "godless" secular education, as one St. Paul's parishioner wrote.[10]

Still, Wyatt's motivations are not entirely clear. Most documentation today, including early pamphlet histories from as far back as 1906 about the School's founding cite the line from the 1853 incorporation papers stating that the Boys' School was a place "for the maintenance and education of poor boys."[11] The fire in the spring of 1854—which ravaged all but a few walls and objects of reverence at the Church—left few documents to analyze; if there is consolation to be had about this loss, it can be found in Wyatt's own words during a sermon the following day at Grace Church, when he said that such a tragedy was but a "momentary interruption to our privileges."[12] Contemporaneous church records and notes are scant, and we know of nothing that would give us some idea about just what happened on that Friday in February when Wyatt sat down with 12 subscribers and decided to start The Boys' School of St. Paul's Parish on February 9, 1849.

Most of what we have to interpret was an appeal for funds he made to his congregation for funds for the Boys' School in 1861. In general, his new charity was to serve "a class most remote from the privileges of education and religion," partly modeled after the Girls' Orphanage founded in 1799, with a similar mission to develop and instruct poor children as responsible members of the community, as well as its call to bind their students out when they were ready.[13] "The main and ultimate object always was and still is," Wyatt wrote in 1861, "to establish an asylum for poor boys, precisely similar in most respects to that which has been so long a source of pleasure to all concerned, the Benevolent Society, or 'Girls' School of the Parish.'"[14]

But Wyatt's intentions seemed more ambitious and practical (and our faithful Wyatt was a pragmatist); the Boys' School, for instance, unlike the Girls' Orphanage, is never referred to as an orphanage in parish documents or in early references. The two institutions were similar "in most respects," as Wyatt said, but not all. For example, this new "boys' orphanage" was operating only during the day until after Wyatt's death, despite the fact that the 1853 articles of incorporation said otherwise; according to these articles, the School was to place any boys who came from "parent or parents, or any Orphan's Court" under the control of the incorporators or those they appointed "until they shall think fit to bind them out, which said corporation shall be entitled to do for any term not exceeding the period at which such boys shall have completed their twenty-first year."[15]

The First Doctor

The Reverend
Dr. William E. Wyatt

I f character can be interpreted by handwriting, the Reverend Dr. William Edward Wyatt's graceful and erudite penmanship speaks to the endearing ministry and social compassion for which he was noted. For years he was a chaplain without pay at the Maryland Penitentiary and apparently gave services in "small clothes, silk stockings and silver-buckled shoes, and always wore a silk gown in the streets," and had pulpit gloves "with one finger cut for convenience in turning the leaves of the manuscript." In one biography, Wyatt was said to be "more universally known than any Protestant clergyman of the city," and as a professor of divinity at the University of Maryland, he was referred to as, affectionately or not, "Dr. High-Church," perhaps because he was one of the most prominent and influential "Anglo-Catholics" who introduced, among other elements, weekly Eucharist and the use of linen eucharistic vestments.

Born in New Manchester, Nova Scotia on July 9, 1789, Wyatt was graduated from Columbia College at age 20, was ordained deacon one year later and a priest at age 24, and in 1814 at the seasoned age of 25 was called to St. Paul's Parish as associate rector. There in 1827 he became the Church's eighth rector and the first to be democratically elected by the vestry (rather than by the appointment of the governor of the Provinces of Maryland), serving in that position for the next 37 years until his death. Along with the Parish, Wyatt reached a golden anniversary with Miss Frances Billop, whom he married in 1812; together, they had seven sons and four daughters.

Wyatt was not only the center of the Mother Church. He was arguably acting bishop in 1830 and a leading candidate for the position in 1838. Serving eight times over the span of 25 years as president of the House of Deputies (the highest office a clergyman in the rank of presbyter can hold in the Episcopal Church), and as deputy to the General Convention for 30 years, Wyatt had influence throughout the Diocese and in Maryland, especially when at age 60 he became president of the General Convention and member of the Standing Committee. Wyatt was also a diplomat and statesman who "brought a united parish through the bitter controversies prior to the Civil War."

When most of the Church burned down in 1854, he called Richard Upjohn to rebuild it on the same foundation. That decision makes the Parish today the sole surviving institution in Baltimore to occupy its original lot since the City's incorporation. A year after the fire, and while in ill health, he still had time to found the Church Home Society, a shelter for the destitute and sick, which later became the large enterprise known as the Church Home and Hospital. So, with the Boys' School reaching its 150th year on February 9, 1999, Wyatt's strengths of faith and posterity have thus proven to keep his projects close to their roots.[1]

"They are school boys, and have first to do all their school work,

and then they have to take out of the hours when other boys

are playing, all the time for practicings and rehearsals—sometimes

in the morning, sometimes in the afternoon, sometimes in the

evening till 10 and after 10 o'clock. This soon ceases to be

fun for boys who have to work so constantly, having to give up

even part of the Saturdays, and oftentimes, every other day. All

through Lent a service every day in the church and twice, or

three times, on Sunday; and all the work of practicing and

getting ready for Easter to be done in addition, for all of which

they receive on an average less than one dollar a month …

Surely, we owe our thanks, if nothing else, to our choir boys."

The Reverend John S. B. Hodges, 1889

In fact, an orphanage was hardly the defining feature of Wyatt's vision for what this school would eventually become. The group of 12 that Wyatt asked to subscribe to his vision in 1849, and then the group of nine who signed the incorporation papers (five were in both groups, including Wyatt and his son Edward), seemed to be busy enough to trouble themselves solely with starting a small shelter for destitute boys. These men were leaders in Baltimore: merchants, statesmen, lawyers, and bankers, most of whom are readily found in historical accounts and biographical excerpts of the city's history. Wyatt's plan was bigger. He aimed to take boys "tested and developed in point of native character and talent … to bestow our privileges upon the most deserving, and to obtain a greater security for ourselves of favorable results; while we multiply four-fold the objects, and widen the scope of our charity, without a material augmentation of expense." Starting an orphanage paled in comparison to piloting an exponentially growing outfit that might redeem the "leagued and emboldened vice upon posterity … [who], like lepers in the East, herd together in obscure districts and remote suburbs, [and] create a moral atmosphere of pestilence." An orphanage that could set its boys on a Christian course and spread the mission to others—here was an idea. "Now, let the patriot look at the same class of children trained in our schools," implored Wyatt, "and matured in the enjoyment of Christian privileges. They are clay in the potter's hand. Awful responsibility! God has placed their plastic and yielding elements of character in your disposal."[16] If Wyatt and his founders could put

St. Paul's Students and Masters, 1912

(From top, left to right) masters Frederick Brown Harrison, Miles Farrow, the Reverend Carl Bernhardt; (fourth row) students Harold King '08, George Hatton '10, Tunis Craven '08, Channing Lefebvre '11, Harry Bicks, Horace Fort '07, Alfred Fort '08, Robert Nelson '10; (third row) William Rideout '11, Pinkney Holmes, Jr. '09, Russell Ryan '08, unidentified, H. Wetherbee Fort '10, Charles Jervis '09, Maurice Hill '06; (second row) Eugene Milby '10, George Thomas '10, Winthrop Heyer '08, Tracy Tyler, S. Page Nelson '12; (first row) Charles McGill, Tommy Craven '09, unidentified.

Like Father, Like Son

The Reverend Dr. John Sebastian Bach Hodges, an English Cathedral boy born in 1830, did not have a familial tie with the famous composer, but his family had a strong psychological and emotional one (his brother, George Frederick Handel Hodges, and his other siblings were also named for composers or biblical figures). His father, Edward Hodges, received his doctorate in music at Cambridge, where he studied the nature of sound and the "abstruse Science of Acoustics," becoming an eminent organist at churches in Bristol, England for the first half (20 years) of his professional career. Then, crossing the Atlantic in 1858 (John was 16), his father continued his "divided life spent in two hemispheres," for the second half as organist at Trinity Church and choirmaster at Trinity School in New York. His daughter—John's sister—described him as a "Musical Missionary," who "in the more pathetic words he loved to apply to himself … was a 'stranger and a sojourner in the land.'"

Thus, his father had marked a clear path for young John. A singer in college and a tenor soloist at Trinity, John Hodges graduated from Columbia College and the General Seminary, and after serving two parishes in Chicago and New Jersey over the course of 16 years, the "priest-musician," as some called him, then left for Old St. Paul's, where he served for 44 years, 35 of those as rector. "[At the] front rank of composers," Dr. Arthur Kinsolving later wrote, "[Hodges] left behind more music of real merit, perhaps, than any clergyman who ever served the

The Reverend
Dr. John Sebastian Bach Hodges

American Church." Perhaps Hodges aimed to hear his own music when he founded the vested St. Paul's Choir of Men and Boys in 1873.

Regardless, Hodges turned his energies to many initiatives. He began the endowment fund of both the Boys' School and the Parish; erected the St. Paul's House; served as chairman of the Church Home and Infirmary; started the first Christian Home for Self-supporting Women in Baltimore; and increased the number of services in the "full Cathedral scheme … beginning at early morning with the celebration of the Holy Communion and ending with choral evensong," focusing on the "dignity, beauty and inspiration of its ritual." He married Lucy MacDonough Shaler of Pittsburgh (where he was eventually laid to rest), with whom he had six children, two while he was rector.

But after all of this, "there is no part of his work in the Parish during the past 35 years," he wrote about himself in 1906, "upon which the rector looks back with so much satisfaction; and realizing [the School's] present condition, with a property unencumbered with debt, with a helpful amount of invested funds, with an admirable system of instruction and discipline, with a most capable master—realizing all of this, the rector looks forward with hope and confidence … that the Boys' School may be a pioneer in this country in the establishment of schools like Eton and Rugby, to maintain and educate boys who may be successful and honorable members of the States, and useful and devout servants of the Church of the living God."[1]

the Parish at the center of this larger, younger missionary effort, they might have better control of an outcome. Here was a remedy as "they [the trustees] worried about the crime and poverty and the future of traditional American values," wrote historian David Hein '72 on the incorporation of the School. "They wanted to curb the evils of society, such as violence and intemperance, and they desired to hasten the socialization process of the urban masses through application of heavy doses of conventional virtues."[17]

Thus the word "school" only partially describes Wyatt's aim, and in fact wouldn't have meant much to his patrons anyway. At the time, schools were either secular and poor, or expensive and elitist. Maryland's approach toward education "hung somewhere between Northern interest in public schooling and Southern regard for the academics that prepared gentleman for public leadership," as one historian wrote, and would not develop as an institution until later in the century, along with the rest of the nation. Only about 15 percent of white school-aged children attended public school, and many upper-class children received private schooling. Not until 1847 did the General Assembly of Maryland even pass an act allowing the incorporation of schools, along with libraries, fire companies, and social, athletic and religious clubs and associations.[18]

As Wyatt devised his own version of this school-orphanage, he had models to follow. He communicated frequently with bishop William Rollinson Whittingham, who seven years earlier had helped start the College of St. James near Hagerstown, Maryland, a southern breed of the New England boarding school movement; by 1848, St. James had jumped in enrollment from 14 to 89.[19] Wyatt also called upon Isaac McKim as a "public and spirited" parishioner, the man credited with establishing the first free school in Baltimore in 1821, with 200 boys and girls enrolled each year. Likewise, Wyatt believed that a Christian education should not be exclusive, and that it was something "of universal importance [that] must be attainable by all."[20]

But Wyatt's plans were stalled by the fire at the Church in 1854 (just a year after he formally incorporated the School and finally extinguished the Church's mortgage debt), and later by his extended illness preceding his death in 1864. Nevertheless, the well-established church architect Richard Upjohn had repaired the edifice by 1856, and Wyatt reported to the bishop that his new school had 50 pupils enrolled for the following two years.[21]

At age 72, when Wyatt directly appealed for funds to his congregation on April 9, 1861, he described an optimistic future for the Boys' School, including plans for a new building. (Classes had thus far been held in the Sunday School room.)[22] But three days later, Fort Sumter was bombarded and President Lincoln called for 75,000 volunteers to defend the capital. Virginia seceded from the Union on April 17; and two days after that, the 6th Massachusetts Infantry Regiment rolled into Baltimore amidst violent rioting. Wyatt's young school and the city were thrown into political, geographic, and military gridlock, right at the gateway between north to south, and were captive to the next four years of war. Other than Wyatt's call for funds, no documentation exists about the School's activity until after the Civil War.

The Parish stood in a painfully divided and damaged city during the war, unsuccessfully apolitical, and mostly siding with their Bishop Whittingham's clear Unionist position among church leaders who readily took either side. Members of Wyatt's congregation argued hotly as they drew the Parish directly into the war; one founder of the School, Mayor Thomas Swann, for instance, was head of the short-lived and riotous "Know-Nothing Party," which "persecuted immigrants and fostered religious prejudice."[23] As president of the Standing Committee of the Diocese, Wyatt had his hands full as he butted heads with the bishop, who was amassing his support for action from other bishops in the North over how and to what extent the Church should be involved. In the end, Wyatt's plans for the School had to be deferred during these trying years.

Wyatt died in 1864, six years after the trustees had formally begun to consider the next step: to admit boarding students and to implement Wyatt's vision fully.

THE MAKING OF ONE MAHAN

The Reverend Dr. Milo Mahan (pronounced "MAN"), Wyatt's successor, was the one who put the "and maintenance" in the School's founding mission "for the education and maintenance of poor boys." A political moderate in the severely wounded post-war city, Mahan's short six-year tenure was actually a pivotal time for the School, during which he fundamentally—even radically—redirected Wyatt's day school orphanage. Mahan, with his assistant C. C. Grafton, wasted no time in making changes. He appealed to the trustees: No, he argued, the Boys' School should not educate just "destitute children" but those who "fail of their high calling for want of a helping hand to lead them onward," as well as students with "better capabilities" who had in their childhood "a more careful nurture." He wrote an appeal in December, 1868 that encouraged the congregation to take an interest in the "thousands of boys of a higher grade" and the "welfare of the rising generation."[24] In short, Mahan wanted to hand-select his boys before they arrived at a place they should call home.

By his second year, in 1866, Mahan had already transformed the School into an "asylum"—meaning supervision, lodging, and board—all made possible through the purchase of a building for $20,000 hitherto occupied by the Maryland Asylum for the Blind about ten blocks west at 258 Saratoga Street, in close proximity of Lexington Market and the neighboring shopping district. The School finally occupied the new residence in 1868.[25]

Although Wyatt, who yearned for a more sophisticated charity school, may have sensed the eddies of a budding boarding school movement, which was expanding outward from New England, Mahan knew hardly any other kind. He had attended St.

Milo's School

The Reverend
Dr. Milo Mahan

High Churchman the Reverend Dr. Milo Mahan was a politician, leader, and scholar for whom, "even in the busiest of his late years," wrote a contemporary biographer, "nothing was more refreshing than to throw himself down on the sofa with dear old Homer in his hand."[1]

Mahan as historian: author of the 700-page tome *The History of the Episcopal Church*, and professor of church history at the General Theological Seminary, where he developed a "scholarship second only to bishop William R. Whittingham in Baltimore."

Mahan as religious student and academician: a boarder at the Flushing Institute (where he took Holy Orders); a teacher of Greek literature at Episcopal High School; a priest ordained in New York at the Church of Holy Communion at age 28; an assistant professor at the General Theological Seminary at age 33; a writer and co-editor of *The Church Journal* (a distinguished national publication of the Episcopal Church); and a public speaker along the Eastern seaboard.

Mahan as politician: a reformist concerned about Catholic defection from the Episcopal Church and its challenges to Christian faith; a progressive discovered at Episcopal High School with "the hated *Tracts of the Times*," a document which linked him to the controversial Oxford Movement within the Church, and subsequently led to his forced departure (by Virginian bishop William Meade, who, when he employed Mahan, "justly thought he had obtained a prize"); and an active

moderate during the Civil War, who tried to find common ground between Unionists and Confederates.

Though born in 1818 a Southerner from Suffolk, Virginia, home for Mahan was New York, thus at first he was very reluctant to move south, particularly to Baltimore when he was called there. But he soon had no choice: the General Theological Seminary where he was teaching at the time was in a financial crisis in the early 1860s, and he had become sufficiently outspoken, seeking "to strengthen the Catholic emphasis in the Episcopal Church," that he lost his job.

He had another particular reason to head south. Mahan had married the "greatly respected and beloved" Mary Griffith Lewis after her first husband, Charles Smith Lewis of Philadelphia, died in 1847. (Incidentally, they married three years after Lewis had organized a separate congregation within St. Paul's Parish in 1844 under the name St. John's Church, Huntington.)

Beginning at age 27, Mahan suffered from what he called a "disease of the heart." His periods of physical distress increased as he grew older, aggravated by a prodigious workload. When he passed away at Old St. Paul's in the summer of 1870 at age 52, Mahan had finally acceded to a renewed offer from the General Seminary, knowing that the strain of parish and pastoral work was not going to lessen. While one could speculate on how the Boys' School might have grown had Mahan lived, the answer is "not much": he had formally agreed to begin teaching again in New York that fall.

Founders and Subscribers

I f one's aim is to begin an ambitious institution to redeem those "most exposed to wants, associations, habits and passions likely to drive them to vice, destruction or ruin," one could hardly go wrong with the established network the Reverend William Wyatt tapped to start his boys' school in 1849. With this credibility, he could in turn provide for his subscribers a natural outlet for upper-class philanthropy.

In almost all cases, the founders were educated power brokers. Frederick W. Brune, Jr. received one of the best educations available at the time. At age 14 he studied at the Round Hill School, later graduated from Harvard College and went on to start a preeminent law partnership with future mayor and prominent judge, George William Brown. A devout Christian, Brune was a founder of the Maryland Historical Society, a charter board member of the Church Home Society with Wyatt, and a member of the General Convention for ten years until his death. Interestingly enough, Brune's son, John, was elected president of the Baltimore Association for the Improvement of the Condition of the Poor in 1857.

Brune was also closely tied by the law profession to founders William B. Perine and Reverdy Johnson Jr, who was a U.S. minister during the administration of President Andrew Johnson, and later president of Union Manufacturing Company of Maryland. Johnson's brother-in-law, Thomas Hollingsworth Morris, also a founder, retired early from law and devoted himself to community service.

One incorporator, Thomas Swann, president of the B&O Railroad in 1849, and later a mayor, governor and congressman, surely knew another founder, Samuel W. Smith, the "oldest stockholder director" of the B&O and son of Robert Smith (Secretary of State under James Madison). Though Samuel had "never been in public life,

all his instincts leading him to avoid the strife and turmoil of modern politics," he became president of the Baltimore Club and later of the Maryland Club.

William R. Travers, another incorporator, was successful enough as a merchant and broker to have five "luxurious domestic establishments" in which to "enjoy a unique popularity"; to belong to some 27 organizations (social, political and athletic); and to start a charitable 350-acre village for "working men." He married and had nine children with Maria Louisa, fourth daughter of Reverdy Johnson; this union made him the brother-in-law of founder Reverdy Johnson, Jr.

Founders Cecilius Coudon Jamison was president of the Bank of Baltimore and held the prestigious role as member, secretary and later vice president of the Society of Cincinnati; Robert A. Taylor was a wealthy landowner and partner in a dry-goods, auction and commission merchant company; and Whig politician and congressman Dr. John Hanson Thomas was president of the Farmers' and Merchants' Bank of Baltimore.

Three other founders, Gustav W. Lurman (partner in his own shipping company); Samuel Owings Hoffman (state senator in 1858); and John Montgomery Gordon (president of the Union Bank) were all part of the distinguished Monday Club, consisting of 25 of "the most influential leaders of Baltimore's social, business and professional circles." And five (Swann, Hoffman, Morris, Smith, and Gordon) were later to become part of the first board of trustees assembled in 1875 for George Peabody's new Institute in Mount Vernon Place.

"Let your charity brood over this unorganized mass," Wyatt appealed to them and others, "as the Spirit of God brooded over the wild waste of waters, and what a splendid creation may arise in harmony and beauty!"[1]

"[The Boys' School has cared] for an average of

24 boys a year for 30 years—more than 800 years

of care of a single boy—or the care of more than 230

boys for a three-year course of a liberal and religious

education. The greater part of these boys are today

honestly and honorably doing their duty, as citizens

and churchmen, in the various states of life opened

before them; some in business, some in professions,

in law, medicine and theology."

The Reverend John S. B. Hodges, 1905

Paul's College (now referred to as the Flushing Institute) under the care of the Institute's founder, the Reverend William Augustus Muhlenberg, an Episcopal clergyman. Muhlenberg started the school in 1828 with its "successful method of impregnating education with Christian principles." The Institute served as home, classroom and family (with rector as father)—a center of Christian stability grounded in faith. At age 17 Mahan became one of the first three teachers (his subject was the classics, Greek specifically) at the "Virginia High School," known now as Episcopal High School (EHS), which began in 1839 and served as one of the oldest beneficiaries: teachers who left the Flushing Institute.[26] Thus, Mahan had graduated from the boarding school prototype (Flushing), and taught for seven years at one of its first replicas (EHS).[27]

Before arriving to the Baltimore in 1864, Mahan must have known Bishop Whittingham and surely would have discussed with him both the Parish, where Whittingham was consecrated in 1840, and the School. Whittingham, for one, had been a primary force behind the founding of the College of St. James in Hagerstown and even asked Muhlenberg to run it. Secondly, Whittingham had studied church history at the General Theological Seminary in New York where Mahan later served as a professor in the same subject. So, if Whittingham had his own vision for the Boys' School, it was likely in line with Mahan's, who also was said to have had "an intense love of children" and a "singular power to attract the personal confidence of others."[28]

On several occasions, Mahan, as principal of the Girls' Orphanage and chairman of the Boys' School, wished "to put [both] on a far more efficient footing than before … I have started our boys' school," he wrote in a postscript to a letter to a colleague in 1869, "seventeen boys to be liberally educated … a splendid teacher and matron with all things working well. Everything is paid always in advance. If we keep up the program, we should have a Church School. If I had you in Baltimore, I could make you *spin*."[29] By then, Mahan was immersed in all of his parish projects, institutions and affiliations that existed when he arrived or that he initiated. A "convinced High Churchman," Mahan added colored altar lights to the Parish services and "still more frequent celebrations of the Holy Communion." He apparently enjoyed the "charming social tone of Baltimore" which he wrote was "the most enjoyable of all of our large cities" and "a constant feast for him." All of this was cause for him to turn down numerous requests to return to the General Seminary to assume a prestigious academic post.[30]

As far as we know, "nine boarders and a few day scholars" constituted the full enrollment of the new Boys' School in 1868, which means that the number of students would double in a year. Mahan apparently handled the religious instruction personally, and, like Wyatt, emphasized the importance of church music, the core classical subjects of Latin and Greek, as well as math, moral and religious character building, and all the "habits and courtesies" necessary to prepare a boy for ministry, teaching, or "any walk of life."[31]

Mahan aimed, as he said, to *create* a church school, not to continue one, and under him, the tone, mission, and philosophy indeed began to resemble that of a church boarding school. If Mahan had an ideal for this school, certainly it was some combination of the Flushing Institute, Episcopal High School, the College of St. James College and, of course, his own scholarly vision.

SAINTS AND SINGERS

The Reverend John Sebastian Bach Hodges still had a "High-Church" foot in England when he succeeded Mahan as rector of St. Paul's Parish in 1870 at age 40. He was Anglican born and bred, seasoned in New York and Chicago, and always "through his father steeped in the English Cathedral tradition." In fact, his father was the organist of the Anglo-Catholic Trinity Church in New York and music instructor at Trinity School, arguably the oldest and most reputable choir school in the country.[32] And any father who names most of his children after famous composers must be serious about music; luckily for young John, he could play an organ and sing at the same time, a man of church music himself who would define the Parish in part by the success of an early and resolute decision to start a vested choir made up exclusively of men and boys.

It took only three years for Hodges to make such a significant change in the musical annals of St. Paul's Church. The choir until then was composed of men and women who "appeared in street clothes, the varieties and contrasts of their dress being somewhat tempered by screening the choir from the congregation." As far back as 1802, as acknowledged in a sermon given by Rector Joseph G. J. Bend, the Parish had supported a trained choir.[33] Seventy years later, in the highest of High Church ritual

Flying Solo

Recent choristers (from left) Stephen Leggin '93, Matt Hankins '93 and Toby Bozzuto. The early years of the Choir also had notable choristers. Housemother Miss Ellen Bryan, who served from 1895-1910, had as "one of her particular charges … a youth of rare gifts," Harry Percy Veazie '06 from New Jersey. "This boy," according to Dr. Arthur B. Kinsolving, "was perhaps the most famous soloist in the Choir of St. Paul's during the Church's history." Veazie was an assistant master at the School for a short time at the end of 1908, but then supported himself as a student at Columbia, and later as a choirmaster, attracting "the attention of a wealthy Washington churchwoman who enabled him to go to Oxford University." He took Holy Orders in England and led a parish in San Francisco. Channing Lefebvre '11 was another notable who actually followed future choirmaster Miles Farrow to New York and taught at the Cathedral School. Lefebvre later became the first assistant choirmaster at the New York Cathedral, the organist and choirmaster at Trinity Church in New York, and headed music instruction at St. Paul's School in Concord, New Hampshire.

the Parish had yet seen, Hodges introduced a more Catholic tradition than ever, and confidently persuaded his congregation that a more organized choir would provide "a dignity and a grandeur befitting this noble building; and of all places most becoming and suitable in this the Mother Church of the city." With that, Hodges added vestments, eliminated women, and inaugurated the Choir of Men and Boys on a day of rejoicing: Easter Sunday, 1873.[34]

In general, church music, choirs, and vestments were a source of heavy debate and discourse through the first half of the nineteenth century in the Episcopal Church. "Churchmen drained their ink wells and dulled their pen points in attempts to convince fellow Episcopalians that music was necessary for worship," wrote Jane Rasmussen, a historian of church music. Some believed, as Maryland bishop James Kemp did in 1827, that trained voices improved the singing—and worship—of a lethargic congregation, the performance of which often served as a litmus test for the enthusiasm of a parish as a whole. Hodges's father, an ardent supporter of choirs and church music, felt similarly: "What hope can be entertained for the restoration of congregational singing," he wrote, "whilst so deadly a feeling as this [shame] prevails among a large portion of those who profess and call themselves Christians?"[35] For those churches which accepted choirs, the elimination of women became an accepted practice: "By mid-century, the ideal choir was thought to be composed of boys, or boys and men." Vestments, however, were more contested. In one case, even as late as 1871, "a clergyman of the Diocese of Ohio was presented by his bishop for trial, on the ground of violation of the doctrine and discipline of the Church … because he had refused, at the bishop's request, to disband his surpliced choir and give up processional singing."[36] This was an extreme case, though it was not until the late 1850s

Home Away From Home

Early boarders in front of the double townhouses at 8 and 10 East Franklin Street, which the Boys' School called home for 40 years. The land itself was once owned by Revolutionary War hero Colonel John Eager Howard who later left it to his sixth and youngest son, Charles. In 1833, Charles sold it to Charles Meyer who erected the current buildings, built in the Greek Revival style. A lawyer and politician, Meyer was also a philanthropist who helped found the Maryland Historical Society and was one of the incorporators of the House of Refuge, which he managed until his death in 1864. Charles E. Weathered, a manufacturer of doeskins, bought the homes at that time, but four years later transferred the property to United States attorney Archibald Sterling, Jr. Eventually, Sterling retired to the country, and sold the buildings in 1883 to The Boys' School of St. Paul's Parish, residents until 1923, when John G. Mathews bought the place to open a fashionable antique shop. After his death, Tio Pepe's restaurant became its last owner and resident. The boys here were not identified.

"The arrangement with Dr. Hodges is I am to teach at the Boys' School four hours a day and to receive for the session $300. This will enable me to get on without other assistance, I hope, and allow me time for study after one o'clock."

Master J. Stewart Smith in a letter written in 1872
to bishop William R. Whittingham

that using surplices gained any momentum.

Bishop Whittingham did not object to adding vestments to the Church's services.[37] Still, Hodges prepared his congregation for the "shock" in an earlier sermon; and though some documents suggest that the news of such ritual and pomp caused great alarm, only two parishioners on record left for another church (and they later returned). If skepticism and discontent still existed, it did not last. Nine months after the first performance, during Christmas of 1883, Hodges combined the Choir and the nearby Peabody orchestra, whose reputation was already becoming national, in a three-hour service for his "wonderfully ritualistic church."[38]

To Hodges's delight, both Wyatt and Mahan had stressed church music at the Boys' School. Where Wyatt saw the makings of a large charitable and missionary enterprise and Mahan a budding Episcopal High School, Hodges saw a training ground for choristers. In fact, the idea was not a totally novel one. "Sometimes," wrote Rasmussen, "especially when choirs were composed of children, the singers were obtained from orphanages." Still, even by the 1840s, only two churches sponsored boys' choirs.[39]

Despite his eagerness to develop a choir, Hodges arrived to find the position of headmaster vacant and other pressing matters to address first. The board of 12 trustees (three of whom were the original incorporators, including Wyatt's son), on which he sat *ex-officio*, authorized him to secure a headmaster for the first six months of 1871, but was eager to "obtain a permanent headmaster from the training School of St. Mark's in England."[40] The search abroad was unsuccessful and that fall, until 1878, R. D. Whittle became the first appointed headmaster of St. Paul's, responsible his first year for about 20 boarders. According to Hodges, who would be hounded by issues of funding for the next 35 years, "twice that number could be accommodated and more reasonably provided for were the necessary means furnished."[41]

Though Hodges, along with his assistant, I. L. Nicholson, managed the School until 1874 when the trustees took the reins, he referred to Whittle as the "Principal" in his Parochial Report, crediting him "for his zealous and unremitting attention to

Early Legacy
of Choirmasters

Though early histories and records rarely, if ever, refer to the Boys' School as a choir school, often as many as two thirds of the boys enrolled sang in the Choir when they lived on Franklin Street. "Without the Boys' School," wrote the musically gifted composer and rector, Dr. John S. B. Hodges in 1902, "it will be impossible to maintain the standards of the Choir in St. Paul's Church which it has attained." The Choir's quick success was almost entirely due both to Hodges's interest and commitment as well as to the fact that the position of choirmaster became a combination of long tenures (like those of the rectors), and persistent recruiting (like the future athletic coaches), both of which resulted in a strong reputation, tradition, and, perhaps most important, reserve supplies.[1]

Miles Farrow filled the first truly combined role of organist and choirmaster for the Parish in 1894, the beginning of what some refer to as the Golden Age of the Choir. A composer himself, Farrow at age 18 had been an organist of a cathedral in his native state of South Carolina, and arrived at Old St. Paul's for the first time in 1892 as a guest organist. When he began there two years later, Farrow assembled a choir that initially had about 12 boys and six men, though this would soon double in size. In addition to daily choral services (one of the few churches in the country that had them, according to Hodges), and three Sunday services, Farrow was also known for the five annual evening musical services which he arranged. A student of English composers, Farrow visited England five times and wrote an instruction guide, *The Training of Boys' Voices* in 1898. (Perhaps he was more recognized by the students, however, for his donation of a "ping-pong table and outfit" in 1902.) According to Hodges's successor, Dr. Arthur *(continued on next page)*

The Choir in the mid-1920s, still with their Eton collars; rector Arthur B. Kinsolving stands in the center of the third row. Edmund Sereno Ender (fourth from the left, top row), who replaced Alfred Willard in 1921, was choirmaster until 1953.

B. Kinsolving, Farrow, "in the assembly of gifts he possessed—liturgical insight, knowledge of what was best in classic Anglican Church music, skill in getting the best out of his boys, awareness of growth and development in Church music in England and in this country—had no outranking rival in this country."

Not surprisingly, Farrow's departure as choirmaster and headmaster of the Boys' School just after his 15th anniversary with the Parish was "the heaviest blow the music interest of St. Paul's ever received," said Kinsolving. Though the vestry offered him a substantial increase in salary and "the whole community joined in a dignified plea" for him to stay, Farrow opted to take a prestigious position as the first professional organist of the Cathedral of St. John the Divine in New York City, where he served for the next 22 years. Attending the Cathedral's first public service on Easter 1911 were the Choir of Men and Boys, Hodges, noted St. Paul's choristers Harry P. Veazie '06 and Channing Lefebvre '11, and Kinsolving, as well as "about 20 bishops and 500 other clergy." Eventually, Farrow, due to prolonged ill health, returned to Baltimore in 1931 where he passed away in "relative obscurity," according to Douglass Forsyth '56, who wrote the most comprehensive history of the Choir.

When Farrow left, a period of transition followed as the Church solicited applications for choirmaster from all over America and England. By recommendation of Hodges and Farrow, Dr. A. Madely Richardson, an organist of Southwark Cathedral in London, arrived in the fall of 1909, but after a "brief and painful interlude" of less than a year, he left for a new position in Newport, Rhode

"The Boys' School was never strictly a choir school, but the necessity of furnishing eighteen or twenty boys with voices, and the line of boys including the entire school in cap and gown marching on Sundays and week days as well to choral services at the Mother Church under the baton of [choirmaster] Miles Farrow, one of the most gifted Church musicians that Baltimore ever had, gave prominence to this aspect of the School."

The Reverend Arthur B. Kinsolving

A Short History of The Boys' School of St. Paul's Parish

Island. "Dr. Richardson," wrote Kinsolving in his history, "while a master of his craft, came to Baltimore with a British disdain of all things American and very soon proved himself a misfit." Again, the Church struggled to fill the post. Charles F. Wilson, a native of New York, succeeded Richardson in the summer of 1910 and served for four years. The Church then replaced him with Alfred R. Willard from Minneapolis, who served from 1913 until 1921, and who "maintained during his time high tradition in church music," also serving as musical director at Goucher College. An experienced choirmaster, Willard was himself a close observer and student of Miles Farrow. He and his "gifted" wife, who had been appointed at Peabody, were apparently greatly missed from the musical circles of Baltimore when they left.

Even years after Farrow had been gone, the Choir was esteemed. One choral performance in January, 1914 apparently attracted 600 people to the Church "in spite of the inclement weather." Through the transition, Kinsolving also advertised across a fairly wide region for "choristerships" to keep the Golden Age gilded. According to Forsyth, the mother of 32-year chorister Charles Stokes '27 learned about a vacancy at the School in the periodical *Southern Churchman* which she picked up 150 miles from Baltimore. No doubt, Kinsolving was heeding what Hodges said in 1891: "It is no easy task to keep up a choir of men and boys, especially of boys. If you lose a man you can as a general rule replace him by another man who can sing and read music … Boys who read music and have voices are not so readily found, if at all. You have to take raw material and work it from the bottom."[2]

BELOW: 1910 baseball team,
captained by Eugene Milby '10.
The six-game 2-3-1 season
included a 20-2 loss, followed by a
20-2 victory, against the "Country
School" of Gilman. The only tie
was against St. David's Choir.
The boys were not identified
in this picture.

the moral and mental training of the boys; and also to the matron, Mrs. Whittle, whose kind and motherly watchfulness over them adds very greatly to their comfort and well being."[42] Students submitted applications to the rector or to the "chairman of the Committee on Applications," and once enrolled, the progress of the boys was marked by a periodic examination in the Sunday School room, which the congregation was invited to attend. (Few actually went: "Had a greater number of persons responded to the invitation … the result we are sure would be a juster appreciation of the work, and an increased practical interest in it.") For some time, until 1874, the School shared space in the Wyatt Memorial Chapel, which seated 130, a project begun by Mahan, who had also proposed to the trustees using missionaries to help run the School.[43]

PRESENTED BY THE EPISCOPAL REGISTER.

Mother Church

The Parish's first home, a small brick church set on a lot that includes its current area, was erected in the 1730s on a hill overlooking the harbor. Parishioner John Moale had secured the land ("Lot 19") in 1729, the year the Maryland Assembly laid out Baltimore Town. The Parish built a second church in 1784, and seven years later, after vestryman John Eager Howard had donated land on Saratoga Street, the Parish added what is still the Rectory, expanded several times over the course of over two centuries. In 1817, St. Paul's finished a third church with a 126-foot tower, balconies, and space to seat 1600; it was known then as the "Episcopal Cathedral." When this building burned down in 1854, English-born architect Richard Upjohn originally had in his designs a five-story tower for the new edifice (pictured above), but the vestry canceled those plans. Two years later, Upjohn completed what is now commonly referred to as "Old St. Paul's Church," originally painted an ocher tone, which today still stands on the original foundation.

"The summer is in many ways a distressing and
depressing time in the Church. The congregation is
so small on Sundays, and so almost nothing on other
days … scarcely any choir boys are left. The music is
so heavy, the little there is of it … there is none of
the life of young children about."

The Reverend John S. B. Hodges, 1890

Perhaps the vestiges of Wyatt's vision of an orphanage lingered, because when Hodges made a seemingly obvious decision—to charge tuition—it would almost shut the School down. For several years, this experiment appeared to be working. In 1873, of 30 boarders, 18 were entirely supported by the Parish's Parochial Charities Fund, the regular tuition charge being $200.[44] "For every hundred and fifty dollars contributed we will place a beneficiary in the School," he wrote in his report on Parish charities. "Three thousand dollars is not too much to ask for the support and education of *twenty* boys, when one thousand is not infrequently expended upon a single boy's schooling." By adding both day and paying students, the following year the School tripled its enrollment (43 boarders and 18 day students), "more pupils than at any former period of its existence," yet the number of beneficiaries (18 boarders and five day scholars) had dropped slightly. Thus, its annual budget had grown in a year from about $4,000 to $7,662, but now only a third came from the Parochial Charities, dangerously dependent on this new revenue stream.[45] "This was a critical time for the institution," wrote Hodges. "Everything seemed prosperous and encouraging." To accommodate the high enrollment, Hodges added several teachers to help Whittle; had repairs made to the property; moved and expanded the dining room to provide space for a "much needed" library; and purchased new furniture.

But "the tide had risen to its height and had turned." Outstanding tuition charges went uncollected, and this new revenue stream hardly rose above a trickle. The trustees grew anxious about the sour balance sheet at the close of 1876, and a year later, "a plan was prepared for the thorough re-organization of the School, and its entire management put under an executive committee."[46]

The year 1878 was one of reckoning for the Boys' School. The trustees moved to close it entirely. But Hodges challenged them and argued that the School's "scope for doing good was great, if only it could be generously sustained for a few years longer, and by the benefaction of the liberal in the way of legacies in the course of time receive permanent endowments to carry on its work." To compound Hodges's problems, the closing years of the decade were hard economically for the city, as the use of machines soon displaced workers and greatly shifted employment patterns; 1878-9, the most trying year for the School, in fact reflected a "slump" for Baltimore. Additionally, the 1870s as a whole saw significant growth in schools as well as charitable institutions, perhaps diluting the value and innovation some initially saw in the Boys' School. Nevertheless, the board gave in, but on one condition: so long as Hodges ensured that the School would close each year free of any new debt, they would concede. With fourteen boarders, all under full scholarship, the trustees rented a house at 95 St. Paul Street to keep the School running, but disposed of the Saratoga property to extinguish the debt. Headmaster Whittle left in 1878, likely because of a shortage of funds, and that August the trustees placed Hodges in full control of the School. Honoring his commitment to the trustees, Hodges feared admitting paying scholars as the crisis lingered. Enrollment fell to twelve and then to nine, and boys were sent to the "Public School, as there was no master. The boys kept together as a family with a matron in charge."

A woman saved St. Paul's. "Favorable breezes began to blow," wrote Hodges, "not so strongly at first, but steadily." After the School moved once again to 44 East Monument Street, enrollment crept back to 15, and in 1882 Hodges hired a master to instruct the boys in a room in the Parish House. Held on only by the tethers of Hodges's good faith, now orphaned from two homes in four years, the School took a new turn in 1884 through the "munificent liberality" of a $3,500 contribution from parishioner Miss Frances Donaldson. This and the sale of the earlier Saratoga property for $11,500 enabled the trustees to purchase and fit out a three-story building at 31 East Franklin Street and acquire the title of the building next door. (These would both be renumbered 8 and 10 East Franklin Street.)[47]

Part of the optimism, at least for the trustees and for the congregation, stemmed from the fact that by this time money annually appropriated from the Parochial Charities Fund no longer was needed to support the Girls' Orphanage of the Benevolent Society; their leased properties were not only covering expenses but bringing in revenue, a result they had been anticipating for some time. For the Girls' Orphanage, Hodges had proven his credibility at managing money, and so used it as an example of how to secure the Boys' School for the long term. Of the three other Parish charities, the Church Home, the Parish Mission, and the Boys' School, Hodges asked for the most from his congregation for the School ($3,000). And even in its still weak state, he claimed that the School was "growing in strength and in efficiency," and emphasized in his short history of the Boys' School in 1905 that "*to-day [the School is] doing more work, and better work, than for several years past.*"[48] He also alluded to an "implied understanding" (presumably with either Miss Donaldson or the trustees) "that the benefits of the School were to be extended as widely as possible, and the grade of the School to be brought up to as high a standard as possible."[49]

THE GOLDEN AGE

And so here, on the steep cobbled hills of Franklin Street not four blocks from the Church, these hardships hopefully past, the School would remain for the next 40 years, and see its own Golden Age with eminent choirmaster Miles Farrow; with the musically gifted Hodges, whose faith in the School had been heavily tested; and with choristers who came from hundreds of miles away. The 1880s were a time of recovery for the School. On the first condition of the new infusion of money—to extend the reach of the School—Hodges was able to "act promptly" and increase enrollment to 21 boys (with only one paying), led by a resident master, a matron and a non-resident assistant master. "The wisdom of keeping the School open soon became evident … especially for the friends of well-born but poor boys who are not otherwise able to secure the benefits of the foundation of a liberal Christian education." Hodges had already begun putting serious thought into creating an endowment for the Parish as well as for the School. Urging his congregation to contribute ("$2,500 is the amount we ask for this year"), he ambitiously aimed to give the School a "position of independence." The School, he said, "is strictly Parochial, in the sense of looking only to our own people for support." While there were a few notable legacy gifts, donations from the congregation ranged from "one pair chickens" to "three dollars" to "bag peas" to "one necktie," even as members such as Dr. A. H. Powell, who acted as school physician, would volunteer their services.[50] In 1886, Hodges made an aggressive move to streamline the Parochial Charities overall by restricting funds only for his Church Home and the Boys' School. Improvements to the Franklin Street building were regular and often expensive; in 1893, for instance, about 40 percent of the total operating budget went to house maintenance and repairs, and a little less than a third to salaries, with the rest split among servants, books and stationery, gas, and furnishing.[51] Some changes were made for students: "An additional large room on the ground floor has been carpeted and furnished as a sitting room for the boys in the evenings."[52] Nevertheless, by the time Hodges left twenty years later in 1905, the School's endowment had climbed to $47,000, providing the School with nearly half its operating money from invested funds, while the Church's $72,000 was not significantly higher—an interesting comparison.[53] Hodges now had his pair of solvent institutions: the St. Paul's Orphan Asylum for Girls, at 10 East Franklin Street, and, next door, his Boys' School at number eight, which seemed to be evolving into a legitimate secondary school.[54]

Now that he had finances under control, Hodges could concentrate on improving the academics, which he admitted were "not so high as some might expect" and which he partially attributed to the fact "that the younger boys applying for admission are received in preference to those who are older, and consequently enter the School with little preparation." By 1887, enrollment generally remained at a stable 30—five greater than the number Hodges believed comfortable—a number that would hold almost perfectly steady until the School moved in 1923. He claimed that

Corralling the Old Boys

"The Association of former members of the Boys' School"—ten years before the School awarded diplomas and had graduates—gathered for drinks in the assistant minister's study and for dinner in St. Paul's House to form the Alumni Association on January 26, 1895. "In previous years the alumni have not been known to the School in general but only to individual boys," noted the students in 1914. "Owing to this fact we have not been able to locate as many of the 'Old Fellows' as we had hoped to."

This first meeting was organized primarily through the efforts of assistant rector and the new Association's president, the Reverend Charles A. Jessup, though "great regret was felt at his absence" at this first meeting of 18 men. Alumnus Frank Gavin presided over the meeting, which included the rector and school physician Dr. A. H. Powell. At this 1895 meeting, one notable action item was implemented—the Alumni Medal: "It was announced that the Association, to show their affection and love of their old school, had offered a handsome prize, to be contested for by the boys at the School, and they hope to continue this feature year by year." The medal is still presented annually at graduation.

Though the association apparently had 60 active members at this time, no record of its work exists. The club stalled in 1900 when Jessup withdrew, and was not reorganized until April, 1913 by headmaster William Elmer, appointing Robert Nelson '10 as its first president. A year later, the "Association of Old Boys," as Dr. Arthur

Graphic from the students' *Triakonta*.

"Maurice Hill '08 is attending Kent School, Connecticut. We hope that he has been able to take up a mechanical course as he would often show his talent while here by breaking up the electric light system."

"Alumni Notes," *Triakonta,* 1912

Kinsolving referred to its two dozen or so active members, met three times a year for the "transaction of important business." At the first meeting, alumni re-introduced the Alumni Medal, described as a "beautiful trophy," though it was actually a gold medal, given to the boy who most excelled in his deportment.

The very notion of alumni—their responsibilities, their loyalty—was just now taking shape as a formal idea; Kinsolving, from Episcopal High School, and Elmer, from Woodberry Forest School, recognized their importance. Other schools, like the Episcopal Academy, which began its Alumni Society in 1878, and the Hill School, which began one in 1894, both in Pennsylvania, were examples of a similar effort to maintain and extend the boarding school family after graduation. To make it official at St. Paul's, Elmer had to give out diplomas first, which he did in his second year in 1914. (Students still had to complete high school elsewhere.) "Now, alumni, it would be very easy for you to drop us a line telling us about yourselves and where you are," wrote students, but, despite their commitment to printing an "Alumni Notes" section in every issue, the boys soon lamented not long after this first solicitation at the lapsing alumni subscriptions. "Several of the alumni have refused to subscribe," commented students, "because they no longer know any of the boys." In truth, the most committed alumni began to arrive with the first high school diploma, awarded in 1927.[1]

"In the past the School has been entirely devoted to the work of the Choir which has always been a great feature, but now other branches are sprouting out. Chief among these is athletics. On October 24, we began the first of a series of foot-ball games, four in number."

Triakonta, 1910

RIGHT: This 1912 soccer team, unfortunately not identified, could not seem to score a victory during their short season against Reid Memorial, St. Andrew's, and the Jefferson School.

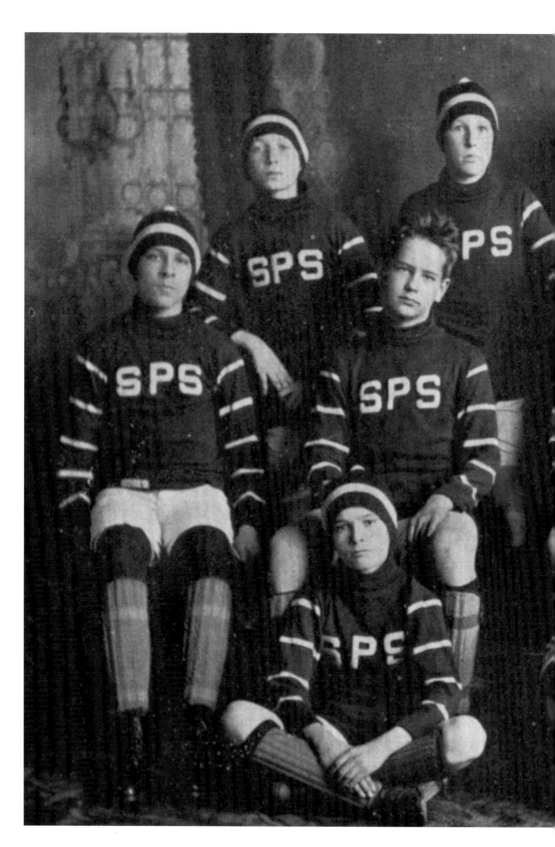

the School "supplies a want in the Church which is not supplied elsewhere in Maryland … There is no reason why the Boys' School should not take high rank amongst the educational institutions of the Church, and extend to future generations the benefits of a thorough moral and spiritual training."[55] For Hodges, raising the level of scholarship sometimes came second to raising the caliber of music, and he occasionally appointed music teachers over other masters. Not until the summer of 1891 did the Choir have August off in the summer, an "experiment" which Hodges proclaimed a success. (And by 1899, choir boys had both July and August to relax.)[56]

At the turn of the century, the curriculum, assessed by regular, public examinations, certainly seemed comprehensive enough, if not overwhelming: writing, mathematics, physiology and hygiene, Latin, German, geography, history, English literature, drawing and bookkeeping, "a long but very useful and excellent list." The School emphasized "reading and spelling, writing and figuring, four things which are very essential to-day in the education of every man."[57] And every Friday, boys were given instruction in church history by a member of the clergy.

Amidst the daily routine, the "Gay Nineties" kept Baltimore active and life around the School both exciting and uncertain. "The confusion of telephone and telegraph wires on tall poles at the intersection of Charles and Lexington Streets was like a maze of a steel engraving."[58] The Orioles took three straight championships in the National Baseball League from 1894-96; the two popular rowing clubs, the Arial and the Arundel, known as the "Patapsco Navy," attracted great attention; and lacrosse took hold in 1888 at Johns Hopkins. Theater expanded "with gusto" at places like the Wednesday Club on Charles Street; Henry Ford tinkered with the gasoline buggy, though the barouche, drawn by two horses, was still most prestigious; the Linotype had revolutionized printing; and people were shouting "Remember the Maine!" when the US declared war in 1898 against Spain after the Spanish fleet destroyed the battleship *Maine*.[59]

Despite this burgeoning of economic and social development in the metropolitan area, a majority of the boys were not local. For the 1892-93 year, Hodges listed all 11 new boys (out of 24 total), only four of whom were from Baltimore, one from D.C., two brothers from York, Pennsylvania, and the others from Calvert, Cecil and Talbot Counties. Even much later—in 1911, for instance—only two of the eight new boys were from Baltimore, the others coming from New York, Pennsylvania and Virginia. Applications for admission, "sought from distant points," had been increasing since the early 1880s, requiring an admission process that was "often a painful duty to have to give an unfavorable reply to such appealing and deserving applications."[60] Hodges claimed in 1895 that if funds were available they could double the 24 currently enrolled. Preference was often given to the children of clergy and communicants. On one occasion, the bishop made a personal visit to the School, requesting that two more boys be enrolled "until they shall be able to enter some col-

Though this picture was taken during the School's visit to Old St. Paul's for the "Lessons and Carols" service, inaugurated by headmaster Robert Hallett in 1985, the Church has not made any significant changes to its interior since it was rebuilt on the same footings in 1856, two years after a fire had burned most of it down.

lege, and eventually take Orders in the Church."[61]

By now, Hodges had created his choir school, which also shared qualities of Mahan's boarding school vision. "It is not an orphan asylum, or a home for destitute and uncared-for waifs," Hodges averred. "We receive boys of a respectable parentage, the children oftentimes of those who have been well-educated, and have occupied a good position in society, but who are not able to give their boys an education." By 1895, all boys in the Choir were pupils in the School, accounting for 15 of the 24 boys total, six of whom were in training. On a few occasions, Hodges turned down boys who applied so he could hold spots for "two to three boys with good natural voices, training not required, who may be of use in the Choir." Otherwise, he did not pack the School with singers.[62] In truth, though Hodges believed the Choir greatly increased the parishioners' interest in the School and therefore in giving to it, and though he claimed the services had risen to "place the name of St. Paul's Church amongst the foremost in this Country," he often reiterated that the School was not simply a training ground.[63]

If a woman rescued the School in 1878, women again boosted it in 1895, when they significantly expanded and solidified the Boys' School. To start with, that year the trustees of the Benevolent Society decided to move their Girls' Orphanage from Franklin Street and hand over the building to the Boys' School. Their move was in part a reflection of the larger suburban development north of the Church, due to the quick spread of "electric transit with annexation," and in many ways a precursor to a decision the Boys' School would make several decades later. Second, two gifts, one of $5,000 from Miss Martha Gray, who that same year would add another $10,000, and another of $1,000 from Miss Donaldson, who enabled the School to make the earlier move to Franklin Street, gave "the rector the opportunity of enlarging the work and bringing it up to a higher educational tone."[64] Immediately, with the added space, the School's enrollment filled and exceed its capacity of 30 boys.

And so, for 25 years, the Boys' School was Hodges's adopted child. He had exercised his most important right, by the authority of the Board, to appoint the headmaster. But in 1902, the trustees resolved that the rector should only select candidates, leaving the decision to the board. The decision was probably a result of a growing tension between the rector and the vestry, who disagreed with Hodges about how to run the Church. "Unfortunately," wrote Kinsolving in his history, "there was considerable friction just before his resignation between Dr. Hodges and the lay trustees, so the fortunes of the Boys' School were at a rather low ebb when Hodges's successor entered upon his duties." Still, Hodges left the School in a remarkable condition when he stepped down as rector in 1905. It was "no longer an experiment," he claimed. Enrollment was steady, an endowment was increasing, and a reputation had been secured for scholarship and music.[65] During the period between rectorships, the trustees appointed the esteemed choirmaster Miles Farrow to be headmaster. Hodges left the Parish on the tail of the devastating fire of 1904, which ripped through half the city of Baltimore and just missed the School.

DOCTOR KINSOLVING ARRIVES

Just as Dr. Arthur B. Kinsolving, the first Virginian rector of the Parish, did not bring the roof of the High Church tradition any lower at first—as some had expected—he made no dramatic changes to the Boys' School when he began on October 1, 1906. Yet with patience he changed the institution systematically and, over the course of his 35 years, dramatically. Perhaps he knew it would take this much time to impart his own vision for the School. It was a vision derived in mission, design and spirit from his alma mater, Episcopal High School (EHS), in Alexandria, Virginia, where he had become a colleague of its 44-year principal, Dr. Launcelot Minor Blackford. Though Episcopal High School was only ten years older than St. Paul's, it had developed much more quickly, with six times the enrollment (186) in 1922. More importantly, Kinsolving could readily apply Episcopal High School's philosophy to its Baltimore cousin without much adaptation. As much as Hodges had created a choir school, he had also set the foundation for a church school, very similar to the way Kinsolving once described EHS in its history (which he finished, incidentally, at St. Paul's Parish): "The grounding he gets in English … the habit of relating knowledge to life…to form sound opinions … to have some knowledge of those international relations … But the thing which makes the High School a place appealing to a boy's deepest loyalty is that it is a Christian school founded and carried on by men of faith and prayer."[66]

Kinsolving also saw that the Boys' School had potential and had proven its viability: consistent enrollment figures; a secure financial footing (all boys received full scholarships); and a strong loyalty and tradition with the "indefatigable and enthusiastic instructor in vocal music" Miles Farrow, who would stay as headmaster until 1909. Kinsolving found a committed group of trustees, such as J. B. Noel Wyatt, grandson of William Wyatt, and J. Marshall Thomas, both of whom reportedly visited the School almost daily.[67] And other influential Baltimore businessmen, including Herbert M. Brune, Leigh Bonsal, John E. Semmes, G. Herbert Boehm, and J. Harry Lee were active in such routine business as securing masters and matrons.[68]

The Parish welcomed Kinsolving and hoped to acclimate him quickly to the mission of both the Church and the School. Members of the vestry as well as the congregation also viewed it as an opportunity to address issues that Hodges had apparently neglected. "The important matter of the systematic religious instruction of the boys and girls in our two Schools is just being taken up," read a short piece in a 1906 *Parish Notes*, just after Kinsolving arrived. "As the new rector was prepared for the university at a Church school, and also served as under-master in two large Church schools for several years, it is natural that this side of the work of St. Paul's should appeal to him … Meanwhile, we beg to assure those who are interested that this sacred claim has not been forgotten."[69]

The stability of the School, however, was not guaranteed when Kinsolving arrived. Headmaster Farrow, for instance, had the assistance of two under-masters who often stayed for a year or less, men who were usually recent college graduates in transition themselves. (Frederick B. Harrison, for instance, who was assistant master from 1907-09, received his Ph.D from Yale while he was still teaching; James D. Pinkerton, assistant from 1911-12, went on to Harvard Law School.) Others seemed to move around to different schools with fair frequency, such as Horace Smith (1911-13), who went on to Gilman Country School. Additionally, students often left during the school year, usually because of sickness, with significant turnover (sometimes half the boys) during the summer. For those students who stayed several years, they might have enjoyed some sense of continuity with headmasters, the Reverend Edward S. Juny (1896-1902); the Reverend R. S. Wood, who served the next four years; and later, the Reverend William T. Elmer, who led the School from 1910-17. Their "beloved"

Patron Saint

The Reverend

Dr. Arthur Barksdale Kinsolving

In a large mural of ten prominent Baltimore philanthropists in Shriver Hall at Johns Hopkins University, the Reverend Dr. Arthur Barksdale Kinsolving stands among George Peabody, Moses Sheppard, Enoch Pratt, William H. Welch, James Cardinal Gibbons, Johns Hopkins, John D. Rockefeller, Robert H. Jenkins and Theodore Marburg. But while this memorial might exalt him as a patron saint of twentieth-century Christian Baltimore, Kinsolving has always been patron saint of St. Paul's School, shaping its most distinctive features over the course of 36 years.

The underlying current in his (and the School's) history is Virginian. The name Kinsolving, thought to be Scandinavian, first was seeded there by his great-grandfather in Albemarle County, where he had only one son, George Kinsolving, a dealer in horses who socialized with Thomas Jefferson at Monticello. George also had an only son, Ovid, who adventured with a black servant over the Appalachians to Kenyon College in Ohio where, inspired by an English group known as the Seventeenth Century Metaphysical Poets, he aspired to the Episcopal priesthood, graduating from the Theological Seminary in

Virginia and becoming the first clergyman in the state to wear a white vestment. Ovid married the sister of the vice provost of University of Pennsylvania, Julia Krauth, but it was Ovid's second wife, Lucy Lee Rogers, a descendant of the Virginia Lees and apparently a woman of "great saintliness and high literary intelligence," who gave birth to Arthur Kinsolving. Thus, Kinsolving had in his Virginian lineage men and women of stature, faith and passion.

Kinsolving was born in 1861 in the rectory of Emmanuel Church in Middleburg, Virginia, a year before his father was incarcerated in a northern prison by the Federal Army at the opening of the Civil War. After his release, his father became rector of St. John's Church in Halifax, Virginia, where he raised Arthur and his brother Lucien. In 1882, Arthur graduated from Episcopal High School, taught there for a year (1883-4), spent a year at the University of Virginia, and was graduated from the Theological Seminary of Virginia in 1886, at which point he led his first parish in Warsaw, Virginia. Not long after, on a call to New York City to seek funds for a church in his parish lost by fire, he accepted the rectorship at Christ Church, Brooklyn; led the second largest parish on Long Island until 1906; and was archdeacon of Southern Brooklyn for five years. He was a deputy to the General Convention of the Episcopal Church eleven times, served as chairman of the National Committee on Christian Education, and was a board member of Episcopal High School, about which he wrote a history. Just before he became rector of St. Paul's Parish and moved into the rectory, he received the degree of Doctor of Divinity from Washington and Lee in 1905. As if he were not busy enough, at age 35 he married Sally Archer Bruce, with whom he had seven children.

Kinsolving was indefatigably human and challenged by the world, but always had wit at his side. With two brothers who were bishops of the Episcopal Church, he watched his wife convert to Roman Catholicism (after all seven of his children had left the Rectory) and his daughter marry a Jewish man. (To this he quipped, "Though I am broad ecclesiastically, I never expected to become a link between Abraham and the Pope.") He tried to raise chickens behind the Rectory in his early years there and failed, attracting "rats and dirt." He fended off a steady stream of burglars, two of whom successfully broke into his home. He had his assistant clergy press grapes into wine in the Rectory basement. As a dinner guest along with the Choir, he "ordered" steak to be considered whale meat in view of Lenten abstinence rules. When he had his eye removed and replaced with a glass one in 1943, no one noticed, and some said his vision was even clearer.

He was an avid golfer and spent summers in Fishers Island, New York where he served as summer rector of St. John's Church from 1911 to 1935, and where he later died. He was close friends with Cardinal James Gibbons; was a member of the University Club, where he spent time with some of the local politicos such as Theodore Marburg and Alfred Shriver; knew King Edward VII (and also William Temple, soon to become archbishop of Canterbury), whom he visited on a trip England in 1908 (and talked about in New York City subways); caught a ride back to Long Island on a garbage truck; and apparently terrorized a bishop on a short practical joke by driving slightly too fast on a car ride to Washington. Having survived a civil war and two world wars, he died on August 15, 1951, when, on his last birthday, he said he "never expected to attain the freezing altitudes of the nineties."[1]

A servant of the community, of the Parish, and of the Boys' School, Kinsolving's *modus operandi* was this: "If you want a man to serve you, get him to love you."

Graphic from the students' *Triakonta*.

A Day on Franklin Street

Think back for a moment. Your week was crammed, your day filled as a student on Franklin Street. This was home for you and 29 others. Rise at 7:30 in one of the five upstairs dormitories. Breakfast at 8:00, prepared by Mrs. Weaver: lumpy oatmeal, usually, wishing it were tapioca pudding, which you dubbed "frog eyes." Then you finished your chores, and from 9:00 until 1:00—though it is a blur to you now—in one of the two large adjoining rooms, you had some arrangement of English literature, mathematics, American history, music, French, and more Latin than you could handle, all taught by two teachers. The rest of your day flew by: lunch at 1:30; three hours of choir from 2:00 to 5:00, broken up—hopefully—with 45 minutes of recreation (when you tried to avoid the "Calvert Street Gang"); supper at 6:00, when you had to watch the teachers enjoy specially-prepared creamed potatoes, milk and lamb chops. You studied from 7:00 until 9:30, and then, exhausted, you put out the lights at 10:00 p.m. This was a five-day routine, from Tuesday to Saturday, but if you included Sundays—with services, Sunday School, and choir rehearsals (unless you were an acolyte)—a six-day routine would be more accurate.

In what little free time you had, you visited the YMCA for gymnastics two blocks away, or Druid Hill Park for football, the Fifth Regiment Armory for track, or the Rennert Hotel for ice cream. You could always use the ping-pong table, the pool table, or the dumbbells at school, and in the winter you might try skiing in Worthington Valley. If you were really lucky, you went to dances at the Girls' School on North Charles Street, or on the Sunday School trip to Tolchester, with swimming and games all day. Hot air balloons, the Baltimore fire with the sky so lit up, tobacco on the streets, Halley's Comet, the Circus Parade and Bob Ula's band, made school in the city both exciting and scary. Perhaps you tired of being a perfect choir boy and spent ten cents on a crystal radio set to listen to a broadcast after lights out or, one winter day, decided to smear Limburger cheese on the radiators. "It was the biggest stink I ever raised," you boasted.

You remember Dr. Kinsolving clearly. Your math teacher who threw chalk at the blackboard. The kindness of Miss Gilman and Miss Harwood, housemother Miss Bryan, Mr. Wyatt, and Mr. Thomas. You even recall playing lacrosse at Mt. Washington—long before the School moved there—with sticks which people thought were crabbing nets. But for you, the Choir was always the heart of the School, and you fondly remember marching in cap and gown to church, waving proudly back at Cardinal Gibbons in the mornings.[1]

The Reverend S. Hilton Orrick served as Dr. Arthur Kinsolving's loyal assistant rector from 1921-53. Orrick was the saint in full charge of the Church through the summer, during which time he occasionally lived with his family at the Boys' School after it moved to Mt. Washington. The 1945 *Crusader*, the student yearbook, is dedicated to him, "a symbol of the Christian virtues."

housemother Miss Ellen Bryan (1895-1910) and Farrow (1894-1909) certainly had the most durable presence. Despite all of this shifting of people, the buildings on Franklin Street were indeed far less a school than a home, with the five dormitories, two bedrooms for the teachers, two dining rooms, two school rooms (one which doubled as a choir room), and a library. Other essentials were not forgotten: a billiard table, "thirty wands and rings," a ping-pong table and a piano.

By 1912, Kinsolving had articulated the School's mission: "The task we have before us is the proper training of boys in body, mind and spirit." In almost every issue of *Parish Notes*, Kinsolving gave reports about the Boys' School to educate his congregation about its mission and purpose. Since he had arrived, Kinsolving carried the School toward what soon became his mantra: *Ut sit mens sana in corpore sano* ("that he may be sound mind in a sound body"), the first manifestation of which was a gymnastics exhibition at the University School on Maryland Avenue in 1907. "In the 'free movements' exercises," he described, "and advanced gymnastics on the parallel bars, the boys' precision, quickness of eye, hand, foot and manly bearing were visible tokens of careful discipline ... The 'play element' was given its proper place in the Indian club relay race and a game of basket-ball." Exercise was still limited to about three hours each week at the nearby YMCA, or calisthenics exercises with the master in the playroom, neither of which seemed to begin until the middle of winter. In his solicitations for support, Kinsolving admitted in 1910 that while activities of the boys had improved, more needed to be done in the area of physical education, and that they needed to renovate a large room in the School for a gymnasium, because "the low sloping ceiling makes it very inadequate."[70]

Despite the fact that usually a third of the enrollment had to be filled each year, Kinsolving never had trouble keeping the School at capacity, though one could sense that he was often scrambling to find boys. In only one year, 1914, did the "very unusual circumstance" occur in which every boy who was enrolled in the spring returned in the fall.[71] In general, the rector, the choirmaster, the Parish music committee, and often members of the congregation were "constantly on the alert" for "boys of intelligence and promise, between the ages of 10 and 12," particularly those "boys with voices." In many cases, the choirmaster was still looking for boys in October, even when all vacancies had been filled for the fall.[72]

High among Kinsolving's priorities was improving the academic quality and standards of the School, a place now "for thirty boys, choristers, sons of clergymen and others who could not otherwise secure the advantages we were giving them," noting an improved curriculum by 1910 for which more "thorough work is being done." Assessment was done through monthly public examinations. More rigorous religious instruction appeared, and boys continued to be confirmed at the School. (In 1911, a typical year, of the 29 boys at the School, 21 were communicants of the Parish, and seven were confirmed at the Church.) Under choirmaster Alfred Williard, music once again became part of the regular curriculum, in part due to the high number of 24 boys training for the Choir. Other changes in the academics were on one hand hardly notable, but on the other significant, because they slowly, but permanently, altered the School. In Kinsolving's first year, for instance, he decided to publish for the first time recipients of commencement awards, as well as the students' "General Averages," in the Parish newsletter, ranking them from highest (H. Wetherbee Fort '10 with a 99 percent average) to lowest (George C. Thomas '10 with an 89 percent average). He could subsequently show his congregation first, that the School had raised its standards when these averages suddenly plummeted the following year, (highest, 83 percent to lowest, 79 percent), and then a year later, that classes had become more competitive as this range now went from 58 percent to 94 percent, a more typical academic spread. The number of commencement prizes had tripled by 1909, and he also introduced two other important prizes for choir boys, one for progress and improvement and the other, the choir medal, for "deportment." These prizes now totaled 15, about one for every other boy.[73]

All this is to say that Kinsolving was clearly shaping the Boys' School using an Episcopal High School mold. His leadership and changes were decisive and lasting and they rounded out the School's offerings. He encouraged the boys to start a literary magazine, *Triakonta*, for themselves and the Parish community in 1909. The Randall Literary Society, an organization for the upper three forms, also began that year. Both were attempts to rally students around academic and intellectual exercises, to provide them a forum to share their ideas and work, and, according to Kinsolving, "to give the boys an opportunity to learn to speak in public."[74] Though the Randall Society included speeches and performances, other public shows began as early as 1906, when the boys gave a "creditable minstrel show" for the Sunday School children. For both diversion and instruction, Kinsolving also invited speakers to the School, such as Dr. Abercrombie, who for many years would give lectures for the students on such topics as "Hygiene." Even Kinsolving's minor changes often made substantive differences. In 1910, for instance, he referred to the older grades for the first time as the "Boys' High School," an important distinction. And the library, for those "many boys" who were "voracious readers," had grown from a few books to 1,200 volumes, bolstered by frequent gifts from people like Elizabeth Gilman, who donated a 20-volume set called "The University of Literature."[75]

Of all this, perhaps the most important aspect of Kinsolving's tenure was that, unlike his predecessors, he did not plan on running this School himself; he believed in others and he delegated. Thus his appointment of the Reverend William T. Elmer was another shaping moment. Elmer, who also served as assistant minister for the Parish, had taught for nine years at Woodberry Forest, Virginia, a rival of Episcopal High School. Although originally appointed for one year, Elmer went on to serve for seven because of the efficiency and thoroughness of his management. Thus with great

The Choir Medal, still the highest honor for a chorister, was first given to Winthrop Heyer '08 and Wallace Everton '07 in 1907.

Graphic from the students' *Triakonta*.

Choirboy Comedy

A *Jokes* section made every issue of the students' first newspaper. Examples:

TEACHER OF MATHEMATICS (who has just given back the corrected exam papers): "The three pupils in the last row are the only ones who had correct answers to the first two examples."
VOICE (from back of room): "good teamwork."

TEACHER: What is the meaning of trickling?
STUDENT: Running slowly.
T: What is the meaning of anecdote?
S: A short funny tale.
T: Correct. Now a sentence illustrating both words.
S: A dog trickled down the street with a can tied to his anecdote.

speed, by Kinsolving's design, Elmer's administration, and the "long experience and warm personal interest" of assistant master Horace Smith, did the School evolve its own sense of identity and unity. At the 1914 commencement, Elmer announced that the School would offer real diplomas, called "certificates of proficiency," for the first time in its history for completing the regular five-year course. The following year marked the first valedictory address, given by graduating student Charles Kloman '15. And students made attempts at the first school song and emblem.[76]

Students tested and rejected other attempts at self-definition, however. In 1911, younger boys formed two clubs, later referred to as fraternities, the Beta Phi and the Sigma Sigma. These were disbanded either due to a lack of interest or perhaps as a result of a larger national debate that questioned high school fraternities. (The boys

"It seems natural to assume that on Mars human nature is fundamentally the same as that on Earth, and that only in its fuller development lies its superiority."

Charles R. Kloman '15, in the School's first valedictory address in 1915.

LEFT: Students at commencement in 1915 with the Reverend William T. Elmer (top center). Graduates of the Class of 1915, now "Old Boys," were: Ralph E. Buxton, C. A. Clark, J. Carroll Johns, Charles R. Kloman, Charles A. Wilson, and Jere M. Wilson.

"We trust that those who have gardens which more than supply their own needs will kindly remember us at the Boys' School, and help us to take care of the large family we have to maintain there. Any autumn vegetables would be so welcome an addition to our larder, potatoes, carrots, cabbages, anything that you have."

The Reverend Arthur B. Kinsolving, 1919

The first indication of a school emblem, featured on the 1915 cover of *Triakonta*, the first student publication.

offered their own opinion on the matter in 1917: "The spirit of the high school fraternity is in direct contrast with the spirit of the true democracy that should exist in our secondary schools and consequently should, and ultimately must, go.") Mostly, though—the emblem, the song, the club, the magazine—fell victim to the coming World War.

IN SPITE OF THE WAR!

"We will do our best to make the paper a success—IN SPITE OF THE WAR!" cried the editorial in the fall 1914 *Triakonta*:

> *A terrible calamity has happened in Europe! The traditions of Christmas have been overthrown even in our own country. Now we are in the throes of panic. What little we can spare is given to the fugitives of the war abroad; mother economizes in household management and father walks to business so that suitable offering may be made … Christmas traditions may be upset but the legend remains.*

Despite such effusive patriotism and anxiety, it is hard to gauge just how immersed the young boys were in the details of the war, though the boys seemed knowledgeable enough, as one program for the Randall Literary Society attested: "Debate: Resolved, that air crafts are better for the destruction of battleships than submarines." Williard's choir, as an added example, performed in December, 1915 at the Lyric for Belgian Relief, raising $1,000. But this was certainly a far cry from the November 17, 1918, Sunday service after the Armistice, during which the Choir sang "Te Deum," Hodges's "Jubilate," and other anthems. Even so, in Kinsolving's most substantive history of the Boys' School, he never mentioned the war except in the most limited references, such as to lament over a headmaster's departure for service.

Still, both School and especially the Parish made many sacrifices and adjustments in war-time Baltimore. Significant labor shortages grew as the number of enlisted men from Maryland jumped from 3,000 at the opening of the war to 62,000 by its close. As a total of 170 young men in the Parish enlisted, women of the Parish also got directly involved with the war effort through such church-initiated efforts as the Red

Thirty Ways Hath September

That the boys could name their first student publication after the number of boys enrolled suggests that life on Franklin Street must have seemed stable enough. So, in 1909 students started *Triakonta*, meaning "30" in Greek, which they published and circulated among themselves, the alumni and the Parish community with fair regularity until the School's move to Mt. Washington in 1923. "This being the only publication of its kind ever produced in the School, the paper naturally cannot be compared with those of larger schools," proclaimed an editorial in the inaugural issue. "But we intend, in the course of time, to increase it both in actual size and amount of literature which at present, owing to the small age of most of the boys, we are not able to do." Rector Arthur B. Kinsolving informed his congregation in 1910 that he hoped it would also be an incentive to the boys to help them develop school spirit.

Equal parts literature, school directory, public relations, alumni newsletter and calendar, *Triakonta* is the clearest window through which we can peek into the small, intimate community of the Boys' School on Franklin Street. In the first years of its publication, most issues listed every visitor to the School in the previous months, while the "News" section included details of daily existence that ranged from tongue-in-cheek ("Several boys were at home for a short holiday sick, but we trust that the coming pleasures of examinations will urge them to recovery") to administrative ("A series of lectures on sanitary hygiene is being given by Dr. Abercrombie of Johns Hopkins every Thursday at 12:00") to the decidedly banal ("Page Nelson has assumed the task of writing out an account of athletics").

The publication was staffed with editors and a business manager (who solicited ads from several dozen patrons), and Kinsolving pronounced it a "very creditable production" at Sunday service. Students often exchanged and critiqued papers with schools such as Landon, Episcopal High School, Woodberry Forest (from which headmaster Elmer came), Taft, and locally, Gilman and McDonogh. If St. Paul's boys didn't see themselves as part of the expanding circle of private and public schools, they were certainly aware of what and who were around them.

One important legacy of the magazine which discontinued in 1922: Beverly R. L. Rhett '21, the publication's business manager in 1921, would later teach at St. Paul's for 15 years and help found and advise the School's second newspaper, *The Monitor*, in 1932.

Franklin Street Rock

The first school song appeared in 1910 but, like many of the traditions of this period, did not survive World War I or the move to Mt. Washington. Initiated by the School's long-time friend J. B. Noel Wyatt, the song below was finished by the boys in a contest; the record also shows that the school song ended the 1912 commencement exercises.[1] The result:

From Saratoga's rugged hill
  where the shadow of St. Paul's
Lies on the ancient cobblestones,
  Besides its tawny walls,
To where on Franklin's fairer slope
  Our pleasant pastures lay,
We *Triakonta* S. P. S. would wend
  our wont-ed way.

(Chorus)
Singing! What's *Triakonta*?
Can't you guess?
Why! *Triakonta* "S. P. S."

And there within the sheltered fold
  Our young ideas would shoot
Attached to "Bryan's" apron strings
  And fed on Latin root,
With "periods" of Pool and Gym;
  Or lured to field and track
We'd march, with Miller in the van
  and Veasy at the back

Singing! &c &c &c

Or else from out the sacred shrine
  Of Music, in the rear,
Would burst forth floods of melody
  To charm the listening ear;
Or tones of such Wagnerian din,
  You'd think the house afire,
And, for the rescue rushing in.
  Would find it was—the choir:

Singing! &c &c &c

"Now as the United States has entered the war, we all should

'do our bit.' This summer the boys can go to the 'farming

camps' to help solve the food problems. At these camps the

boys will have military drills and will be prepared for the

army so they can join as soon as they are old enough. The

younger people of America ought not and will not be behind

in helping in the great fight for Liberty, for a world peace,

and for humanity ... We therefore are bound to help bring

this terrible conflict to a climax as soon as possible and

above all 'Stand by the President!'"

Triakonta, 1917

Cross committee, producing large quantities of surgical dressings at St. Paul's House and creating a "club" for service men at Camp Meade, which was very popular for weekend leaves.[77]

Raising funds for the operations of the School became more challenging, but despite money being diverted toward war funds and the increase in the cost of supplies, Kinsolving did not seem to have significant problems until later; even in 1918 he remarked on how well the School was doing in its instruction and enrollment figures. This optimism was soon tempered by "considerable difficulty," when, before that year closed, headmaster Thomas DeCourcey Ruth and both of his masters were called into service.[78] The situation had become even more difficult when the trustees had to ask his successor, headmaster Harry Converse, to resign after one year of service, making that summer "rather an anxious one [since], of course, that of house-mother, Miss Yancy went with it [his resignation]." Financially, since a weak dollar strained resources overall, times were extremely tight for the School in the closing years of the decade. The price of coal, "another abuse," in Kinsolving's words, had almost tripled between 1911 and 1921, an increase "for which there seems to be no excuse" and which heavily taxed the heating budget of the Church and its six buildings.[79]

While war filled the larger emotional and political context in which the School operated, changes in the urban landscape, especially around Franklin Street, were dramatic too. In the early 1900s, "auto owners began redesigning the city" and "sharp entrepreneurs began adapting ... to the new form of locomotion. Charles Street, Cathedral Street, and Mt. Royal Avenue ... instantly became auto-oriented." Half a million people watched the first airplane fly over the city on November 7, 1910.

Though Baltimore was "still a horsey town" and "did not give the impression of a highly mechanized city, introductions of dozens of mechanical, electrical, and automotive devices excited a sense of futuristic changes and visions of comfort, speed, and youth. But the quality of urban life, for better or for worse, was essentially human and animal, rather than mechanical. It was this quality—the human tempo—that after the war became the object of nostalgia."[80]

On November 11, 1918 at 11:00 am, whistles blew signaling the Armistice. Both City and School erupted in joy, and everybody traveled downtown to celebrate. "Nobody returned until dark," claimed an editorial in *Triakonta*. Celebrations were somewhat quelled, however, by an influenza epidemic which closed the School that same autumn for several weeks.

The war disrupted and delayed the formation of a budding school identity, one that had been evolving since Elmer began as headmaster. Once he left, the School lost continuity during a wave of six different headmasters the trustees appointed between 1917 and 1923, the year the School moved to Mt. Washington. Kinsolving still noted in 1920 "a perceptible improvement in the morale of the School."[81] Through this time of change, the trustees created various committees to address the ongoing needs of the School. One committee, composed of women, oversaw the "domestic arrangements" while three others, house, finance, and school, were made up of trustees who handled most of the important operational and administrative tasks. One policy change of note, enacted in 1921, was to reconsider the "arbitrary limit" of a boy's stay at the School and to create a post-graduate year for three students who completed the sixth form.[82]

MAKING THE MOVE

While the cost of running the School in the city was expensive—doubling in ten years—the move from Franklin Street to the Mt. Washington suburbs in 1923 was motivated by an accident. James Chapman III '23 was struck by a cab during one of the thirty-minute evening recesses—and thereafter claimed, almost proudly, that he helped move the School.[83] This was not the first accident: an earlier student, Donald King was hit by a car in 1915 while roller-skating and suffered serious injuries.[84] The danger came as no surprise. "To reach their athletic field at Homewood or Roland Park, a street car journey of many blocks was necessary," noted Kinsolving. "Younger boys playing out in the street in front of the School were sometimes struck by passing motor vehicles." In Kinsolving's characteristically positive manner, he added, "Yet even in those cramped quarters, by reason of the fine school spirit, a very happy life was led." Thus, with the traffic in the streets and the lack of a nearby playground, and several decades of a capacity enrollment (often well over its "comfortable" 30 by four or five students), the vestry and the trustees knew that the School's urban future looked grim, an issue Kinsolving had been aware of since he arrived in 1906.

"Of the many lessons which the war has taught us, there is one of paramount importance and that is that culture and education are insufficient in themselves to prevent wars and bring about peace which the world is yearning for … We believe that education will be used for man's destruction unless it is suffused with true Christian idealism."

Headmaster Ernest H. Forster, 1919

But both the vestry and Kinsolving recognized the significance of such a move as well as the potential negative and heavy impact created by this new distance between Church and School, eliminating the "customary sight of the traditional marching, winter and summer of the St. Paul's choir boys down Charles Street to the Church in their choral robes and caps … two abreast, each pair of boys matching as to size, with the smaller ones in the front ranks."[85] The vestry naturally worried about keeping a steady stream of choristers, a problem other churches shared, such as one Episcopal church in Boston: "In addition to the continuing demands of our own parishes—together with the total absence in our own country, save in isolated instances, of the advantages of the choir school afforded in the English Cathedrals—render no easy task the maintenance of an efficient choir of boys."[86] But after serious thought, the vestry agreed that the trustees (many of whom were members of both) had a right to select a new site, and the vestry pledged "all possible aid" to relocate the School in a place that was still convenient for the boys to come to Old St. Paul's. As chairman of the vestry, Kinsolving appointed a separate committee composed of himself, three members of the vestry, Robert W. Johnson, Sr., Leigh Bonsal, and Herbert Brune, and three trustees, W. G. Bowdoin, Jr., T. F. Cadwalader, and E. H. McKeon, to determine a course of action.[87] Soon, Kinsolving related the details of the move to the congregation in a fall, 1922 letter titled "The Future of the Boys' School," which acknowledged that "a difficult period in the life of the School had been reached."

After deliberating over several potential sites, the board secured eight acres at 2101 Rogers Avenue for $27,500, between South Bend and Hyland Avenues, its home for the next 29 years. Cost to renovate the School was estimated to be an additional $40,000, not including several thousand dollars to level the athletic field and convert the nearby stable into a small gymnasium. The sale and purchase were a good exchange because of inflated real estate values in downtown Baltimore. The two houses on Franklin Street sold for $55,000, still about $10,000 shy of the total cost of outfitting the new site. Regardless, the School had been in a good financial position since its $10,000 remaining mortgage had been paid and its endowment had more

"It is because it is no part of the function of a University

to teach religion, or for that matter have an oversight

of either character or manners, except in a general

and ineffectual way, that the function of the Christian

school is becoming increasingly important."

The Reverend Arthur B. Kinsolving, *The Story of a Southern High School*, 1922

than doubled to $109,000 from the time Kinsolving had arrived.[88]

The slight shortfall in financing, however, motivated one significant decision by the trustees who, seeking funds, authorized themselves "the power to add to their [trustees'] number to secure subscription." The importance of raising money—and having the hands to do it—was already made apparent by the Episcopal Church's "Nationwide Campaign" to raise $4 million for the missions, a number set by the General Convention. Kinsolving alerted his congregation that "we shall soon need canvassers, active workers, those who sufficiently believe in the cause to work for it, to sacrifice time," and had to explain that the two fund-raising efforts—for the School and for this campaign for missions—were not in conflict. In some ways, this moment would later help explain Kinsolving's guidance in making the Boys' School more independent. With only so much money that could be raised, Kinsolving also recognized a lingering tension between securing money for the Church and for one of its premier projects.[89]

Initially, the capacity of the Mt. Washington building was 35 boarders. The suburban community, just beginning to grow, also seemed a strong prospect for paying day students "whose tuition would be practically velvet [certain]" and would "supplement the income from the boarders, thereby making more certain the School's ability to meet its carrying charges." Led by trustee and architect Howard May, plans began immediately to enlarge and renovate the manor house for school purposes. While the goal was to start the 1922-23 academic year in their new home, the fall "Michaelmas" term was held at Franklin Street; the boys thus enjoyed the longest St. Paul's Christmas break in history, about six weeks, and the ladies of the Parish held the first rummage sale for the School to help provide funds for much-needed equipment.

With this move, the School's engine, which had been puttering for a few years, would still continue to putter for the next ten years while it adjusted to the new accommodations, to uncooperative and mostly incompetent headmasters, and to a thirty-minute ride from its Church.

Choirmaster Donald McDorman '33 leads the Choir in the Parish undercroft before it was renovated. A few choir facts, according to a 1992 compilation done by former librarian Ethel Hardee: first appearance of daily evensong (1895); first performance in a concert hall (1905); first radio broadcast (1926); first televised Christmas Eve service (1948); first performance of a commissioned work (1968), written by Wilmer Welsh; and first performance at the White House (1985).

Training for the Good Fight

by John T. Ordeman

The Boys' School of St. Paul's Parish as we know it today is a very different institution from the one the Reverend Dr. William Wyatt founded in 1849. Wyatt's school, which began as a parish outreach project, did not serve the children of parishioners, but was "an institution for the maintenance and education of poor boys."

Wyatt's successor, the Reverend Dr. Milo Mahan, was, in a sense, the founder of St. Paul's School. A classicist at Episcopal High School for seven years before taking Holy Orders, he introduced a curriculum designed to prepare graduates for matriculation in institutions of higher learning. Mahan opened a boarding facility and stated that the School would be seeking students of "a high grade and better capabilities," rather than "the most wretched class of boys."

The Episcopal High School, which had been founded ten years before St. Paul's School, was apparently Mahan's model for St. Paul's. Mahan would certainly have applied to the Boys' School the mission statement written by the Reverend William N. Pendleton, the principal of Episcopal High School when Mahan served as classics master:

The object of the school is to educate youth on the basis of religion; to apply the instruction of the Bible in the work of training the mind, influencing the heart and regulating the habits; to provide for boys during the critical period of middle youth and incipient manhood the safest and best superintendence, the soundest and most healthful moral influences and the most faithful Christian guidance, associated with the most useful and extensive course of learning practicable. In a word, it is to make full trial of Christian education in training youth for duty and for heaven.

Much has changed in a century and a half, but one thing has remained constant, a characteristic that distinguishes St. Paul's School for Boys—and St. Paul's School for Girls as well—from all of the other excellent independent college preparatory schools in the area. St. Paul's is—as it has been steadfastly since its founding in 1849—an Episcopal school and a parochial school. It is the Schools' affiliation with Old St. Paul's Church that is the essential difference between our Schools and all others; to my mind, this association with the Mother Church of Baltimore gives us distinct advantage over them.

Since leaving St. Paul's in 1985, I've served as headmaster of three other schools—all non-religious independent college preparatory schools. I've had the opportunity, therefore, to reflect upon the difference between a parochial Episcopal school and schools that have no religious affiliation. I recall the words of a friend who is an alumnus and a trustee of a distinguished, nondenominational Baltimore school. In an address to the St. Paul's trustees, he observed that he envied our School's opportunity to deal directly with the spiritual aspect of life, something that is difficult—if not impossible—in an institution which professes to be religiously neutral.

If one accepts the classical ideal of a sound mind in a sound body as the apogee of education, the non-religious school can provide all that is expected. If, however, one hopes that a child will also develop spiritually, only a school with a religious component to its curriculum and its program of activities can provide a complete educational opportunity and experience.

Few churches make available to bright, inquiring adolescents a systematic study of theology or an explanation of the doctrines of the Church, and few parents are sufficiently well-versed in these matters to supplement this teaching at home. Where else but in school is a student to get the knowledge he will need to defend and maintain his beliefs against the formidable opposition of the anti-religious forces or the more subtle enticements of the proselytizing religious groups present on college campuses?

I believe that the willingness—indeed eagerness—of many college students to reject traditional Christianity for humanism or the practices of one of these seductive groups is largely the result of ignorance of the bases and tenets of Christianity. Those who have learned little of the Christian faith since they left Sunday school, where instruction was on a level appropriate for a child, have a knowledge and understanding of Christianity which is not sufficient for them to be able to uphold or defend their religious position against a persuasive atheist. Their naïve beliefs are easily shattered, and they may fall for any ideology or philosophy which offers assurance, companionship and comfort.

I am not arguing for a minute that students should be protected against philosophies and ideologies which are un-Christian. Indeed, if educational institutions are not places where conflicting ideas abound and are freely discussed and given the honor that all creative intellectual achievement deserves, the minds of the students are unlikely to expand or mature. However, I do believe that Christian students should be as well-armed for intellectual combat as are their adversaries.

All St. Paul's students are required to attend regular chapel services, conducted by an Episcopal priest and based on the liturgy of *The Book of Common Prayer*, services which are now held, at last, in a handsome chapel design to foster spirituality. The prayers are traditional and meaningful and beautifully phrased, as opposed to the generic sort used in a non-denominational setting—prayers which are apparently designed to offend no one, not even God.

St. Paul's, in addition to having a central religious purpose, is also an academic institution which is ethnically, culturally and religiously diverse. This dual identity creates tension and, at times, conflict which must be resolved in order to re-establish an equilibrium—a delicate balance of the forces pulling the School toward each of the desired objectives. Just as a Christian person, well-intentioned and devout though he may be, can never attain the Christ-like perfection for which he strives, the Christian school will inevitably fall short of achieving the lofty ideals which it espouses. The School is, after all, only human.

There is something even more important that distinguishes the church school from the non-denominational school: the ethos of the school—the essential character—the atmosphere, something which is sensed intuitively by the students and by the teachers and which affects both their actions and their relationships.

A Christian school does not simply add religion courses to its curriculum and services to its daily schedule, nor is religion merely a veneer to improve its appearance. Rather, religion must be an inseparable force, an influence on all phases of school life. When a school professes to be Christian, it assumes an awesome obligation. If it is to fulfill this obligation honestly, and be an effective witness of the Church, all decisions—from the decisions which establish broad policies to the myriad daily decisions made by teachers and administrators—must be made with the consciousness that the School accepts and endorses the fundamental Christian concepts of the worth of Man and the dignity of the individual. High ethical and moral standards must be upheld, and love must be a basis for action, not merely an abstract ideal.

It seems to me that non-denominational schools, by taking no stand and ignoring religion, hope they can avoid having any influence on the religious beliefs of their students. Such is not the case, however. If religion is not a part of daily routine, boys and girls will assume that it must be something that exists only at special times and in special places. A school which excludes religion is therefore not neutral; it is irreligious.

St. Paul's accepts students of all religious persuasions—or of none, for that matter—but it is, in its very essence, an Episcopal school. As such, St. Paul's takes seriously the responsibility to educate our students in the beliefs and the practices of Christianity. Still, the School is not and would not want to be a school exclusively for Episcopalians, or even for Christians. Students belonging to other religious groups should not have their faith undermined or be made to feel uncomfortable in class or in chapel. But all students, we hope, regardless of their religious affiliation, will benefit from their participation in the religious activities at St. Paul's. The Anglican tradition, according to the Most Reverend Frank T. Griswold III, the presiding bishop, "because of its 'graced pragmatism'—its reasonableness formed by Scripture and tradition—possesses a unique capacity for diversity, and the ability to discern and welcome truth in its various forms." Unlike the schools of most denominations, Episcopal schools manage to be Christian without being narrowly or rigidly doctrinal.

The people who have directed St. Paul's for fifteen decades have never lost sight of the fact that the School was and is and shall remain, first and foremost, a Christian institution which has at its vital center traditions and teachings of the Anglican Communion. If religion is to become a central force in a person's life, it must be an integral part of his most important activities. For students, these activities take place in school. Religion—vital and relevant—should be there too. The church school's role, as I see it, is to put it there.

St. Paul's has something very precious in its heritage as an Episcopal school and as The Boys School of St. Paul's

Parish. I hope and pray that all who have authority and responsibility for it will see that this heritage is preserved for future generations. When a school manages to operate successfully on the basis of Christian principles, the campus truly becomes a place where "all good learning can flourish and abound." May it ever be so at St. Paul's.

John Talbot Ordeman served as headmaster from 1966 to 1985.

OPPOSITE: The Choir of Men and Boys inside Old St. Paul's.

Notes: 1849-1923

1   William E. Wyatt, "To the Members of St. Paul's Parish" (St. Paul's Parish, Baltimore, April 9, 1861), 2.

2   William E. Wyatt, *A Discourse on Christian Education* (St. Paul's Parish, Baltimore, 1833), 28.

3   Sherry H. Olson, *Baltimore: The Building of an American City* (Baltimore: The Johns Hopkins University Press, 1997), 103-140.

4   Wyatt, "To the Members," 8.

5   Frederick W. Kates, *Bridges Across Four Centuries* (St. Paul's Parish, Baltimore, 1957), 32.

6   Weldon Wallace, "Old St. Paul's—Social Force for 275 Years," *The Sun*, 29 October 1967.

7   Arthur B. Kinsolving, *A Short History of The Boys' School of St. Paul's Parish Baltimore, Maryland, 1849-1945* (St. Paul's Parish, Baltimore, 1945), 13.

8   Wyatt, "To the Members," 5.

9   In 1800, the Benevolent Society of the City and County of Baltimore was incorporated as a parish charity, organized by Eleanor Rogers, who founded the school at St. Paul's Church in 1799. In a similar effort, the Parish opened its first Sunday School in 1817 for 21 boys, adding about two students each week that year, which led to an enrollment by the following fall of 103 (though oftentimes half were marked absent). Ten years later, girls were admitted, and enrollment would remain high. Establishing a Sunday School was actually part of a larger widespread movement which began in England in the late eighteenth century.

10 "Education," *The True Catholic: Reformed, Protestant, and Free*, 8 (1851), 537; The word "godless" comes from this article written by St. Paul's Parish vestryman Hugh Davey Evans.

11 Charter Record, Liber E. D. 1, f. 236, "Articles of Association Incorporating The Boys' School of St. Paul's Parish" (1853).

12 Francis Beirne, *St. Paul's Parish Baltimore: A Chronicle of the Mother Church* (St. Paul's Parish, Baltimore, 1967), 103.

13 David Hein, "The Founding of the Boys' School of St. Paul's Parish," *Maryland Historical Magazine* 81 (1986): 149-159.

14 Wyatt, "To the Members," 18-22.

15 Articles of Association, 1853.

16 Wyatt, "To the Members," 9-19.

17 Hein, "The Founding," 155.

18 Robert J. Brugger, *Maryland: A Middle Temperament, 1634-1980* (Baltimore: Johns Hopkins University Press, 1988), 249; Maryland General Assembly, "An Act to Authorise Incorporation in Certain Cases" (8 March 1847); The Act limited the "property, real or personal, or capital stock" of new institutions to $10,000 without application to the legislature.

19 Garner Ranney, interview by author, Baltimore, Maryland, 6 January 1999; William Francis Brand, *Life of Bishop Whittingham* 2 vols. (New York, 1883); The College of St. James was arguably Bishop Whittingham's most prized project. For the only book-length treatment of the College of St. James, see David Hein, ed., *A Student's View of the College of St. James on the Eve of the Civil War: The Letters of W. Wilkins Davis* (Lewiston, NY: Edwin Mellen

Press, 1988). For a more condensed history of St. James see: "A Brief History of St. James School" (The College of St. James, Hagerstown, Maryland, 1997); James McLachlan, *American Boarding Schools: A Historical Study* (New York: Charles Scribner's Sons, 1970); Most believe that the model for the modern family-oriented boarding schools, and the movement itself, came from the Round Hill School in Massachusetts and then the Flushing Institute, in Flushing, New York, which was founded by Episcopal clergyman the Reverend William Augustus Muhlenberg. "The basic models and intellectual inspiration for Round Hill, the Flushing Institute, and the College of St. James had been a combination of the American college, Swiss and German schools, and romantic ideas about education," said historian James McLachlan. The Boys' School had a direct connection to these models. First, rector Milo Mahan graduated from the Flushing Institute. Secondly, Whittingham had a close relationship with the first headmaster of the College of St. James, the Reverend John B. Kerfoot, in the 1840s. And finally, Mahan spoke at St. James in 1851 and on occasion visited there. These connections, however, require much further exploration. As a final note, the Flushing Institute had one of the earliest boys' choirs to be sponsored by an Episcopal Church; the St. Paul's Choir followed closely behind, and today is the second oldest of its kind.

20 Beirne, 99-100; Wyatt, *A Discourse on Christian Education*, 17-18.

21 *Parish Work* (St. Paul's Parish, Baltimore: 1894): 8.

22 Wyatt's appeal, "To the Members," is in fact the earliest written record of the founding of the School and its work before 1861.

23 Beirne, 109.

24 John Sebastian Bach Hodges, *Sketch of History of the Boys' School of St. Paul's Parish* (St. Paul's Parish, Baltimore, 1905), 8-9.

25 *Parish Work* (1894): 9.

26 Henry John Hopkins, ed., Preface, *The Collected Works of the Late Milo Mahan D. D.* 3 vols. (New York, 1875), i-il.

27 Mahan would be the first in a line of future leaders of St. Paul's School who came from Episcopal High School: among others, rector Arthur B. Kinsolving and headmasters George S. Hamilton and John T. Ordeman.

28 Alvin W. Skardon, *Church Leader in the Cities, William Augustus Muhlenberg* (Philadelphia: University of Pennsylvania Press, 1986).

29 Mary Bready, *Through All Our Day, A History of St. Paul's School for Girls* (St. Paul's School for Girls, Baltimore, 1999).

30 Hopkins, xl.

31 Our earliest documented masters were the Reverend Henry T. Lee, headmaster for one year in 1869, and William Harwood, his assistant.

32 James Elliott Lindsley, *This Planted Vine: A Narrative History of the Episcopal Diocese of New York* (New York: Harper & Row, 1984); Jane Rasmussen, *Musical Taste as a Religious Question in Nineteenth Century America* (Lewistown/Queenstown: The Edwin Mellen Press: 1986).

33 Personal gratitude from the author to Dr. Garner Ranney, archivist of the Episcopal Diocese of Maryland, for supplying this sermon: the Reverend Joseph G. J. Bend, "Church Music" (Baltimore, 1802).

34 Douglass B. Forsyth '56, *Boys With Voices: The Choir of Old St. Paul's Church, 1873-1992* (St. Paul's Parish, Baltimore, 1992); A part-anecdotal, part-historical record of the Choir of Men and Boys of Old St. Paul's can be found in Forsyth's book, a combinaton of research and interviews. Choir rosters, as well as a listing of award winners, choirmasters and other miscellaneous data, were compiled by St. Paul's librarian Ethel Hardee into a separate document, "St. Paul's Choir of Men and Boys, Historical Record." This and Forsyth's well-organized notes, materials, and articles, are all available in the St. Paul's School archives. Both documents were put together in celebration of the tercentennial anniversary of St. Paul's Parish.

35 Rasmussen, 58, 71-72, 319, 370-79.

36 Leighton Coleman, *The Church in America* (New York: James Pott & Co., n.d.), 325.

37 Hodges and Bishop Whittingham were close associates, first because Whittingham aimed to make Old St. Paul's the Cathedral of the Diocese, and second because Hodges married Whittingham's daughter. After Whittingham's death, Hodges gathered the funds necessary to craft a stained-glass window in his memory, which can still be found in the Chapel of Old St. Paul's.

38 Beirne, 129; The statement was apparently made by the poet and noted flutist in the orchestra, Sidney Lanier.

39 Rasmussen, 321, 348.

40 Why exactly the Boys' School trustees looked abroad, or to St. Mark's specifically, for a headmaster is unclear, but it was at least in part an idea of Hodges, who was born and raised in Bristol, England. The trustees of the Girls' School, including Hodges and many of the Boys' School trustees, took a similar path in 1873 when they assigned the management of the School to three Clewer Sisters, an order of the Church of England. The authority to select and appoint the headmaster was not returned to the hands of the trustees until 1902; the first headmaster to be appointed this way was the Reverend R. S. Wood.

41 Whittle also had an assistant, Frank Mackall. *The Parish Almanac of St. Paul's Baltimore* (St. Paul's Parish, Baltimore, 1872); On the cover of this annual publication it reads, "Faith, if it hath not works, is dead," and includes details about all of the Parish charities: the Boys' School, the Church Home and Infirmary, its mission work, and the Orphan Asylum for Girls.

42 *The Parochial Charities of St. Paul's, Baltimore* (St. Paul's Parish, Baltimore, 1875): 11.

43 *The Parish Almanac* (1873): 9.

44 Students were assessed for the tuition charge in accordance with their ability to pay. While Kinsolving's history stated that the amount of financial aid at that time was based on need, Hodges did not mention anything about it in his own history.

45 *The Parish Almanac* (1873): 9; Of the School's $4,000 operating budget, the largest line item was $1,123 for "Provisions and Marketing" and then $980 for teachers.

46 Hodges, *Sketch of History,* 12.

47 Olson, 199; Hodges, *Sketch of History,* 15; Hodges does not identify Miss Donaldson in his history, except that she was "a lifelong friend." It is also true that in the 1883 *Parochial Charities* report he does not name her either, implying that it was much later that anyone realized who had made the contribution. His successor, Dr. Arthur B. Kinsolving, later commented in his history, however, that Hodges "was able to persuade" Miss Donaldson to give $2,500 of the total amount to secure the property, and the remaining $1,000 for operating expenses through the year for coal, a "heating apparatus," and furnishings.

48 *The Parochial Charities* (1883): 4-5. In 1872, the Parish committed $1,886 from its Parochial Charities Fund to the Girls' Orphanage, whereas ten years later, the Orphanage was entirely self-sufficient.

49 Hodges, *Sketch of History*, 16.

50 *The Parochial Charities* (1883): 7; (1885): 4-5, 15; (1886): 4.

51 *Parish Notes* (February, 1893): 4.

52 *The Parochial Charities* (1883): 7; (1885): 4.

53 Arthur B. Kinsolving, *Twenty Years in an Historic Parish* (St. Paul's Parish, Baltimore, 1926), 13; The second legacy gift (the only other was actually 30 years before) to "place [the School] on a firm and permanent foundation" came from a non-parishioner, William G. Harrison, in 1883. Apparently Harrison was a part of the Parish but then was removed, which "the whole Diocese of Maryland so deeply feels and so sincerely laments." Later, however, another reference in an issue of *Parish Notes*, said, "That young man is to-day a member of St. Paul's congregation, and not yet an old man, when the endowment shall be completed and the [Boys' School will] no longer be compelled to go from door-to-door seeking the means of doing the work for which it was created—'the maintenance and education of poor boys.'" As an additional note, the first recorded legacy gift, mentioned in Hodges's *Sketch of History*, was in 1854, left by a Jacob Albert and valued at $10,000.

54 To what degree and extent the young boys and girls interacted at this time is not detailed much in early documents, aside from an occasional note in newsletters about Parish-sponsored events that occurred between the two.

55 *The Parochial Charities* (1885): 4-5.

56 *Parish Notes* (October, 1890): 1; (October, 1891): 2.

57 *Parish Notes* (February, 1895): 4.

58 "At Baltimore's Crossroads: Baltimore of 1890" (The Fidelity Trust Company, Baltimore, 1946); Brendon Hunt, *Homeliness and Godliness in Baltimore Dens, An Oral History* (1999).

59 Francis F. Beirne, *Baltimore … a Picture History: 1858-1958* (New York: Hastings House, 1957), 72-85.

60 *Parish Work* (1895): 6; *Parish Notes* (February, 1893): 3.

61 *The Parochial Charities* (1886): 4-6.

62 On only a few occasions were choristers not also students in the Boys' School, such as in 1897 when "all but two" were pupils.

63 Hodges, *Sketch of History,* 26-27.

64 Olson, 212.

65 A fair bit of renovation was necessary for the Franklin Street building, including new boilers, radiators, and bathrooms.

66 Arthur B. Kinsolving, *The Story of a Southern High School* (Baltimore: The Norman, Remington Co., 1922).

67 "Few persons have ever done more for the School as much as [trustee] Mr. J. Marshall Thomas," wrote Dr. Kinsolving at Thomas's sudden death in 1911, "and to it the loss seems now irreparable."

68 In 1910, the trustees found matron Miss Thompson, who had come from Gilman Country School, and who followed long-time matron Miss Ellen Bryan. St. Paul's and the Gilman Country School communicated regularly in these kinds of ways. In 1921, Gilman's headmaster Captain Wardlaw Miles gave the commencement address on personality, in which he "commended strongly to the boys the singling out for study and imitation of the great characters in history." It is interesting to note that the following year, a commencement speech given by the Reverend Benjamin Lovett of St. Andrew's Church was titled "Character Building."

69 *Parish Notes* (November, 1906): 2; Beirne, 157.

70 *Parish Notes* (May, 1907): 7; (April, 1911): 7; (November, 1912): 6; (February, 1914): 6.

71 The good fortune of having all of the boys return in 1914, however, resulted in a later dearth of choir boys—since fewer boys were in training—requiring that the trustees authorize opening five more spots exclusively for choristers. The fact that every boy returned in 1914 means that this year is the only one in the School's recorded history that did not have graduates. This was the same year, ironically, that Elmer announced he was introducing the first diplomas.

72 *Parish Notes* (October, 1911): 5; (October, 1914): 8; (May, 1922): 4.

73 Not surprisingly, prizes were often named and awarded by benefactors, such as one of the School's "most faithful friends," Miss Asenath Harwood, who for several years covered the School's entire annual coal bill. Upon her death in 1911, Miss Harwood (daughter of Judge James Harwood of the Orphan's Court of Baltimore) who lived with her mother and half-sister nearby on Saratoga and Calvert streets, had been, during the last two years of her life, the largest individual contributor to the School and the largest benefactor to the Church in its entire 219-year history. Her bequest left $50,000 for the School, $25,000 of which was for the endowment. The prizes themselves ranged from a "five dollar gold piece" to a set of books. The School gave two prizes for spelling, one for history, arithmetic, Latin, one for the highest average in each of the six forms, and later one for sacred studies.

74 With elected officers (including a "Librarian and Censure"), the boys in the Randall Literary Society were faithful to Saturday night meetings and a monthly program that included recitations, debates, and essays, as well as occasional trips with J. B. Noel Wyatt to such places as the Walters Art Gallery. Programs were published in the boys' *Triakonta*.

75 The headmaster appointed one boy as librarian and six older boys as monitors who helped with routine library responsibilities. The first recorded monitors, listed for 1902-03 were Theodore Heywood, William H. B. Evans '03, William M. McGill '03, William Hechman, Frank Crayne, and Ernest Coffroth.

76 Charles R. Kloman's valedictory speech, printed in full in the November, 1914 *Triakonta*, is worth further review. The theme of the speech is "utopia," and it discusses elements of a perfect commonwealth, human nature, and Utilitarianism. "Each of us has his face set toward some Utopia," he wrote, "which he is to build of his own ideas and efforts and dreams."

77 Olson, 295; Beirne, 163-64.

78 *Parish Notes* (October, 1918): 4.

79 Kinsolving was not alone in his disgust with the high price of coal. Honorable J. Charles Linthicum, parishioner and husband of the woman who later left the largest bequest to the School, was one of many who protested the inflated prices in the early '20s.

80 Olson, 287-88.

81 Kinsolving, *A Short History*, 12-17; Thomas DeCourcey Ruth, an instructor at Princeton University, served the 1917-18 academic year, but late in the year was called for "war work." Ernest H. Forster held the position until Henry A. Converse became headmaster (1918-19), who "was a fine classroom teacher but was not successful as an administrator, and therefore was not re-appointed the following year." Forster, who was still master then, "would have been offered the headmastership had it not been for an appeal made in the pulpit of St. Paul's by Bishop L. H. Roots [to teach in China]." Harold Hastings, a teacher at St. Paul's, Concord, then took "temporary charge" until June, 1920. A "clerical headmaster," the Reverend T. J. M. Van Duyne followed, serving for a single year, and was replaced in October, 1921 by the Reverend Percy Coulthurst, who filled the post for three years until February, 1924, when he returned to parish work. As an aside, the first indication of the shift from "Head Master" to one word, "Headmaster," appears to be during the 1917-18 academic year. For the purposes of this history, "headmaster" has been used throughout.

82 The first three post-graduate students were Robert Lee Bull '21, Beverly R. L. Rhett '21, and Frank D. Mead '21.

83 The survey was completed by James Chapman III '24 and conducted by faculty member Louis Dorsey Clark in 1970; photostats of this and others can be found in the School archives.

84 "Most reprehensibly," described Kinsolving, "when these people had injured and run over this dear boy, they at once put him into their machine to take him to the hospital, and then, thinking it would injure their good names, laid him out on the street again and went their way; he was found an hour or two afterwards."

85 Frank L. LaMotte, *The First Hundred Years of The Boys' School of St. Paul's Parish* (St. Paul's School, Baltimore, 1949), 12.

86 *The Parish of the Advent in the City of Boston: A History of One Hundred Years, 1844-1944* (Boston: The Parish of the Advent, 1944), 133.

87 Kinsolving, *A Short History*, 16.

88 *Parish Notes* (December, 1917): 8; (October, 1922): 2.

89 *Parish Notes* (November, 1922): 5.

The First Doctor
1 Kates, *Bridges Across Four Centuries*, 28-29; Kinsolving, *A Short History*, 14; "St. Paul's Parish: Three Hundred Years in Witness, Worship and Service" (St. Paul's Parish, Baltimore, 1992), 2.

Like Father, Like Son
1 *Parish Notes* (May, 1915): 2-3; Hodges, *Sketch of History*, 28; Faustina Hasse Hodges, *Edward Hodges* (Baltimore, 1896); Miss Hodges died in 1896 before completing the biography of her father, but her brother, the Reverend John S. B. Hodges, finished it while he was rector at St. Paul's Parish.

One Mahan, One School
1 Hopkins, *The Collected Works*, i-il; One of Mahan's first and most notable speeches in 1851 was called *A Christian Odyssey*, given at the College of St. James in Hagerstown, during which he used literature as an entry point into deepening one's faith, a common rhetorical device of his. His biographer, John Hopkins, incidentally, was also a co-editor of *The Church Journal* with Mahan along with John Henry Hobart II; Kates, *Bridges Across Four Centuries*, 32-3; McLachlan, 149.

Founders and Subscribers
1 Wyatt, "To the Members," 9; *Baltimore Past and Present* (Baltimore, 1871), 466; David Hein, "The Founding," 149-59; A significant number of these details, including the one here about Reverdy Johnson, Jr., were found in this article. Hein also draws from an article in the *Maryland Historical Magazine* for information about the Monday Club. Much biographical material on the founders and incorporators can be found at the Maryland Historical Society. G. W. Howard, *The Monumental City* (Baltimore, 1889).

Early Legacy of Choirmasters
1 Forsyth, *Boys With Voices*; Miles Farrow was organist and choirmaster from 1895-1909 and served as headmaster of the Boys' School from 1906-09.
2 "A Short History of Music at Old St. Paul's," *Maryland Churchman* (January, 1959); Despite the fact that Dr. Richardson was forced to leave for some unexplained reason, the vestry gave him a $1,000 gift upon his departure in December, 1910.

Corralling the Old Boys
1 Many students, if they did not first find employment, finished their education in an area secondary school. On one occasion, Kinsolving urged for the sake of the School's history that alumni write down their memories, but as far as records show, such work was never completed. Layton Smith, first president of the revitalized Alumni Association, soon added an alumni page and the annual meeting's minutes to *Triakonta*, but it rarely materialized. The Association seemed to be mostly a social enterprise, and with the exception of announcing the winner of the Alumni Medal, chosen by recommendation of the headmaster, most early "pleasant gatherings" were confined to planning a date for the next year, set annually for the Saturday nearest St. Paul's Day, electing officers, and admitting new members.

Patron Saint
1 T. Benson Musgrave '27, interview by author, Towson, Maryland, 7 November 1998; William N. McKeachie and James Cantler '43, interview by author, video recording, Charleston, South Carolina, 3 September 1998; Lucinda Leigh, phone interview by author, 14 December 1998; Sally B. Kinsolving, *Biographical Data of the Reverend Arthur B. Kinsolving, D. D.* (1954); The mural was named in the will of the late Alfred Shriver, and the artist engaged to paint it was Leon Kroll. The most recognized portrait of Arthur Kinsolving by the St. Paul's community, however, is the one which currently hangs in the Brooklandwood Mansion; Kinsolving is seated in a Florentine chair, wearing a maroon velvet jacket with black satin lapels and cuffs. Commissioned to Stanislav Rembski, the portrait was formally presented at the Boys' School commencement, June 3, 1941, the year before he retired. As an aside, a curious connection between Christ Church in Brooklyn, New York, where Kinsolving served as rector, and Old St. Paul's Church: both were designed by the nation's foremost ecclesiastical architect, Richard Upjohn. A final note: Lucy Lee Kinsolving died in May of 1862, leaving a second son who was 13 days old.

A Day on Franklin Street
1 Most of the information in this piece is drawn from surveys that Louis Dorsey Clark sent out in 1970 to those alumni who were students on Franklin Street. Those who answered were in the classes between 1906 and 1923, but the author takes some creative liberty here in merging years. Other details come from a printed interview of Eugene W. Milby '10 conducted by George Hamilton and Louis Dorsey Clark, "St. Paul's Was Everything to Me," *St. Paul's School Currents* (Winter 1980-81). The Reverend James Valiant '24 mentioned the "Calvert Street Gang" in his survey and said that, on the choristers' march to Church, they were "sometimes attacked," resulting in a "choir with black eyes!" The lacrosse sticks apparently were brought by school physician Dr. Abercrombie from Johns Hopkins. Full names of those cited in this text: Miles Farrow, Ellen Bryan, Ethel Weaver, Elizabeth Gilman, Susan Asenath Harwood, J. B. Noel Wyatt, J. Marshall Thomas, H. Graham Dubois, Dr. Arthur B. Kinsolving, Cardinal James Gibbons.

Thirty Ways Hath September
1 *Parish Notes* (February, 1910): 4; (March, 1910): 4.

Franklin Street Rock
1 J. B. Noel Wyatt, nephew of Dr. William E. Wyatt, was a devoted parishioner of St. Paul's Parish and a significant contributor to the School. A few interpretative notes: the first literary magazine, *Triakonta* (meaning "30" in Greek), was the School's usual enrollment while on Franklin Street. "Bryan's apron strings" refers to their long-time housemother, Miss Ellen Bryan. "With Veasy [sic] at the back" presumably refers to chorister Henry Veazie '06, though why he is "at the back" is unclear.

LEFT: Choristers in the late '50s under Donald McDorman '33. (From left) Melvin E Minter, Jr. '68, Christopher R. Hardee '68, and Warren Liddell '67.

PREVIOUS PAGES

First 'A' Conference Championship Team

The 1940 champions after 24 straight victories and the first of seven straight 'A' Conference lacrosse titles. (Third row, from left) John A. Pierson '42, G. Brown Hill '42, Key Compton '42, T. Clay Groton, Jr. '41, H. Franklin Knipp, Jr. '40, Malbon R. Wood '43, (second row) coach Robert P. Fuller '39, Dennis M. Hoffman '40, Newell T. Cox, Jr. '40, Edwin H. McFeely '42, Donald B. Stewart '42, M. Beach Schultz '42, J. Donald Connor '40, coach Howard Myers, Jr., (front row) Charles W. Moxley '39, Randall C. Coleman, Jr. '39, J. Lyon Rogers, Jr. '40, Howard W. Smedley '41, John R. Cook '40, Norman M. Torrence '40, E. Tileston Mudge, Jr. '40, Marshall M. Austin '39, John L. Robertson III '41, M. Raymore Greene '41.

by Harrison Davis, Class of 2003

Class is over. I think, *Yes, recess.* I put my books away and run down to the basketball courts in the gym. *Oh no,* I think to myself. The gym doors are closed. I run up to them to take a closer look. *Yes,* they are open. I look inside. The hockey players have taken one side of the gym, and the basketball players have taken the other side. *Uh oh.* No eighth-grade basketball games are going on. I know that I could rumble with the hockey players or put 'em up with the basketball players. I know that if David Brooks is in the basketball game he will dominate or if David Cornbrooks is in the hockey game, he will dominate. I can join any game I want because I am in the eighth grade. "This power is great," I say to myself. I run in, *wham,* I nail the basketball out of the player's hands. *What a steal.* I hear voices in the background: "You got nailed!" and "In your eye!" Someone covers me, *zoom,* I run by him. *Yes,* I think to myself, *bucket, bucket, bucket, three in a row.* I know someone will call "three-D." I feel bad for this person because I know I will school him. "Recess over!" a teacher calls out. Back to reality.

The Student in the Athlete

by Martin D. Tullai

*"If we work upon marble, it will perish; if on brass, time will efface it;
if we rear temples, they will crumble into dust; but if we work upon immortal minds,
and imbue them with principles, with the just fear of God and
love of our fellow-men, we engrave on those tablets something
that will brighten to all eternity."*

Daniel Webster

My first impression of St. Paul's School was formed in 1953, when my wife Jean and I drove down from New Jersey for my interview with headmaster S. Atherton Middleton and trustee Frank Mead '21, regarding the position of athletic director, football coach, and eighth-grade history teacher. Prior to my meeting, a gray-haired gentleman, Louis Clark, greeted us cordially with a friendly wave and gentle demeanor which will always be with me. I have thought many times about that moment—what a wonderful first impression of the School I received from that courtly man.

When my employment began and I became immersed in the daily routine, it became quickly apparent that the most telling aspect of this institution was the general philosophy which emphasized three significant areas—the mind (academic), the spirit (religious) and the body (physical-athletic). These main principles have

Martin "Mitch" Tullai and J. Tucker Radebaugh '95.

been constant and have insured a positive school atmosphere where students can grow to their full potential.

Are we the same school as when I first met Louis Clark? This could hardly be true. However, while we have kept pace with change, we have certainly maintained those values and traditions; our core philosophy is strikingly sound.

Certainly the "physical-athletic" aspect is unquestionably an integral part of St. Paul's. Over the years our athletic program and our teams have been highly successful; anyone evaluating what we've achieved in this dimension cannot help but be impressed by the record of accomplishments compiled by our players and coaches.

It is disturbing to realize, however, that sometimes rumors, half-truths and misrepresentations have fostered a misconception that we are a "jock school," that we have been so heavily devoted to athletics that our educational objectives have been given short shrift.

CONTRIBUTOR'S ESSAY

While the following article was written as a defense of football, I'm taking the liberty of presenting it as originally written because, I would submit, it is germane to an overall philosophy of athletics, to the other sports we offer, and, more importantly, to those bridges between the field and a student's whole education. In sum, it is a philosophy far removed from developing "jocks." No one claims that football or any sport is an end in itself. It is, however, a significant experience in life through which a boy can learn to better prepare himself for whatever he will ultimately become.

FOOTBALL: ANOTHER VIEW

Over the past several years, a series of magazine and newspaper articles have raised questions regarding the value of football as a worthwhile American sport. "The desecration of autumn by football has begun," railed one writer. "Abolish football!" said another. This is unfortunate. As thousands of young men throughout the nation are once again undergoing preparations for another football season, I would respectfully, and emphatically, disagree with the critics of this great American sport. Indeed, football serves many positive functions.

*Provides for a high degree
of physical conditioning.*

Having been associated with football for over 50 years as a player and as a prep school football coach (more correctly, as a prep school history teacher who also coached football), I believe that parents who deny their sons the opportunity to play football—if the boys are physically able and if they desire to do so—are depriving them of a mountaintop experience.

Teaches one to disregard minor pains and bruises.

Football on the scholastic level is worthwhile, because above all else and if nothing else, it helps a boy to understand himself—to learn how hard he is willing to work to achieve a desired objective. He discovers his capabilities and learns that through determination and pride he can go well beyond his presumed limits; he learns about how he fares under varying conditions, the

Mitch Tullai in costume during his annual birthday celebration of President Abraham Lincoln. With him are (from left, front row) John L. Sindler '86, Robert A. Burgin '86, Steven M. Blair '86, (back row) Steven Reid, Edward L. Morton '86, Bryan C. Doak '86, and Trent W. Nichols III '86.

optimal as well as the dismal; about how to get lost, for a moment, in something bigger than himself; about how to discover his latent strengths, particularly those he never knew he had.

*Teaches one to control and
command one's own powers.*

In his essay "Football and Education," the editor and writer, John Chamberlain, pointed out that the sport "teaches many valuable things ranging from discipline to the proper adaptation of means to an end ... Football may be the school's most enduring contact with the world of discipline, of sharp thinking, of a demonstrable connection between what one puts into a thing and what one gets out of it at the other end."

*Teaches one to subordinate
one's interests to that of the group.*

In short: discipline.

That all said, after discussions with a number of respected alumni—both prior to my tenure and since— as well as through my own experience over more than four decades, I believe these claims of athletics being overemphasized are false and unsound. They are exaggerations beyond proportion both to numbers and extent. St. Paul's has never been a "jock school" as this term is generally applied.

For example, I remember when we—like a number of other private schools—accepted post-graduate students, a legitimate program allowing high school graduates to take an extra year to improve their academic standing. Some of these young men turned out to be fine athletes, but it was often overlooked that they also contributed a great deal in other ways.

Provides a sense of
accomplishment from an honest
and dedicated effort.

Of course, as sometimes happens, misrepresentation of the facts can and did occur. In the mid-'50s, as Middle School faculty member Mike Rentko and I were preparing for a football game against one of our rivals from outside the Baltimore area, a local newspaper there reported that our squad was led by a post-graduate student named Lincoln "Link" Bogart, a grizzled, 22-year-old ex-Marine who weighed in at 195 pounds and starred for the Marine Corps team while in the military service. True, Link was a post-graduate, but, in fact, he was an 18-year-old scrawny-looking kid who weighed all of about 160 pounds soaking wet, had never been in the military service, had never played high school football and, obviously, had never played for a team in the Marine Corps. He had played end on a recreation team in Baltimore County.

Actually, Link had enrolled at St. Paul's unbeknownst to Mike and me. Headmaster Appy Middleton brought him down to the field the day before fall camp opened and

> # I WOULD RATHER BE A FAILURE AT SOMETHING I LOVE THAN BE A SUCCESS AT SOMETHING I HATE.
> GEORGE BURNS

> # BETTER AN OLD STORY THAN A BLANK PAGE.
> YOGI WIMPLE

Two of over one thousand signs in Mitch Tullai's collection, most colored by students during Saturday detentions.

explained that he had just admitted a fine student who would like to try out for football. "I hope you have room for him on the team," the headmaster said. "Room for him!" Mike and I were delighted. After all, he was our 22nd player: now we could scrimmage!

Offers a young man a chance to enjoy
his "place in the sun."

Perceptions change slowly. The "ex-Marine" story hung around, and for a time people believed it, embellishing this "jock school" image. (Incidentally, Link turned out to be an outstanding student as well as a terrific football player, despite his lack of size and experience. Not only was he elected captain, along with Nicholas Ratcliffe '56, but he kicked off, returned points, played defense, and led the team in running, passing, and punting. Mike Rentko once observed that Link put more people out of work than McCormick's reaper!)

Have athletics been important? You bet! But to imply that it has overshadowed the rest of the School is specious; one need only examine the fine accomplishments, college attendance, and our graduates' contributions to society to realize how fallacious this thinking is.

Teaches one not only to want
to win but the necessity
of developing the willingness
to work to win.
(To have a "wishbone" is fine, but
to develop a "backbone" to realize
one's wish is even better.)

The truth is that our coaches have succeeded because they have shaped those students who "walked in the door" and came to St. Paul's because they belonged here, not simply because they were good athletes. From time to time one hears that we ought to recruit and proselytize, something which I neither favor nor believe is in the best interest of St. Paul's. Under the Maryland Scholastic Association, it was illegal. In my time we did not practice it, and again I say I hope it never will be accepted here. We have enjoyed plenty of success without it, and will continue to do so because of what we have to offer.

Teaches one to think fast
and realistically.

While our enrollment has increased appreciably in recent years—placing us on par with most teams we play against—this has not always been the case. How then have we been able to compete so successfully? Certainly, a primary factor has been the hard-working, knowledgeable, and inspired mentors who have made their mark. While they have mostly been classroom teachers, we also were lucky to have part-time coaches who understood our philosophy. True, these men have directed, molded, and inspired students to play to their ultimate, but they have focused on the School's overall educational goals.

Significant too is our own version of a feeder system. The stick work the young players have developed by the time they arrive to the Upper School, for instance, has been tremendously helpful in our lacrosse program. All sports, to one degree or another, have reaped great benefits from the fact that the Lower School, and especially the Middle School, have these programs in place.

Looking back over 41 years as a coach, teacher and administrator, if I had to cite one factor which impelled our student-athletes to achieve as they have—at times against tough odds—I would credit the importance of *pride*.

Obviously, I don't mean egotism or exaggerated self-esteem. Rather, pride meaning an unwillingness to accept mediocrity, a dissatisfaction with being second best. Pride as a frame of mind: in essence, a constant desire to work harder to ensure that when you play you are fully prepared to do your best. (*Preparing* to win—not just winning—is what is important.) Pride meaning a desire to be somebody who has accomplished and achieved,

who has accepted a challenge to strive and to sacrifice. Pride meaning spirit. And while team spirit bespeaks enthusiasm, it also demands a positive attitude, intense desire, commitment to cooperation, and keen self-discipline.

These qualities and our core set of values, our own "Seven Pillars of Ethics"—respect, honesty, cooperation, fairness, caring, empathy, and moral courage—I'm proud to say that since my first days at St. Paul's have been an important part of our ethical hallmark, including the athletic dimension.

We can exult in the fact that the history of this place is a history of care and concern reaching across generations of students, uniting us all in the steady consideration of the welfare of this venerable place in Brooklandville: St. Paul's School.

Mitch Tullai has been a faculty member since 1953 and served as athletic director from 1953 to 1978.

1923-1952

MIND, BODY, AND SPIRIT ON ROGERS AVENUE

School archivist and faculty member for 62 years, the late Louis Dorsey Clark aptly framed and titled his draft history of this era: *The Maturing Years, 1920-1960*. For here, in the blocky manor house on Rogers Avenue in suburban Mt. Washington where "a happier group of boys one rarely sees," atop a 9.5-acre site overlooking the Jones Falls; here, within sight of downtown Baltimore, the hustle of streetcars and bustle of pedestrians, the growing urban sounds of combustion engines; here, where there was finally room to grow, the School hurried through its own adolescence. When students arrived in 1923, the School had a newspaper, but stopped printing it; it was almost high school, but still didn't graduate seniors; it played sports, but won nothing for the trophy cabinet. By 1952, it had all of the above, and more. The Mt. Washington decades were ones of identity, self-consciousness, pride, confusion and, most of all, *masculinity*. And these elements—made manifest in sports and activities, shield and song—would soon appear in such reckless over-abundance that later, like the maturing teenager, the School would need to rein itself in. And rector Arthur B. Kinsolving, surveying this new home in 1923 felt that with space and a promising location he could finally fulfill his Episcopal High School vision of cultivating students in spirit, body, and mind.

But this vision was neither easily nor immediately realized. The last—the mind—proved the most elusive for Kinsolving. Finding qualified teachers and a competent headmaster—a problem since William Elmer left in 1918—would prove the single greatest challenge for Kinsolving and the trustees until George S. Hamilton arrived as headmaster in 1932. In this endeavor, the '20s marked Kinsolving's most difficult decade, just as it marked the first step in the School's explosive growth. "This was the period when small gains were large victories in themselves," wrote Clark, "as well as symbols of progress."[1]

Other than the hectic six-week move during Christmas 1922, the School's physical transition to Mt. Washington was fortunately smooth enough. Canadian headmaster the Reverend Percy Coulthurst opened the Mt. Washington campus with 41 students for its first semester that spring. But after a year, a specially-appointed vis-

OPPOSITE: A typical Mt. Washington scene as these students walk from the main building down to the athletic fields. (From left to right) H. Eugene Agerton III '50, August W. Schell, Jr. '50, John B. Yellott '49, and R. Cyrus Griffith '51.

Ernest "Ernie" Bowles on the kitchen steps of the Mt. Washington manor house one day during his 34-year tenure (1924-58) on the maintenance staff. "I would find it difficult indeed to single out a more valuable, dedicated, loyal member of my staff than Ernie Bowles!" wrote headmaster George Hamilton. "He was always there, strong as an ox, and general handyman *par excellence*. Trimming the hedge, mowing the lawn, filling in holes in the kitchen driveway, donning a white coat for a gala occasion—but his heaviest, most difficult, and most essential responsibility was the antiquated, hand-fired coal furnace. The dark regions of the cellar, under the front hall, were Ernie's domain— his castle—his 'office.'"

Beverly Randolph Lee "Pop" Rhett '21 was a gentleman of Virginia and of Washington and Lee University, was a banjo player in an age of banjos, raised horses and loved horseracing (the "sport of kings" he once said), and brought a field of literature, ideas, and academics to St. Paul's for 18 years. Faculty admired him (George Hamilton asked him to be the godfather of his daughter). And students dedicated their 1943 yearbook, *Spirit*, to him, just before he went into the Navy and later to Hawaii to work in communications, the industry in which he spent the latter part of his life. Among other contributions, Rhett created two essential icons of the Boys' School: the emblem (1933) and the school song (1939).

"The world of today is vastly different from that of five or six years ago. It was comparatively easy then to get a job. There was hardly any competition. We will soon be out of school and we want to be prepared."

The Monitor, January 20, 1933

iting committee of trustees (Kinsolving's new mechanism for quality control) felt that the "big and powerful" Coulthurst, a man of few words and "not a lot of malarkey," as one alumnus described, was not a responsible administrator and should not be re-engaged. Unsuccessful at finding a replacement, however, Kinsolving permitted Coulthurst to return, but soon found "conditions indicating a lack of discipline on three different visits. On one occasion no master was present … and only ten of eleven boys were on the premises. After about half an hour, the headmaster returned but could not satisfactorily account for the absent boy." Coulthurst resigned in February, 1924 to return to parish work and was replaced by William Anderson, principal of the Alleghany Country Academy of Cumberland, whose wife also joined the staff as a teacher and assistant.[2]

With Anderson working competently during his first year, Kinsolving and the trustees turned their attention to assembling a consistent roll book of masters, but despite their desire to have teachers with some tenure, the School had five different headmasters and some 24 different masters from 1920-30; alumnus Beverly Rhett '21, and his cousin Harry Rhett were actually the only teachers to stay longer than two years.[3] If there was any continuity on the staff during these early years, it was because of the caretaker and janitor Ernest Bowles, the housemother and dietician Sally Barron, the cook Ethel Weaver, and the choirmaster Edmund Sereno Ender, all of whom most alumni remember with great clarity. Ender, who would stay until 1953, could at least help Kinsolving with the new task of commuting boys to two, sometimes three services on Sundays, by trolley or car—a prescient indicator of massive administrative headaches to come as the trustees honored their promise to the vestry to keep the School close to the Church.[4]

To take his first step towards developing a real academic institution, Kinsolving also had to graduate students. Commencement had become tradition, but not until 1926 did the School offer—and students rightfully claim—a graduating year. Simultaneously, he and the trustees recognized that boys were basically *sans corpore sano*; other than sports at Druid Hill Park and the nearby dirt tennis courts for "healthy, open-air exercise," athletic competition had begun only sporadically under Benjamin Thomas, the first documented "Director of Athletics," in 1924 with area schools like Boys' Latin, the Donaldson School, the Marston School, and Mt. St. Joe. (Public

Gridiron

The cold hard truth is that the original St. Paul's colors were not blue and gold. We know this from the first documented football team described in an 1889 issue of *Parish Notes*. The short clip, which also listed one of the earliest recorded roll book of boys, said the players had decided on orange and black jerseys, "the same as worn by the Princeton Club." Tastes changed, and this combination did not survive the turn of the century.

Although over the next 30 years football found a place in early student publications and occasionally in the board minutes, not until 1932 did rector Arthur Kinsolving, with humble pride, report to his congregation about a St. Paul's victory over his alma mater, Episcopal High School. With the addition of a more organized athletic program under Frank Mead '21, the School celebrated its first 'B' Conference football championship in 1934 (as well as their first gridiron banquet) with 156 total points to their opponents' 13. At that point, Mead gave Clark V. Hoshall '35 what appears to be the precursor to the first monogram sweater and awarded 17 varsity letters.

Howard Myers, Jr. took the team and made them run with a championship and an undefeated season his second year in 1936, another title in 1937 in the 'B' Conference, and a three-way tie in 1938 with Boys' Latin and Friends. It took a good five years before the squad could schedule enough games to qualify at last for the 'A' Conference in 1941. That season, Frank LaMotte's well-attended fall banquet, a tradition he renewed in 1937, was certainly a good way to celebrate an 8-1 record, one Myers repeated his last season in 1945.

Like most of the sports at St. Paul's, the early '50s proved challenging on the new fields of Brooklandville.

Finally, in 1956, after Mitch Tullai had been athletic director and varsity coach for three years, attendance at games improved, and varsity closed with a winning 5-3 record for its second consecutive year. He and Michael Rentko, tired of losing so many in a row, did a "masterful job the entire season," according to *The Crusader*. Within a decade, football grew in strength and ability. The "Team of 1966" Tullai would later claim as one of his best (8-1; 314 offensive points, a record; and 57 points allowed), and registered the first championship in the 'C' Conference as well as a hard-fought victory over 'B' Conference champion Gilman.[1]

Varsity opened the '70s with its first undefeated season since 1936 and to a new Memorial Field, winning the championship two years straight in the newly-formed Tri-County Independent Football League. With winning records for half of its seasons, the '80s became a strong lead-in for five straight 'C' Conference championships from 1989-93. After a 41-year coaching career, Tullai stepped down in 1994 with 210 football victories, two undefeated seasons, and 11 of the 16 School championships.

The '90s remained strong. Coached by Brian Abbott '85, himself a player for Tullai, the varsity took two straight undefeated championship seasons, including a 19-game streak over the course of 1995 (10-0) and 1996 (9-0). (Incidentally, the 1995 championship appropriately marked the dedication of the game field to Tullai.)[2] Abbott's five seasons included five All-State players, and record-breakers Conor Gill '98, with an all-time season passing record of over 1,100 yards, and Chris Berrier '96, with a record 33 career touchdowns and a season record of 1,837 rushing yards in just ten games.[3]

1932 Football Team

(Third row, from left) coach Lewis Tignor '25, R. Donald McDorman '33, Michael L. Rodemeyer '33, James Galick '36, Ralph Hain '34, Randolph Alridge, coach Frank D. Mead '21, (second row) Oscar L. Moritz '34, George O'Connell '35, Elmer H. Kilian, Milton F. Meador '34, S. Vincent Kelly '38, (first row) James D. Beck '33, Dabney H. Cruikshank '36, Jason M. Austin Jr '33, Henry Hastings '34, Robert D. Maccubbin '36.

Outside a New Gym

Students stand by a Ford
"Woody" station wagon as the
builders complete the first Kinsolving Gymnasium. Designed by
the father of Howard Myers, Jr.,
the gym was "in no sense a luxury,
but a necessity" with a "floor of
gumwood with a covering of
Bakvar." Myers added showers and
dressing rooms, and built it using
"the skyscraper principle, the slate
roof being supported by structural
steel girders." The gym officially
opened December 8, 1937,
dedicated by headmaster George
Hamilton to Dr. Arthur B. Kinsolving. While it served the 140
boys well, its use went further
than the students: three nights a
week for badminton, particularly
in the early '40s when alumni,
parents and the community played;
one night for faculty and alumni;
Mondays for the Mt. Washington
Club; and, of course, dances,
proms, speakers, assemblies,
films, and bazaars during all
other free moments.

*"And intelligent educators recognize that athletics, under
competent supervision and direction, furnish a moraliz-
ing and stabilizing influence in the life of a youth."*

Dr. Arthur B. Kinsolving to the students in the new
Kinsolving Gymnasium, 1938

schools, "with big players who chewed tobacco," were too strong for anything more
than "friendly contests"). Bulldozers thus took their turn at the hilly backyard of the
manor house which, even when graded by 1925 at a cost of $7,000, would be too
small for practices and games until an expansion into the woods much later in 1940.
(And the red clay earth would always be painfully rocky enough to be known by all
as the "Rock Bowl," excellent and ample stony fodder for disciplinary measures.)[5]

These hitches tolerated and glitches addressed, by the mid-'20s, Kinsolving's own
Episcopal High School seemed well within reach as it improved its facilities and added
students. The first major expansion to the manor house was a 60 by 25-foot west wing
called the 'A' Dorm "for a minimum increase of 14 scholars" added in 1926. The new
space provided enough room to double enrollment to 65 (59 boarders and six day
scholars), enlarge the dining room, leave more space for Edmund Ender's choir, and
add bedrooms for three masters. The trustees had already authorized advertising the
School, which apparently yielded a "flood of applications." And with a strong base of
paying families in the Mt. Washington area, Kinsolving thus could more actively
enforce the tuition charges and be more selective about whom the School would

The First Seal

Just before Crusader lacrosse ravaged Baltimore and just after a school newspaper was running to press, George Hamilton realized something was missing. For among all of his achievements in the land of tangibles, he was a man of symbols too. In the winter of 1934, he chaired an ad hoc committee with masters Donald Pierpont and Beverly Rhett '21 to design the School seal and "coat of arms." Initially, Rhett looked to the Church for some guidance, and they assembled a derivation of a shield once used by St. Paul's Parish, which consisted of two Roman swords crossed over a book with the motto *I have fought the good fight*. "We wanted an attractive, meaningful design," wrote Hamilton, "with the symbols that stood for the essential characteristics of the School and its objectives, its Christian philosophy and background, its strength of purpose and willingness to fight hard for Christian ideals." Everything became easy after that.

The Monitor reported that using the motto on the shield "reminds us of the continual effort on the athletic field even if one is not first on the team; it stands for taking time out and contributing your best to some school organization; it means steady, hard work on lessons." Rhett and Pierpont left

Emblem used on the 1933 diploma.

Emblem used from 1934-1998.

Current emblem.

the swords with which to fight this good fight, crossed for effect, or, in agrarian terms, to "beat … into plough shares."

The acorn was obvious: that from which great oaks grow. Greatness from small things. "The tremendous impression that even so small a school as St. Paul's can make her sons grow to full stature."

The rope: one fabric of many strands, or "St. Paul's men inter-twisted inextricably," described Hamilton, "enriched and strengthened by each addition, each personality." The knot of brass fittings symbolized a unity of its members.

The cross in the border: salvation, resurrection. The three interior crosses: the Red Cross, peace, unselfishness.

The border around the shield, usually in blue "as frequently seen surrounding the virgin": purity.

The date: 1849, the founding, of course.

And finally, the Latin motto, *Veritas et Virtus*: Truth, virtue, courage. This was in fact Hamilton's idea, and the boys would interpret it however they liked: "the Latin inscription on the scroll," a student editorial said, "*Veritas et Virtus*, reminds all Crusaders of the two virtues which St. Paul's tries hardest to instill—truth and manliness."[1]

*"A growing boy is
a destructive animal."*

The Monitor, April, 1933

Boys Will Be Boys
Students posing behind the main building of Mt. Washington soon after the School moved in 1923. Enrollment would grow from about 30 to 60 in the first ten years at the School's new campus, but would catapult to 217 in the second ten. The boys here unfortunately were not identified.

"Sometimes the masters who were not on charge would go to Pimlico late at night for ice cream at the local drug store, but their life was full of the monastic existence at school. There was a rule, unwritten or otherwise, that undermasters should not be married and should live in the building. By special dispensation from the rector, Dr. Arthur Kinsolving, Louis D. Clark was the first undermaster to marry; and Dr. Kinsolving performed the ceremony himself in 1931."

Louis Clark, *St. Paul's School: The Maturing Years, 1920-1960*

admit. The Boys' School was certainly no longer a school for orphans, but rather for "families of moderate means who could not be at any other School but for ours," Kinsolving explained to the trustees. "The School should serve a cross-section of the community and not any single class. It is far better for the boys themselves that this should be so." As these initial conversations evolved about whom the School should admit, its future seemed to have the "brightest prospects in its history." Headmaster Anderson hoped "in another year [1927-28], the School would fully reach the position of college preparatory." With a promising enrollment (in 1927, several boarders were even housed with neighborhood families) and a steady stream of tuition income, the Boys' School had many reasons to feel encouraged.[6]

The School's optimism—and coming financial anxieties—were a reflection of the times and typical of Baltimore. Life in and near the city was a delicate combination of park and factory, buoyancy and growth, a decade, in H. L. Mencken's words, of "the boosting, the booming, the go-getting, and the ballyhoo." Despite a migration of the affluent outward from the city's center, St. Paul's Parish also prospered in the '20s, though sometimes things frayed unpredictably. The Benevolent Society, as a specific instance, had to close its Girls' School for two years in 1927 and sell its Charles Street home. But the stock market crash, of course, soon set tone and context for everyone; nothing was certain, and that very notion was disconcerting: "Suddenly quieted, when construction stopped and the factories laid off workers by the thousands, Baltimore pursued its agenda, like a mirage on the horizon."[7] St. Paul's Parish and School, like the city, continued.

It was not the 1929 stock market crash, however, that stalled the School's progress and ambitious plans. Rather, it was the irreversible and contemptible reality that

A typical dorm "room" of a Mt. Washington student, though about half of the 60 boarders did not even have partitions between beds. Unmarried faculty members like Charles Heller and Bayard Berghaus '36, who provided this picture, stayed in a double alcove nearby.

"And it is the days of youth that are the precious days,

for it is in these days that character is formed and codes

of honor are assimilated, in which youth see visions and

dream dreams."

Dr. Arthur B. Kinsolving, 1949

William Anderson turned out to be a pedophile. "A charge of immoral relations between William Anderson," documented the trustees in the minute books, "and one of the boys of the School was made by Messrs. [Beverly and Harry] Rhett. Harry Rhett stated that he saw the occurrences through the keyhole of the door that separated his bathroom from the headmaster's study on the night of March 16th [1927], after the Choir concert. The suspicions of both Rhetts had been aroused previous to that by various circumstances and by information imparted to them by another of the boys." According to alumni of that time, Anderson had propositioned students the summer before he started in 1924, but this act of "gross immorality" (as Kinsolving called it in his own history of the School), was not detected earlier for a number of reasons. For one, Anderson proved himself a "good executive and able disciplinarian." In fact, a year before the incident, Kinsolving remarked in his twentieth anniversary sermon, "We owe the success [of the School] almost entirely to the intelligent management of an interested board of trustees and to the wise administration of the present headmaster, Mr. William Anderson." And Anderson's background, aside from having 18 years of teaching experience, was strong enough. He graduated from Virginia Polytechnical Institute and completed graduate work at the University of Michigan; served as a principal of the Cumberland Academy for four years, where he increased enrollment from 43 to 147, was identified with the work of the parish in Cumberland, and was said to be "an enthusiastic instructor and master who has devoted his life to work among boys"; and his wife was noted as "an accomplished woman," a graduate of Smith College. Kinsolving explored rumors he had heard about Anderson before he was hired, but found nothing out of the ordinary; only later did he realize that the letters of reference he had received were not authentic.[8]

Less than 24 hours after Anderson was discovered, he was tried by the enraged trustees and ordered to gather his things, never to return to St. Paul's or to teach again. Trustees seriously considered prosecuting but feared the "accompanying publicity would put an ineradicable stigma" not only on the "eight or ten" boys who came forward but also on all the other students as well as on the School. "Dr. Kinsolving spoke of the distinction between mercy to sin and mercy to the sinner, and that whatever he might do for the latter he could do nothing to expose any other boys to the danger of such contamination." Anderson's wife pleaded ignorance and admitted that

Corporal Punishment

The first and last recorded incident of corporal punishment was in 1924 when a boy was whipped with a belt by a master. Testifying in front of the trustees, the student "admitted using some bad language, … and the [master] administered the whipping in spite of his resistance … The boy complained that the whipping was excessive, but on exhibiting his bruises they did not appear to be serious." Later, in 1930, "[Headmaster Henry] Holladay … brought up the question of corporal punishment, which was discussed, and being resolutely opposed by [two trustees], it was understood and agreed that such a punishment in general should cease, but that in the event of a serious breach of discipline the boy's parents would be advised of the alternative between expulsion and switching before the latter should be administered."

"there was much insanity in the family." But to the charges, "Mr. Anderson made no answer except in these words: 'I submit my resignation to take effect at your convenience.'" When Anderson did not show up that Monday, the 59 boarders and six day students were told that he was a corrupt man whom they would never see again.[9]

Thus the years of work and signs of progress were regrettably tainted. Kinsolving kept the School under control, but most decisions for the next five years were made defensively. Following the incident, yet another round of headmasters filled the post: Dr. Wyllys Read for one month, followed by the Reverend S. Janney Hutton '10, recommended by two Gilman headmasters, from 1928-29, and then Walter B. Lawrence, a graduate of Taft School and Yale University, who left after only a year.

Finally, some continuity came with Henry Thompson Holladay who had been Lawrence's assistant and who would serve as headmaster for the next three years. Still, in 1930, not only was Holladay relatively new to the School, but so was every teacher, as future mainstay Louis Clark had left to try his hand at business and Rhett had transferred to another teaching position. Holladay was in his early thirties, had graduated from Episcopal High School (obviously attractive to Kinsolving) and from Hamden-Sydney in 1922, and had taught Latin and languages at several schools around the country. When he arrived, he hired his 26-year-old brother Lewis Holladay, Jr., listed as "Senior Master" in the first School catalog (1931-32). Though Kinsolving would later request his resignation, Henry Holladay was probably the best person to steer the School through the initial crash and the first quaking years of the Depression. A stern man of discipline, Henry Holladay ran a cleanly—most alumni of that era say spotlessly—organized ship. Students, as an example, were not allowed to talk during dinner and were "schooled to extreme deference to masters." Rules and regulations, for Holladay, were perhaps a good tonic to the threat to hope and stability the Depression presented. Holladay managed money well, and readily articulated a serious need to increase the endowment and to address the "constant inquiries from parents of worthy boys who find it impossible to meet the full cost."[10]

Though unknown to the boys, 1930 in fact would be the first year that the School would have the right combination of masters who would bring an unusually lasting and creative energy to the School: Frank Mead '21, a strong athlete from University of Virginia, would build the framework of a robust athletic program; Clark, who returned a year later, would stay with St. Paul's until his death in 1989; Donald Pierpont, from University of Richmond, would found the Lower School and the arts program.

While Holladay brought a "much needed order" and planted the seeds of longevity with his hires, he soon "antagonized trustees, staff, faculty and parents by his autocratic and uncompromising attitude toward the running of the School" and was not re-engaged for the 1932-33 year.[11]

Once again, Kinsolving had not found the right leader for the School he wanted to build. But the bad streak had come to a close. During the coming period of total

The manor house
of St. Paul's School at
2101 Rogers Avenue.
Only "privileged" seniors
were allowed to spend
time on the front porch.

Lessons in Stickwork

Lacrosse star William U. Hooper, Jr. '47.

That it took only four "agitators"—without a coach, or a full-length field, or even one player who had some remote experience in lacrosse, and with an athletic director who "didn't know A from B about" it—to start a team in the spring of 1933 in a school of 58 at the peak of the Depression seems improbable enough. But it is just as astonishing that in no less than a decade the game was a central, dominating force in the School, in Baltimore and throughout the mid-Atlantic, a game in which St. Paul's continues as a powerhouse today. Like the origins of the Choir, St. Paul's affixed itself to an atypical idea (few private schools had even considered the sport) and performed with an intensity that was at once profound and single-minded.

Perhaps lacrosse took hold because it was a natural extension or the next best thing to football—only in the spring—more fluid, at least as rigorous and equally as aggressive. Also, as one of the first team members suggested, its attraction stemmed from the School's rekindled student body, enlarged and diversified by an influx of "day dogs" who brought new ideas and raw athletic ability. It also helped that lacrosse was right next door to the Mt. Washington Club. A family friend of the Boys' School, Fritz McDorman (brother of future faculty member and choirmaster Donald '33) coached a team of 12 and got mauled 15-1 in the School's first interscholastic game against Donaldson, a school which would close the following year. (Consequently, two of its stronger athletes, Theodore Poole '34 and A. Merriman Casey '35, defected to St. Paul's, as well as future coach Howard "Howdy" Myers, Jr.)

With $100 from a parent, and "the few dollars the School had," All-American Gordon Pugh, replacing Fritz McDorman, began molding the team two days a week. In short order, Pugh took St. Paul's to a winning record for the first two years they played, moving up to the 'A' Conference his third and last year. By 1936, with an enrollment of 105, students filled two varsity squads and a jayvee team. They knew they could win. And they did.[1]

**The Importance of
Being Pierpont**

No two descriptions are alike
in the world of master Donald
Pierpont. Over the course of his
12 years (1930-1942), he started
the School's first drama club,
organized the first library, began
the first Lower School, spoke on
Rembrandt and prehistoric art,
performed his own one-act plays,
and helped design the School
emblem. "So, if you have a naturally mean streak," he said to one
assembly on the topic of using
one's latent abilities, "look around.
Perhaps someone is looking for a
man to scare little children off a
vacant lot." The "Renaissance
Guy," as master Louis Clark called
him, also had a 70-pound, police-
trained Great Dane named Marcus
that licked fried eggs off a plate
and interrupted football games.

economic stagnation and until World War II, St. Paul's would witness a period of significant growth. Indeed, arguably the greatest surge of energy in the School's
history—powered by adrenaline and inebriated with raw spirit—occurred during the
most economically trying time in this country's history. It was the Hamilton Surge.

THE HAMILTON SURGE

The new headmaster, George S. Hamilton, loved to sing and tell jokes. Perhaps this
combination of humor and music equipped Hamilton with his armor and shield—
and his faith with a horse to ride—not only to sustain his maturing School through
the heart of the Depression but also to expand, deepen and enrich it. The oldest
teacher there at age 28, Hamilton opened St. Paul's in 1932 with 36 boarders and 24
day students; a devoted cadre of masters like Donald Pierpont, Beverly Rhett '21,
Frank "Speedy" Mead '21, Louis Clark, and Lewis Tignor '25; and a committed staff
including dietician Sallie Barron, matron Noel Bush, and caretaker Ernie Bowles.[12]

Hamilton also had a sturdy foundation: Dr. Arthur B. Kinsolving's faith and his
quarter century of experience in Church, City and School; a plot of suburban land
rough and ready near a dependable source of day students; a stirring sense of Virginia,
of the South, and of Episcopal High School, where Hamilton had already taught; and,
most importantly, a mission—to become a school. In truth, as area independent
schools had themselves begun maturing, competing, and defining themselves, St. Paul's
lagged behind. Since World War I, deepened by the torpid and irregular 1920s with
its many different teachers and headmasters, scarred by Headmaster Anderson, separated by location from its Mother Church, and remaining an unremarkable presence
athletically and academically, St. Paul's was well past infancy as an institution, but just
not ready for high school.

For the boyish Hamilton and his handsome, new-fledged teachers, work toward
this mission certainly seemed painless and quick enough; it was as if everybody
there—masters, students, and trustees—had tired of waiting. Their faith was all the
stronger. In fact, as more established schools suffered in the Depression between 1930
and 1935, such as Calvert (enrollment dropped seven percent in 1933 alone), Gilman
(enrollment fell 26 percent, boarding plummeting by nearly 75 percent), and Boys'
Latin (a 25-percent drop), St. Paul's took off. The School nearly doubled both its operating budget ($14,971) and its enrollment in these five years (105 students, its capacity)
and would quadruple both ($55,165 and 235 students) in another five. Tuition rev-
enue remained steady; in 1934, for example, only two of the 88 boys received a full
scholarship. And it also remained affordable; in once case, Hamilton reported to the
trustees that only three schools on the East Coast had a less expensive boarding tuition
than the $400 the Boys' School charged. Where St. Paul's lagged in 1932, it began to
gain ground quickly. The School had firsts that finally lasted: emblem and shield, varsity sports, school newspaper, victory bell, drama club, mascot, gymnasium, athletic

field, Lower School, cheer rallies, yearbook. And from this list of firsts arose the single most animating force in an institution's evolution: spirit. Hamilton's era (1932-44) had none like it.[13]

Neither the trustees nor Hamilton took for granted their good fortune during these dismaying times. Through the Depression, they found creative strategies to make ends meet. In one case that almost forever changed the School, the trustees, examining the costly renovations the manor house needed, laid out detailed plans to merge with the Donaldson School in Ilchester, Maryland, a new institution founded through a bequest of a loyal Old St. Paul's parishioner and long-time School friend, Miss Frances Donaldson. The plans detailed how the combined board of trustees should be organized and how the School would re-locate. Ultimately, the negotiations fell through, but it serves as only one example of trustees seeking opportunities to keep things solvent. They encouraged faculty to earn money during the summers to support themselves, paid salaries in whole or in part by room and board, and targeted the suburban—and wealthier—day population of students who overall were less expensive to matriculate.[14] This strategy to increase day students was most efficacious. Though they paid a third of a boarder's tuition, day students were not only less expensive but also were easier to accommodate since the dormitory—almost always full—could handle at most 60. In 1934, the number of day students equaled the number of boarders for the first time, and every subsequent year, boarders became the minority by an increasing percentage (43 percent in 1936, 29 in 1941). Steady tuition fees during the Depression enabled Hamilton to pay off the mortgage and even give faculty raises in 1934. Remarkably few problems ever resulted from uncollected tuition. Later, in 1940, for instance, with 58 boarders and 123 day students, only $400 went uncollected. Interestingly enough, the early '30s marked the period when St. Paul's weaned itself from its financial dependence on the Church, which, according to Kinsolving, had been "one of the Church's heaviest obligations financially." In fact, in 1934, Hamilton asked for only a third of the roughly $5,000 the Church had been giving the School annually since the '20s, and paid off a long-due $1,200 outstanding debt to the vestry the following year.[15]

Mostly though, the Depression closely unified trustees, faculty and students and galvanized school spirit. St. Paul's was now big enough to hold the contours of a community but small enough to remain a family. The dining room had rectangular tables of ten, each with a master and one circular table of faculty children. No one sat until Hamilton had said grace. Dorms were rows of alcoves, cabinets, beds and shelves, swept, tidied and given the "white glove" check for dust every morning. The campus always needed cleaning, and boys always needed prodding (or detention) to do it. The School voted Democrat in a student poll (Roosevelt and Garner over Hoover and Curtis), were pro-New Deal, and wanted the U.S. to join the United Nations.

The new family almost couldn't keep up with itself, too anxious for its own col-

Sports That Never Were (Though Might Still Be)

Not a comprehensive list, but worth noting a few: track in the '20s and '30s. Badminton Club, 1939, centralized at St. Paul's with some 100 adult members, one of the largest in the city, with young pro Robert Wentworth '49. Boxing, 1949, under Ray Greene '41. Archery, 1948, under Woodruff Marston, one of the Baltimore Oriole Archers. Box lacrosse, 1950. Several decades of softball under Michael Rentko and Mitch Tullai, later Carel Beernink, 1950. Fencing, Guy Kagey, 1954. The "friendly" Gun Club, 1955, under Angelo Gentile, with skeet shoots against Gilman, reemerging in 1965 under Samuel Williams. Ski Club, 1966. Ultimate Frisbee, 1983. Varsity ice hockey, begun by Derek Stikeleather in 1996, has been the latest to test the athletic waters. Graphic by August W. Schell '50, from the 1948 *Crusader*.

Just STP in yellow chenille—
That's all you see, sez you?
Think of the boys who,
years before,
Won a letter like this, too;

Who cherish it still and always will
Till the end of their earthly trip;
They know it's a symbol
of courage,
Of the best in sportsmanship.

Excerpt from

George S. Hamilton's

well-known poem "STP"

lective adulthood to linger through adolescence. Consider Hamilton's first year, 1932-33: eight full issues of *The Monitor*, the student newspaper which followed the ten-year absence of *Triakonta*; the first library (a remodeled recreation room); the first varsity lacrosse team; and "an old ship's bell" which rang for the first time after a lacrosse win against the Catonsville jayvee on May 12, 1933.

And in his second year: a school seal; faculty-run summer programs; a student government called the "Old Boys' Club" (oldest of the "old boys" was 16) designed to promote fellowship and school spirit; an honor system; membership in the Maryland Private School Association; and, "in keeping with the trends of education among Baltimore preparatory schools," a division of Upper School and Lower School (at first called the Preparatory Department), under Pierpont, with its own dormitory, two classrooms and 23 students.

Of these initiatives, the honor system was perhaps the most significant. It was also an obvious addition: almost every faculty member was tied to a Virginian school, and Kinsolving and Hamilton both held the Episcopal High School tradition close to their hearts. The honor system was indeed based on Episcopal High School's, one which had been in practice there for over 50 years since 1877 under Launcelot Minor Blackford, Kinsolving's friend and colleague. "The discipline of Episcopal High School," wrote Blackford, "is based on the principle that … [the teacher] not neglect to inspire, if he may, such sentiments of honour and moral responsibility as will lead the pupil to govern himself."[16] Former headmaster Henry Holladay, an Episcopal boy too, had in fact initiated the effort by 1931, and noted that it was managed by the five appointed student prefects, the "favored few," Holladay said, "to which every boy should aspire." But it was Headmaster Hamilton who both fully embodied and actively promoted the system, and who put it into full effect by 1935. "We feel that by developing confidence in honor," remarked an editorial in *The Monitor* that year, "one of the most serious troubles with which a school can be threatened will be overcome—namely, mistrust among students." In short, the goal was to "stamp out dishonesty."[17]

With honor, faith, students, and money, Kinsolving also found, at last, his *corpore sano*, his "Athletes of God," as he described them—students with opportunities to harness their "spiritual power." Holladay had at least made some strides with the intramural track meets (his preferred sport, and, incidentally, Hamilton's) in the winter, baseball in the spring, and the occasional interscholastic "Fifth Regiment Games." But when Holladay claimed that "in athletics St. Paul's is outstanding," he was mostly referring to the fact that students had a place to exercise in a small gymnasium, which was actually a barn, "adequate for the physical training of the smaller boys." He noted that the older boys enjoyed "outside training" on the football, basketball and soccer teams, which sometimes competed in the Interacademic League.[18] Still, the St. Paul's Saints (not yet Crusaders and not yet with uniforms) were hardly benchwarmers in

"As I write, I am picturing you in my mind's eye just as though you were sitting before me on the bleachers in the gym ... as fine, as loyal a bunch of fellows as any headmaster could wish for. I get a thrill of pride whenever I face you and think of the many splendid things we have accomplished working together shoulder to shoulder for 'our dear old school St. Paul's!'"

George S. Hamilton in a letter to his students during the summer of 1938

George O'Connell '35, during his 68 years to date with St. Paul's, has been a student, choir member, football player, charter member of the Spectator Club, parent of two alumni (one of whom was also a faculty member), trustee for 36 years (1952-87, 35 years as secretary, 22 of those as treasurer), first elected alumni trustee with a right to vote, historian, archivist and, since 1987, alumni-development liaison. For appropriate posterity, O'Connell now has a room, a portrait which hangs opposite that of Dr. Arthur Kinsolving, and a scholarship in his name.

the high school athletic world until Hamilton instituted the first athletic requirement when he arrived in 1932. He and Mead, who had not associated well with Holladay, took the School to the playing field. As the first active athletic director, Mead immediately introduced the School to the Maryland Scholastic Association (MSA) and mingled with others in the league. Early St. Paul's coaches like Lewis Tignor '25, who replaced winter track with wrestling (which was soon usurped by basketball in 1936) received pointers from seasoned Gilman coach Ed Russell, who offered his jayvee team as opponents.

Lacrosse appeared that spring, but it was football which proved in 1933 that the crusading boys could contend; indeed, that year's gridiron team was the first in a long string of the proverbial "Greatest Teams Ever," just missing a 'B' Conference championship that year and acquiring its first title against the strong Boys' Latin team in 1934. "In winning the championship, St. Paul's has demonstrated clearly what can be done in a short time," wrote *The Monitor*. "A few years ago, the School was practically unknown athletically. People thought of St. Paul's as a fine old choir school." Though the Choir was still the School's principal activity (all students were given a vocal examination when they entered), more boys meant more energy to channel. Thus, the sudden explosion of sports was hardly a surprise; by 1935, nearly every boy was playing some sport—"from the youngest to the oldest," Hamilton proudly reported to his trustees.[19]

AND THEN THERE WAS HOWDY ...

By way of a woman who once saved the School and a lacrosse game the novice Saints expected to lose, Howard "Howdy" Myers, Jr. arrived at St. Paul's in 1935 and would complete permanently and entirely the transformation Hamilton had already begun to make. Lacrosse coach Fritz McDorman, with a team of 12, endured a 15-1 loss on the Mt. Washington field against Myers's team, which came from Miss Donaldson's

When Days of Old St. Paul's Carry On

"Adrian Hughes, Class of 1876, is a well-known lawyer in Baltimore.
It has been mainly through his interest in the Alumni Association
that it has continued in existence."

Alumni Notes, *Triakonta*, 1922

Little else is known about this Adrian Hughes in the above note, but plenty is known about Charles Stokes '27, who sparked the Alumni Association to life in the late '30s, building off of the work of such people as W. Carroll Mead '19. Through the '40s, Stokes and others expanded the Association, began a series of vaudeville entertainment shows called "Alumni Presents," held concerts, and launched such events as "Varieties Drives" to raise money for a scholarship fund. Since no alumni association could be without the breaking of bread, the crusading alumni certainly had food, such as the annual banquet at Park Plaza Hotel in 1948; but they also had sports, designating the Poly game in 1941 as the School's official "Homecoming Event" at Homewood Field. They also enjoyed helping students, sponsoring college visits (to see "several fine fraternity houses"), teaching classes on finance, running lacrosse clinics, and everything in between.

When the School moved in 1952, no alumnus could pretend Brooklandville was Mt. Washington. The Old Boys felt disoriented. This wasn't their school, some said. Sure it was, others replied. Still, activity slumped. The Hunt Cup fell on homecoming weekend. *The Monitor*, which kept alumni connected, lost focus. And the Association was not sure where or what to call home. Credit a new birth to president Ned Pendleton '54, who restructured the Association in 1962; to Headmaster Middleton and people like Fredricka McDorman, who helped bring about the bull roast in 1963 (inviting parents in 1966), the Outstanding Alumnus Award, and class agents; to Headmaster Ordeman and Robert Randolph, who organized records and developed events; and to Headmaster Hallett and Joan Abelson, who fleshed out publications and engineered an efficient development arm.

Keeping track of alumni was challenging enough, so events soon required a consistent calendar. Traditions began. The bull roast, though it had heydays in the '70s, with turnouts of 800-plus (1976), has in recent years emerged as the main fall jamboree, while "Blue and Gold Day" (soon, an entire weekend), inaugurated on May 12, 1979, has become the most significant alumni event of the year. Silent auctions, athletic contests, and new events like the pancake breakfast over Christmas, begun in 1993, have brought more alumni together, a body of graduates that numbers some 2,430. And the annual fund drive has never been stronger: half of the alumni contributed a total of $219,027 in 1997, compared to $4,500 given when the annual fund-raising effort formalized 40 years before.[1]

"How can I explain it to you ... that elusive, intangible thing that we call the St. Paul's spirit? Words are inadequate. They sometimes render flat and lifeless a thing that is vital and very precious ... The value of spirit cannot be assessed. Without it, a school lacks true life."

George S. Hamilton, *St. Paul's School Catalog, 1939-40*

The victory bell, which first appeared in 1933, quickly became a tradition to ring after defeating an opponent.

Donaldson School (which closed that year). Myers turned down a higher offer at Friends' School to work at St. Paul's, an offer made by the trustees with Mead's recommendation. Thus, Myers came to coach a team he had just annihilated on the field, and he would reverse that order quickly.[20]

As the new athletic director, Myers systematically shredded opponents over the next 11 years with relentless energy and success: 15 championships, including five MSA 'A' Conference titles with his last five teams (football, basketball and lacrosse), six straight 'A' Conference lacrosse championships his last six years, basketball his last three (after moving to the 'A' Conference), and a football team (1945, his last), one of the most successful to date with an 8-1 record. Like a choirmaster, Myers's musical scores were his plays, his songs, his games.

Soon, Myers was busing his football team 250 miles at a stretch to crush the competition, like the Christ Church School in New York 53-0 in 1937. That same year he started school two weeks early for his football players to practice, work out, and study plays at his family home in Cape May, New Jersey. His drive was indeed fierce and continuous, but Myers had license to lead. Hamilton—buoyant, charismatic, quick, and determined—and Myers, with a martyr-like commitment and the force of a freight train, shared a common instinct about how to teach character and honor. Not everyone, however—Hamilton included—could always dodge a freight train; some did not even want one on their tracks. Thus Hamilton found himself in the difficult position of trying to manage Myers, someone who could alienate faculty and students just as expeditiously as he could rally them, whose teams were now defeating opponents three times their size. Here was a man drawing a new kind of attention and prestige that the School had not yet experienced; and, ultimately, this meant strong enrollment, a deepened alumni base, and improved access to better resources. Myers was in many ways the strong-armed headmaster—without the title—who pushed his agenda. Factions within the School grew and dissolved; students could fear, hate or love him, depending on how Myers felt about them. Hamilton still recognized that nothing could do more for a School than spirit, and Howdy Myers shaped its healthy core. Even for those students who were not his fans, this new spirit was infec-

It's Howdy Myers Time

His work ethic was Protestant, his conservatism Victorian, his principals Puritan, his "religion" was honor and character, his scripture was an open field, a team and an opponent. Howard "Howdy" Myers, Jr. (1935-46) is indeed one of the easiest figures in the School's history either to imagine or to remember, but also the most complicated to explain and to understand.

His object was partly to win, but even on championship games he would, and did, pull starting players from the team if they broke training rules, even curfew. He once turned down an NFL coaching job while breaking records as athletic director at Johns Hopkins and at Hofstra University—where, over his 25 years there, he became known as the father of Long Island lacrosse. No one, even his daughter, can recall him swearing; in fact, Myers may be the first man to be taken seriously when he shouted his most effusive invective, "Geazie Peazie!" He wore ties to games, lined up his toothbrushes perpendicular to the sink and got upset when they (like his children and his students) were out of line. He ran his modest Peugeot into the ground. Even on holidays, Myers, in his near obsessive-compulsive behavior, would spend 14 or 18 hours a day working on the infinite variety of X's and O's; the geometry of what he taught in the classroom could forever translate to the geometry of plays he devised for the field. Myers was about timing, short

"Great Caesar's ghost!"

Howard "Howdy" Myers, Jr.

scrimmages, and repetition, and his philosophy had little room for anything other than black and white; either you were an honest man or a fink, a believer or a traitor.

Some recall this figure with a kind of loosely defined terror, even animosity; others see him as their only father. Myers was distant with all of his players, less remote with a privileged few, but on whichever side of the Myers field you sat, his presence was enormous. Quipped *The Monitor*, "Have you noticed all the heavy rains now that football practice has stopped? Coach Myers's influence with the Weather Bureau has long been rumored."

"Lacrosse is the house that Howdy built," remarked coach George Mitchell '44, though he would later amend these words to, "*St. Paul's* was the house that Howdy built." Indeed. Myers and his teams brought thousands to games, and when alumni talk about the spirit of St. Paul's—relentless and unconditional—they are referring to the time when Howdy walked the ground.

Father of Dorsey and Howard III, Myers was neither a staunch patriot nor a church-goer, but he was a stubborn missionary for staying busy, advising at one point or another almost every activity that St. Paul's offered. When he did stop at night, his food was roast beef, his pleasure straight and to the point: bourbon on the rocks and a pipe.

And two final notes to close: Myers never played lacrosse. And he liked football better.[1]

LEFT: Seated here behind the first Kinsolving Gymnasium, Lilyan Lorenz worked for 40 years (1945-85) as secretary for headmasters Appy Middleton and Jack Ordeman, the longest employment of any St. Paul's staff member. When Lilyan took the position, her friend informed her that the amount on her paycheck would remain the same. Not until she received her first check from St. Paul's did Lilyan realize that this "same" amount appeared only twice each month. Apart from her clerical duties, Lilyan played an integral role during the move to Brooklandville, planted a sapling of a Wye Oak in 1953, which now stands tall in front of the mansion, and lived in the north gatehouse from 1975 until her retirement. In her *Baltimore Sun* obituary in 1994, Ordeman recalled her famous wit in response to a woman who was angry that birds had messed her windshield. "For some of us," Lilyan said to her, "they sing."

tious, with qualities central to the School's mission—honor, camaraderie, sportsman-ship—and would turn an otherwise good decade into a Golden Era altogether, not just in sports but in the full school experience.[21]

Though Myers brought with him the conviction that character and integrity, not muscle and speed, were qualities that made up what he called "manliness," sports and winning had become by 1940 no less than an obsession. Faculty that year sacrificed their annual salary increases to help pay for a full-length lacrosse field.[22] To be presi-dent of the Monogram Club, the most prestigious and most rigorously-regulated club, with their own room, medal, and clothing, was the highest honor, the second being varsity team captain. Even student editorials written the first year Myers arrived voiced new concerns that sports not take up all of a student's time.

No doubt, part of Myers's success was owed to the times. Athletic competition and sports were an obvious way to toughen young boys into tough young men in a very tough time—emotionally, physically, mentally. The country slid from a Depres-sion straight into a world war. The School's growing obsessions were neither unique nor without equal (City College football players, for instance, were rumored to practice four hours a day). Athletics was less a matter of personal victory or of a team's achievement, than of a collective acknowledgement that there was no better way to become a man.

Myers insisted on fitness and routines to embed these ideas. Everyone attended games. Bonfires became pre-game celebrations, banquets ended seasons, strict training rules and codes of conduct were steadfast expectations. He gave athletes their own tables in the dining hall on game days, regulated their diet (typical spread: dry roast beef, baked potato without butter, peas, toast, and tea), and engaged boys as young as possible (known as "Little Weeds" in the classroom, "Little Cruisies" on the field). By luck or by persuasion, Myers always had players. By the end of the decade, students were carrying their lacrosse sticks to the movie theaters and transformed the dining hall into a football field for the prom.[23]

When Myers re-awakened basketball, the barn-turned-gym was hardly spacious enough. Spearheaded from the pulpit by Kinsolving, the fund-raising effort for a new gym began in early 1935, and when it was completed in 1937 at a cost of $30,000, it was said to be one of the best in Baltimore.[24] Thus, within Myers's first five years, St. Paul's had all the elements of a true athletic program: fields, uniforms, a gym, and plenty of opponents who hated to lose.

BELOW: George Hamilton with wife Vyvyanna and daughter Welby, in one of three station wagons mostly used to commute boys to and from games. The mother of George O'Connell '35 secured the first Model T Ford station wagon for the School, and also had the circular driveway paved in front of the manor house.

Hoop Dreams

The earliest indication of organized "tub-thumpers" appears with the 1920-21 basketball team, which played and practiced at the nearby YMCA on Charles Street, though this "new branch of athletics had been introduced" in 1916. Wrestling generally had been the winter concern, until Howard Myers, Jr. found basketball the best bridge from football to lacrosse. During his first year in 1935, he brought the basketball team into official varsity status with a 28-game schedule, held practice in a gym in Hampden, and played games at Johns Hopkins until the first Kinsolving Gymnasium gave the sport a home two years later. By 1938, Myers had enough boys to create two equally good teams that alternated quarters, and beat an historically stronger Boys' Latin to become the first area school to win all of its league games.

Myers left his 11-year coaching career in spring 1946, having just concluded three straight 'A' Conference basketball championships. His successor James Boyer (1947-49) took the team to a victory over Lawrenceville in New Jersey, a private school championship in 1948-49 and an undefeated season in the league. James Ratcliffe (1949-55) would see the team through the beginning of a lull as the School moved to Brooklandville in 1952 and had nowhere to shoot hoops, requiring a frequent and inconvenient trek to the old Mt. Washington courts. The loss of all five starters in 1952, the "most dismal basketball season in St. Paul's history" (2-15), would also help explain a three-year losing streak that preceded its first victory on the new campus against McDonogh in 1955. Once the new gym was completed (1954), wins came with it. When Mitch Tullai (1955-61) coached his first team, he gained a second-place ranking in his division, and in the following season had the first winning record in seven years, later assisted by Valentine "Dutch" Lentz (1957-59). Though a 1966-67 jayvee championship was a proud moment for Tullai, varsity's second place run in the MSA Private School League in 1959-60 and in 1961-62 under George Mitchell '44 (1960-63) and Mike Rentko (1961-64) was as far as they would get until Tom Longstreth became coach in 1964. Over the next 22 years, his team took division titles in the 'B' Conference in 1976, 1977, and 1983.

Succeeding Longstreth in 1987, Rick Collins (1987-97) and his teams made aggressive drives to the hoop. In his second year, 1988-89, varsity earned its first MSA championship in 43 years. Over the course of the next ten years, he would accrue an overall record of 201-83, with two straight MSA championships (1990-92), back-to-back MIAA championships (1995-97), an Independent School championship (1991-92), and second-place ranking in three other seasons (1988-90, 1994-95). His work done, Collins left the team in the hands of Tony Meyers.[1]

"It has been said that St. Paul's turns out the best-dressed athletic teams in the city and the worst-dressed students."

The Monitor, 1948

ST. PAUL'S vs. CALVERT HALL

Friday, February 16, 1945, 8:30 P. M.

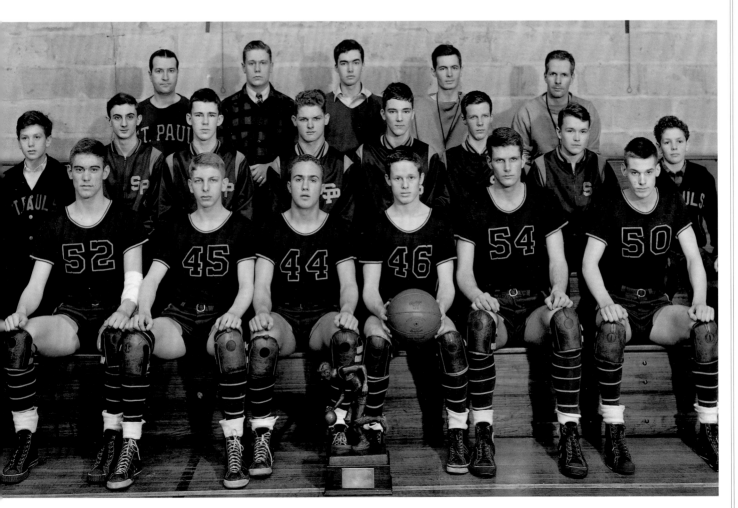

First Maryland 'A' Conference Basketball Champions, 1943-44
(Third row, from left) trainer James Boyer, Sloan Griswold '47, manager Raymond A. Gore '44, assistant coach Marshall Turner, coach Howard Myers, Jr., (second row) manager Bill Wyman, John A. Turner '44, William U. Hooper, Jr. '47, Thomas W. Gough, Jr. '46, Stewart McLean '44, Carter O. Hoffman '45, C. Herbert Sadtler '45, manager Edward Leonard, Jr. '47, (first row) A. Hamilton Bishop III '44, Charles B. Compton '46, Robert E. Sandell, Jr. '45, William F. Crocket '44, George L. Mitchell '44, James F. Adams '46.

BUSINESS AS USUAL

Meanwhile, Hamilton had to concentrate on building a school. The gymnasium was one of many much-needed physical improvements, and between 1935 and 1938 alone, the manor building faced significant renovation. Some changes were cosmetic—a fresh coat of paint, new gardens, shutters, a parking lot and a paved circle. Other changes included better Lower School quarters, a new 'B' wing dormitory to accommodate 15 more boys, and a new furnace for which "after 15 years of a venerable 'horse-and-buggy' type of heating," said the students, "we have been given a New Deal."[25]

A growing school tested Hamilton with an entirely foreign set of management and operational issues. In a handwritten note to himself, he began with "We are too busy to" and itemized a long and overwhelming list, including "teach boys how to study; get yearbooks on time and done properly; utilize cultural influences of Baltimore; inspect dorms rigidly; give sex talks to adolescents." He also described the causes as "too full a class schedule; too many games—intramural, jayvee, varsity; too long practices; no weekend plans."[26] And at the bottom of this note, he jotted some solutions: cut a study period to leave time for publications, begin a student body "town" meeting, and initiate a work program. The best Hamilton could do was to figure things out as they popped up.

George Hamilton was not, however, building his School in the dark or without pattern, even though Donaldson School's closing meant that St. Paul's was the only Church boarding and day school, which, according to Kinsolving, "is widely recognized as one of the most effective agencies in Maryland for training boys of moderate means into wholesome, Christian manhood." More importantly, the enterprise of private college preparatory schools was itself developing, and Hamilton had the foresight to involve St. Paul's beyond the work that Myers was doing athletically. In 1937, the entire St. Paul's faculty, for instance, attended the second annual conference of the Private Schools of Maryland. In fact, at the end of the decade, Hamilton was elected president of the Private School's Association of Baltimore, which at that point included 18 private schools. All this was designed in part to expose the School to the outside world. Despite the new publicity Myers had attracted in local newspapers, Hamilton also actively marketed the School. In one typed note, titled "Is It Worth the Cost?", Hamilton defended the added expense of private education. "If a boy gains from private school not only a thorough scholastic training but also the moral soundness, the ideals of civic responsibility, and the courageous spirit that will enable him

Chief Builder

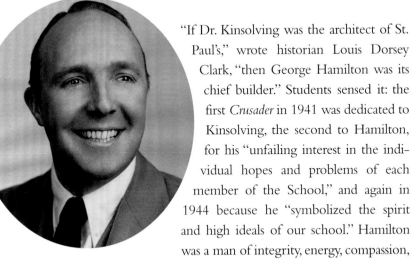

George S. Hamilton

On a particularly unremarkable day, George Stanton Hamilton found himself deciding something particularly unremarkable on his way to work at an advertising firm in New York. He thought he would walk—for the first time—on the other side of a wide New York avenue, an avenue he had been strolling down for months. And there, something particularly remarkable happened: he bumped into an acquaintance which, in turn, led to a lunch date where he was offered a very different kind of job.

"There's a little school in Baltimore looking for a headmaster," this powerful man, Brooke Stabler, said to him.

"Headmaster!" replied George who at this point had just recently, and secretly, married 20-year-old Vyvyanna Sanz of Rio de Janeiro, a woman he met and wedded within three months. "But I'm only 28!"

Stabler looked at George seriously and replied: "It's a very small school."[1]

Within a few months, Hamilton was driving with Vyvyanna in his Ford Roadster to a school they had never heard of, in a city they had only passed through. Ernie Bowles handed them mint juleps on the porch of the manor house on the Mt. Washington campus. The decision was not difficult.

An alumnus of Randolph-Macon and an English teacher at Episcopal High School for five years (1925-30), Hamilton and his mentor, Dr. Arthur Kinsolving, shared a common ancestry of sorts, not just in alma mater but in what each felt should be the code and conduct of a school.

"If Dr. Kinsolving was the architect of St. Paul's," wrote historian Louis Dorsey Clark, "then George Hamilton was its chief builder." Students sensed it: the first *Crusader* in 1941 was dedicated to Kinsolving, the second to Hamilton, for his "unfailing interest in the individual hopes and problems of each member of the School," and again in 1944 because he "symbolized the spirit and high ideals of our school." Hamilton was a man of integrity, energy, compassion, and hard work who preached these values to his students every morning.

Hamilton's father was a sheriff in the smallest of small towns called Warrenton, Virginia; his mother raised his two sisters and two brothers, though one passed away when he was young. Academic scholarship was ambient sound, not the driving music, of Hamilton's work; his legacy was honor and character. He believed in the second chance, in ideas, in a student's ability to grow. Under him, most things St. Paul's—newspaper, emblem, athletics, mascot, and more—were formed.

First Lady of the headmaster, the beautiful Vyvyanna, who had appeared on Broadway but was most popular at school for her movie reviews in *The Monitor*, was on occasion asked by students who came to the house if they could speak to her father—that is, George. Two daughters, Diane and Welby, would make these errors less frequent.

George and his wife knew how to have fun, spent time with other faculty families like the Tignors and the Meads, ran lemons on the windshield to keep it from freezing, raised Easter chicks—all the while listening to George's notoriously bad jokes … and his catchy limericks.[2]

1923-1952 - MENS SANA IN CORPORE SANO

The Student Voice

Students in chapel in the Kinsolving Gym at Mt. Washington. A little background on their mindset and beliefs, using several polls reported in the 1947 issue of *The Monitor*. Of 164 students who voted, 85 percent would elect Thomas E. Dewey for President, 7.5 percent Franklin D. Roosevelt, and 7.5 percent had no opinion; 75 percent would not choose a career in politics, and 66 percent said that the voting age should *not* be lowered to 18. (Two years later this number dropped to 51 percent.) In a 1945 poll of 91 St. Paul's students in high school who answered the question, "Do you think that girls should plan a career other than homemaking?" 44 percent said yes, 34 percent said no, and 22 percent had no opinion. How about a job with a labor union? Ninety-five percent would decline, though only 51 percent would take a career in professional services (e.g. doctor, lawyer) and 15 percent in government. The remainder indicated a wide range of career choices.

(From left) James M. Jordan III '41, H. Franklin Knipp, Jr. '40, Key Compton '42, and
John W. Wyatt '40 studying in master Beverly "Pop" Rhett's apartment.

"There are few schools from which we have drawn boys whose representatives as a whole rank better than the boys from St. Paul's School, Baltimore."

Dean Gilliam, Washington and Lee University in a letter to George Hamilton, 1939

to face adult life successfully, it is worth every penny of its cost."[27]

Hamilton also concentrated on improving the School's academic quality and rigor. In 1933, he reported to the trustees that all but one master was a college graduate and a year later noted that students could take the College Boards; by 1935, he proudly announced that Johns Hopkins was willing to accept graduates from St. Paul's.[28] To Hamilton, his teachers were colleagues and friends. "In the smoke and chatter of our long meeting last night," he wrote to his faculty, "we accomplished a good deal of important business." To be sure, not all was fraternal. "It is true," wrote Louis Clark, "that occasionally there were on the staff men of choleric disposition to be endured by their associates. Their presence could break progress; however, they supplemented the eccentric quality of a school of individualists." Regardless of the causes, the issues were demanding. Hamilton always had his hands full with the minutiae: reinforcing table manners and "combating unjust and irritating criticisms of meals by informing the students who 'gripe' how difficult it is to obtain the food we want and the necessary servants"; consolidating an unwieldy set of school regulations; or punishing students "hooking off bounds after lights out." At the same time, Hamilton was now beginning to plan a framework to "develop a definite and sound system of scholastic credits and promotions within the School itself," a goal which included placement and qualifying tests to enter "Intermediate School" (sixth through eighth grades) as well as high school.[29]

As St. Paul's came to terms with itself—with who and what it was—one particular challenge Hamilton faced was how to maintain the connection between Church and School, a link which had been weakening since the move to Mt. Washington. In 1936, a typical year, only eight of 120 boys enrolled were from families of the Parish. In fact, Kinsolving hoped that, since most of the St. Paul's boarders went to Sunday School at the Parish, they would actually be a good source of prospective communicants, namely their parents.[30]

In any case, efforts were made to strengthen the tie between Church and School. Hamilton, like many faculty, was Christian to the core. He re-instituted the weekly Sacred Studies course and urged teachers to worship. "More Church attendance by the masters would have a good effect upon the boys," Hamilton said, "not to mention its possible effect on the masters!"[31] Trustees sometimes stepped in: "Mr. [Thomas] Cadwalader raised the point, as to the part of the training at the Boys'

"As I sit by a window looking westward, and day

after day am reminded by the setting sun of the 'night

that cometh wherein no man can work,' I rejoice in

retrospect more than words can express in the privilege

of having through 36 years as rector of St. Paul's and

chairman of the board of trustees been able to

make a contribution to the life and expansion of

the Boys' School."

Dr. Arthur B. Kinsolving, 1949

School, of the apparent inadequacy of their instruction in the use of the prayer book while in the Church … and advised correcting any laxity." To make things more challenging, while Kinsolving maintained a presence at the School, he would turn 70 in 1941, and his visits were limited—as far as the students were concerned—to those when he spoke on broader topics such as church history or the well-rounded gentleman. Though Kinsolving was the students' most reliable link to the word of God, he more frequently provided a strong link to the rest of the world around them. He posed to them such imponderables as "Who made God?" as often as "What color is square?" and invited prominent guests to speak on such things as politics or selecting the right career. He did not seem to be actively promoting Old St. Paul's or the Parish at the Boys' School. Furthermore, the School's new-found fiscal independence weakened ties as well. "With such a completion of our plant [the addition of the gym]," noted Kinsolving to his Parish congregation in 1936, "we will also be able to take one step further toward making the School entirely self-supporting—a consummation devoutly wished."[32] The Parish, at least, wanted to relieve itself of the heavy burden of helping the School financially. But this independence had a symbolic price. Later, in 1938, perhaps in an attempt to recover some control, a heated argument arose when vestry members of the Parish insisted that they take over the invested funds of the School; the Boys' School trustees refused, and the the debate ended. In truth, though, there were more pressing concerns—recovering from the Depression and preparing for war—which kept these men far more preoccupied and worried. The long-term consequences of their decisions concerning the relationship with the Church were impossible to predict anyway. If there were a time, however, when the School had begun to part ways, it was now.

The faculty in the Mt. Washington library during headmaster S. Atherton Middleton's first year, 1945-46. (From left) James Boyer, Marshall Turner, John F. Dunn, Morgan H. Pritchett, Charles E. Danner, Jr., assistant headmaster Beverly Rhett '21, Headmaster Middleton, Robert P. Fuller '39, Howard Myers, Jr., John Tuton, Sturges Ball, Robert C. Mosher, Michael Fay, Howard E. Wooden.

LURKING TENSIONS AND THE SECOND WORLD WAR

A disquieting anticipation of coming global crises clouded the second half of the 1930s. Topics of the first senior speeches, for instance, which began as a requirement in 1936, included propaganda, Hitler, and Mussolini. (Needless to say, other less grave topics included botany, breeding homing pigeons, and drum fishing.) As the European conflict escalated, Kinsolving described to the boys "the true picture of ghastly international strife and threat" and how they "should watch out for class prejudice causing conflict in the world of labor."[33] Debates over the media and censorship flowered, and open discussion about politics and war were encouraged. In one speech to the student body, Louis Clark reiterated his conviction in Voltaire's axiom: "I don't believe a word you say, but I will defend to my death your right to say it."

Beginning in 1940, the most significant and immediate impact of the war was the sudden loss of so many teachers to service. "Considerable anxiety was caused by the drafting of two of our best teachers, Messrs. Stewart Lindsay [who had been there two years] and John Neely [who had been there one]," wrote Kinsolving. Similarly, Hamilton, who himself was part of the civil defense team for the Mt. Washington neighborhood, worried in a letter that year: "We have on our hands at present a good many boys who are weak in their classes ... because they were tossed around by the sudden losses of such men as [Donald] Pierpont, [Robert] Kinnaird, [Bayard] Berghaus '36, [Lewis] Tignor '25, [John] Alnutt '35, and Clark ... We must work

In 1944, the year this picture was taken, of the 24 graduates, five went into the Navy and one each to the Marine Corps, U.S. Army, Air Corps, Maritime Service, Naval Academy, Virginia Military Institute, and the Navy V-12 program.

"The watchword of the day is 'speed.' War emergencies

wait for no man. Yet there is one thing upon which

the hope for the future rests: character—sound

character—for the youth of today and the citizens

of tomorrow … Without fanfare, without spectacular

speed, we shall go on trying to give each boy a

sound, honorable character."

George S. Hamilton in a letter to parents, 1943

together. We must hold the lines at all times and to all boys on this slogan: 'You have a hard job. You cannot dodge it … You must sacrifice anything absolutely necessary for good work in your classes.'" In one case, trustees even petitioned the Draft Board to postpone enlisting Pierpont, "as the key man where any loss of the registrant will have a disastrous effect upon the Lower School." The strategy worked for a year, but by spring of 1942, he and four other masters also went into service, replaced by teachers Howard Wooden, Morgan Pritchett, Charles Danner, Jr., Edmondson Hussey, and the Reverend John Tuton. Twenty-one alumni were in civilian or military college courses as well that year. An explosion of applications for admission further strained a short-staffed faculty. St. Paul's had all boarding and day vacancies filled a month before it opened in 1942, and for the first time in ten years, Hamilton capped enrollment, informing the board that "the School is much handicapped to carry on the high plane as in the past."[34]

The School quickly made a variety of "war-time adjustments," announced in a letter to parents: a radio and commando course, which was "but one aspect of our sensible emphasis on physical fitness"; a greater emphasis on English, math, physics, and chemistry; and pre-flight training for the older boys by naval aviation instructor Robert Kinnaird. Air raid drills interrupted the school day as students and faculty huddled in the darkness behind covered windows. "We are not for a moment forgetting that this new training is valueless," Hamilton reassured parents, "unless it is supported by constant attention to each boy's character and attitudes. In spite of the many handicaps and inconveniences under which we must all work, you can be sure that your boy is being trained thoroughly and correctly."[35] Adjusting to the dramatic rise in normal living expenses and setting aside money for emergency funds and defense, the School was sorely strapped. "The war must be won," wrote Hamilton. "Luxuries, then, must go." Non-luxuries meant food, clothing, health "safeguards," and "the proper schooling for our children." St. Paul's adapted rapidly, and as a result

Councilmen, Athletes, and Missionaries

THE GOVERNING BODY

Every school has its student council. At St. Paul's, a governing student body called the "Old Boys' Club" dates back to the mid-'30s. According to the 1942 *Crusader*, however, the student council did not officially begin until 1941, its three representatives having "earned the highest honor St. Paul's has to offer—that of representing and governing its two hundred students." Long advised by Louis Clark, the council, until the mid-'60s, also assumed the role of an honor council, which in its early years included only one student from each form and three senior councilmen. A constitution appeared in

1954-55 Student Council. (Standing, from left) Louis Dorsey Clark, Nicholas M. Ratcliffe '56, Alan D. Jones '56, W. Bruce McPherson III '58, William N. S. Pugh '57, (seated, from left) Stephen W. Fertig '55, Charles M. Jankey '55, William G. Patterson, Jr. '55.

1951; members soon were publicly sworn in; and charity drives became a significant responsibility. In the '50s, the Middle and Lower Schools created their own student councils, and the Upper School added three representatives for each grade, in addition to having a president–vice president ticket. A formal honor council, composed of a separate body of students, appeared in the '60s and has remained under the tutelage of Tom Longstreth.

GUILD AND VESTRY

The first signs of a formalized student vestry actually came by way of rector Harry Lee Doll in the form of the Acolyte Guild in 1946, also known as the "The Order of St. Paul." The young Order spoke to the Church's interests in priming young clergy and was "not only to have the boys assist with the services but also to familiarize the students of the School with the proceedings of St. Paul's Church." For about two decades, the Guild remained strong (20 students), primarily under the Reverend James Cantler '43, who became the School's first full-time chaplain in 1955 and soon formed the first student vestry in 1956. Unlike the Guild, the Vestry helped centralize student community service activity, "bring the students closer to the religious life of the School," and assist with chapel services, acquiring needed additions such as a memorial plaque for those who died in war, flag holders, and a Bishop's Chair. In less than ten years, the Vestry and the student council were said to be the "two foremost school organizations." By the early '60s, though the Order had faded, the Vestry remained an active club for a committed set of students, and one was added in the Middle and Lower Schools. Complete with their own constitution and projects, such as tutoring programs, clothing, food, toy and blood drives, and a sock and mitten tree for the needy, the vestries have remained strong, supervised by chaplains like the Reverend Frank Strasburger (1971-75) and later the Reverend Donald Roberts (1991-98). Of particular note is the range of religious backgrounds of its wardens in recent years: Jewish, Muslim, and Catholic.[1]

1949-50 Acolyte Guild. (From left) George M. Trautman '51, J. M. Dryden Hall, Jr. '50, J. M. Perry Archer '50, W. C. B. Young '51, James E. Rutledge '52.

TWO LETTERS, MANY BOYS

"One of the strongest ambitions of every student at St. Paul's is to become a member of the Monogram Club," said one of many editorials in the '30s and '40s. The club was indeed quick to rise in number and prestige. Certificates of achievement in sports were first awarded by Frank Mead '21 in 1934, the same year that the Monogram Club, originally an arm of the Old Boys' Club, charged 20 cents for dues and handed a varsity letter to its first elected members. Soon, under advisor Howard Myers, Jr., the club organized its own dances, where "some of Baltimore's most attractive girls will be on hand"; ran pep rallies; and raised money by selling raffle tickets, candy, athletic equipment and later Christmas trees, megaphones and ice cream. They also invested the dues and earnings *(continued on next page)*

in trophies, an "amplifier" and a whirlpool bath, "which had become [trainer Jim] Boyer's pride and joy." But "most helpful," said one student editorial, "has been the club's practice of trying to show erring students their shortcomings."

Over time, the Monogram Club established new rules for selectivity and new forms of initiation, including dressing as a woman, rolling a stone around the Mt. Washington driveway with one's nose, and forbidding talking for three straight days. "The most amusing activities," as the 1953 *Crusader* described, is "to see a boy covered with lipstick, duck-walking up the walk quacking like a Canadian Honker." The club was in most characteristics a fraternity, often run by "a council of seven" or a complex of committees who could lead the "august body" properly. It also had the particular privilege of its own room by

In their less than athletic pose, students relax in the Monogram Club room, the only place indoors where smoking was allowed. (From left) E. Ross Wagner, Jr. '49, S. Kirk Millspaugh '49, Russell G. Henderson '49, John B. Yellott '49, W. Waller Wilson '49, Basil B. Bradford '49, Philip F. Dice '49, G. Gordon Gatchell, Jr. '49, Thomas C. B. Howard '49, J. Gainor Stehl '49.

1936, outfitted by Myers, with trophy cabinets provided by rector Arthur Kinsolving. For over 60 years now, the Club has kept a strong roll book, but soon a Spirit Council (1955) would handle the rallies, as the "hoofers" stayed busy with the three-day initiations and "spinning popular disks [so that] their dates could swing and sway."[2] In recent years, the club has dwindled in numbers, with only 10 members in 1995, compared to 26 in 1945 and nearly 50 in 1965.

the shuffling in staff was sometimes erratic and confusing. As one example, Myers's wife, who had been Hamilton's assistant, became the School's treasurer and replaced trustee W. Carroll Mead '19; he in turn had replaced his brother Frank; and Frank in turn had replaced Leigh Bonsal—all within a span of two years.[36]

Hamilton otherwise still managed to make steady progress through the war. "Regardless of Hitler, of bombs, or of taxes," he said in a confident four-page declaration to parents, the School would play on. During this time, in the spring of 1941, trustee Thomas Young secured a "very fair bargain" from the Johns Hopkins University and Hospital, a small 15-acre piece of land on Enslow Road for $14,000, adjacent to the current campus and "much of it on high ground"(a very nice addition to their low, muddy fields).[37] The School, adding this and another five acres, now had a campus of 30 acres and a more suitable building to house the Lower School, converted at a cost of $2,000 that summer, and at first run by Helen Clark and John Alnutt '35. For the first time, St. Paul's felt it could legitimately publicize having two schools teaching grades three to twelve between them—just shy of the full K-12.

By 1942, the country's concerted effort to win the war spared little for secondary schools. Single male teachers were already being called; students between 18 and 19 faced the draft starting that January, married teachers within the year; and soon "all will be called except physically unfit, older men, and women." Hamilton grew anxious about non-specialized schools being forced to close. That academic year was particularly trying, as Hamilton realized that his 26 oldest students and his remaining faculty would likely be gone before year's end. He grew disheartened about having

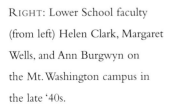

RIGHT: Lower School faculty (from left) Helen Clark, Margaret Wells, and Ann Burgwyn on the Mt. Washington campus in the late '40s.

"older and feeble teachers ... a more limited curriculum, a school of younger boys." To help, the trustees formed committees to handle the budget, housing, admissions, and, interesting enough, a "Committee to Study Reduction in Student Aid."[38]

War was now the reality. While many boys signed up for programs like the Navy's V-12, which allowed students to finish high school and promised a college education, Hamilton also initiated a plan to graduate some older boys by February or March in 1943 in fear of their early drafting. "Everything possible should be done to allow our boys to graduate from high school," he argued. "They have worked for years toward it in good faith ... They must be helped in avoiding a future stigma that they do not deserve." Soon, the School hailed its own service flag. Alumni and faculty returned to give speeches. And the Work Program began, "an organization of boys (choir members and varsity athletes exempt) who clean ... and keep the grounds free from trash since servants could not be secured for the manifold duties of maintenance." (The program actually continued into the '50s as part of a scholarship incentive.) In 1945, the School could not get more classroom chairs due to war-time restrictions. Masters

ABOVE: The Lower School building, added to the Mt. Washington campus in 1941. When this picture was taken for the 1950 yearbook, the Lower School, run by Edmondson Hussey, offered grades three through five, and within two years would add kindergarten through second grade.

Graphic by Keith McBee '43 in *The Monitor*, October 6, 1939.

A Day in Mt. Washington

1940s. Haircuts at the Pimlico Barber Shop, "The St. Paul's Barber." It's the fall dance, says the Cotillion Club. But you're also on for Stunt Night; you're one of three "members" of the KAB (Kale Against Boys) and one of twenty in the Poster Club; and you better attend the pipe-smoking club meeting and bare your collection of "briers." Now someone has you by the sweater and you're off to the cave in the woods drinking sassafras tea, knowing it's not the best idea before running 80-yard sprints for jayvee football practice; nor do you want to pick up your share of rocks or walk around the front circle for three hours again. You've missed your weekends. You deserve some fun. You, a hepcat? You, a square?

At least you managed to avoid the garbage battle in the history classroom, *thank God*, and tested your strength in the mad race for the bookstore every recess for candy and drinks. Anyway, you need your rest. Rise at 7:30 a.m. Make beds, sweep, clean by 8:00. Breakfast. Chapel at 9:00. Classes. Recess. Classes. 12:00. Lunch, 45 minutes. Choir practice. Sports. Coats and ties, again, for 6:10 dinner. Little time for lacrosse before 7:00 p.m. study hall, all

two hours of it. Lights out at 10:10. No sneaking out tonight. There are never closed doors around here. Of course, you always have one backup plan if things get boring: get sick. The infirmary, with Miss Barron, is always a nice way to change the scenery.

Either way, this was the era when you cleaned your plate. Diced a grease ball—breakfast sausage cooked black. When you sat, as a family, among wooden rectangular tables of ten, a master at the head. When boys had chores, serving (some variety of) meat, potatoes and something green, from platters passed around. The cook, Mrs. Ethel Weaver, an entire family tucked into one woman had the spirit of a saint and the energy of a horse; she was the kitchen, the cook, and the cabinet-maker. Masters taught you manners. Teams sat together before games. You did not complain.

Life, indeed, seemed simpler then, and St. Paul's seemed closer, more intimate. Boarding has that effect, you think. True. But no school, as far as you can tell, ever had that spirit and honor that turned heads in envy, some in fear. And for you, St. Paul's was a challenging, tiring, and very special place to be.[1]

Literati

THE MONITOR

Under advisor Beverly R. L. Rhett '21 and editor Jason Austin, Jr. '33, *The Monitor* (a name chosen by a school-wide contest) began the same year as headmaster George Hamilton. "St. Paul's now has a full-fledged school paper," the first four-page issue reported. "*The Monitor* is your paper. It will be your official voice to the outside world." The paper, like its predecessor *Triakonta*, also served as yearbook, alumni newsletter, and moral voice. Early editorials encouraged good behavior, hard work, and keeping the campus neat. Winning many first- and second-place awards from national competitions like the Southern Interscholastic Press Association (SIPA) and the Gold Medal award from Columbia Interscholastic Press Association, its first move away from strictly news and editorials began in the March 7, 1958 issue when it published two poems. Further steps were taken in 1961 when the magazine absorbed the new,

"Once every three weeks [the editor] and his cohorts would disappear into that maze of glue, wastepaper, battered typewriters, old decayed lunches, and mangled furniture known as 'The Monitor' room. Many Cokes and blasphemous interjections later, these stalwarts would emerge from their smoky retreat …"

The Crusader, 1952

but short-lived literary publication *St. Paul's '58* (and its successors *St. Paul's '59* and *St. Paul's '60*). Supervised by Robert French '50, *The Monitor* became a 16-page quarterly magazine with a staff of 25 and five editors, a quick hop from its modest eight pages a few years prior.

As early as the '40s, students tested the might of print. "The Confidential Corner" in 1943 was devoted "to scandalously revealing unguarded moments of both students and faculty," while others poked fun, such as "Pot Luck" by Richard Owen III '56 and the "Roving Reporter" by Henry "Punch" Peterson '57. Not until the '60s and '70s, however, did the content, design, and art grow notably provocative, even psychedelic. Censorship by the administration seems to have become a serious issue for the first time in 1965, which, as one student hyperbolized, "caused so much furor that the editor had to leave the state the morning after graduation." Farcical as it sounded, the administration now had to watch out. The magazine proceeded unafraid, with fold-out photos of students smoking; polls about girls' schools and parties; sophisticated photography; and debates over Vietnam. After 1976, when *The Monitor* excised most of the news and journalism by creating a more periodic newspaper, *The Page*, it has since remained an outlet for the students' creative voice. Printed at varying intervals, it is now in its 67th year.

THE CRUSADER

Beginning in 1941, Carroll P. Cole '41 edited and Howard Myers, Jr. advised the first yearbook, dedicated to Dr. Arthur Kinsolving. Over the decades, the yearbook has assumed the role of documenting students, faculty, sports, and activities, waning in and out in quality and thoroughness over the last 30 years, no doubt due to the daunting task of tracking a growing school. Some stats. The first 1941 yearbook, featuring 200 students, nine faculty, and 19 seniors, had 50 pages and a staff of 11; the 1997 yearbook, with 835 students, 58 seniors and 88 faculty, had 162 pages and a staff of 18. In 1941, the editors covered eight grades, three sports, and five activities. In 1997, this jumped to 13 grades, three student councils, three honor councils, four singing groups, five theater productions, three publications, and some eight active clubs. First published senior elections, called "Vital Statistics": 1950. First color spread: 1962.

SPECTATORS

Afternoons turned literary at Mt. Washington after a 12-year drought when the Randall Literary Society faded in 1923. Not until 1935, under Beverly Rhett '21, did the Literary Club form, which, with guest speakers, seminars and literary reviews, soon took the more stylish name, Spectator Club, named after Addison and Steel's popular eighteenth-century English periodical. A medallion, called the "dangler," awarded at the annual gala banquet, became a symbol of complete membership, given by cast of vote after "a well-prepared, well-delivered, and informative speech." Limited to juniors and seniors, Spectators' activity depended on the year. Some examples: "To stimulate student interest in literature and contemporary events" (1942); for students taking an "active interest in the world" (1943); or a club "for development in the field of modern thought." In 1945, this Saturday afternoon club drew up its first constitution under Howard Wooden, but in the late '40s, participation dwindled to seven students, and at Brooklandville, the club, advised by Louis Clark, was primarily for boarders who usually met on Monday nights. The club appears to have disbanded by 1963.[1]

ABOVE: *The Monitor*, May 3, 1940.

Graphic by Keith McBee '43.

were overjoyed when "new waste baskets—almost impossible to obtain in these times—were found and purchased." Faculty member Charles Danner, Jr. sold war stamps in the bookstore. Students studied the new GI Bill and planned for college after they returned.[39]

These adjustments, in perspective, may sound more dramatic than they actually were. Perusing issues of *The Monitor*, or in interviews with alumni, one notes that the daily life for students continued relatively uninterrupted even at the war's height in 1942-44. Students discussed the honor system and athletic over-confidence; Myers created an "Anti-Boredom" program for dorm students; a science club was formed; sports columns and articles, starting line-ups and scores filled the student newspaper. The volatile world brought erratic changes to the School, but it still seemed safe enough. "Hitler seems to be for most of us far removed from St. Paul's," wrote one. "But is he?"[40]

What alumni from the early '40s remember, in fact, was not the war, but the peak of this unprecedented spirit and athletic dominance that shadowed the '30s *esprit de corps,* as Louis Clark described it, a spirit which would surpass all possible expectations of what a small school of 235 students was capable of in a decade frenzied by sports and adrenaline.

Middleton Vitality

S. Atherton Middleton

Samuel Artherton Middleton found himself in the world in 1901, just before his family would relocate to the Corsica River farm near Centreville, Maryland; here, good education was as distant as the neighboring Chesapeake was wide. To fill this educational void, his grandparents, an old English manor family, thus started the Gunston School in 1912, which had a governess, a tutor, and the neighborhood children for students, a school that flipped from all girls to coed, day to boarding. So, while his grandparents evolved their own school, Middleton was previewing his own long career in education, first as a boy at the Marstons School (and later a teacher there for a short period), and then as the force behind Camp Gunston using the facilities of his grandparents' school during the summers. He then went on to teach at Episcopal Academy in Philadelphia, where he coached football and wrestling, and then received his Masters in Education at University of Pennsylvania, where he coached the varsity lacrosse team.

Nicknamed "Happy" (shortened to "Appy" during his college years at Johns Hopkins University), this "H" deletion was certainly not out of angst. Appy was president of his class, voted "Most Popular" and "Best Athlete" by his peers, and, as a lacrosse and All-American football player, a scholar, and a gentlemen, Middleton was not just one who knew the social graces, though he knew those

too. Interestingly enough, Middleton, his mother and his wife, Kitty, were Episcopalian, and his father was devoutly Quaker.

It might be noted that Headmaster Hamilton had one thing that his successor Middleton didn't: a nice singing voice. If there was one thing on which Appy might have exerted his headmaster's influence, it was to have his grandson (the first male descendant) sing in the Choir; he made it to the probationary round, but had a terrible time. Appy sighed. Even as a true Christian, and so very proud of St. Paul's, he still had to acknowledge the cacophonous cards he had been dealt.

Middleton led St. Paul's for 22 years, the longest tenure to date; accredited the School and moved it to Brooklandville; raised academic standards; expanded enrollment and invited the first black student to attend; and hired critical St. Paul's luminaries. When he left in 1966, the head of Gilman advised him to "cut the cord," which he reluctantly did, though Middleton would continue to serve as a trustee.

Students admired him. "In recognition of his eleven years of faithful service," said the dedication of the 1955 *Crusader,* "his wise and successful academic leadership, and his unflagging interest in all the individual problems and aspirations of the student body, we proudly and respectfully dedicate this yearbook to our headmaster."[1]

A Lacrosse Hall of Fame

Jerry Schmidt '58 was the first and only lacrosse player ever to appear on the cover of *Sports Illustrated*; Scott Bacigalupo '90 was the second player to be featured inside it, followed by Tim Whiteley '92 and Mike Watson '93. These facts are well known. But the composite scoreboard of athletic achievement of lacrosse players from St. Paul's certainly makes a more profound and compelling statement. "To name even some of the outstanding lacrosse players from St. Paul's," said former Boys' Latin coach, Claxton "Okey" O'Connor, who sponsored St. Paul's admission into the MSA in 1935, "would be like counting sheep on a sleepless night." True, but a few firsts to be noted: Donald McDorman '33, who scored the first St. Paul's goal, but against his own team; then Oscar Moritz '34, who scored the School's second and only goal in a 15-1 loss to Donaldson School.

Then the stars, a partial list generated from written histories and interviews: Edgar Boyd '36 and Hunter Cole '37 are perhaps the first noted greats, and since then, the lists only get longer: Ray Greene '41 (the School's first All-American in 1943) and Howard Smedley '41 opened the '40s; Billy Hooper '47 and Jim "Ace" Adams '46 were a devastating pair. Add to them: Joshua Brooks '42, George Mitchell '44, Robert E. Sandell, Jr. '45,

Thomas Gough '46, Charles B. Compton '46, Thomas Tongue '46, and goalie William Clements II '46. In the '50s: James Grieves '51, Walt Mitchell '51, James Lewis '53, Ernest Betz '54, Alfonse Kelz, Jr. '56, Nicholas Ratcliffe '56, Henry Peterson '57, R. Streett Whiteford III '57, Ross D. Parham '58, and Schmidt all played a part in nine title games, capturing five. A select few will mention player Will Vercoe, who went to St. Paul's for one year as a post-grad in 1958 and made first team All-American his first year.[1]

Kent "Skip" Darrell '60, George C. O'Connell, Jr. '61, Carl Ortman '63, Robert MacCool '66, Leslie Mathews '69, and goalies James Shreeve '60 and David Kommalan '62 were noted stars. The '70s had Wayne Eisenhut '71, David Warfield '71, Wicky Sollers III '73, goalie Robert Clements '76, and Steven Stenersen '78. Larry LeDoyen '82, one of only three students to earn 12 varsity letters in high school, finished his career scoring the winning goal (136 total) after a face-off in a 10-9 overtime victory in the 1981 championship game against Loyola. Other '80s stars included Peter Sheehan, Jr. '83, Steven Mitchell '83, and Michael Morrill '84.

And, finally, for the '90s, strong seasons mean quite a list of strong players: Bacigalupo, Kyle Durkee '91, Whiteley, Watson, Ben Strutt '93, Tucker Radebaugh '95, Chris Berrier '96, Chris Kakel '96, Rich Reid '96, Rich Yost '96, Conor Gill '98, Michael Satyshur '98, Scott Marimow '98, and Pat Tracy '98, who set the single-season goal-scoring record of 56.[2]

OPPOSITE: Thomas C. Hasson '64 (33) making a save against Joe Cowan during a 1963 game against Friends School. Marty Cain '64 (39) and Dudley Shoemaker III '63 (54) stand ready.

"To see your school life gliding by, and sinking into dusky

shadows, is difficult. 'Surely,' you say, 'this is just an

extended holiday before me, and I shall return when it

is done. Then I shall hear once more the vigorous slap of

a football on the field, and the soft snatches of music from

a choir rehearsal below 'A' Dorm. Then I shall tell stories

again after 'lights' at night, and 'hurl pillows from alcove to

alcove'… St. Paul's has taught us that which we can never

leave behind—the beauty and power of Christian ideals."

The first *Crusader* yearbook, 1941

THE SPIRIT OF ST. PAUL'S

The re-grading, renaming, and expansion of the athletic field in 1940 was an appropriate beginning to the seven-championship, 72-game lacrosse winning streak that lasted until spring 1946.[41] Students waved their lacrosse sticks in unabashed pride and raced to the victory bell.

That said, an aside. Lacrosse star William U. Hooper, Jr. '47 might be the first to say the simple secret to lacrosse is this: passing the ball is faster than running with it. And to pass the ball requires teammates. And teammates require a coach. And both require a School that can teach students to understand, to corporealize the simple wisdom that passing is, in fact, more effective than running. Perhaps in the peripatetic movement from classroom to field and back, students recognized this wisdom, one bound in fundamentally human principles and values, for to pass is the ultimate athletic gesture of teamwork. It was not the score the team cared about, but the assist. From this emerged the essence of a spirit: St. Paul's knew how to pass in the 1940s.[42]

When alumni and faculty speak of the first half of this decade, they will almost invariably mention winning streaks and statistics that are dumbfounding for a school that was often a third the size (in enrollment, in resources, and physically too) of its opponents yet chillingly dominant, and shake their heads with a misty pride. But what they quickly try to articulate is the profoundness of St. Paul's Spirit (capitalized by intent). The only yearbook that did not take the name *The Crusader* was the gold-covered 1943 book, titled *Spirit*. The Crusader uniforms were the sharpest around, a gift of Kinsolving's son-in-law. All students went to games, an unwritten rule which was, of all the rules the School had, the most quietly and heavily enforced. To miss one was to be bedridden or ostracized. In many ways, that rule covered everything.

OPPOSITE:

Dressing for Success

Sidney C. Lusby '51 (seated) stringing a lacrosse stick with Charles K. Bibby '49. To the right of Bibby is William Hunter '49.

DEPARTURE

While students cried victory, the '40s were an emotional time in other ways for the School, and perhaps the most arduous in its history. To begin with, the close of the war, while alumni and faculty returned, created a new kind of anxiety. Suddenly, for students, service was not the next step. "The end of the second world war brought some of our old masters back to us, and that was very helpful," one student wrote. "But this unrest and confusion and the uncertainty concerning the draft, [which] made definite plans for the future impossible, have naturally been felt here at school."[43]

The war was but one compelling reminder of just how fragile unity and stability actually were. The core set of characters who had molded St. Paul's in spirit, character, and honor disappeared, all within five years. Kinsolving retired in 1942, replaced by the Reverend Harry Lee Doll. A man of stature and grace, Doll also placed new pressures on Hamilton and the administration. Twenty-year housemother Sallie Barron left in the fall of 1942, as did Edith Bush, the assistant housemother for twelve years.[44] George Hamilton left in 1944, Howdy in 1946. The passionate, beatific center of St. Paul's was suddenly gone, that rare combination of sport (Myers), spirit (Kinsolving), mind (Hamilton), and love (Barron) which—while brittle at some links—had a common and well-understood mission.

Actually, tensions at the administrative level had been percolating through the early '40s. For one, the School was particularly divided over whether to become accredited. Myers, who was acting assistant headmaster, was a representative of one large camp which felt that the process of accreditation would sabotage this spirit and tight-knit community, diluting it with bureaucracy and academic requirements (such as requiring masters to have a college degree, which Myers did not have). In short, it meant abdication of much authority to visiting committees and commissions whom no one knew. Hamilton, in the other camp, believed that accrediting the School was a necessary—if not long overdue—step in preparing St. Paul's for a bright, if not competitive, future. And Doll, strongly on Hamilton's side in this matter, strongly asserted his views on how the School should be run. Further complicating the matter was the fact that while Doll and Hamilton concurred on this point, they strongly disagreed about how best to manage Myers, and therefore how best to manage the School.

Most believed Hamilton would never leave, but he did, for several reasons. The first was financial: his salary simply would not support three children. The second, Doll's arrival, affected the first. In a letter dated February 1, 1944, a week after he had submitted his letter of resignation and four months before he would leave, Hamilton said to Doll, "Unquestionably you are personally aware of the acute hardships worked upon teachers and preachers by terrific tax demands and a sharp increase in daily living … My own case is typical." Hamilton explained that despite a $30 per month raise the trustees authorized in 1942, one year later Federal tax withholdings cut his salary by $40 each month, so Hamilton was "with less income than I had been unable to

In addition to a long list of contributions to St. Paul's, W. Carroll Mead '19 (left) was a trustee for 46 years (1933-79) and chaired the campaign to raise money for not only the first Kinsolving Gymnasium at Mt. Washington, completed in 1937, but also the second one on the Brooklandville campus, completed in 1954. With him in this picture, taken in 1953, is rector and president of the board for 13 years (1942-55), the Reverend Harry Lee Doll, a man of influence and presence, who would be consecrated as Suffragan Bishop of Maryland on May 24, 1955.

Safe at home

New York Yankee manager
Casey Stengel, on June 26, 1949,
has a word with American League
umpire James Boyer at Yankee
Stadium in a 6-2 victory against
the Detroit Tigers. Boyer, who
doubled in the fall and winter as a
St. Paul's trainer and coach (1932-
49), signed this photo for his good
friend and St. Paul's headmaster
George Hamilton.

live on before the entry into the war … I simply must have reasonable assistance in
making 'buckle and tongue meet.'" Hamilton's plea extended to faculty members Ann
Burgwyn, Tignor, and Myers, the only ones whose salaries were not "substantially
raised" the year before, a fact that was, he believed, "somewhat ironic, too, that the four
of us have had greater School responsibilities than ever." He concluded the letter:
"The total amount involved in my proposal will not exceed $650 (less than we paid
Mr. Bresnan for his unauthorized and useless sodding extras!). This year's budget can
easily absorb the above figure." Despite both the need and its apparent legitimacy,
Hamilton's proposal was not passed.[45]

Financial reasons aside, Hamilton left in 1944 because he was deeply saddened that
so many of his faculty were still overseas—with no guarantee of their return—and felt
a keen sense of loss after Kinsolving retired. Many took Hamilton's departure hard,
especially alumni in service who sent letters of regret, gratitude and great surprise. "To
say that I am shocked to hear of George's decision to leave St. Paul's is putting it
mildly," said one letter in the spring of 1944. "What in the world are these kids going
to do? George was, to them, the combination of all of the state championships rolled
into one. He was always the true motivating factor behind the 'Spirit of St. Paul's' …
I am forced to greet news of his resignation as nothing short of tragedy."[46]

After Hamilton's departure, the latter half of the decade saw a school trying to
manage and recoup from very serious losses. Even in 1945, when Myers was begin-

A Club for All Seasons

Leave it to several hundred boys to make life interesting, and busier. Lots of clubs came (in the '40s and '50s) and went ('60s and '70s); the critical ones stayed: newspaper, yearbook, student council. But a little background, for these were signs of the times.

Philosophy Club, 1945. Seven charter members under advisor Howard Wooden. Dinners and speakers. Reinvigorated under Tom Longstreth in the mid-'60s, evolving into a "place for open and frank discussion … Although very little philosophy is discussed, the name has become traditional and acceptable, perhaps because much student philosophy is revealed."

Stamp Club. Twenty strong in 1945. "One of the fastest growing organizations in recent years." Trips to Washington D.C. Contests. A constitution for buying, selling, and "obtaining philatelic items." Student leaders for the "United States stamp division" and the "foreign stamps branch." Faded in membership, revived in the '50s, faded again.

Camera Club. Begun in 1946 under Beverly Rhett '21. Use of the "Speed Graphic camera in taking pictures of games and other school activities." *The Monitor* and *The Crusader* get noticeable facelifts. Contests. Plans to build a darkroom with a significant $75 gift from the Mothers' Club in 1951. Took a dip after the move from Mt. Washington, but returned as the *Photography Club* under Francis Dice and president Alan Powdermaker '56 in 1955. Active and prolific through the '60s and '70s, under faculty Howard Emsley, Jr. and William Polk.

Science Club. 1952. Popular through the end of James Ratcliffe's St. Paul's career (1972). "During the Golden Era of science, St. Paul's is contributing its part to this phase of a pupil's education," said the 1953 *Crusader*. Science assembly, 1961. "Severe membership restrictions" when the club's participation reached the "point of unsuitability." A new science building in 1965 helped.

Chess Club, revived in 1961 under chaplain James Cantler '43, and, after "inconsistent existence" in the late '60s, stayed active under Frederick Leist. In 1982, headmaster Jack Ordeman reported that the chess team, "the Cerebral Crusaders," beat Boys' Latin during Blue/Gold Weekend.

Language clubs arrived in the '50s: *French Club*, George Blackburn; *Spanish Club*, Robert Bracken. *Latin Club*, Angelo Gentile. A merged *Language Club*, 1956. *Foreign Relations Club*, 1959, with Carel Beernink and his "immense knowledge of Europe." A *Europe Club*, 1966, for students planning to travel.

Hiking Club, 1952, Wilfred Heller. Overnight trips. *United Nations Youth Organization of Maryland*, 1953, for one junior and one senior. *Hobby Club* for younger students, 1951. *Debating Club* (an offshoot perhaps of the 1951 *Rhetoric Academy*), forming in 1958, with a win over Gilman, reappearing in 1965 under Walter Frey IV (beating McDonogh on the topic of movie censorship), and then again in 1978. *Creative Writing Club*, 1965. *Rocket Club*, 1968.

And a few in recent years: *Model United Nations Club* (1987) under John Patterson; the *Chromatics* (1986) quartet, begun by Jeff Gemmell, and the student-run octet *Route 81* (1992), guided by George Johnson; *Amnesty International* (1989); *Environmental Awareness Club* (1990) under Edward Brady; *Black Awareness Club* (1990) under Jay Bond; and the *Technology Club* (1993).[1]

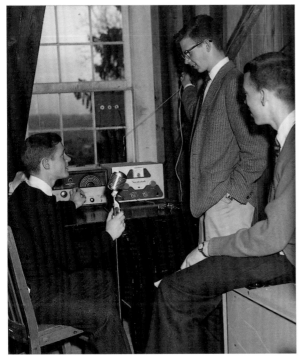

ABOVE: The 1944-45 Model Airplane Club in its first year, with a future replete with air shows and gas motors.

NEAR LEFT: Gerald D. Sylvester '48 in a 1945 group shot of the popular Poster Club, which had the start of its strong 20-year run in 1940, with contests, pins for members, and a boost from artist August W. Schell, Jr. '50. Posters reappeared under a revived club in the mid-'50s but left for good in the '60s.

LEFT: Robert E. Robertson III '60, Barry E. Birch '60, and Stephen A. Barney '60 with the Radio Club, which began in 1954 and soon had lessons in Morse Code, qualifying entrance tests by 1958, and all the equipment needed for a radio station, helped by the Fathers' Club. As described by the yearbook: "The club's functions, other than each boy working toward his personal goal of acquiring a radio operator's license, are setting up the public address system … and assisting in matters touching on its field."

"I know and love every stick and stone, every nook and cranny of our School. I cherish the memories and friendships of the boys and masters with whom I have worked for so many years ... Believe me, fellows, it nearly broke my heart, but I simply had to do what I thought was the right thing. Don't think that my giving up the headmastership means that I shall lose touch with you, or lose interest in St. Paul's. 'I'm a Crusader born, / I'm a Crusader bred, / And when I die / I'll be a Crusader dead.'"

George S. Hamilton, in his last year as headmaster, 1944

ning to say his own good-byes, an editorial claimed that the spirit wasn't what it used to be, though athletic teams were in fact doing superbly. Complaints about uncooperative younger boys appeared as editorials focused on such topics as "consideration for other people," which noted the students' dismay at the declining support given teams that spring. Discipline problems increased. Another editorial lamented the fact that students could no longer be as close to faculty, because many were ridiculed for "slurping" (in modern language, "brown-nosing"). Most of this, of course, revolved around the idea of spirit. In 1949, as another instance, a student in his senior speech announced that his topic was "spirits," not "spirit"; but the reporter, not hearing the difference, claimed that everyone was about to fall asleep because they were going "to hear, more or less, the same thing they have heard time and time again each year."[47] In short, a nagging fear—that the spirit of the early years was waning—took hold and grew. It was not so much that the rallies ended altogether or that the quality of the "locomotive" cheers deteriorated, but that the School lacked a synergy, an energizing force. In its place grew a new apathy. "It's now November," wrote one boy. "Whether the majority of students and parents know it or not, this is the School's one hundredth anniversary year. Hardly anything has been mentioned about this occasion."[48] Even two years later, in 1951, in response to the team's low morale, the trustees considered dropping the football team from the 'A' Conference.

And so it was that in 1944 the incoming headmaster, S. Atherton "Appy" Middleton, found himself awash in subtle and complex problems wholly different from those that challenged Hamilton just 12 years before. For the Golden Era in St. Paul's history most certainly was coming to a close.

Proms and Cotillions

A cotillion is an elaborate dance. The Cotillion Club thus was a small social club that held elaborate dances, in particular the prom and the Anniversary Dance (the "main winter social event") held in such places as the Fifth Regiment Armory or the Emerson Hotel; organizers handed out tiny gold-inscribed blue booklets which contained blanks for eight dances. Cotillion members disbanded in 1943, not because of the war but because 12 of its 13 members graduated and its advisor Lewis Tignor '25 went into the Navy. This left W. Wardlaw Thompson, Jr. '43, "the only seasoned socialite," and the Monogram Club to take the responsibility; soon, advisor John Dunn revived the club in 1946 "to replace the haphazard incumbent system of putting on dances." While the move to Brooklandville sent the club into the extra-curricular woodwork, the Anniversary Dance continued for some time, though ultimately only the prom would survive through the century.

St. Paul's
Cotillion Club

ANNIVERSARY SUPPER
ST. PAUL'S SCHOOL
2101 Rogers Avenue
TUESDAY, FEBRUARY 19th
7 O'clock

Persons desiring to play bridge, please bring
and score cards.

The
Senior Prom

St. Paul's School
Presents
RUDY KILIAN
AND HIS KADETS
On
FRIDAY, MARCH 8, 1935
$1.00 Couple or Stag

Lacrosse Tradition

Anyone who knows St. Paul's lacrosse knows about the 72-game, seven-championship winning streak from 1940-46, including four-straight MSA All-star victories (1943-46), under coach Howard Myers, Jr. That achievement only jump-started half a century of unparalleled success in the sport. As other schools caught on to the fastest game on two feet, the victories sometimes grew even sweeter. All great teams have great coaches, but even to follow Myers (cumulative record: 135-18-2) was daunting enough. The list: Robert "Pic" Fuller '39 (1947-48); Ray Greene '41 (1949-50); James "Ace" Adams '46 (1951-53); Tommy Tongue (1954); Gene Corrigan (1955); George Mitchell '44 (1957-63, 1968-84); Mike Rentko (1964-67); James Andrew (1985-88); Mitch Whiteley (1989-94); and Rick Brocato (1995-99). Streaks were broken, but the Crusaders remained no less strong.

Lacrosse coaches George Mitchell '44 (left) and his assistant George C. O'Connell, Jr. '61.

Numbers don't always tell the whole story, but in this case, it helps. In 65 years, the School has had over 100 collegiate All-Americans (including 10 goalies), 11 players and coaches who went on to head college teams, 13 High School All-Americans, ten National Lacrosse Hall of Fame inductees, 12 Kelly Award winners, 23 MSA championships (twice that of any other school), and a cumulative record of 649-224-8.[1]

Beginning as head coach in 1957, Mitchell, assisted early on by Adams and Neil Pohlhaus '45, continued to crush opponents with his teams, winning three MSA championships and six private school titles by 1963. When the first private-public school competition began in 1952, the "Crusies" won every year but 1954 and 1956 for the first ten years, with six private school crowns. In fact, it would take 35 years (1968) to have its first-ever losing season, despite championships in the year prior (Mike Rentko's last year) and the year after (1969, the undefeated "They Did It All" team). After nine MSA championships and a cumulative record of 225-81-4, Mitchell stepped down in 1986, "possessor of the winningest lacrosse tradition in America," as one article aptly put it.[2]

A quick aside: all of this success was not about luck. Jayvee coaches like James Ratcliffe (three championships in the '50s) and Tom Longstreth worked hard to train the younger students, and most point to coaches like Louis Clark for the early, consistent training the "Little Crusies" received.

Though the Crusaders took a co-championship in 1981 and one outright in 1982, the 1990s proved a true return to dominance when Mitch Whiteley, a player for McDonogh and Dartmouth College, took the team. As 1991 Baltimore Coach of the Year, Whiteley won two championships during his six years, including a 35-game winning streak. Rick Brocato became head coach in 1995, making the play-offs in his first four seasons and the finals in 1996 and 1998, the year he earned himself the accolade of Baltimore City/County Coach of the Year.

The abridged version: no high school in the country has more MSA/MIAA championships, All-Americans, or Hall of Famers.[3]

Varsity coach George Mitchell '44 on the Lower Fields at Brooklandville. By 1962, after nearly 30 years, varsity lacrosse had an 84 percent win-loss record (193-35-1) with 13 championships and one losing season, ranking second place seven times. Mitchell's most memorable game was the 1957 9-2 victory over the strong Long Island team, Sewanhaka, breaking their 92-game winning streak.

For Sale

W. C. B. Young '51 (left) and
J. Michael Sheehan '55 in the
book store on the Mt. Washington
campus. The price of a lacrosse
stick when the sport began at St.
Paul's in 1933: $15. In 1999: about
$80. Not only have prices jumped
(a candy bar was five cents), but
today the book store, run by Lee
M. Mueller, has seven departments,
14 parent volunteers (two working
each morning and afternoon), five
student employees during the
summer, over 1,100 different items
for sale, and a $150,000 inventory
(five times what it was in 1983
when inventory was first tracked).
Books, which now cost on average
$70 each, represent a $100,000
stock each year alone, minimally
marked up by about 25 percent to
cover overhead. Since Mueller
took the reins from Cathy Wellner,
who followed her mother, Pete
O'Connell in 1986, the Brooklandville bookstore has moved
twice, and now handles busing
for special events, ordering (from
blackboards to student t-shirts to
notebooks to desks), and most
ticket sales, such as those for
shows at The Center.

Pipe-smoking All-American lacrosse player James Ratcliffe brought science and an often-noted strict discipline to St. Paul's for 23 years (1949-72). The science building, his pride and joy, was dedicated to him in 1972, his last year. Ratcliffe coached (jayvee lacrosse, varsity basketball); served as assistant headmaster every year; revamped the boarding department and the demerit system, "from a Saturday to an afternoon affair"; and opened the first all-school Field Day in 1952. Extremely tough, but fair and compassionate, to most, Ratcliffe was known as "Jimmy the Rat," but this was in fact an affectionate label.

THE MIDDLETON STRETCH

"A headmaster's job," Appy Middleton once confessed, "is a glorified janitor." For 22 years, Middleton's custodial art, then, was to serve as the loyal guardian and administrator of his Church-affiliated independent day and boarding school whose goal, he knew, was to prepare its boys for college. A coach and noted lacrosse player himself, Middleton loved sports as much as any other, but coming from the more established Episcopal Academy and supported by Doll and the trustees, his highest priority was to improve the School academically and place St. Paul's on the accredited list of the Middle States Association of Colleges and Secondary Schools.

Middleton arrived, of course, just at the height of an athletic frenzy which, if not one of monomania during the final years of Howdy Myers, was at least threatening to eclipse the School's primary mission of learning. The lacrosse teams were still tanks, rolling in, crushing, and rolling out. In 1945, they scored 261 points to their foes' 25 in 14 games; in 1946, 224 to their opponents' 45. The young Robert "Pic" Fuller '39, who replaced Myers as athletic director and lacrosse coach in the fall of 1946, and then James "Ace" Adams '46 (1951-53) led the School to continued successes. Athletics drew attention to the School from across the city as the Crusaders broke records, frustrated every neighboring school, and shamed Princeton and Navy in repeat and stunning lacrosse victories. Middleton reported to the trustees upon his arrival that he "had never experienced more loyalty to the school or a better school spirit than that displayed by the students and alumni."

Though the Middle States review later found the intangibles of spirit and honor "very desirable and distinguishing features," Middleton viewed this energy as a potential snag in the pursuit of accreditation. "The scholastic standing was not what it should be," he said to the trustees his first semester, discovering "that there were no systems of testing the student; that the curriculum was limited—no manual training, no music appreciation, no study of art; that the School was not prepared for college boards; that the discipline was not yet what it should be; and that there were a number of problem students, some not qualified [enough to be enrolled]." With that, Middleton administered remedies quickly and systematically. Almost immediately, he and the trustees developed the School's first true mission statement, which seemed comprehensive enough: to provide "courses in the essentials of Christianity; ... a program of athletics for all; ... aid for worthy boys in financial need insofar as the school is able" and "sufficient scholastic background to meet the entrance requirements of the colleges of their choice, and to give to those students, who for varied reasons will not go on to college, the education necessary to enable them to live as useful and happy citizens of the community."[49]

Middleton quickly attended to the vast array of details to realize this mission. His first three years witnessed a new chemistry lab and a recreation room; "modern indirect lighting" to replace the high-glare overhead lights; a card index for every book in

70 Years, Three Choirmasters

Edmund Sereno Ender

EDMUND SERENO ENDER

When you live to be 101 (1886-1987) as Edmund Sereno Ender did, 32 years as choirmaster of St. Paul's (the longest yet) is still only a chapter. The rest was about music, Western Europe, and academe: head of music departments of the State College of South Dakota (1910-12), organist and choirmaster of Gethsemane Church in Minneapolis (1912-18), professor of music theory at Carleton College in Minnesota (1918-21), and later, professor of music at Yale, where he received his degree. He had strong mentors of note, including Dr. Horatio Parker of New Haven, "one of the most gifted composers of church music in this country," according to Dr. Arthur Kinsolving. Ender toured cathedrals and their choirs in England, and studied under renowned faculty at the University of Berlin, in Paris, and at Oxford. Well-bred and all the wiser, he arrived in Baltimore at the age of 45 where, in addition to his full-time duties with the Choir, he taught at the Peabody Institute and directed the music department of Goucher College. His 32 years (1921-53) at Old St. Paul's were undoubtedly the second Golden Era for the choir, as it advanced its local and national reputation in choral music in both the Anglican and European traditions. He had been honored with his own scholarship funds in 1932 (a substantial $350 given to choristers, established by Mrs. John Nicholas Brown) and later gave the School money for a choir room on the third floor of the Middle School in 1969. He was born in New Haven, retired twice in Florida, first at age 67, then at age 78, and passed away in Oklahoma. Notwithstanding, Ender had plans for posterity, perhaps a first attempt being prodigy and protégé Wilmer Hayden Welsh (student and soprano soloist from 1943-46), who indeed led the Choir as organist with only two years of instruction while Ender was on leave. "15-Year-Old to Run Choir" stated *The Sun* headline in December 1949, though Welsh unfortunately left soon after.[1]

DONALD MCDORMAN '33

But the noted protégé of Ender was choirboy Donald McDorman '33, who served as organist and choirmaster from 1953-72 and as part- and full-time faculty member at St. Paul's from 1941-72, a term interrupted only by WWII, when he served as a naval lieutenant. McDorman graduated from Johns Hopkins University and Peabody Conservatory, took organ lessons from Ender, and practiced at Old St. Paul's. He performed with the Choir at the Lyric Theater; brought them into the television age with an annual Christmas Eve mass first broadcast on WMAR in 1954; started the first Glee Club; served on the faculty of St. Paul's School for Girls; farmed future talent with a new junior choir; and daringly took the boys on their first trip to England. "There is virtually no one in the great family of these institutions," wrote rector Halsey Cook about him in 1972, "who has not been in some way touched by the gentle, patient teaching he has given or the extraordinary music he has evoked from our children."

RODNEY HANSEN

And so it was that organist Rodney Hansen, who followed McDorman from 1972-91, became but the third of just three choirmasters who served across a span of 70 years, key to its long-standing success. Hansen faced and overcame a growing set of challenges too: the high priorities of a school coming of age, with the three A's (athletics, academics and activities) competing for time. Still, no matter. Under him, boys followed the *Pride of Baltimore* in 1986 to England to sing, visiting there again in 1989 in a fitting exchange with a choir from Bristol (where founder of the St. Paul's Choir, Dr. Hodges, was raised); sang with the Berlin Opera Company at the Kennedy Center for five performances of Puccini's "Tosca" in 1975; sang for President Ronald Reagan in 1985 at the White House; and were featured frequently in local television broadcasts and newspaper stories. Hansen was named Organist Laureate at Old St. Paul's and played a virtuoso series of organ concerts during the Parish's tercentennial celebration in 1992. He thus left a substantial and well-trained group to continue what is now an astonishing 125-year tradition.[2]

TOP: Rodney Hansen leads the Choir during a performance for President Ronald Reagan and the First Lady during the Christmas season in 1985.

BOTTOM: A typical scene as Donald McDorman '33 leads practice with the entire Choir in the Church's undercroft.

The Character of Louis Dorsey Clark

Three hundred and fifty people turned out to celebrate Louis Dorsey Clark's fiftieth year at St. Paul's in 1977, the same year he was inducted as an honorary alumnus, and twelve years before he would pass away—at the age of 84 (1905-89)—on the tennis court, his home away from home. Few think of St. Paul's without thinking of Louis Clark, the first of 11 siblings all born in just 15 years, four miles west of Ellicott City. When he began as a teacher in 1927, he would interrupt his 62-year history with the School just twice: once for two years in 1929 to try his hand in the telephone business, and once to serve his country in WWII for three years, made Lieutenant in 1944. He continued in the Naval Reserve until he retired from it in 1965, having been promoted to his final rank of Commander in 1956.

While at St. Paul's, he filled almost every role: history department chairman, assistant headmaster, senior master (a title created by the trustees in his honor in 1970), dean, and archivist. Instrumental in accrediting St. Paul's in 1946, Clark shaped St. Paul's in large and small ways, such as developing a burgeoning advisor program in the mid-'50s, and overseeing the School's first full literary magazine in 1940, *The Scribblers* which contained 32 pages of poetry, fiction, and

Louis Dorsey Clark

serious articles about the war. For years, Clark supervised the student council (the then judiciary arm of the honor system), the long-lived Spectator Club, and was instrumental in coaching future stars with the "Little Crusies" program in football and lacrosse. He began the annual campus debate (featured in *The Crusader* for decades), helped to induct the School into the Cum Laude Society, energized current events in the classroom, and was a loyal Old St. Paul's parishioner, bibliophile, and friend. His wife of 58 years, Helen, joined the Lower School faculty in 1934 to assist Donald Pierpont with the instruction of what was then 16 boys. While at Mt. Washington, Louis and Helen raised Michael '55 and Judith.

It is impossible to document fully the work and character of Louis Clark and the influence he had on students and teachers alike. As long-time colleague Tom Longstreth said in a tribute to him in 1989, "We live in a world increasingly in moral confusion and chaos … For there seems to be no accepted standard of behavior, and everything seems to be flying out of control. But in this world, Louis Clark lived by the quiet, steadfast, abiding virtues—loyalty, honesty, faith, brotherhood, and sisterhood—without which we are lost."[1]

the library; a scoreboard and stands for 450 fans; tablet arm chairs instead of desks; a shift from a coal furnace to oil; lockers and a new training room; another "sorely needed" field (requiring 50 truckloads of dirt and pipelines for draining), as well as a drainage system for the Alumni Field to relieve the constant mud problem; and a second tennis court. One enormous headache was organizing bus and car routes for Ruxton, Homeland, Roland Park, and Towson every year, a service both expensive and exasperating. While many boys walked, the School added to its fleet an Oldsmobile station wagon in 1946 and its first school bus, seating 20 and painted all-blue with the letters "SP" and a single gold stripe.[50]

Of all these improvements, as important in Middleton's first year was to adopt a standardized testing and grading system running A to E; "This letteral system," said *The Monitor,* "is now used by schools and colleges all over the country." Shortly after, another small but important tradition began in 1946 when the School inaugurated the Headmaster's List for boys whose marks included "nothing lower than a B" or "more As than Bs."[51] Similarly, commencement prizes that year included new awards such as the Politeness Prize, Best Informed Student, Proficiency in English Grammar, and what is still the highest St. Paul's honor—the Kinsolving Fellowship Award, given to a boy who most embodied the spirit, honor, and character of St. Paul's. The criteria used to select the award-winners became the necessary benchmarks against which faculty could assess their students' performance and improvement.

Middleton understood that, like championships and all-star athletes, St. Paul's also needed these other quantifiable measures of academic achievement to improve what would become the most important list: college admissions. Acceptances remained generally strong, Virginian and parochial. In 1947, a typical year, 22 out of 24 graduating seniors planned to attend college, about half choosing University of Virginia, Johns Hopkins, or Washington and Lee—a pattern which would remain relatively constant. No question that going to college was important to students: "Men who have the best education will find themselves on the head of the list [of job applicants]," said a student editorial. "Decide what field you wish to enter and pick a university that gives you a good training in that field."[52]

Meanwhile, Middleton also had to manage the School's reputation and image. Some were content with the way things were in their own Rogers Avenue world, spinning outward only to nab victories. If St. Paul's lurked in the shadows of other more developed prep schools, it trailed them more as a threatening pest than out of emulation; recognition alone was not reason enough to win games. One of Middleton's daughters remembers while a student at Garrison Forest, a local girls' prep school, telling classmates there that her father was headmaster at St. Paul's, to which they usually responded, "Oh, St. Paul's, Concord, how nice." Standing corrected, they inquired, "St. Paul's, Baltimore?" For those who chose to acknowledge it, St. Paul's was less a prep school and more a place where the dress code was coat, tie, and lacrosse

Fathers and Mothers

As if a school full of boys weren't enough, the Fathers' Club of St. Paul's opened its first year in 1947, by way of athletic director Robert P. Fuller '39, who sent out a letter to four fathers and organized the first successful meeting on December 3, 1947. Their goal was to create "an organization which could perform an outstanding duty toward achieving success with your son as a student and athlete and also provide new moral and spiritual support for the teams on which he plays." After the first official gathering on January 21, 1948, the club soon had father-student-faculty discussions, elected officers and set plans for the centennial celebration; by that November, the club had 38 members, 70 a year later.[1] Besides "recommending the School to high caliber prospective students," the club's objective quickly turned to raising scholarship money and organizing fund-raising events such as the first turkey dinner and bazaar in 1949 under president Ramsey Leigh, with carnival games and three Hollywood can-can dancers.[2] Headmaster Appy Middleton was pleased: "Ethel [Weaver], the School cook, whose figure was an advertisement for her cooking, outdid herself in preparing turkey, gravy and stuffing, three or four vegetables, hot biscuits, and homemade pie." After all this eating, the most important club venture was the School's future move to Brooklandville, a serious collaboration between fathers and trustees to secure the financing and location of a new site.[3]

Soon the Mothers' Club formed on February 8, 1950, "possibly being a little envious of the adulation being given the Father's Club for their good work for the School," said the students. The Mothers' Club provided such things as draperies for the infirmary, organized the magazine drives, assembled a fall "Fashion Show and Tea," and held the Christmas Program in the new Kinsolving Gym.[4]

After some discussions, in 1964 the two clubs merged into the Parents' Club, and since then, auctions, cocktail parties, spring fairs, Las Vegas Nights, and father-son athletic dinners have rallied this important constituency. In 1979, the Parents' Club sponsored the first annual "Night of the Arts," during which students danced, sang, played music, and displayed their sculptures, paintings, art, and film productions. As significant, the Parents' Club has taken new leadership roles and responsibilities, particularly in the '80s when it began addressing such issues as drugs and alcohol, an ever-growing source of anxiety. The Parents' Club sponsored symposia on the topic and with the faculty formed a drug and alcohol committee which also concentrated on values and self-esteem building. Soon, the club also underwrote the School's entire drug and alcohol education program, and in one case, 60 percent of the parents signed a pledge card to enforce the School's policies about drinking and hosting parties.

Over time, the Parents' Club became known as the Parents' Association, assisted by a full-time administrative liaison, Dee Bendos. Today, an executive board of over 20 members coordinates parent volunteers who oversee everything from health awareness programs to a second-hand clothing store to fairs throughout the year.[5]

stick, a jab City College players preferred. Partly in response, Middleton soon became acting chairman of the Evaluating Committee for Middle States, president of the Private School Association in Baltimore, and a member of the Country Day School Headmasters' Association.[53]

As St. Paul's garnered an enviable reputation in athletics, admissions became more sophisticated and competitive. Word of mouth was not necessarily enough to gain entrance. As enrollment held steady at about 240, prospective students now had to pay a hefty $25 application fee and take entrance and placement examinations, a big step from the 1936 application, which only asked for name, address, age, and: "Is the candidate choir material?" St. Paul's was also attractive because it was relatively inexpensive; tuition remained comparatively low for the post-war inflationary period, made possible because the School was now free of mortgage debt. Boarders paid $770 and day students about $300 in 1946-47, 25 percent less than inexpensive area schools like Boys' Latin, which charged $400 for day students. Scholarship money was almost nonexistent, however, mostly limited to an average gift of about $75, and usually only for choristers (particularly substantial was one provided by Helen Linthicum). While St. Paul's assisted children and families of limited means with new financing packages, almost the entire student body still paid in full.[54]

After two years as headmaster, Middleton had succeeded in getting St. Paul's accredited. An evaluation by the Commission on Secondary Schools in 1946 found the Boys' School above average among independent schools in the northeast, particularly for its library, staffing, student activities, and administration.

Improvements in the curriculum and the academics, however, had not come so easily. The committee found a "lack of knowledge on the part of the faculty … of philosophy of the curriculum" and "no evidence of much thought to … the content of courses." Faculty, according to the report, appeared to be mostly using the table of contents in their textbooks to structure courses, could not assist those boys who lagged behind, and provided few opportunities for creativity.[55] In all fairness, Middleton really could not rectify this situation quickly. The source of highest anxiety for him was, in fact, retaining and finding qualified and committed teachers, though the 1946 report had actually commended the School for providing new incentives like a retirement plan and having the "best available staff members at a time when the supply is admittedly meagre." But almost ten years later, in 1954, Middleton shared a survey with the trustees which revealed that the median cash salary for teachers at St. Paul's was only $2,500, hardly competitive with other day schools ($3,300) and boarding schools ($3,800).[56] Further challenging him was that with a succession of capital projects since 1923, the endowment had been whittled away to a paltry $10,000. Although raising tuition seemed an obvious way to find more money to pay teachers, Middleton feared that quick hikes were not the solution, especially since the School could not offer a range of programs and classes comparable to those of other

"The use or possession of intoxicants of any kind, or any form of gambling, will subject a boy to immediate dismissal. Boys are not permitted to have at the School motorcycles, radios, or firearms … Boys are not allowed to keep food in their alcoves."

Headmaster Henry Holladay,

St. Paul's School Catalogue, 1931-32

OPPOSITE: (Standing, left to right) Joseph F. Garver '49, E. William Davis III '50, William N. Stellmann '48, and (seated) George E. Webber, Jr. '48.

schools. Middleton faced a dilemma that would extend well into the '80s, and which, over time, would slowly drive up the operating costs of the School and thus the cost of tuition.

With 240 boys, twelve teachers, two physicians, a matron, a secretary, a choirmaster, and an athletic trainer, Middleton had his hands full. To assist him, he made his first administrative appointment in the spring of 1946: business manager Harry Love, who handled the growing number of incidental, time-consuming issues relating to finances, maintenance, and the plant (though Love also coached intra-murals and taught a math class). In 1949, Middleton enlisted James Ratcliffe, who also came from Episcopal Academy and who for the next 23 years would bring a strong and long-needed order and discipline. And considering the opening words of the 1946-47 School catalog—"The provisions of this publication are not to be regarded as an irrevocable contract … The School reserves the right to change any provisions or requirements at any time within the student's residence or attendance at school"—Middleton, upper level administrators and the trustees felt at least a budding, and equally disconcerting, sense of liability.[57]

And then there was the life of the Lower School "Little Weeds." With three teachers, its own building, library, dancing classes, and recreation room, the "Weeds" (third and fourth grade) truly grew in their own field, within a separate set of boundaries. Led primarily by Edmondson Hussey, who followed Donald Pierpont, the Lower School had its own academic lists and a "Conduct Honor Roll", as well as a novel concept termed the "Departmental Idea" which emphasized extra home-room time for students needing help or guidance. The "Weeds" also indicated what wouldn't grow: the School discontinued the Lower School boarding department in 1948, about 25 years before the entire department would be eliminated. Middleton primarily wanted to extend the Lower School into the first and second grades, the absence of which he felt was compromising the School's ability to attract new students. To help, the $300,000 centennial campaign in 1949 included money to enlarge the Lower School. "Will you help guard St. Paul's supply line?" asked the School's earliest campaign brochure in 1950: "Many of our own Alumni have been disturbed by this situation [only admitting third graders or older] … Loyalty to St. Paul's came into conflict with the best interests of their child's early schooling." Middleton noted the bumper crop of "war babies" beginning to reach school age as an incentive for "prompt, effective action now."[58] These additions came quickly; by 1952, St. Paul's was a full first to sixth form (twelfth grade) school.

Certainly Middleton, an Episcopalian, also wanted to maintain and strengthen the Church-School connection. Some incentive came by bequest of Helen Linthicum, who left $30,000 in jewelry for the eventual construction of a chapel, the largest gift the School had received of its kind. Middleton had arrived to find religious instruction at St. Paul's inconsistent, a discovery mirrored in Dr. Arthur Kinsolving's

Richard A. Moore '53 (second from left) and Joseph P. Martin, Jr. '53 in a 7-4 victory over Gilman in 1953.

observation that an "effort to use the secular faculty … has not been entirely success-ful." Rector Harry Lee Doll adopted a more forceful approach. With his assistant, Robert Caperton, he immediately formed an Acolyte Guild to train boys to admin-ister all parts of the service except the Sacraments, added short daily chapel services, and developed a far more comprehensive curriculum in religious studies. He began a weekly address to the students, both from himself and from visiting clergymen, took a column in *The Monitor*, and in 1945 began giving students the Bible as part of com-mencement for the first time, a tradition which continues today. (Another event that year—a graduation party hosted by Old St. Paul's—was lost, however.)[59]

The Choir still served as that concrete link between Church and School, but with its 35 boys under the direction of Edmund Ender, it represented only 15 percent of the student body. Still, they remained extremely active, performing seasonal and annual recitals, such as well-attended concerts for Shepherd Pratt, or one at St. James' First African Church, from which the proceeds went to the George S. Bragg School for Colored Children. Visits from groups like the London Choir School; trips to places like the Naval Academy, the YMCA, and Kopper's Company; Christmas caroling, Sir John Stainer's cantata, "The Crucifixion," and oratorios—all continued with variety and at an aggressive pace. Nevertheless, in the din of lacrosse cheers, the Choir became a "little publicized activity here at St. Paul's ... The harmonized voices may not be familiar to the students, but it is to the regular members of Old St. Paul's Church." The Choir generally had strong turnouts and was noted in articles and school catalogs as being the School's principal activity. Under choirmaster Donald McDorman '33, who began in 1953, interest in various choral groups increased. Of course, there were other incentives for students to be supportive: "St. Paul's School can justly be proud of the outstanding work of the Choir this year. It not only brings fame but does its part in raising money for the gym fund."[60]

THE SCHOOL MOVES, AGAIN

By 1952, the School had once again outgrown itself, and the steady rate of expansion was not improving the situation. (Charlie Stokes '27 even said in 1948 that the School had evolved "beyond recognition" in 20 years.) The Middle States Evaluation that year—with strong marks overall—found physical facilities dismally lacking. The criticism was not surprising. The time-worn buildings; the "deterioration of some of the neighborhood"; a city proposal to widen the roads, which would include cutting into the athletic fields, and rumors of a "superhighway," which would become Northern Parkway; and the lack of any prospective land to add space—all added to a deepening anxiety about the School's future that the trustees had long felt.[61]

The School's decision to move was inspired in part by a "sizeable check" of $10,000 by parent Harry Dundore, money initially earmarked for expanding the science laboratory. Feasibility reports soon revealed, however, that the "school building was termed a 'tired building' and the advice was not to add to it as it would be money poured down the drain." It was actually the suggestion of the executive committee meeting of the Fathers' Club to move the School and to urge the trustees to take action. For some time the Greenwood School in Ruxton was targeted for relocation, but it had been sold by the time the trustees had agreed to move. At the next meeting, a small group of fathers, led by Dundore, proposed the Emerson Estate and "Brooklandwood" in Brooklandville. But trustees continued to debate the move, anxious over the estimated $270,000 expense that would send the School back into debt; the potential impact it would have on the overall character of the School; and an estimated 25 percent drop in student enrollment because of the distance and added tuition charge. (In fact, enrollment would increase the first year at Brooklandville from 227 to 335, nearly 70 percent.)[62] No one questioned the intimate bond between place and school—and St. Paul's had done all of its growing in Mt. Washington.

The Benevolent Society, as if repeating its 1883 act of grace when it helped finance the School's move to a larger home on Franklin Street, once again provided the necessary leverage the Boys' School needed, aided by the $10,000 and a valuable piece of land, also given by Dundore. Had it not been for the $100,000 for a mortgage using the corporate funds of the Society, soon to re-establish the St. Paul's School for Girls on the same estate, the move likely would never have happened. But after many "apparently insurmountable" problems were solved—and with the help of an additional $20,000 from the Society—the School purchased the grounds.[63]

In return, the Benevolent Society earned four spots on the Boys' School board of trustees, which was increased in size to 20. And a rationale had been developed for the new Boys' School publicity material: "Recognizing that a coeducational school might not appeal to its alumni, the Boys' School ... explains the admission of girls to the Lower School as an act to simplify life for the parents of both sons and daughters; now mothers would need to deal with only one carpool." While the Boys' School accepted the additional liability of more students, some decisions, such as awarding scholarships and methods for collecting tuition, were separated.[64]

Trustees William F. Stone, Jr. and Vernon Stehl were formally recognized by the board for their efforts in making the quick but difficult move over the summer of 1952, a property which "is the pride of the board, an advancement of the cause of the Church, and an outstanding asset to the entire community." The adjustment for students was reasonable enough: "In spite of some last-minute turmoil and confusion of building and moving," students wrote in *The Crusader*, "the class quickly fell into stride." For coaches Louis Clark, Gene Corrigan, James Ratcliffe, Carl McEntire, and athletic director James Adams '46—especially without a gym—maintaining the athletic tradition was a high hurdle, and would in fact take several years to recover.[65]

When the School accepted 22 girls into kindergarten through second grade classes, with the option to continue through the fourth grade, it had consequently obviated its very name, at least the "for Boys" segment. Thus board president Harry Lee Doll in 1952, by issue taken up by the Benevolent Society, pushed for one final change: the School would be recognized and referred to not as St. Paul's School for Boys, or as the Boys' School, but as "St. Paul's School."[66]

"If you really want to hear about it…"

by Tom Longstreth

I recall an unusual and wonderful chapel service. First, a religiously skeptical student reads a paper he has written for his English class, on the subject of spirituality in the poetry of W.H. Auden. Then an older member of the Maintenance Department eloquently shares his experience of having attended the Pope's celebration of the Mass at Camden Yards the previous Sunday. Next, a recent alumnus now working in maintenance sings and plays some of his original music, which to my ear is deeply spiritual. Finally, our Upper School custodian, a Baptist deacon, preaches a powerful, moving sermon, at the conclusion of which he leads us in prayer as the Upper School community joins hands. I feel confident that, in differing ways, some of our students have had their eyes opened this October morning, sensing that the mysterious beauty latent in human life is all around us if we take the time to look and listen and open our minds.

When I coached the varsity basketball team, we once played a five-overtime game against McDonogh, losing finally by one point on a shot which, in the opinion of virtually everyone in the Kinsolving Gym except the referee whose call it was to make, was released after the game-ending buzzer had sounded. The claim that we "really" won seemed hollow when the next morning's newspaper reported a win for our opponent

Tom Longstreth in his typical literary effusion, probably teaching either William Faulkner or *Catcher in the Rye*.

and a loss for us, hollower still when the league standings for the rest of the season continued to concur with that perception of the game. In the real world, where real facts must be reckoned with, the truth was that we did not "really" win at all; we really lost, and twelve young men had no choice but to accept that hard truth, however "unfair" it may have seemed. Kids are resilient. They can accept, and bounce back. They can handle lots of things, especially those that aren't a matter of life and death, like losing a game. In this way, I believe, they are given an early indication, an insight into the nature of life: that it isn't always fair, and that we should not expect it to be.

When I was coaching our jayvee lacrosse team in 1969, Edmondson was one of our 'A' Conference rivals. I remember a very hard-fought loss on their field, a major upset for sure. Late in the game, one of our midfielders took an over-the-shoulder, "buddy" clearing pass from our goalie and, sight unseen, was simultaneously upended by an opponent's perfectly clean and legal but incredibly hard hit. The Edmondson player scooped up the ball and headed downfield; our kid did a mid-air somersault, landed on his rear end, bounced up, grabbed his stick and ran back to stop their fast break, as if he hadn't just had his clock cleaned. Immediately after the game, most of Edmondson's team came over to congratulate him and to marvel at his resilience. The two teams left the field together talking about that play. It was a great moment, only a year after the rioting in Baltimore following Dr. Martin Luther King's assassination.

It's not an officially stated policy; it's just something we do intuitively, all the time, without even thinking about it or defining it as such. We recognize opportunities for our kids to have learning experiences, some of them in most unlikely situations.

One of our great strengths has always been our relatively small size. At St. Paul's, if a boy makes up his mind not to, he won't get lost in the shuffle. Be it in academics, athletics, or the arts, we want each student to find out what he is really good at, what he really enjoys and does exceedingly well, and then work hard to maximize his potential. In this way we envision our kids experiencing the tremendous feeling of satisfaction which will come from honoring their gifts by using them productively. In my mind this arduous process of self-discovery is the greatest benefit of education.

As far as our teaching methods are concerned, they are as different as we are as individuals. It is another strength of St. Paul's that the faculty is left free to be our own best selves. While our styles differ, we share the common goal of bringing out the best our kids have in them.

Class sizes are relatively small, rarely exceeding 18 kids. If we haven't already taught, coached, or advised him, we get to know each student. The classes tend to be interactive, involving discussion and give-and-take rather than lecture. We try to get our students to learn to think for themselves and make connections, rather than merely learn specific facts. It's wonderful, for example, to see a student recognize the parallels between the Salem Witch Trials of the 1690s and Senator McCarthy's anti-Communist scare in the 1950s. We are not throwing out information; we are teaching our kids as individuals. We want them to participate, literally to have a voice in their own education.

We want them to understand the world they live in,

so that they may better cope with its demands. We want them to learn to evaluate competing claims and make informed judgments, including moral judgments. We try not to stop when we have dealt with *how* something happens; we think it very important whenever possible to deal with *why* it happens, whether that be in studying the humanities, the sciences, mathematics, or foreign languages.

Take, for example, *The Catcher in the Rye*. Everybody knows that Holden Caulfield is depressed; he tells us that repeatedly. But what he doesn't seem to know, or even consider, is why he's depressed. If depression results from repressed anger, Holden's may go back to his little brother's death from leukemia three years before the story is told. Holden says that on the night Allie died he broke all the windows in the garage, and tried to break those on the station wagon too, and that consequently his parents were going to take him to a psychiatrist. As heard by a grieving, frightened kid: Buckle up, get hold of yourself; if you don't we'll put you into an insane asylum. So maybe it's all that anger he's been holding in that's made him depressed. And if he seems to be a good deal less depressed at the end, maybe that's because he's shared his feelings with you.

Let us not forget, too, how much learning goes on, for the cast and crew as well as the audience, when one of our dramatic productions is staged. *I Never Saw Another Butterfly* and *The Diary of Anne Frank* let us feel the horror of the Holocaust in a way that is impossible through reading, for now the victims have a human face. *The Runner Stumbles* and *Hush* take us into the tragedy of sexual exploitation; again, we feel the pain and sorrow in a way that we can't access through reading. And what better way to understand and sense the tension in crucial eras of American history than to witness *The Crucible*, *The Night Thoreau Spent in Jail* and *The Grapes of Wrath*?

I realize that the above discussion of teaching and learning sounds very idealistic. Obviously, we don't always succeed. But I hope I have fairly described the goals towards which we aspire.

We are, quite obviously, a college preparatory school.

The whole issue of college looms increasingly larger as a student moves through his Upper School years. And that brings us to the point that our mission is not just to get young men into college. It's to prepare them to succeed in college, and success will be much more likely if the young man is in the best college for him, which is not necessarily "the best" college in the eyes of everybody else. And he will be more likely to succeed in college if he has some notion of why he is there and what he wants thereafter.

We also hope that we are preparing our graduates to succeed in later life. And this means that the emerging young man must sooner or later start to determine what he means by "success"—or, more likely, what he wants to do with his life, what his ultimate purpose will be. It would be a terrible thing if this goal were somehow lost sight of.

When we occupied the new Chapel in 1996, we re-instituted the "senior speech," which each member of the class must deliver. In a word, these meditations, by and large, have been quite remarkable. Many have been deeply personal, some have been truly eloquent, and all have been serious, thoughtful and sincere. Had my 1950s prep school class been faced with this requirement, I am certain that the majority of us would have given a standardized summary of our schoolboy careers, concluding that the Episcopal Academy had made us who we were. We wouldn't have taken the huge risk of revealing who we really were, as our seniors do today.

(It's not just our seniors. From time to time under-classmen do it too. Particularly memorable was a chapel talk given by a junior, a devout Muslim, who set forth his religious view of Jesus's birth: that he was without a human father, that his mother Mary was a virgin, but that he was not divine, as in Christianity. And more: it was clearly organized, insightful, precisely worded, and deliv-ered most effectively. Even more remarkable was that it inspired a totally unexpected spontaneous lunch-table discussion among five or six of his teachers, leading to some heartfelt sharing of our individual religious views, something we don't often do, especially in groups. It was

as if the student had been the teacher, setting forth the agenda, and we older people had been the students, responding: a model class.)

Another avenue for self-expression is *The Page*, an issues-oriented, in-depth contemporary exemplar of high school investigative journalism. It flourishes because the students are given the freedom to produce the newspaper. They take pride in it because it is their publication, not a publicity arm of St. Paul's School. Its editorial direction is determined by them. There have always been faculty advisors, who have put in huge numbers of hours and much caring, but they are not censors. The students have tackled, in depth, very sensitive issues, some dealing with the School's image and perception in the community, others (including drug and alcohol use, sexual behavior and orientation, academic cheating, verbal harassment and disrespect among students) having to do with the reality of daily student life. To its credit, the St. Paul's administra-tion has not censored or limited *The Page* in what it wants to say or how it wants to say it. And this trust has been justified: the students have rarely abused or violated it, but rather have recognized their obligation to exercise their freedom in a responsible fashion.

It is obvious that the success of *The Page* is a function of the trust extended by the School and honored by the newspaper. In truth, because we have an honor system, our entire community, at least in theory, is based on trust. We want to believe, for example, that when a student does well on a test or paper it is his own good work that we are see-ing; we want to believe that when he tells us why he's late for school or class he's telling us the truth; and we want to believe we can leave our classrooms open when we aren't in them and find nothing missing when we return. It's an idealistic view, and obviously we fall short of its expecta-tions, but it's what we want to believe we can be.

Our honor system exists in order to draw a clear dis-tinction between ordinary violations of school rules and matters of personal integrity. Chronic lateness, cutting a class, or parking in an unauthorized space may result in demerits, but usually no hard feelings. But when a student lies, cheats, or steals he has weakened the trust we want to live by, and weakened our sense of community. The students elected to the Honor Council hear the case, make the call and recommend the penalty. It's their system, and we trust their judgment. Some of us, when we have a particularly complicated disciplinary case which boils down to whom to believe, or whether to believe, turn it over to the Honor Council to decide, for they often have a better feel for such situations than we adults do. Again, it's a matter of trust. Over the course of a year the students on the council, as well as those who appear before it, learn a lot—which is the goal implicit in everything we do at school.

My personal practice in cases where it's a close call whether or not to believe a kid has always been to do just that, to believe him. I'd rather make a mistake believing a kid who's lying than to make one by disbelieving a kid who's telling the truth. In the former case the student has to live with his lie and deal with it; in the latter case the damage is irreparable, for he will never forget and never forgive, and rightly so. For me, which way to go in such cases is clear to see.

I wish there were room enough to give their due to the other organizations which have arisen over time from student demand and now flourish in the Upper School. All of them have faculty advisors and student members who put in inordinate amounts of time and do good works which are labors of love. We offer a wide range of opportunities in dramatics, vocal and instrumental music, painting and drawing, photography and film studies, as well as in service clubs and student government. There is something for everybody, and many young men over the years have found themselves by participating in activities which bring out the best in them and help them better know themselves. One of our college counselors always tells our students that no alumnus in his experience has ever returned to school saying that he wished he had done less while here.

When I first came to St. Paul's, I was told that in addition to teaching English I would also be asked to "help out a bit with some of the undersquad sports," as every-

body else did. Sixty-eight seasons later, 38 of them on the varsity level, 32 of these as a head coach, here I am.

Helping to start baseball at our school and coaching the varsity team through its first ten seasons gave me tremendous satisfaction. But basketball has always been my great love. It's the only game I really enjoyed playing, the only one I was truly passionate about. It's the only one I've coached every year I've been at St. Paul's, including a number of seasons with the varsity.

It's very hard to explain, but there is a certain beauty in seeing your team play the game right, with the ball and the players in constant motion, with seemingly perfect timing, with crisp passes leading to good, open shots, and with everybody working hard to make your man-to-man defense too tough for the opposition to beat. It's rare when this all happens, and when it does you want to savor it.

Once in a while you have a season which ends up being a wonderful experience. Not only does your team play the game right, but something more than that is happening: everybody pulls together, everybody knows his role, everybody gives his best, and the whole is somehow greater than the sum of its parts. It becomes not mainly a sports experience, but a human experience. It becomes a glimpse of human nature at its very best. It's a rare achievement, which for the players can't be duplicated in later life. It's a kind of harmonious perfection which maybe only kids playing a game can achieve. My coaching colleagues will, I am sure, understand me here.

I may have given the impression that, while our students do a lot of things on campus, they don't do much beyond it. Nothing could be further from the truth.

For many years we have given food at Thanksgiving, and on other occasions, to the entire Claremont Community in East Baltimore. More recently we have engaged in Christmas clothing drives, for Claremont as well as for other needy communities. While these projects have been managed by the Vestry, they have enjoyed wide support from the student body and faculty. Another vestry initiative has been its sponsorship of our program to support the Homeless Shelter at Old St. Paul's Church. Students and faculty have spent many a night on-call in the shelter, enabling it to provide meals and lodging to needy people. During the 1990s St. Paul's has forged a wonderful relationship with the Coldstream Elementary School and the surrounding neighborhood in Baltimore City, offering after-school tutoring by our students and the wonderful Coldstream Summer Enrichment Program for six weeks on our campus. The seniors of 1998, for their class gift, donated money to support a school-wide community service project in the Coldstream neighborhood, reminding us that we must be part of the much wider world outside St. Paul's.

Before closing, I want to address an issue that concerns me deeply.

Over the years, our small number of minority students have tremendously enriched the quality of life at St. Paul's. As far back as 1976, an African American student was the recipient of the Kinsolving Award, and in 1978-79 another was the president of the student body. In scholarship, leadership, athletics, and the arts, minority students over the years have made St. Paul's a better school.

Demographics are changing rapidly. Today's America is vastly different from the one which existed when I first came to St. Paul's. We need to make use of the whole talent pool which is available to us. We need to make St. Paul's more representative of the larger outside world in which our students will be living and competing in a new century.

We must make a commitment, of the kind we have made to build The Center, the Chapel, and the Athletic Center, to recruit and retain minority students and faculty. The resources have become available for everything else we have wanted to do. We need to do it again.

Our mission statement and our Christian heritage enjoin us to intensify our efforts to embrace all of God's children. We must do so for our own good, as well.

Some personal reflections in closing:

I haven't mentioned any names because it would be impossible to include everybody, and equally impossible to leave so many good people out while mentioning others.

Our Maintenance Department is superb. The campus is beautifully cared for. The men and women who maintain our buildings and grounds give us all a wonderful environment to work in.

Thanks also to our colleagues who work in the mansion. There is so much to do in the operation of a school that we aren't aware of, or take for granted. You guys really do a job.

To the headmaster: St. Paul's has never been in better shape.

To all of you in the Lower and Middle Schools: you keep sending us fine, well-prepared kids. Thanks!

A very positive development over the last decade has been the addition to the faculty in all three divisions of a number of bright, enthusiastic and caring young people. The School is in good hands for the future.

As for myself: I continue to enjoy and be energized by my life at St. Paul's. Over the years the students by and large have been good people. They usually come through for you when you really need them to. My colleagues have been and remain talented, interesting, stimulating, caring, and hard-working people, and endowed with the saving grace of marvelous humor which has gotten us, individually and collectively, through the tough times. I count many friends. Thanks.

Tom Longstreth has taught and coached at St. Paul's since 1962.

Notes: 1923–1952

1   Students left Franklin Street in December of 1922 knowing only that they should wait for either a telegram or a telephone call to signal their return to Mt. Washington. Louis D. Clark, *Notes on The Boys' School of St. Paul's Parish: The Maturing Years 1920-1960* (St. Paul's School, Brooklandville, Maryland, 1970), 189; *Parish Notes* (October, 1923): 2. Members in the chapter's opening lacrosse picture identified by Thom Hook '41.

2   Charles Stokes '27, interview by Louis D. Clark, video recording, "Recollections: An Oral History of St. Paul's School," Brooklandville, Maryland, 22 May 1986; *1910 Minute Book of The Boys' School of St. Paul's Parish* (St. Paul's School, Brooklandville, Maryland), 173-191.

3   This data was collected from issues of *Parish Notes*. In each issue, the Parish listed the trustees as well as the masters of its institutions, including the Boys' School; in fact, aside from the minute books, which did not always document who worked at the School, these lists are the only record existing of who taught.

4   As an example of teachers coming and going, Benjamin Thomas, "in special charge of athletics," was replaced by John Lovett in 1926; Robert W. Pearman and Harry P. Rhett, Jr. (first cousin of Beverly Rhett '21, student at Episcopal High School and one of many in Baltimore who left for Manhattan to string stocks with the roaring '20s silver lining) soon replaced him, but they both only stayed for two years. As an aside, apparently Beverly Rhett and his musical partners often performed several times a year at a bar on Solomon's Island about 90 miles away.

5   Graduates of the original Class of 1927 were: James Hundley, Arthur Musgrave, and Charles Stokes; the three from the Class of 1926 who returned to receive their diplomas were: Dunnell Baker, John Gallup, William Gould, and Hugh Higgins. *Parish Notes* (October, 1924): 4; (October, 1925): 6; Most point to Frank Mead '21 as the first athletic director for the School, since earlier appointments like that of Benjamin Thomas did not seem to yield lasting results, nor is it clear just what the responsibilities were.

6   *Parish Notes* (October, 1924): 4; (April, 1932): 3; Kinsolving, *A History of the Boys' School*, 18-20; Kinsolving and the trustees reduced the tuition supplement that choristers received from $75 to $40 in 1936, and removed any choir scholarship for former choristers in 1937.

7   Bierne, 174-175; Although the Girls' School closed, through the generosity of Mr. and Mrs. William Buckler, the Benevolent Society was able to rent another residence known as "Evergreen" further up Charles Street and to reopen the school in 1929 with eight girls.

8   *Parish Notes* (March, 1924): 4.

9   *Parish Notes* (October, 1923): 4; Kinsolving, *A History of the Boys' School*, 17-20; Kinsolving, *Twenty Years in a Historic Parish*, 11; *1910 Minute Book*, 235-241; Kinsolving later learned about and subsequently ended a teaching position Anderson apparently had taken in Illinois after the incident.

10 *1910 Minute Book*, 271-275; The three masters were: William R. Reynolds, of Harvard; Thomas Stearns, of St. John's; and Herbert C. Moore of Baltimore, none of whom stayed for very long. Clark, 177; *St. Paul's School Catalogue for 1931-1932* (St. Paul's School, Maryland, 1932), 18.

11 Clark, 178.

12 Beverly Rhett '21, who had taught for several years in the '20s, returned from the Tome School, which was in decline and later closed due to the Depression. As an interesting aside, the way people learned about the School was rarely accidental: Edith Bush (maiden name Rogers), whose mother died when she was ten, was under the care of Dr. Arthur B. Kinsolving when he was rector at Christ Church in Brooklyn, where Edith later met and married her husband, Noel Bush; Edith took the job at St. Paul's soon after. Frank Mead '21, as another example, was hired during the Depression, and also represented the providence that favored the School during this time. When he received his "pink slip" from a New York City brokerage house in 1931, Mead traveled back to Baltimore to see if his brothers (all of whom were involved with the School) could help him find a job. Frank Mead would soon found the School's athletic program.

13 *1932 Minute Book of The Boys' School of St. Paul's Parish* (Baltimore, Maryland), 43; Walter Lord, "Gilman in the '30s: a No-nonsense, No-frills Education," in *Gilman Voices*, ed. Patrick Smithwick (Baltimore, MD: The Gilman School, 1997), 73-79; Margaret Worrall, *Calvert School: the First Century*, (Baltimore, MD: Calvert School, 1996), 37-43; Tom Buck, *Jack Williams and Boys' Latin, 1926-1978* (Baltimore, MD: Gateway Press, Inc., 1983), 23-40; Hartford Gongaware, *Bombay Run: New Hope in a Roebling Masquerade* (n.p., 1997).

14 *Parish Notes* (October, 1933): 2; Kinsolving, *A Short History of the Boys' School*, 24; In 1884, Miss Donaldson gave rector John Sebastian Bach Hodges the financial leverage he needed to move the Boys' School to Franklin Street. When she died, most trustees, especially Kinsolving, anticipated that Miss Donaldson would leave her estate entirely to the School and to the Parish, and for some time she had planned to do so. However, when she changed churches toward the end of her life, she also re-administered her

money to go toward the Donaldson School. "It was a heavy blow to the new rector and to the members of St. Paul's when the contents of her will were revealed," said Kinsolving. The disappointment was aggravated by the fact that the Donaldson School quickly became insolvent and closed during the Depression, during which time the trustees of the Boys' School made a "moderate bid" for the estate in 1934 after failing with the earlier plan to merge. (The plan failed because the two boards could not compromise on several management and operational issues. The Donaldson School eventually sold for $40,000.) The Boys' School finances improved by "God's good providence" when the bequests of Miss Asenath Harwood, another earlier and significant contributor to the School, "brought us comfort and encouragement." Meanwhile, in the summer of 1934, the trustees accepted the offer of faculty members Frank Mead '21, Lewis Tignor '25, Donald Pierpont, and Beverly Rhett '21 to conduct a six-week summer program for tutoring boys. In exchange for the use of the building, the trustees took ten percent of the receipts, while the rest supplemented teachers' salaries.

15 Kinsolving, *A Short History of the Boys' School*, 23-28; *Parish Notes* (April, 1932): 3.

16 John White, *Chronicles of the Episcopal High School in Virginia* (Dublin, NH: William L. Bauhan, Publisher, 1989), 74, 256-257, 287-293; While historians of Episcopal High School assume its honor system was modeled on that of University of Virginia, which set up its system in 1842, there is no documented connection. (An alternative source is West Point, which had the system in 1802.) As an additional note, the honor system at University of Virginia began after a tragic incident in which a student killed a faculty member on the "Lawn," leading to a serious disciplinary crackdown. One reaction to the trauma, designed to ameliorate the tension between students and faculty, was that they were asked to sign a pledge: "Acceptance of that relatively simple certificate, quite similar to the first part of the present pledge [at the University of Virginia], was regarded as a show of confidence in the students by the faculty, and thus began an Honor System which allowed the students to establish their own standards for ... conduct, and procedures for dealing with violations." Episcopal's pledge was almost identical to the University's, and the pledge St. Paul's adopted was likewise taken almost verbatim from Episcopal.

17 *St. Paul's School Catalogue for 1931-1932*, 9-13; *The Monitor* (9 November 1934): 2.

18 The track team, according to Holladay, won the Interacademic League championship for the second time in 1931. He also said that the School "made a splendid showing in football and baseball."

19 *The Monitor* (23 November 1934): 2; *1932 Minute Book*, 33. The '20s and prior were in fact dotted with occasional basketball and football contests, but they amounted to little more than a handful of games. Frank Mead '21, for instance, recalled master Ed Ashton, an athlete from Bucknell, and their "one basketball game with him against Public School #9."

20 See footnote 14 regarding the founding and dissolution of the Donaldson School.

21 *The Monitor* (8 October 1937): 1.

22 *1932 Minute Book*, 103.

23 Phone interview with George Mitchell '44 by the author, 1 February 1999.

24 *Parish Notes* (January, 1938): 3; *The Monitor* (8 October, 1937): 1; The gymnasium was designed by trustee Howard May, and its price cut by a third due to the help of architect Howard Myers (athletic director Howdy's father). A committee, made up of George Hamilton, Dr. Arthur Kinsolving and trustees Thomas Young and W. Carroll Mead '19, led the fund-raising effort. Ultimately, they raised $8,000 and secured the rest with "part of our corpus." The old gym was completely remodeled to house Louis Clark and Howard Myers, Jr., and included extensive landscaping around campus, including a picket fence, beds of tulips, and jasmine and evergreens in front. The landscaping that year inspired the creation of "Arbor Day" on April 1 during which students beautified the campus, though it is not clear how long this tradition continued.

25 *The Monitor* (18 December 1936): 2; The 'B' dorm was also designed by trustee Howard May, built to match the 1928 'A' dorm.

26 These and other notes were uncovered at the house of George Hamilton's daughter Welby Loane. It was bundled with other documents from 1942-43; along with the fact that the work program is mentioned, Hamilton most likely wrote this note after 1939.

27 *Parish Notes* (November, 1936): 4; (March, 1937): 4; *The Monitor* (2 June 1939): 1; Undated letter by George S. Hamilton, "Is It Worth the Cost?"

28 *1910 Minute Book*, 281; *1932 Minute Book*, 11; Having well-trained teachers had been a topic of discussion and concern among the board members for several years. Trustee Leigh Bonsal made the first formal suggestion in 1930, "that in his view we should have a policy of employing as teachers only men who have degrees or certificates qualifying them to teach in accredited high or secondary schools."

29 Clark, 52; Letter by George S. Hamilton, "To All Masters," 1939.

30 *Parish Notes* (February, 1937): 5; (March, 1937): 4; Kinsolving saw

the School as a means to introduce students to the Church. In 1939-40, for instance, 66 (of 181 enrolled) students were Parish communicants from the Boys' School.

31 Sacred studies had been sporadically scheduled throughout the '30s. Kinsolving could not always teach the class and members of the Church like Arthur Blythe assisted him as instructor of religious education.

32 *1932 Minute Book*, 75; *Parish Notes* (November, 1936): 4; (November, 1941): 8; *The Monitor* (4 November 1938): 1.

33 *The Monitor* (8 October 1937): 1; In February, 1937, certainly by Kinsolving's design, students raised $21 for the "floodstricken areas of our country," not the first or last of the drives to help others in the community.

34 *Parish Notes* (October, 1941): 6; George S. Hamilton, "Faculty Meeting," 14 April 1940; *1932 Minute Book*, 100-120; Letter from Alfred Tyler to William H. Kirkwood, Local Draft Board No. 12, 5 May 1941.

35 Undated letter from George S. Hamilton to parents, 1942.

36 A draft novel by alumnus Thom Hook '41 is worth reading for a more personal interpretation of how St. Paul's managed through the war. A copy can be found in the St. Paul's School archives. Thom Hook, *St. Paul's Preps for War!* (n.p., 1996).

37 This reference comes from an undated letter from George Hamilton to parents, titled on the back: "Your son has a priority rating too!"

38 George S. Hamilton, "Faculty Meeting," 14 October 1942.

39 *The Monitor* (2 February 1945): 2; (20 April 1945): 2; Perhaps the headmaster realized the value and education in student labor. After the war ended, seniors supervised between three and five boys for each classroom in the building during the 15-minute period after the last class and before athletics at 3:00.

40 *The Monitor* (2 October 1941): 2.

41 The enlarged athletic field was funded primarily through the Alumni Association (and consequently called the Alumni Field) under the leadership of Charles Stokes '27 and a committee of trustees. The scoreboard and stands added later were also made possible through a substantial $1,200 gift of the Association.

42 William U. Hooper, Jr. '47, interview by author, 2 May 1998.

43 *The Monitor* (5 June 1946): 2.

44 Housemother Miss Sallie Barron was replaced by Mrs. Henry Burgwyn of Virginia, who shared the duties with Mrs. Katherine Tignor.

45 Handwritten letter from George Hamilton, 1 February 1944; It is important to note that we do not know for sure if this particular letter, found in Hamilton's personal files, was ever sent to Harry Lee Doll. We do know, however, that the two discussed topics relating to the details of Hamilton's financial situation.

46 Letter from Charles Blake Duff to Mr. and Mrs. George S. Hamilton (27 May 1944); Letters like this one are numerous.

47 *The Monitor* (16 February 1945): 2; (15 April 1949): 1.

48 *The Monitor* (14 February 1947): 2; (10 December 1948): 2.

49 Report by the Commission on Secondary Schools, "Cooperative Study of Secondary Standards: Educational Temperatures," St. Paul's School for Boys, Baltimore, Maryland, 8-9 April 1946; *1932 Minute Book*, 150-164.

50 The card index fell under the supervision of faculty member Charles Danner, Jr.; *The Monitor* (10 May 1946): 1; The transportation headaches compounded when General Motors delivered the School's first bus half a year late.

51 *The Monitor* (October, 1944): 2; It is interesting to note that several months after the change in grading systems, the number of boys who made the honor roll, after grades were re-adjusted, jumped from nine to 23 students. Other kinds of lists faded, however, like the Commendation Program, begun in the spring of 1947 to recognize students for doing well or working hard.

52 *The Monitor* (31 January 1936): 2; (16 February 1945): 2.

53 Students did make an effort to learn about what other schools were doing beyond sports. On December 4, 1944, for instance, members of the student council attended the Inter-High School Congress, which included most schools in the city and which had a mission to understand each other's school.

54 Buck, 51.

55 The accreditation and review process has not changed a great deal since the '40s. Composed of headmasters, teachers, and principals, a committee examines in great detail all aspects of a school, including its physical plant, enrollment, curriculum, athletics, and teaching.

56 *1951 Minute Book*, 25 January 1954.

57 *St. Paul's School Catalog, 1946-47*.

58 Campaign literature, "Will you help guard St. Paul's supply line?" 1950.

59 Kinsolving, *A Short History of the Boys School*, 34; *The Monitor* (25 October 1946): 1; Courses included, for instance, the Old and New Testament; the life of Christ and his teachings; comparative religion; "man, his relation to God, and to his fellow man"; and Christian ethics.

60 U.S. Naval Academy Chaplain Merle N. Young, letter to Edmund S. Ender, 26 April 1952; Letter from James H. Bevier of the Young Men's Christian Association of Baltimore to Edmund S. Ender, 13 May 1952; "Souvenir of the Visit of Old St. Paul's Choir to Kopper's Company, Inc.," 21 December 1944.

61 *The Monitor* (27 January 1947): 4; (10 December 1948): 1; *1932 Minute Book*, 168.

62 S. Atherton Middleton, "The Parents Club 1947-1972," *St. Paul's News* 4 (June, 1973): 4; *1951 Minute Book*, 25 February 1952.

63 Letter from Harry Lee Doll to the Members of the Board of Trustees of the Benevolent Society, Maryland Diocesan Archives, 7 August 1952. "Certain unforeseen exigencies," however, required that the original loan to the Boys' School be increased by $20,000 to pay for a costlier electric light contractor, movement of a sewage disposal plant, fire code requirements, and damage done by a "terrific" storm on July 8, 1952. The Society's generosity proved itself once again after it provided a second $20,000 loan from their unused income in the fall of 1954 to help underwrite the construction of the second Kinsolving Gymnasium.

64 The decision to add four women trustees from the Society was based on the relative proportion of the agreed-upon maximum number of girls in the Lower School, or 75 of 300 students. The agreement in terms of management and expense reporting is spelled out best in the *1951 Minute Book*, "Survey of Proposal to Relocate School at Brooklandwood," 2 February 1952. The legal agreement can be found in the meeting minutes dated 8 April 1952. Thirty years before, the Boys' School trustees had once considered and then rejected the idea of adding women trustees: "The question of adding female board members to the Board of Trustees was then discussed. On motion, duly seconded, it was resolved that the Ladies' Advisory Committee be increased to a number not exceeding five" (*1910 Minute Book*, 187).

65 *1951 Minute Book*, 11 October 1952; *The Crusader* (1953), 18, 55.

66 Bready, 33.

Gridiron

1 Fifty years of football can hardly be summarized in a few paragraphs. The following observations, notes, and data were compiled by Mitch Tullai. (For statistics, game records and other information, Tullai has the most complete archives for football prior to 1992, though it still needs compiling. Statistics for the latter part of the '90s can be found in the School's athletic department.)

By Mitch Tullai: The football program at St. Paul's has promoted worthwhile values since its inception—and it continues to do so. Going back to the 1930s, when championships were won in 1936 and 1937, and continuing through the 1940s, when teams trod the gridiron in 1940, 1945, and 1948, football was a positive and strong force. It has been a high privilege for me to have coached football at St. Paul's over the span of 41 years. I'm proud of our players who have worked diligently, sacrificed willingly, and achieved a high degree of excellence.

Asked to make some observations, I offer the following. First, over these 41 years, our hardworking athletes recorded 29 winning seasons (11 championships and two undefeated seasons), 11 losing seasons, and one 4-4 season. Second, through 1965, when many of those seasons we played an independent schedule, our strong teams well might have been in contention for addi-

tional championships if we had played in a league. Third, one of the finest memories is how even those teams faced with a losing season maintained a high level of dedication and an energetic work ethic, even in the last week.

My sincere appreciation to all the terrific young men who represented St. Paul's on the gridiron and who established their credentials with such determination, desire, and pride. And thanks to the coaches who did such fine work in building football teams as well as helping young men develop to the best of their abilities.

Coaches have performed yeoman service in preparing these boys for the next level of competition and challenge. These coaches included Howard Myers, Jr., Gene Corrigan, Jack Molesworth, Michael Rentko, Tom Longstreth, Neale Smith, Jr. '58, George O'Connell, Jr. '61, George Mitchell '44, Mark Curtis, Rick Collins, Mark Reuss, and Brian Abbott '85.

Teams with winning records in the '50s: 1955 (5-2-1), Mike Rentko's first season, opening with a tough 7-6 victory over Gilman, the success due to his well-coached defense, and coupled with the heroics of Lincoln Bogart '56; 1956 (5-3), a cohesive group; 1957 (5-1-1), well-balanced; 1959 (5-3), determined.

In the '60s, seven teams stand out: in 1960 (7-1), the lone loss to Landon stung, but victories over Gilman and McDonogh were bright moments; 1961 (6-2), a team with size, speed, and great effort; 1962 (4-4), perhaps the best 4-4 team ever, especially considering a 14-15 heartbreaking but inspiring loss to a great Gilman championship team; 1963 (4-3-1), a team with desire and determination; 1965 (6-2), winners of the first season of the newly-established MSA 'C' Conference championship, and record breakers with 314 points in the season and only 57 points allowed defensively under coaches Longstreth and Smith; 1969 (4-3-1), a team with great effort.

The '70s were extremely productive, with St. Paul's winning 71 percent of its games; 1970 (6-0-1), the first undefeated season since 1936; 1971 (7-1), winners of the first Tri-County Championship, with 51 points in eight games allowed under coach O'Connell's well-drilled defense; 1974 (5-3-1), a team winning second-place in the Tri-County with a willingness to work under pressure; 1975 (7-2), a great effort as second place winners in the Tri-County; 1976 (5-4), another second place ranking in Tri-County with a consistently good effort; 1977 (6-2), second yet again in Tri-County, after a tough loss in a well-played game against the strong Boys' Latin team, coached by St. Paul's alumnus C. Ridgely Warfield '62; 1978 (5-4), a hard-working group; 1979 (7-2), a well-earned and long-awaited Tri-County championship.

The '80s produced two champions among overall strong seasons: 1981 (6-2-1), a hard-working, persevering team earning second place in the Tri-County; 1982 (7-2), a cohesive team with a well-deserved Tri-County championship; 1984 (5-3-1), willing workers; 1988 (5-3), a team of great desire and effort; 1989 (7-2), a well-focused group who won the MSA 'C' Conference championship, the first of five straight.

The '90s, especially 1990-93, produced teams of great proficiency, winning 89 percent of their games with strong defense—on average, just 36 points against them *per season*: 1990 (8-1), champions, a tenacious group allowing 45 points defensively; 1991 (8-1), champions again, an aggressive team allowing 55 points defensively; 1992 (9-0), champions for a fourth time, a team marked by speed, strength, and high determination, with Rick Collins's well-schooled and aggressive defense, which established a record of only 21 defensive points in nine games; 1993 (7-2-1), champions for a fifth time, allowing but 24 points over ten games.

2   *Parish Notes* (April, 1889): 4; (November, 1932): 3; Boys listed on this early football team: captain H. Frank Mellier, Layton Smith, Norris Kelly, Read Johnson, Edward Hinton, Philip Wright, John Wiegand, William Walker, Howard Hutchins, Vernon Smith, and George Davenport. *The Crusader* (1957); The Memorial Field was made possible in 1970 by the help of the Ensign C. Markland Kelly, Jr. Memorial Foundation and was dedicated at the October St. Paul's-Severn game.

3   All-State players: Brandon J. Bortner '96, Christopher Berrier '96, John K. C. Payne '97, Scott Kim '95, and Nick Alevrogiannis '99.

The First Seal

1   Letter from Louis Dorsey Clark to Jack Ordeman, "The St. Paul's Seal," 23 January 1974; *The Monitor* (10 May 1946): 2; George Hamilton was said to have credited Donald Pierpont for the final design of the seal, though Beverly Rhett '21 and he were very involved in the content, depiction and selection of symbols and ideas. Historian Dr. David Hein '72 gave a Cum Laude address on "Veritas et Virtus," printed in the summer *Currents*, 1984. Hein translated "Veritas et Virtus" as "truth and courage," and added that "Virtus" could take on meanings of moral excellence, manliness, valor, and bravery.

Lessons in Stickwork

1   Those "agitators" were Robert Maccubbin '36, Donald McDorman '33, Henry Hastings '34, and Oscar Moritz '34; Frank Mead '21 interview by Louis D. Clark, video recording, "Recollections: An Oral History of St. Paul's School," Brooklandville, Maryland, 16 September 1986; Lord, "Gilman in the '30s," 77.

When Days of Old St. Paul's Carry On

1   From 1950-86, the Alumni Association awarded what was called the Outstanding Alumnus Award, first given to A. Aubrey Bodine '21. Then, in 1988, it was renamed the Distinguished Alumnus Award, given to W. James Price IV '42, the only alumnus to have received both. (Price was named Outstanding Alumnus in 1972.) *The Monitor* (19 May 1950): 1. The first *St. Paul's News* came out

in May 1970, when the alumni edition appeared, and though the alumni news was intended to be quarterly, it rarely was. *News from St. Paul's School* (Spring, 1966); Michael Mills, *Nuts and Bolts of the Alumnus* (Jamestown Distributors, n.d.).

Hoop Dreams

1   Coaching years in this essay gathered from *The Crusader*. Tom Longstreth, interview by author, Brooklandville, Maryland, 2 February 1999; Rick Collins, email interview by author, Brooklandville, Maryland, 2 February 1999; *Triakonta*, (March 1916): 15; *Maroon and White* (Boys' Latin School, 1928), 23; *The Crusader* (1953), 50.

It's Howdy Myers Time

1   *Hofstra Report* 1.5 (Hofstra University, April, 1975): 3; Dorsey Myers Donnelly, interview by author, Cape May, New Jersey, 20 November 1997; *The Monitor* (18 December 1936): 2; (10 May 1946), 1.

Chief Builder

1   Hiring George Hamilton was not as serendipitous as it seemed. In addition to a recommendation from the Reverend Albert Lucas from St. Alban's School, Dr. Arthur B. Kinsolving was an acquaintance of Archibald R. Hoxton (son of his long-time friend Colonel Llewellyn Hoxton), principal at Episcopal High School, from whom he gleaned key information about Hamilton's ability.

2   Welby Loane, interview by author, Brooklandville, Maryland, 21 November 1997; Vyvyanna Hamilton appeared in the Broadway show "Good News." Diane Boynton, interview by author, Brooklandville, Maryland, 28 October 1997; George S. Hamilton, interview by Welby Loane and Diane Boynton, audio tape, Baltimore, Maryland, 1984.

Council, Athletes, and Missionaries

1   *The Crusader*, (1947); (1952); (1956), 34; (1959), 21; (1966), 87; *The Monitor* (Fall, 1965): 2; *The Epistle/The Page* 9.4 (13 December 1984): 3. Most students in the Acolyte Guild became licensed lay readers in the Diocese of Maryland, and those who excelled were awarded silver crosses and could serve as a Gospel server and flag bearer; from that point, they received a blue acolyte cross as an "an ardent Epistle server"; and lastly, the lay reader's cross was "bestowed upon those boys who have also served flawlessly as being Crucifer." Robert Wolf '57 was the student Vestry's first senior warden. Incidentally, the Vestry began the same year as regular communion services in the School's chapel, 1956-57.

2   *The Crusader* (1942), 36; (1943), 26; (1946); (1953), 29; *The Monitor* (24 April 1936): 1; (17 March 1950): 1; *The Page* 10.2 (18 October 1985): 6; Many of the dances in the '30s, usually sponsored by the Monogram Club, were entertained by the orchestra of alumnus Jack Keene '23. Members of the club received letters

and a sweater, then "danglers" (seven letters), and finally, if one had the ultimate position of being captain or coach of a championship team, silver cups. In 1951, under James Adams '46, the "School leader jackets" appeared. In 1953, Mitch Tullai became the club's advisor.

A Day in Mt. Washington

1 Full names of those mentioned in this piece: Louis Dorsey Clark; Edith Bush, Sallie Barron, and Ethel Weaver. The author has taken some liberty in merging years and notes from interviews with alumni. Michal Makarovich, *Gustafson's: My Heart, My Home, My God!* (n.p., 1945).

Literati

1 *The Monitor* (16 October 1941): 1; (25 January 1946): 2; (19 November 1948): 1; (17 March 1950): 2; (6 February 1959); (Fall, 1965); *The Crusader* (1943), 25; (1945), 34-35; (1954); (1960), 80; The dangler medallion had an inkwell and quill on a book across a silver key, and the Spectator Club banner is scrolled across the front. The member's initials were engraved on the back.

Middleton Vitality

1 *Queen Anne's Record-Observer*, Section A, 12 January 1983, 5; Emily Durham and Carter Bond, interview by author, Reisterstown, Maryland, 1 December 1997.

A Lacrosse Hall of Fame

1 Joshua Swift, "St. Paul's Lacrosse: Coming Back Strong," *St. Paul's Magazine* 5.1 (Winter, 1989): 15-17; Rick Brocato, email interview by author, 15 December 1998, Brooklandville, Maryland; George Mitchell '44, interview by Charles Lonsdale '89, video recording, "Recollections: An Oral History of St. Paul's School," Brooklandville, Maryland, 13 June 1988; Frank Mead '21, interview by Louis Clark and Mitch Tullai, video recording, "Recollections: An Oral History of St. Paul's School," Brooklandville, Maryland, 16 September 1986; Alexander M. Weyland and Milton R. Roberts, *The Lacrosse Story* (Baltimore, MD: H & A Herman, 1965). The first of two of the best compilations of St. Paul's lacrosse history, players, and statistics was a publication (referred in its postscript as a "brochure") titled the *History of Lacrosse at St. Paul's* assembled after the 1964 lacrosse season by trustee and first athletic director Frank Mead '21 and headmaster George Hamilton, edited by Walter Herman '44 and William Tanton '49. In it, Howard Myers, Jr. lists his two "All-Star" teams, from which most of the names from the '30s and '40s are drawn here. Since then, a very well-written and statistically rich second publication called *Stickwork/Teamwork: Half a Century of Lacrosse* was printed in 1984, by Douglass B. Forsyth '56 with data compiled by Robert Schlenger, Jr. '80. Names and data used here are based on numbers in these publications up to spring, 1983. Both publications list for St. Paul's: all-time lacrosse alumni; coaching records and summaries; all-time scores against opponents; all-time lacrosse scores; St. Paul's vs. all-comers; and high school and collegiate All-Americans. Many thanks to Steven B. Stenersen '78, executive director of USLacrosse, Baltimore, Maryland and Bill Tanton '49, senior associate editor of *Lacrosse Magazine*.

2 Some additional notes about players: William U. Hooper, Jr. '47, the first St. Paul's lacrosse player to be placed in Maryland's Athletic Hall of Fame, was also the only high-school student ever to play first string for the prestigious Mt. Washington Club; Bill Keigler '47 was one of the few to play for the Mt. Washington team as a freshman undergraduate. The two other students who earned 12 varsity letters were M. Raymore Greene '41 and George Trautman '51. Charles B. Compton '46 was nominated first team all-MSA for seven of his nine varsity seasons.

Scott Bacigalupo '91 was a four-year All-American at Princeton University, and three students were All-Americans at University of Virginia: Mike Watson '93 (four years), Tim Whiteley '92 (three years), and Tucker Radebaugh '95 (three years).

All-time St. Paul's scoring records: Conor Gill (235), Whiteley (234), Larry LeDoyen '82 (224), who set this record in 1982, and Watson (222).

A Club For All Seasons

1 *The Monitor* (1 June 1945): 1; *The Crusader* (1946), 29-37; (1947); (1948), 34; (1949); (1953); (1954); (1962), 60-73; (1964), 93-99; (1967), 120-127; (1968), 44. Most information has been collected by fairly detailed summaries in the early yearbooks, the first of which began in 1941.

Lacrosse Tradition

1 Championship seasons and their coaches: 1940-46 (Howard Myers); 1951-53 (James Adams '46); 1955 (Jim Corrigan); 1957, 1960-61 (George Mitchell '44); 1967 (Mike Rentko); 1969-71, 1979, 1981-82 (George Mitchell '44); 1991-92 (Mitch Whiteley).

Players and coaches to go on to coach at the college level were: Howard Myers, Jr. (Johns Hopkins and Hofstra); Randall Coleman '39 (who started lacrosse at Drexel and renewed energy in the sport at University of Virginia); Marshall Austin '39 (who started lacrosse at UNC); John Alnutt '35 (who started lacrosse at Washington and Lee); Junior Kelz '56 (Cornell); Jerry Schmidt '58 (Cornell, Hobart, Navy, and Princeton); James Adams '46 (Army, Pennsylvania, and University of Virginia); George C. O'Connell, Jr. '61 (Washington and Lee); Carl Schulteis '62 (Navy); George Mitchell '44 (University of Baltimore); Don Zimmerman '71 (Johns Hopkins and UMBC); Dennis L. Childs '77 (who played while he coached at Stanford); and Gene Corrigan (Washington and Lee, University of Virginia, and Notre Dame). Two of the three rookie coaches ever to win college national championships came from St. Paul's: Howard Myers, Jr. and James Adams '46.

St. Paul's collegiate All-American goalies were: William Clements II '46 (1950), E. James Lewis '54 (1956-58), Jim Shreeve '60 (1963-64), J. Dave Kommalan '62 (1966), Leslie Mathews '69 (1972-73), Robert Clements '76 (1979-80), Peter Sheehan, Jr. '83 (1986-87), Stephen W. Mason '87 (1991), Scott Bacigalupo '90 (1991-94), and Niels K. Maumenee '92 (1996).

In 1971, the United States Lacrosse Coaches' Association instituted All-American awards for high school players, up to five each year. St. Paul's High School All-Americans were: Wayne Eisenhut '71 (1971), Al Sadtler '71 (1971), Robert Teasdale '75 (1975), Peter Eisenbrandt '76 (1976), Michael Schuler '76 (1976), Jeff Cook '78 (1977), William Ness '79 (1979), Larry LeDoyen '82 (1980-82), Peter Sheehan, Jr. '83 (1982), Tim Whiteley '92 (1992), Michael Watson '93 (1992-93), Tucker Radebaugh '95 (1995), and Conor Gill '98 (1998).

St. Paul's alumni in the National Lacrosse Hall of Fame: M. Raymore Greene, Jr. '41, Ivan M. Marty '43, Joseph Sollers, Jr. '45, Robert Sandell, Jr. '45, James Adams, Jr. '46 (coach and player), William Hooper, Jr. '47, Stewart Lindsay, Jr. '51 (left St. Paul's in 1948), Ernest J. Betz '54, Austin F. Schmidt III '58, and Leslie S. Mathews '69. Coaches in the Hall of Fame: Howard Myers, Jr. and Gordon S. Pugh.

The Kelly Award is given to the best high school player in the MSA/MIAA. St. Paul's winners were: William U. Hooper, Jr. '47 (1946), Richard Britt '52 (1952), Henry Peterson '57 (1957), Kent Darrell '60 (1960), Gerald Bresee '64 (1964), John B. Ellinger '67 (1967), Leslie Matthews '69 (1969), Peter Eisenbrandt '76 (1976), Larry LeDoyen '82 (1982), Tim Whiteley '92 (1992), Michael Watson '93 (1993), and Conor Gill '98 (1998).

The expansion of competitive sports in independent schools and throughout the country led to the formation of the Maryland Independent Athletic Association (MIAA), a successor to the Maryland Scholastic Association (MSA). In a St. Paul's brochure printed for the 1998 lacrosse season, it describes the MIAA as "widely regarded as the premier high school lacrosse conference in the world." By far, 23 championships is more than any Baltimore area school. This brochure can be found in the St. Paul's athletic department.

2   Jeffrey Wilhelm, "George Mitchell Hands Over Winning Lacrosse Legacy," *St. Paul's Magazine* 2.3 (Spring, 1986): 18; Tom Longstreth, "George Mitchell: Scholar, Athlete, Coach," *St. Paul's Magazine* 8.1 (Spring, 1992): 12; Mitchell was noted for his membership in the U.S. Lacrosse Coaches' Association's Double Century Club for his 225 career wins. *The Crusader* (1959); *Columns* 7.1 (April, 1993): 6.

3   Mitch Whiteley's son Tim '92 was high-school and collegiate All-American and was all-time scoring leader for the School with 234 points, an astonishing record that was, even more astonish-

ingly, broken by Conor Gill '98 in 1998 by just one goal. If one needs evidence of the competition in the late '80s and '90s, note that during Mitch Whiteley's 35-game winning streak, 17 were won by a single goal, including the '91 and '92 title games. Close games continued: a 1993 8-7 triple overtime victory over Gilman played in a "monsoon"; four overtime games in 1996, including extremely close wins over Gilman and Loyola to rise to the championship game; and one overtime game against McDonogh 13-12 to gain a spot against Gilman for the 1998 title.

70 Years, Three Choirmasters

1   Ender's other instructors which are mentioned in biographical material about him: Dr. H. B. Jepson, Maestro Giorgio Sulli, E. A. Parsons, and Gaston M. Dethier. Ender followed choirmaster Williard, who had known of him before he was selected by the music committee, made up of the trustees and vestry; Kinsolving, *A Short History of the Boys' School*, 36; Charles Eugene Claghorn, *Biographical Dictionary of American Music* (West Nyack, New York: Parker Publishing Company, Inc., 1973), 142-149.

2   Letter from the Reverend Halsey Cook to the "St. Paul's Family" 8 May 1972; "Edmund Sereno Ender, Organist and Choirmaster of Old Saint Paul's, Emeritus," *Parish Notes*, (September, 1987): 1-2; "15-Year-Old to Run Choir," *The Sun*, 26 December 1949; Wilmer Welsh also had music in his blood: his mother was a soprano soloist, his father was a baritone chorister, and his sister was a member of the American Guild of Organists. Later, Welsh transferred to City College when his voice changed and focused mostly on the organ.

The Character of Louis Dorsey Clark

1   Charles B. Clark, Thomas N. Longstreth and Martin A. Tullai, "Louis Dorsey Clark: 1905-1989," *St. Paul's Magazine* 6.1 (Spring, 1990): 12-14; Kent Darrell '60, "174 Years of Distinguished Service," *St. Paul's Magazine* 4.2 (Winter, 1988): 4-5; *St. Paul's School News* (Spring, 1975); (Summer, 1977); Louis Dorsey Clark, interview by Penelope Partlow and Michal Makarovich, video recording, "Recollections: An Oral History of St. Paul's School," Brooklandville, Maryland, 7 May 1987. There is also another videotape of Louis Clark with faculty members Michal Makarovich and Penelope Partlow, and former headmaster's secretary Lilyan Lorenz, during a trip to the Mt. Washington campus just before the manor house was razed. On the tape, Clark gives a tour of the campus and recalls moments in the School's history and life (May, 1986). The tape can be found in the St. Paul's School archives.

Fathers and Mothers

1   S. Atherton Middleton, "The Parents Club 1947-1972," *St. Paul's News* 4 (June, 1973): 1-4; The best history of the Parents' Club was this one written in celebration of the club's 25th anniversary. The recipients of this letter to form the first Fathers' Club were fathers: A. J. Hunter, Paul Morgan, Edward W. Wilson, and George

W. Tanton, Jr. The meeting was attended by the athletic staff as well as by Headmaster Middleton. The first president of the Fathers' Club was Ed McGinty, and the first president of the Mothers' Club was Mrs. Owen G. Bennett. Though Middleton's history of the Parents' Club spans only to 1973, it seems appropriate here to list those he felt should be recognized for their service: Hugh French, Russ Forsyth, Charlie Pforr, Cab Darrell, Lee Goodwin, Roy Mayne, Sam Smith, Earl Lewis, Charlie Peace, Francis Marbury, Paul Jones, John Jankey, George Evans, Charles Shaeffer, Mickey Darrell, Walter Loevy, Lewis Scheffenacker, and Bob Hoyt. "While the above and many others gave unselfishly of their time and energies for the welfare of the school," Middleton wrote, "it seems proper to single out two for special commendation for their outstanding service. They are Harry Dundore and the late Vernon Stehl, original executive committee members of the Fathers' Club who later became members of the board of trustees." As an additional note, the Parish had a well-organized and established Men's Club which functioned in a similar capacity for the Church. On occasion it had its monthly meetings at the School and became involved with such affairs as fundraising for the gymnasium in 1937.

2   Most of the club's fundraising, during such events as card parties, originally was targeted for athletic equipment and scholarships. The later merged Parents' Club was active in raising small amounts of money for gifts to the School, but according to Middleton, records of the donations were either not kept or not to be found. (He did estimate nearly $100,000 had been given during the first 25 years of its existence.) As an aside, card parties, would not continue as fund-raising events because the School did not want to endorse activities which Old St. Paul's Church prohibited and considered inappropriate for church groups.

3   William F. Stone, Jr. and H. Vernon Stehl were said to have "spent every spare minute they had during the summer of 1952 to supervise the construction and remodeling necessary to make it possible to open the school in Brooklandville in September." Howard Gilbert and Paul Mallonee's contributions to this effort were also recognized in Middleton's history of the Parents' Club.

4   *The Crusader* (1952); The first "Brooklandwood" bazaar was actually held under tents before the new Kinsolving Gym was built.

5   *The Monitor* (28 April 1950): 1; According to Middleton, Ramsey Leigh sent a letter to the mothers on October 31, 1949 soliciting their help and suggesting that they also coordinate themselves into a club.

III

by Bill Launder, Class of 1999

B uilding. Shape, size, and structure; mind, soul, and body. Our time at St. Paul's has been one of growth: the campus, its horizon and scope; and for ourselves, its students. Such overt symbolism might seem a bit elementary or contrived, but real change and growth on campus cannot be denied, day by day and brick by brick.

As third-graders watching the burning and reconstruction of the Lower School, and later as middle and high school students watching the growth of The Ward Center and the Chapel—we, the class of 1999, have lived this era of construction.

Yet the shape of St. Paul's and the shaping of its students cannot be defined in terms of classrooms and grades, gyms and fitness, or chapels and prayers. This might ring on the side of a glossy brochure, but renovations and construction have produced an entirely new school. New facilities have enhanced academics and technology, sports, the arts, and spirituality.

Building and buildings are temporary. What remains vital to our experience as students is something constant: the unique spirit and character of St. Paul's as an institution and community. St. Paul's has embraced us as students, as both children and adults. Our growth has been a product of traditions. Physical growth, the continuation and celebration of these traditions, and personal development—our perspective is based not only on these fundamental elements of St. Paul's, but more importantly on our own growth, a reflection of the School itself.

LEFT: Seen here are the original gates to the campus, widened in 1972.

PREVIOUS PAGES: Students from the 1959-60 kindergarten class, the only grade in the Lower School at the time that did not require uniforms. (From left) Mark L. Walsh '72, Benjamin Winneberger, Jr. '72, Francine Kennedy, unidentified, John Weisheit, John Simmons, Ashley Long, Elsa Gaeble, Andie Yellott, and Jamie West. The dog cart was apparently brought in for show-and-tell.

Through Their Eyes

by Michael Schuler '76

Middle School students at St. Paul's attend chapel three times each week. They enter rather noisily in small clusters, usually paired up by grade levels. Moments later, in silence, they listen to the words of our chaplain or guest speaker. Then, when the service closes, the boisterous momentum rebuilds quickly as they depart the Chapel for classes and activities and the rigors of the day.

To understand these students and their swings, you need to look at them closely during a varsity lacrosse championship game, their faces painted blue and gold, shouting cheers at the top of their lungs to bring their St. Paul's heroes success. Or watch them working together in small groups in a science lab, ghoulishly probing the inner workings of a frog. Or witness their release of energy in the span of two minutes during recess in a game of supposed "touch football," diving to make the catch for a touchdown in the end zone by the bush. These stakes are high.

Good Middle School teachers understand this vision of life: what it means to slide down a banister fast and far, to leap down three or four steps in a single bound; to sprint down the beach on summer vacation—all while

sitting in math class; the subtle (or not so subtle) feelings around a young girl, the panic of actually speaking to her. These are the teachers who remember that feelings can be easily hurt, who know how to restore confidence with a pat on the back or a simple expression of praise.

Consider the fifth-grader: polite, respectful, anxious to please. Pass him in the hallway, say hello, and you can expect in return, "Good morning, Mr. Smith. How are you today?" Nothing seems to limit his thirst for knowledge in the classroom or his desire in extra-curricular activities, but for one factor outside of his control: maturity, which he tries desperately to manage.

And then, the eighth-grader: detached and cynical, a moody entity whose articulation rarely expands beyond monosyllabic. Polite manners seem like a distant memory, except perhaps during an undesired meeting with the principal; effort and achievement have been waylaid until the grades "really count" in high school; extra-curricular work is important, perhaps, but only in so far as to impress a member of the opposite sex rather than to please himself or (heaven forbid) his parents. Offer a friendly greeting to the eighth-grader and one can anticipate a well-thought, "Hey." Unoffended, we as teachers know to translate this to mean: "Hello, things are fine. Sorry I can't make more of an effort to talk to you now, but maybe next year …"

These years of transition between fifth and eighth grades can be emotionally traumatic, mentally exhausting and physically disorienting—no doubt the greatest emotional and physical changes of their lives. Teachers at St. Paul's try to understand and sympathize with this, knowing that with transitions come transgressions. Even the best and brightest of our young men, not just those who have a tendency for trouble, run into difficulties.

An example. Not long ago on a warm spring day, two seventh-graders were running a few minutes late to athletics. Headed down the St. Paul's hill toward the fields below, the boys had an epiphany: wouldn't it be interesting to visit the Girls' School for a few minutes? And so, after a leisurely tour of the facility and a few pleasant greetings along the way, they determined it was too late to go to athletics. Rather than bother the coach and the team with an explanation, the students climbed back up the hill, stopped for Cokes in the mansion, acquainted themselves with the maintenance staff, and then headed back to the locker room and home for the evening. Try that again? Sure! They couldn't pass up the same opportunity the next day, nor could five others they recruited to join them on a romp around campus during athletics. All such dominoes fall. The teacher noticed. The search was on. An hour later, the students suddenly found themselves making a detour to the principal's office with the head of discipline.

These students, two of whom were members of the student council, were generally responsible; their parents would have been surprised if they were five minutes late to homeroom. The difficult part, as always, was how to respond with appropriate consequences for young men still boys at heart and in deed; they need clear expectations for their behavior as well as some leniency. The truth is that sometimes the silly attitude of a Middle School student can be a delight to observe.

A few years ago, the entire Middle School gathered in the dimly-lit theater for our weekly assembly at The Cen-

ter. A nervous eighth-grader was making his way up to the stage to speak to the audience. (Each eighth-grader must give a five- to eight-minute presentation, now something of a rite of passage.) As he approached, a classmate "accidentally" thrust his leg out, causing the speaker to trip and fall. The principal asked him to wait in the hall. Here was a highly respected young man who had lapsed in judgment. With a good period of time to reflect, the boy later apologized for "the little devil within me that took control over my body and made me do it." His eager search for an explanation for his behavior was partly due to the fact that he had never been in trouble before. He was not flawed in character but had simply made a mistake, an impulsive burst that embarrassed a classmate, but did not disparage or hurt him. These are the distinctions teachers look for in working with Middle School students at St. Paul's. Teachers must advise, understand, appreciate.

But not all Middle School learning experiences are based on difficulties. Nothing is more exciting than seeing a concept finally hit home or a project come to fruition. I vividly remember teaching a group of sixth-grade math students the relations among measurement, area, and perimeter. A diligent student had been working for days to put it all together when he suddenly shouted, "Wow! I get it, but I'm thinking so hard that my head's on fire, and there's smoke coming out of my ears!" The teacher offered him praise, then summoned the fire department.

Group projects are critical at this level to engage them in hands-on activities and the experience of working with other students. One of the best projects I have witnessed at St. Paul's involves groups of heterogeneously mixed seventh-grade mathematics students put to the task of building a bridge of toothpicks attached to a cardboard base. The project involves researching the historical perspective of bridge building, designing plans, supervising construction, and minding the budget (materials must be purchased and do not come cheap). Although days of effort and work go into building them, it is the culminating competition that captures the spirit of these students: each group attaches weights to the center of their bridges to determine strength, and they breathlessly watch as the bridge holds more, and finally breaks into a thousand pieces.

So who best understands the young men of this age? A parent, perhaps, but this relationship may have to be temporarily put on hold. And friendships may seem everlasting one moment, while at other times subject to natural whims. But a teacher who honors respect, integrity, and compassion, who acts firmly but with flexibility, can be a student's lifeline during these years. A teacher who rejoices in their enthusiasm, takes pride in guiding them, and believes strongly that impulsiveness, energy, and creativity should not be altogether abandoned, can indelibly mark a young man. This teacher knows what being in the Middle School means and enjoys seeing life through the eyes of a thirteen-year-old.

Michael Schuler '76 spent 12 years as a student at St. Paul's, served as a faculty member from 1985-92, and since then has served as the Middle School principal.

OPPOSITE: Until Headmaster Ordeman erected a free-standing Middle School in 1969, the mansion provided space for fifth- to seventh-graders after Middle School head Paul Long moved it from the Lower School stables in the 1950s. (From left) seventh-graders J. Edward Johnston III '74, William Lamdin and Charles F. Hoot '74 on the mansion's first floor. Two sixth-grade classrooms were located in the mansion's basement.

1952-1999

BUILDING OF A PREP SCHOOL

OPPOSITE: Kindergarten students in 1952, the first year at Brooklandville and the first year with girls in the Lower School. Almost the entire Lower School faculty was made up of women, supervised at that time by Ruth Warfield and then Katherine Smith. The instructor here unfortunately was not identified.

Atop the hill at Brooklandville, the view was higher, more expansive, and much farther away from downtown Baltimore, Old St. Paul's, and the vacant Mt. Washington buildings. This campus had space, less commotion, distraction; it had fields; it had an old mansion, stables for classrooms. It was a rustic, idyllic place for 30 boarders among 338 students of The Boys' School of St. Paul's Parish, and 17 girls who attended that year for the first time.

The presence of girls in the Lower School and four women on the board of trustees provided a preview of how the School would adapt to changing pressures, ideas, and motivations over the next half century. But for now, and for the headmaster, S. Atherton Middleton, St. Paul's needed to decide just what kind of school it was trying to be. Was it a place primarily for the most athletically degrading of terms: jocks? Perhaps. The Crusaders, proud, even arrogant, were almost reckless tyrants in lacrosse; the "Little Crusies" were under the able guidance of people like Louis Clark and the varsity under George Mitchell '44—and no one could blame these skilled boys for wanting to win in their uniforms. A church school? Unlikely. St. Paul's was now even more remote from the Mother Church, with an even smaller percentage of choirboys and acolytes among them; rectors Harry Lee Doll and Frederick Kates would make important changes, but their influence could hardly counter the watershed '60s. A college preparatory school? Hopefully. St. Paul's had well survived the evaluation reports of the Middle States, sent nearly all of its seniors to a broader range of colleges, and was poised to expand and revise.[1]

Indeed, welcoming the "first" first grade in the fall of 1950 and then kindergarten in 1952, St. Paul's had at last become a full K-12 college preparatory school. And as the lacrosse team—to the despondency of opponents—strung together victory after victory, Middleton and his 16 faculty members concerned themselves with more advanced notions of continuous curriculum, professional development, and teaching methodologies. If the '30s and '40s were decades of precocious adolescence for St. Paul's—of identity, testing, formation—the '50s and '60s were ones of emulation and of seeking a style, a personality, and a niche. Like the high school freshman who

"Education at St. Paul's, and in all Christian education,

puts God and religion where they belong, not outside

the curriculum, but in the heart of it and all through

it … We would far rather grant a diploma to a boy who

is an average scholar and only a mediocre athlete but who

is honest, honorable, and morally good, then send out into

the world a boy who is a mental genius and a three-letter

athlete but a moral imbecile and a spiritual leper."

Rector Frederick Ward Kates to students, September 29, 1957

realizes he is among older, more refined, and more socially-equipped boys, St. Paul's School was maturing among its more developed fellow institutions like Friends, Gilman, and McDonogh. With an enrollment in 1954 of 426, once again nearly doubled in a decade, St. Paul's now could measure itself—necessarily—by trends rather than by individuals and in relation to groups like the Private Schools Association. Middleton also knew that the School's 1946 accreditation was certainly an achievement but one in no way guaranteed in the future. Coming additions to the curriculum such as French and German for younger students, mechanical drawing, or a slide rule class, helped forge a more robust academic framework.[2]

Enter the Middle School. Students needed a place to grow up, for the leap from Lower to Upper School was simply too long and too far. In the fall of 1953 Middleton separated the fifth and sixth grades within the Lower School stables, called it the Middle School, and soon appointed Paul Long, with three years of the Mt. Washington experience (1948-51) under his belt, as its supervisor, a title he would hold for the next 13 years. When the stables soon proved less than accommodating, Long moved the Middle School to a wing of the mansion, added the seventh grade, and set a new standard for the division under strong faculty like Don Hughes, Donald McDorman '33, Jay Taylor, Michael Rentko, William Polk, Farnham Warriner, Helen Clark, and Bunny Schmidt, often helped by Upper School teachers like Mitchell, James Cantler '43, and Sam Williams. Long introduced the faculty to methods for teaching remedial reading, which led to an extensive program in free afternoon tutoring, attracted local recognition for Middle School curriculum design, and had trustees attend faculty meetings to hear reports on every student.

Meanwhile, the Lower School, with its first female head, Ruth Warfield, who replaced Edmondson Hussey, situated itself in mostly autonomous form with its five

RIGHT: Lloyd E. Sample III '53.

grades, female students, and an enrollment of 125. "Since most Upper School students are out of contact with the Lower School," admitted the 1953 *Crusader*, a first glance at the unbalanced attention given to the upper divisions, "they frequently tend to overlook it." Katherine Smith, who became supervisor in 1954, and her 12 female teachers would indeed navigate their Lower School successfully among the potential obstacles represented by a male-dominated administration and student body.[3]

Libraries were now beginning to bulge. First re-organized by grammarian and Anglophile Farnham Warriner in 1956, and later in the '60s by Ethel "Penny" Hardee (the first Upper School female faculty member), the library had jumped in quality to a much higher shelf. "What has been the greatest improvement at St. Paul's this year?" asked a student editorial in 1960. "The library. In no previous years has it been more used or contained more information, more timely periodicals, more forms of educational material, more classic—or varied—literature."[4] Over 20 years, Hardee would turn a small room and a handful of books into a three-library enterprise.

But despite improvements in the academic infrastructure, the rise of the new Kinsolving Gym in 1954—while an occasion for optimism and excitement—reminded

ABOVE: A typical crowded study hall in the '50s. Faculty member Valentine "Dutch" Lentz tries to maintain order in the original Upper School library, located in the former stables, a space now used for the Lower School dance studio. Among the boys here are K. Rodney Turner '59, William J. Kerr '59, Thomas L. Lilly '59, David B. Patterson '62, Robert A. Gore '59, Carl H. Schultheis, Jr. '62, Walter Toy '59, John B. Toy, Jr. '62, John H. Wight '61, Wilson K. Barnes, Jr. '60, and John R. Bland '60.

all that St. Paul's now had an image and attitude largely defined by lacrosse and a stuffed trophy cabinet. The year after Middleton retired in 1966, the Crusaders won championships in varsity football and lacrosse, and in jayvee basketball and lacrosse, and regularly brought several thousand fans to watch the big games.

In truth, however, athletics were not blinding distractions—though at times they could be—and the substance behind the image did tell a different story. An eligibility committee created in 1950—led by Clark, Long, and later Mitch Tullai—to focus on athletes' "effort not ability," and Clark's guidance program initiated in 1952, were designed to ensure that students were not enrolled just to score goals. In the early '60s, the trustees actively discussed a strategy for obtaining accreditation by the Maryland State Department of Education, and had obtained their approval by the end of the decade. St. Paul's was elected as an official member of the Cum Laude Society in 1965. And Middleton discussed "sectionalizing" grades so that there could be continuity between them from first to twelfth. All represented significant improvements that balanced the prominence of athletics.[5]

RIGHT: Lower School girls at the School's narrow entrance in the early '60s. After 103 years as a single-sex school, St. Paul's enrolled 17 girls in 1952, and rector Harry Lee Doll proclaimed that the "Boys' School" should now be referred to as "St. Paul's School."

"Kit Donaldson's red hot car … provides the ideal place
to meet because it has pin-striped decals on the outside
and everybody knows from that sign that a real cat
owns that vehicle."

The Monitor, 1958, about the "Senior Social Society"

Students on the whole were just beginning to acknowledge college opportunities and their competition, and to recognize that their performance on the Scholastic Aptitude Test (SAT) and College Entrance Examination Board (CEEB) mattered. Additionally, students had begun applying to a more diverse set of colleges since the '40s; in June of 1964, for instance, Middleton reported to the trustees that 34 seniors planned to enter 27 colleges. Most students, though, continued to matriculate in a narrowly-defined set in the south: the University of Virginia, Washington and Lee, and Hampden-Sydney. The process of college admissions was evolving as well, a process slowly formalizing the simple handshakes between the college representative, the guidance counselor (Clark, and later Sam Williams), the headmaster, and perhaps the athletic director. There is no question, however, that college acceptance lists—an important metric of success—were now a significant element of school life.[6]

Like the limber moves of an attackman, Middleton readily cradled new sets of numbers and statistics to prove in fund-raising efforts that St. Paul's was becoming a stronger school. In 1962, after ten years at Brooklandville, he stated that enrollment had doubled from 258 to 510 (clergy children from one to 21, alumni children from two to 38), faculty had grown from 16 to 40 (and from one with an advanced degree to 14), college matriculation rose from 72 percent to nearly 100 percent, and the mean college board score jumped by 139 points.[7]

At the same time, St. Paul's tried to remind itself of its Church connection. "Our education is fulfilled in three major categories," remarked a 1957 editorial admonishing students for their irreverence in Chapel. "The first two are obvious: mental and physical. The third, however, is not recognized as much and is just as important. It is spiritual education, which will be a part of our entire lives." When Harry Lee Doll was elected Suffragan Bishop of Maryland in early 1955, the School lost the austere presence of Church; in his place was an eccentric rector, the Reverend Frederick Ward Kates, who began on June 1, 1956 and who, despite his continued innovation, did not possess Doll's dominant aura. With the School's more secular board and administration, and in the context of a society rendered either paranoid or distracted by McCarthyism and the chilling political climate, Kates faced, needless to say, an uphill battle in his campaign to infuse into the School the Church's faith.[8]

This is not to say that the trustees or their president had lost a commitment to bringing the Episcopal tradition to the new Brooklandwood home. To the contrary. The Helen Linthicum Chapel, with its final decorations placed by April, 1954, was finished before a new gymnasium, which was constructed that same year. But even with a place of worship—the School's first in 30 years—and a sacred studies course, a new student vestry, daily chapel service, and, more important, a full-time chaplain beginning in 1955, the Reverend James E. Cantler '43, the School's spiritual mast swayed. Either Kates could not inject the right antidote to the strengthening secular bug, or the School simply was unwilling to put out its arm for the serum. The School, especially with Cantler's guidance, nonetheless affirmed its commitment. In a 1961 campaign brochure, for instance, the trustees emphasized their "firm conviction about the role of the church school … as a means for making Christian values central in the education and life of our children."[9]

All this—academics, sports, church—is also to say that this new home in this very different decade reminded students, faculty, and the administration that the intimate era of the boarding school had passed. The tight quarters of Mt. Washington and its close proximity to many day students and faculty better facilitated the elusive idea of "community," one which had lost its spark and fuel upon the departures of Howard Myers, Jr., George Hamilton, and Dr. Arthur Kinsolving in the mid-'40s. No one could explain exactly what was missing or how to replace it. Spirit created community, true, but behind this feeling of emptiness was nostalgia for the past, for security.

BELOW: Lower Schoolers among a crowd of 1,500 during the dedication ceremony of the new Lower School on November 26, 1990, nearly ten months after a fire had destroyed most of the original building.

White House on the Hill

Two and a quarter centuries ago, things started hopping at "Brookland Wood" in the vast countryside of Jones Falls, a one-day or nine-mile journey north of Baltimore City. By 1791, soon after the Catholic aristocrat Charles Carroll of Carrollton bought the 467.5 acres from John and Thomas Cockey in 1788 (and increased this holding to 1400 acres by 1812), he had the important convenience of the Falls turnpike road. With that he could add a summer home of domestic Georgian character with gabled roofs, built for the first of his three daughters Mary, nicknamed Polly. Charles Carroll was healthy (he lived to the age of 95), wealthy (one of the wealthiest men in America), and wise (a Federalist, a signer of the Declaration of Independence, and a representative in the first Federal Congress). He liked to build (seven mansions), hobnob (with the likes of George Washington), and live in luxury (with regular feasts of terrapin, fowl, and oysters). Wealthy landowners and pretty, powerful daughters continued to occupy the estate until St. Paul's School, its fourth "family," secured 39 acres in 1952.[1]

To her father's discontent, the legendary beauty Mary Carroll married the British-born Protestant Richard Caton, who had many debts but rarely a job.[2] With him, she had five daughters, Anne, who died as a infant, Mary Ann (later Marianne), Elizabeth, Louisa Catherine, and Emily; the latter three were reportedly the most beautiful women in the country, "The American Graces," and would later marry a duke, a baron, and a marquis in England.[3]

The original Brooklandwood estate had the current semicircular terraces, all of the facilities for a plantation, and over 20 servants. Large rooms on the first floor in which to carouse and plenty of bedchambers made a house styled for entertaining.

The Brooklandwood Mansion, over two hundred years old. Photo given by A. Aubrey Bodine '21 during the Crusade for Excellence Campaign in 1969.

By 1812, the estate had a two-story brick house (the mansion's current central block), two henhouses, a smoke and ice house, three orchards, a wash house, a brick dairy, and one frame house, complete with well-equipped stables. When ten-month-old Ann Caton died of cholera, the family added one of the several reported graveyards on the estate.[4]

In 1845, George Brown, head of Alexander Brown & Sons, purchased the estate, now seven tracts totaling 1,792 acres, for $72,000 for his son Alexander and daughter-in-law Colegate. They soon held the Brooklandwood Tournaments—and first mentioned "Crusaders" there in the 1870s—on a mile track at the foot of the hill; these included "fair ladies" and "knights" who leapt hurdles as they rung hoops with their jousts. George Brown was named "Knight of the Oak," parading the Brooklandwood colors of crimson and gold to the tune of "Maryland, My Maryland."[5] In 1894, and intermittently thereafter until 1906, they hosted the first Maryland Hunt Cup, as well as the first Grand National Point-to-Point, which ran almost continuously until 1935. When Alexander Brown's son inherited the property, his daughter-in-law Fannie gave the mansion a facelift in 1892, changes which gave it the appearance it has today. The estate passed on to their son Henry Carroll Brown in 1902 when the stables burned down and were rebuilt—some 50 years before housing St. Paul's School and 88 before it was again gutted by fire.[6]

A chemist from North Carolina and the inventor of Bromo-Seltzer, Captain Isaac E. Emerson acquired the estate under a lease in 1911 and by title in 1916. Emerson razed all but two barns, constructed dairy farms fit for 100 head of cattle and a bottling house, and tapped the Brooklandwood spring (providing some 20,000 gallons per day).[7] In addition to his yachts and several Rolls Royces, Emerson set up a golf course and a grass tennis court, a circular reflecting pool behind the mansion, a fire department for the farm, and two Navy search lights on the roof facing north and south, along with a captain's walk and a siren. (Apparently his wife had been threatened with kidnapping.) Soon, Mrs. Emerson converted the greenhouse into a chilly enclosed swimming pool—one of Baltimore's first—which the School would later use during the summers, close down, and eventually fill in 1998.

Emerson's step-daughter Ethel Looram, Brooklandwood's last resident, received the deed to the estate in 1949, and would see her son, Francis MacAdoo, married there with President Woodrow Wilson and many of the President's Cabinet as guests. Two years later, Mrs. Looram sold Brooklandwood for $262,500 to a syndicate, from which the School made its purchase in 1952. Now, the St. Paul's Schools possess together 96.5 acres of the original tract. This was not the first appearance of St. Paul's on the estate, however: in the 1890s, the Choir of Men and Boys sang at a wedding in the mansion.

The interior of the mansion, circa 1918. The summer home turned school was placed on the National Register of Historic Places in 1972.

"The independent school is presumably free from political

pressures and government control. Free to create its philoso-

phy and curriculum to standards selected by its

administration; and free to give religion its central importance

as the foundation of ideals and moral values."

News From St. Paul's School, on the need for annual giving, 1966

"Problems You Can Solve with a St. Paul's Education"

"A blond is five feet tall and has measurements 36, 22, 36. A wet rabbit weighs 650 grams. The rabbit runs 730 miles per hour faster than a male deer fly. What is the blond's phone number?"

The Crusader, 1961

"The letter to the editor shows a deep concern, typical of St. Paul's, over spirit," said one editorial in *The Monitor*, "which is undoubtedly not as bad as is sometimes lamented, but which is nevertheless way below its past heights." The spirit council, inaugurated in 1955 and advised by Eugene Corrigan, was one example of students searching for ways to revitalize this sense of community. Lacrosse hero James "Ace" Adams '46, featured at its first rally and bonfire, also reminded teams of a bygone era, and not one exclusively in lacrosse. Adjustments and additions that improved the School and created new opportunities could only partly compensate for the fact that, at heart, there were fewer and fewer people who thought of St. Paul's as home.[10]

INTEGRATION

The May 17, 1954 Supreme Court decision to abolish segregation in public schools came just after the School's move to Brooklandville. Area independent schools had been developing formal admissions policy statements proclaiming that candidates would be chosen regardless of race or color: McDonogh in 1959; Gilman in 1961; Roland Park Country School in 1962. Associations followed suit: the Convention of the Episcopal Diocese of Maryland formally expressed its approval of integrating Diocesan-affiliated schools in 1961; the National Association of Episcopal Schools (NAES) demanded from its members documented evidence of an open admissions policy in 1963; the National Association of Independent Schools (NAIS) had developed a policy in support of open enrollment by 1964.

By the early '60s, St. Paul's trustees had given Middleton liberty to interpret, but not explicitly state, the School's admissions policy as being non-discriminatory. The first documented black applicant appeared during the summer of 1963, but Middleton turned him down because he was not qualified, concluding a letter to the boy's parents: "I am sure it is not necessary for me to state that the fact that Benjamin is a Negro does not in any way enter into our evaluation." In a half-hearted compromise as to whether to openly accept black students, the trustees resolved on October 14, 1963 that, while Middleton could accept students regardless of "race, creed, or color," a second 11-10 resolution deemed that this information would not be made public.

RIGHT: By the time St. Paul's moved to Brooklandville, the School had upgraded most of its station wagon transports to a fleet of buses driven by the maintenance staff and by volunteers like Pete O'Connell. The School subcontracted its busing in 1967, but this solution had mixed success. By the mid-'60s, the School had its own fire engine as well.

"In the same way that books and geometrical instruments float over a surface on our cover [of The Monitor*], our schooling is a thing apart from everyday life. But as we use the books and instruments to draw diverging paths, to define horizons, and to record experience, our schooling is, whether we like it or not, ruled in lines, defined, and continually recorded."*

The Monitor, 1961

Although ultimately there seemed to be little surprise or shock when the trustees finally and openly proclaimed in 1964 that the School would accept black students, the practical outcome of the decision was not obvious. In that same year, for instance, when the trustees of the five-year-old St. Paul's School for Girls (SPSG) resolved in 1964 by a "substantial majority" to admit students regardless of color, Thomas F. Cadwalader, also a Boys' School trustee, and his son resigned from its board.[11]

Unable to anticipate exactly what the community's or the trustees' reaction would be, Middleton made it clear in his last year as headmaster that the first black student would begin in the fall of 1966, so that his successor, John T. Ordeman, would not have to endure the potential backlash arising from his having accepted a black student his first year. Ordeman nonetheless prepared himself. "It seems likely that I shall accept a Negro student for the tenth grade in the next few days," he wrote to a trustee the summer of 1966 before he started, "and it occurred to me that you might be able to prepare those members of the board who would be opposed to this action for the blow which is about to fall."[12] Nevertheless, the year passed smoothly, an obvious and natural step in the life of the School. Even in minute books of that year and years after, race and integration were rarely, if ever, mentioned. No doubt private rumblings continued, but they were rarely documented or made public.

Policy aside, students and faculty working on the quiet land of St. Paul's, made quieter in its new location, seldom had had to think about the uncomfortable, challenging topic of diversity. Attitudes had to change. Statements shifted from the regrettably ignorant (as in a 1958 *Monitor* describing an assembly speech: "[The senior] then stated that the Negro is human and has some degree of intelligence") to—at least by the mid-'60s—partially enlightened, more insightful, and, within the students' rhetoric, liberal. "A form of discrimination is prevalent in the North, especially among the upper classes," argued one editorial in 1961. "These people profess the beliefs of equal opportunity and non-discrimination because of race and are somewhat tolerant in the working world. But they also feel that because of their position it would be a loss of dignity to associate socially with Negroes." This does not mean that the School was suddenly becoming more open-minded. "The assembly was informed that when Negroes do come to St. Paul's," remarked a 1964 editorial, "we could no longer discuss racial problems with the freedom that we enjoy today ... Many of our students claim that they will leave when Negro students come to St. Paul's. Until these narrow-minded individuals either change their bigoted attitudes or do leave, I do not think that we can honestly call ourselves a Christian school."[13]

RISE OF A CAMPUS
In this context, Middleton also averted an onslaught of financial obstacles and challenges. Settling into Brooklandville, the School had to contend with a basically non-existent endowment of under $20,000; average teacher salaries a good 25 percent below those at Baltimore County public schools; available scholarship money actually falling from $8,600 in 1947 to a meager $4,820 five years later; and a nagging debt as a result of building the Kinsolving Gymnasium. A formalized annual giving program begun in 1958 under David E. Ryer '47 and Kinloch N. Yellott, Jr. '46—with choir concerts, dances and cocktail parties, alumni-varsity basketball games, and plans for a newsletter—helped rally the constituents, as did efforts by trustees like Frank Mead '21, W. Carroll Mead '19, and Wilson Oster. Over the course of the decade, tuition increases and more concerted fund raising kept the problems at bay.[14]

As the School quickly outgrew the cramped stables and mansion, the trustees devised a long-range master plan in 1962 and prepared to raise funds for four major projects: a new dormitory, a dining hall, a new science building, and a renovated Middle School in Brooklandwood. These would address the Middle States evaluation that St. Paul's was doing a "superior task" but "sorely needed facilities," and would reclaim

OPPOSITE: Though a handful of boarders would linger until 1972, the trustees voted to suspend the boarding department at the close of 1970, a decision made easier since half of the 14 boarders that year were seniors. "The hope [of the board] was universally expressed," wrote headmaster Jack Ordeman in 1971, "that the suspension of boarding would be a brief one." A return to boarding never materialized, and the Ordeman family would actually be the last "boarders" in the mansion until 1985. Today, the old dormitory pictured here, also used as the student bookstore as well as the former *Page* office from 1976-84, houses Middle School classes, renovated at a cost of $285,000 and dedicated to John T. Ordeman in 1993.

The Craft of Leadership

Long before Jack Ordeman knew what a "Crusie" was, he had worked at Columbia University with e. e. cummings for his masters thesis on the relationship between the artist's writing and his paintings. cummings responded to Ordeman's paper with edits and commentary; Ordeman's interpretations were sound, cummings said.

If Ordeman's vision of the School when he started could be captured in a painting, it would be perhaps romantic, deep in concept, and delicate in color, a work in progress both when he began in 1966 at age 36 and when he left 19 years later. Compatriot of ideas, Ordeman found strength in people and always defended his and their convictions, sometimes to the disgruntlement of skeptics. He and his colleagues made innovation their handiwork. Ordeman also had the background, certainly, to know what a school and an education could be: Phillips Andover Academy; Williams College; assistant headmaster and admissions director at Episcopal High School, where he began the school's first lacrosse club; and captain in the Marine Corps for two years, with the tattoo to prove it.

Ordeman, who on the side published books on art history, including his 14-year labor of love, *Frank W. Benson: Master of the Sporting Print*, carried St. Paul's through deep transformations. But when asked his profession, Ordeman even now would reply that he was a teacher who had administrative responsibilities.

Nothing should be said about Jack Ordeman and St. Paul's, however, without saying something about his

(From left) Board president Halsey Cook, headmaster Jack Ordeman, and Middle School supervisor Mike Rentko at the laying of the cornerstone of the Middle School, named S. Atherton Middleton Hall.

wife, Mary, who indelibly marked the School with character and atmosphere as mentor, hostess, art teacher, mother, and chef. A talented artist, Mary knew when and where the canvas needed more color.

Similarly, the Reverend Halsey Cook was a principal architect with Ordeman in the larger design of St. Paul's. Just as Cook, by moving his family to become the eighth occupant of the downtown Parish rectory in 1964, boldly demonstrated that place meant commitment, presence, and economic wherewithal, Jack, with Mary and family of four (Jennifer, Lee, Elizabeth, and Jessica), was the only headmaster to live and work in the mansion; this was a symbol of a professional and personal relationship that spanned nearly two decades.

The woodworker in Cook perhaps gave vision to turning mansion and stable into campus and classroom for 600. Cook was a man of the Church, but he was also a civil engineer, mechanic, and licensed electrician and plumber; an all-star bridge player at Columbia University, where he earned a degree in English; a hunter; and a sports fan who was later made an honorary member of the Monogram Club. When Cook resigned and stepped down as board president and chairman in 1981, Ordeman remarked that he "steered St. Paul's through the rough waters of the '60s and '70s, and there is no one who cared more, no one who accomplished more, and no one who is more entitled to take pride in the progress of St. Paul's School than he." Surely Cook would have reciprocated this praise.[1]

A 1967 first grade class

(First row, from left) Harry C. Dundore '79, Win Hobbs, Suzanne DeGarmo, (second row) unidentified, Thomas B. Lalley '79, (third row) Allison Babelar, Buckley Winsholt, (back row, standing) unidentified, Marty Hermann, Dicky Grieves, Lisa Tullai, Ray Knapp, Christopher N. Kandel '78, unidentified, Mark Hughes, Frank Williamson, Steven B. Stenersen '78, and Leslie Trazzi.

for it a boarding school status. Middleton, with the help of trustees like Vernon Stehl, launched what became a wave of construction. The capital campaign begun in 1963, jointly developed with the young St. Paul's School for Girls, was a struggle, but under trustee Wilson Oster, St. Paul's successfully reached its own capital goal of $300,000 for a science building. "It is hard for those of us closely connected with St. Paul's," said Middleton, "to wait patiently for the day when all the dreamed-of buildings will be completed."[15]

On April 21, 1964, the Right Reverend Harry Lee Doll, Bishop of Maryland, officiated at the ground-breaking of the first of these buildings, a new science building, which opened in February one year later (with two labs, classrooms "uniquely adapted to the instruction for major physical sciences," an office, a language lab, and a faculty room). "The building," wrote one student, "is truly a modern and impressive building … and has become an integral part of the daily life of the School." By now, the campus—like the School—was growing up.[16]

"I do not suggest to the seniors to burn their draft cards, nor

do I urge them to participate enthusiastically in the well-run

war machine that our society fosters. If the United States

wants to fight the Communists then let us declare war and

hit Peking with everything we have. If not, then let us pull

out of Vietnam and save the lives for better use."

The Monitor, 1965

CHANGE OF HEADMASTER, CHANGE OF SCHOOL

In 1966, after 22 years, Middleton left St. Paul's a larger, more deliberate institution. He had moved the School to Brooklandville, developed the Lower and Middle Schools, hired key faculty like Martin Tullai, Thomas Longstreth, Jeanne Shreeve, and Michael Rentko, and bulldozed a path for the quick rise of new buildings—all while the School found itself, as usual, financially strapped and with its future threatened by competition not only among wealthier independent schools but among a bumper crop of private academies spawned by the integration of public schools.

The time had come to grease the financial wheels, as it were; to persuade people to give or to give more; to take seriously the endowment and the long-term health of St. Paul's. Just one pressing issue when Middleton retired: a dangerously high 95 percent of the School's income came from tuition, compared to a national average of about 60 percent. The trustees, wielding their staff of fiscal oversight, now had to acknowledge more actively the School's market (able students and their tuition), its product (solid college prospects), and its competitive edge (the essence of what the School was). That these high-priority financial responsibilities would fall on the shoulders of the headmaster was hardly to be expected when John T. "Jack" Ordeman took the headmaster's position at St. Paul's School in the fall of 1966. At that time, the trustees earnestly assured Ordeman that these issues would be insignificant demands, if they existed at all. But 19 years later, details of operations and fundraising absorbed the bulk of his time, a transformation that he certainly never embraced, yet seemed at times actively to encourage. Only by doing so could he create a better, more robust St. Paul's. Improvement, after all, ultimately boiled down to time and money. And so Ordeman, with his board president Halsey Cook and a strong group of trustees, found a school of 400 and left it a very different institution of 700, and a very different business.[17]

Despite his self-proclaimed inexperience in that area, Ordeman instituted what would become the School's development department, and in 1967 hired seasoned director of development Robert Lee Randolph. Trustees resisted what seemed like an

The St. Paul's Summers

Few at school could bear to see the wide, green Brooklandville campus lying idle. A summer day camp thus began here for the first time in 1955, and took long strides under people like Paul Long. The "St. Paul's Day Camp," also run by Howard Emsley, Jr., later evolved alongside a Lower School summer enrichment program for 21 kids begun in 1973 by Barbara Mills. By the late '80s, operations had been consolidated, and all the programs fell under the direction of Mary Pfrommer and Winnie Flattery. Together they managed an umbrella program which soon covered 38 different camps for some 500 students, with K-12 programs in everything from SAT prep to woodworking to a very popular program in lacrosse under Mitch Whiteley—all of which continue to grow at an explosive rate. Interestingly enough, for many years, the Lower School summer program had a particularly compelling outreach element that often gave scholarships to verbally gifted kids from public schools, some of whom were later enrolled. Pictured here is the campus as it looked after the School added its first building, the Kinsolving Gymnasium (at left), in 1954. The mansion is in the center of this picture, with the dormitory to the left and the reflecting pool on the lawn in front. The rooftop of the Lower School, peeking out of the trees, can be seen above the mansion.

ABOVE: Inside the School's first chapel, dedicated to its benefactress Helen Linthicum and housed in the Lower School; the Reverend James E. Cantler '43 became the first full-time chaplain in 1955. As a side note, the Reverend Mark Gatza was the only chaplain ordained on the Brooklandville campus, in a ceremony conducted in the Kinsolving Gymnasium on January 25, 1983 by bishop David K. Leighton.

unnecessary and expensive addition—since no other Baltimore independent school had one—but Ordeman pointed to Episcopal High School, where Randolph sat on the board, as a successful model. Ordeman also recognized that the School's alumni base—and best source of ongoing funds—was a loyal group, but small, cultivated almost single-handedly by the hard work of the first true alumni secretary, Fredrica McDorman (wife of faculty member and choirmaster Donald '33), and strengthened by the efforts of people like J. M. Dryden Hall, Jr. '50 and William N. Clements II '46. A full-time development director, Ordeman knew, could help organize and expand the effort. Sensible marketing followed, as the administration introduced a formalized publicity and public relations effort, creating an award-winning 1971 school catalog and expanding the *News from St. Paul's School* from a functional four pages to 20 of much higher quality and depth, with sections and entire issues for alumni. Finally, a 1970 Middle States evaluation gave credence to Ordeman's earlier request for someone to handle operations and financial management, formerly under trustee George O'Connell '35, who "spent untold hours with ledgers and budgets and account books, trying to run, in his leisure time, a business operation with a three million dollar plant and nearly a million dollar annual budget." Even so, as with a director of development, the board strongly questioned the affordability and need of a business

The Fellow in Fellowship

St. Paul's has been built brick by brick, dollar by dollar, person by person. Of the entire $18 million endowment—six times what it was ten years ago in 1989—$12.3 million of it is comprised of 40 restricted named endowment funds. No better place to start a brief overview of these than with W. James Price IV '42, parent, grandparent, alumnus, and trustee. Price first helped David C. Pritchard find a compelling reason to leave $200,000 to St. Paul's in 1974, at that point the second largest gift in the School's history, now worth $1.16 million. Ten years later in 1984, Price oversaw the transfer of $1 million (now worth $4.4 million) to the School from the estate of Walter and Mariam Smith, in memory of their son, Walter S. Smith, Jr., with whom Price served in Germany during WW II and who was killed in action in the Ardennes. This and the first endowed faculty chair, the William J. and Frances R. Price Chair in English, established in 1995 with a current market value of $730,000, means that Price, not including his role in raising funds for the Middle School, the Kelly Gym, and the Price Manual Arts building, has been directly responsible for bringing in about 35 percent of the current endowment.[1]

The other 65 percent is also built upon hard work, legacies, and generosity. To name a few of the funds: the Kelly Memorial ($430,000) for plant maintenance; the Mead Brothers Scholarship Fund ($260,000), in memory of John '17, W. Carroll '18, and Frank '21; the Clements Family Fund ($270,000); and the Thomas A. Foley, Jr. Memorial ($318,000) for boys with "heavenly voices," as

W. James Price IV '42

Thomas's mother, a member of the Parish, specified in her bequest. Many are for financial aid, like the Thomas B. Scheffenacker Memorial Fund ($535,000), established in 1984 in memory of Thomas Scheffenacker '86; the William S. Polk, Jr. Scholarship Fund ($579,000), named in memory of a Middle School faculty member and coach; and the W. Alton Jones Scholarship ($350,000) for minority students, established in 1983.

After headmaster George Hamilton left St. Paul's in 1944, he would never again find a mentor and friend like Dr. Arthur B. Kinsolving, a man of intellect and spirit, leadership and humility, wisdom and wit. In his and the century's late '70s, Hamilton took it upon himself to establish the Kinsolving Memorial Endowment Fund in 1982; valued today at $1.5 million, the fund has supported efforts like the outdoor education program, community service initiatives, the eighth- and tenth-grade bike trip, and the honor system. What Hamilton thought of Kinsolving, many thought of Hamilton, and when he died at age 81 in 1985, headmaster Jack Ordeman and the trustees renamed the fund the Kinsolving-Hamilton Fellowship.

In another commemoration of service, the trustees established the John T. Ordeman Endowment for faculty development in 1984 through a $55,000 gift (now valued at nearly $200,000) from Mr. and Mrs. Talbott Bond. "There is nothing to which the trustees of this school should give higher priority than faculty development," Ordeman later wrote, "and nothing to which I should rather have my name attached than this particular fund."[2]

LEFT: View of the Middle School, built in 1969, and named after headmaster S. Atherton Middleton. The Kelly Gym, added that same year, extends behind it. Sitting on the terraced hill are students John L. Sindler '86, John Linsenmeyer '86, and Allen R. Shutt '86.

OPPOSITE: Austin X. Dopman, Jr. '83 (left) and Regan Marshall.

manager, and most believed the position would eventually be terminated. Nevertheless, with the appointment of Paul Lowenthal as full-time business manager, Ordeman in his first five years had jumpstarted, as he put it, "a major change in the administrative set-up of St. Paul's." Headmaster, business manager, and director of development—with board president Halsey Cook at their side—were now fixed as the fulcrum of strategic planning and decision-making. By the time Wayne Porter, who installed modern systems of budget controls, accountability, and debt collection, became business manager in 1978, and Peter Hussey followed Randolph in 1981, this triangle of administrators would be a mainstay in the operational make-up of the School, and would soon require small staffs of their own.[18]

Meanwhile, Ordeman continued what Middleton had begun to address: St. Paul's at Brooklandville was not yet a campus. After the addition of the science building in 1965, most expected a large dormitory when the School publicly announced plans for a $4 million dorm sufficient for 100 boarders, with a separate kitchen, indoor pool, and recreational facilities, slated for completion by early 1966 and apparently to be one of the nicest of its kind in Baltimore.[19] But Ordeman, hired in part to apply his experience in boarding, questioned the idea when he found a disorganized and weak boarding program at St. Paul's, monitored mostly by college students. Noting a declining interest and enrollment in boarding schools both in Baltimore and nationally and only a few boarders at St. Paul's to begin with (30 on the new campus in 1952, less than 10 percent of the enrollment), Ordeman felt hard-pressed to proceed in this direction. The trustees canceled construction plans, but most believed that at a more opportune time, the School would steer itself back toward the direction of boarding,

"To everyone's pleasant surprise, there was carpeting on the third floor [of the new library building], where classes were held in the comfort of one's home, except for unfortunate electrical shocks. The blackboards were perhaps the biggest shock of all, for they were full-length, magnetic, pastel walls. The boards' ledges were originally movable, but were eventually anchored to the walls."

The Crusader, after the 1966 dedication of the
Grover Hermann Library Building

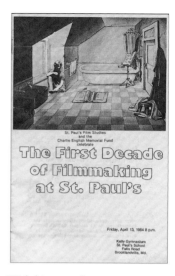

the presence of which they felt lent an important intimacy and character to the School. "The members of the 1966-67 boarding department," as *The Crusader* claimed, "have continued to carry on the core of the St. Paul's spirit." Even in 1970, when boarders numbered only a handful, the trustees recommended only a temporary suspension of the department, but "not the elimination of it."[20]

A library came next, boosted by a large $100,000 gift from philanthropist Grover M. Hermann, a Chicago industrialist and business associate of trustee William Burgen. When Ordeman arrived, Middleton had just broken ground during the 1966 commencement for a classroom building south of the science building, with an additional $30,000 earmarked for an arcade and an underground passageway that would avoid the "wasteful journey between distant buildings." The new building would house the humanities, with a library tucked away on the second floor. With Ordeman's encouragement, the library would soon become the building's nucleus. Guided by Ethel Hardee, the library quickly doubled circulation to 16,000 volumes. Hardee accepted and catalogued donations of old books, and her successor, Penelope Partlow, an experienced librarian, also helped centralize, organize, and expand the School's offerings.[21] Within ten years, the library had grown from a full-time untrained staff of two in the corner of the Lower School, fit for about 13 students, to become one of the first automated school libraries in Baltimore, with trained professionals in each division and a total of 27,000 volumes. The libraries were made up of the Lower School library, dedicated to beloved first-grade teacher Mabel Bennett (1956-66) in 1966; the Middle School library, built later in the decade and dedicated to the revered English teacher Farnham Warriner in 1986; and the Upper School's Grover Hermann Library, named after its benefactor and refurbished in honor of Louis Clark in 1990 by Anna May Austin, widow of Marshall Austin '39. All three attested to Ordeman's claim in a 1977 letter to the trustees that "the area in which the most dramatic improvement in facilities and services has been accomplished is the library."[22]

With his super-8 mm cameras, Michal Makarovich began film studies in 1974 and had near immediate success, especially with significant support later from the Charlie English Memorial Fund. Students in the class like Scott Buckler '78, Ian McCausland '83, Lorenzo Milan '88, and Brendon Hunt '92 recognized these new creative opportunities, and others like Mark Pellington '80 would make careers in the industry. Annual assemblies and events like the First Decade in Film Studies (1984) celebrated the students' artistic venue, and what eventually totaled 34 county, 12 state, and 13 national awards, won by over 500 films and videos produced in 20 years. The cover shown above is a self-portrait in a Disney scene drawn by film student Michael A. Gettier '75.

The Message is the Medium

By the end of '60s, Upper School faculty member Nelson Sweglar had begun the first "Television Techniques" class, a new credit course which met three times a week and which was partly enabled by the donation of audio-visual equipment, a Ford Foundation grant of $25,000, and a collective effort to install a full closed-circuit television network and studio. The first production in 1968 broadcast student speeches, debates, and results of the U.S. presidential elections. With the help of people like the Reverend Herman diBrandi, students produced a 25-minute show (WSTP) for every Upper School classroom one morning each week.

With plans to wire and broadcast to the Lower and Middle Schools, the television show, unique among area schools, had its fans and, of course, its skeptics, but most look back on the program as a significant and unusual achievement, with comedy included. To note: Headmaster Ordeman posing on a spoof about a hair weave at "Mr. Ray's"; French teacher Gertrude Wolf's cooking show; and students' live interviews with sports celebrities like Johnny Unitas. By 1978, the show had dropped to two Monday morning assemblies a month. When Sweglar left four years later, so did the program.

Alfred B. Sadtler '71 (left) and Grant E. G. Healey '71 below the Grover Hermann library in the Hamilton Audio-Visual Room, outfitted by way of Marshall Austin '39 in honor of the former headmaster.

Halsey Cook, Ordeman, and the trustees sustained the momentum of construction and fundraising. By 1971, an astonishing $1.6 million in capital money had been raised in ten years. Consider the campus additions over Ordeman's first decade, 1966-76: three faculty houses (1967), built to attract experienced masters, designed and erected by future assistant headmaster Sam Williams; a new Middle School (1969), dedicated and named S. Atherton Middleton Hall, and made possible through the $550,000 "Crusade for Excellence" campaign; the $70,000 Kelly Gymnasium annex to the Middle School (1969), secured through a capital campaign chaired by trustee Charles H. Peterson to match a gift from the Ensign C. Markland Kelly, Jr. Memorial Foundation; the restoration of Brooklandwood (1970), funded by a $400,000 gift from the Grover Hermann Foundation; the William J. Price III Manual Arts Center (1973), by way of a gift from Mr. and Mrs. John Engalitcheff, Jr.; the Harrison Wing of the Lower School (1974), made possible largely through the generosity of trustee emeritus George Harrison; and an expanded dining facility added to the existing one in the Kinsolving Gymnasium (1976). Looking back over these active years, Ordeman summarized, "We can now say that the physical facilities of St. Paul's are in very sound condition. We're not 'playing catch-up' anymore."[23]

GIRLS ARRIVE

Meanwhile, all through the '60s, girls had been just down the hill. Nine years after the original St. Paul's Girls' School had closed, it re-opened in 1959 newly-outfitted and renamed St. Paul's School for Girls (SPSG) under the auspices of the Benevolent Society, and led by headmistress Rosalind Levering and board president Thomas F. Cadwalader. The Girls' School initially offered grades fifth through ninth, planning to add a high school grade each year. Despite common board members (namely, Middleton, Cook, and Cadwalader), its proximity, and its name, SPSG largely carried on an academically, athletically, and administratively independent existence in the '60s.

In 1957, when a land committee made up of members of the Parish vestry, the Boys' School, and the Benevolent Society, found available acreage at Brooklandville, the argument to erect a girls' school there was in part made financially compelling by the ideas of shared resources and management with its brother school. Vestryman William L. Marbury, chairing a committee with trustees John Walton and Richard R. Harwood, Jr., developed a coordination plan approved by the Boys' School trustees in late 1965. The committee found that, while separation was important, remaining legally independent entities seemed unnecessary. Though the report found no philosophical difference between the Schools, their "continuation as separate academic entities is highly desirable [because] to attempt to merge the two into a single educational pattern would sacrifice much that is valuable in both institutions." In short, the Boys' School urged the Girls' School trustees "that coordination be at the policy-making level, rather than only in cooperation of maintenance matters."[24]

"What Would Happen?"

"If Mr. Ratcliffe ran out of tobacco? … If coaches were planted at the Hunt Cup? … If the yearbook editors could print what they wanted to print? … If the bookstore ran into bankruptcy because of its lack of the highly demanded Androcles and the Lion? … If Windy Valley were deprived of the boarders' secret patronage?"

The Monitor, 1964

ABOVE: Students Silvia Menendez and Robby Pantoulis reading in the Lower School bathtub, a rare privilege that comes only when you learn to tie your shoes. Former Lower School librarian Carol Pieper found the tub in 1974 and later painted Dr. Seuss characters around the side with her daughter, Darby. There is a second bathtub now, and the original, its legs weakened after so many years, sits in a wooden cradle.

After rejecting the proposal in February, 1966, the Girls' School "expressed a desire to cooperate and coordinate," but nothing more formal. "Was it our definite decision that we should operate our school independently of the Boys' School?" wrote William L. Reed, SPSG trustee. "Without vote, it was the definite agreement of all the board that we should do so." The Girls' School, with an enrollment of 86, thus proceeded to design its own philosophy, financial structure, and mission to educate girls beyond the fourth grade. Conversations of collaboration soon turned to more sensitive issues like redirecting the scholarship money currently being advanced to the Boys' School for young girls, a difficult request since the financially-strapped Boys' School had already foregone $4,500 in annual financial support from the Benevolent Society to support its Lower School operations.[25]

Nonetheless, the Boys' School trustees had early on indicated to Ordeman, who himself had attended both a single-sex boarding school and college, that a merger was inevitable, especially given compelling feasibility studies and a national trend toward coeducation in schools and colleges. All that emerged, however, was a mixed bag of honors courses and arts classes, each of which took extraordinary amounts of time and planning. Mary Frances Wagley, SPSG headmistress in 1970, commented that she did not want a "shotgun marriage," as trustees, students, and faculty from both Schools saw plenty of ways to coordinate but surprisingly few ways to see their ideas materialize. Already a hybrid with girls in its Lower School, the Boys' School could serve as a convenient feeder for the SPSG fifth grade, but little else seemed necessary.[26]

The arts actually proved to be the most efficacious (and neutral) means to coordinate, since there existed a Boys' School dramatics club (first under Robert French, and later Albert Cauffman) and an auditorium at the Girls' School, where they performed the first combined theater production in 1961. Rector Halsey Cook, who had children in both Schools, also used the Church as a non-threatening link. In symbolic efforts, he initiated unifying events like the combined Baccalaureate service at Old St. Paul's in 1964, a tradition that has been maintained since.

Boys seemed only faintly aware of the existence of the Girls' School, even at the end of the '60s when more active coordination seemed just around the corner. Slowly, boys and girls acknowledged one another. The theme of the 1970 *Monitor*, for instance, was "The Battle of the Sexes": photographs of armed girls at the base and boys at the summit of the Brooklandville hill show the girls peering up after an "inspiring bra-burning ceremony inside the captured male fortress" and waiting for the men to "put down their accurate .45 caliber lacrosse

RIGHT: Commencement, set in its traditional spot on the Brooklandwood lawn. Headmaster Ordeman speaks from the mansion's back porch. In the foreground on the left is Lower School teacher Emilie Durham, daughter of headmaster Appy Middleton.

sticks." The metaphor of a battle was obviously exaggerated, but still interesting. (The magazine also concluded with Oscar Wilde: "Life is an Imitation of Art.") As the defensive, younger and smaller Girls' School strengthened and gained self-confidence over the course of the '70s, student editorials voiced stronger opinions toward coordination: "To force a student to pass through eight years of his or her life in an atmosphere void of members of the opposite sex can only serve to stunt and distort the learning process."[27]

Three girls from another nearby girls' school, Maryvale Prep, actually attended the very first coordinated class at St. Paul's in 1972, advanced placement English taught by Ordeman. And a year later—14 years after the Girls' School had opened—coordinated classes with SPSG began, due in part both to Ordeman's continued offer of free tuition to girls who took classes at the Boys' School and to the new headmistress, Mary Ellen Thomsen, whose husband sat on the board of Gilman, a school which had begun exploring coordination with neighboring schools Bryn Mawr and later Roland Park. Girls' attendance in advanced placement courses and drama classes increased, and in 1979 Upper School teacher Michal Makarovich started a journalism class, the first to be coordinated from the beginning—so popular that twice as many students signed up as could be accommodated.

Even through the '70s and '80s, the Girls' School remained protective of its own identity—understandably so. With too much coordination, the Boys' School presented a threat with its more developed operational infrastructure, financial stability, athletic program, and reputation. If early SPSG catalog supplements, annual reports, and other public-

"PARTIES: Anyone in the Upper School is eligible for the
grand prize given by the seniors to the person who has the
best party. All parties until May 22 will be eligible."

The Page, 1978

ity material described opportunities for coordination with the Boys' School at all, they buried them within the text. The National Association for Independent Schools (NAIS) had warned that mergers like these often meant the absorption of the smaller and younger school, advice which the Girls' School board has heeded since. Even in 1995, when Dr. Evelyn Flory arrived as the new headmistress, the public announcement claimed that her chief interest in taking the position lay with three principles of the Girls' School philosophy, one being "a commitment to single-sex education." But both schools would continue to take advantage of what came to be considered as the best of both worlds: coordination, without being truly coordinated.[28]

MAKE ART, NOT WAR

As through most of the School's history, the reaction to global and national movements—from civil rights to Vietnam—came a bit slower than that of the rest of the country. The invasion of news was only as dramatic as its potential local impact. Some 100 Upper School students, for instance, unsuccessfully petitioned for a day off when the Vietnam War concluded. "In simple terms," they wrote to Ordeman, "we have never known what it is like to live in peace, for we have never lived in peace." At the top of the hill, of course, things were plenty secure, and if life was as tough as students claimed, "perhaps they are even tougher," retorted Ordeman, "in some places than they have been in Ruxton and Roland Park." Nevertheless, discussions of death, patriotism, gun control, and Communism were still serious, confusing, and immediate. Drug use was as local a threat to stability as any, and trustees soon wrote policies that expelled students unconditionally for possession and use. No doubt, the student mindset was in a much different place than in the '50s. "In ignorance," wrote one student, "there is an education we will never know.'"

Indeed, as St. Paul's circled the periphery of much of the national discussion, the primary consequence of the tumultuous ride of the '60s and '70s was a persistent skepticism and objection to anything worth objecting to; controversial and sensitive ideas challenged a wavering school spirit and pride. Students waxed liberal, then conservative, wondered about ethics and morality. "Where are today's heroes?" asked one. "We have none that I can think of. Maybe that's why we're going downhill so fast." Underscoring the problem for students was what appeared to be a collapse of central values in society and in the world. "Is honesty dead?" asked *The Page*, the student

ABOVE: Middle School faculty member Donald McDorman '33 (far right) herding choirboys, all shouldering their music bags, from what is now the entrance to the Lower School in 1969. (From left) Paris P. diBrandi '75, Eric W. Hardee '71, (at the doorstep) G. Brock Johnson '72, Michael J. Seets '74, H. Bruce Funk '74, John Francis, Glen Stewart, and Glen Wills.

newspaper, in 1977. "People see the president [Nixon] of their country painted as a liar and cannot help but wonder why they should be any more honest."

In turn, an arts program—a means to express these doubts and ideas—seemed to be a natural progression in the '70s, as much as it helped to unify the School. "We dedicate this issue of *The Monitor* to the concept of 'Community,'" the same theme adapted by the 1972 *Crusader*. Attitudes about art had certainly evolved. Consider one 1962 editorial: "To most of the students with whom I have spoken concerning the subject of an art appreciation course, the very idea is repulsive." Few outlets existed. One innovation, an art club organized by Katherine Duer in 1964, had apparently been in the making for years, its goal to "nurture our new experiment in cultural education … which marks the beginning of a new era; each student shall find available the facilities for a broad, truly liberal basis for his education." Although art had been taught in the Lower School for some time by Barbara Trotter, it was in 1967 when Mary Ordeman shaped an otherwise non-existent element for most into a more structured art department. She and faculty members like Peggy Fox, crammed into the Upper School attic, found ways to teach art, though a good 20 years would pass before new department head Sally Fronk found better facilities in the Lower School.[30]

Still, *The Monitor*, a creative space for only a minority of students; periodic low-budget drama productions in the tight quarters of the Kelly Gym; and classes like television techniques could hardly accommodate the expression of a large student body. If students could sing, Donald McDorman '33 knew who they were, leading the glee clubs until 1972, but not until the early '80s did alternative music clubs appear, including a handbell choir directed by Sue Gibbons and a jazz band started by John Thorpe and Marcus Romani. The Choir of Men and Boys, under Rodney Hansen, was still a strong and an important activity, but was mostly relegated to a small group of Middle School students who disappeared to the Ender Room every morning. Said one 1972 editorial, "Although progress has been made in many areas, and the academic and athletic standards at St. Paul's have been steadily rising, the clubs seem to be falling farther behind every year. Who still remembers the rocket club, gun club, ski club, Spectator's club, philosophy club, chess club, jazz club, debating club, poster club, music appreciation club, Europe club or golf club? The dramatics and audio-visual clubs have evolved into half-credit courses. The only existing clubs are the science club, guitar club, and the recently reformed photography club, but even these have few members." If there were arts in the '60s and the early '70s, they were localized instances that few today recall. Most point to Michal Makarovich, who joined the faculty in 1973, as the one who added new colors to the School's blue and gold palette, designing classes in film and journalism, launching a second student publication, *The Page*, and spearheading important events like the first all-school "Night of the Arts" in 1979.[31]

The vocal minority of faculty, complaining about non-existent facilities and an overall weak arts program, had thus become a vocal majority by the '80s, as events demonstrated to the community just how much was happening in so little available space. Several committees, with outspoken leaders like Makarovich, Gibbons, Cauffman, Nelson Sweglar, and others, assembled with Ordeman to identify exactly what purposes something like a shared arts center would serve; they even had preliminary designs from architect John Stetson. The 1978 long-range planning committee began talks of an "institute" for the arts for both Schools and made public announcements. "The planning of a new activities center is underway," said SPSG headmistress Mary Ellen Thomsen, though "underway" would turn out to mean another ten years.[32]

INNOVATION IN THE CLASSROOM

Ordeman's successful acquisition of the first "digital computer" of any secondary school in Maryland in 1967 serves as a good example of the kind of innovation and vision he and a faculty with such varied talents—like television enthusiast and math department head Nelson Sweglar, manual arts teacher Charles Emig, or Lower School science teacher Penny Miller—brought to St. Paul's. Not only did the School proceed with its mission to serve the individual student, but it did so as creatively as possible.

Parallel and Independent Minds

A self-declared learning disabled student, faculty member Ann Stellmann was a guiding force in a new approach to teaching students challenged by the basic skills and who needed more individualized attention. Supported by Lower School head Jeanne Shreeve and headmaster Jack Ordeman, the Parallel Program, as it came to be called, was as organic as it was innovative, beginning in 1973 with a small group of students. Soon it included parallel sections in grades one through four, aided in part by Roger Saunders, a local psychologist and learning specialist. In the Middle School, "parallel" students, better understanding their abilities, transitioned to classes without individualized teaching. By the early '80s, the program, as the School newsletter claimed, "was generally regarded as one of the most successful programs for helping children with language disabilities in operation anywhere." Indeed, no program or provision for learning disabled students existed in any other area private or public school with as concentrated and structured an approach. After much publicity and despite a higher tuition, by 1985, 20 percent of Lower School students were enrolled in the program, or 60 of 300 students.

Ann Stellmann with fourth-graders Harris Thompson '96 (left) and Austen Gardiner in 1988.

The perception and the reality of the program were also like parallel lines, and the two, at a distance, merged into one. Despite the steady success, some trustees, parents, and faculty found the program risky and potentially hazardous to the School's college preparatory reputation; they worried about being branded as a school for the learning disabled, and others felt that "parallel" students often seemed too isolated. Advocates like Ordeman wrote letters of support. "It can be argued from statistical evidence," he said, "that the children in the regular sections progress more rapidly because their teachers do not spend an inordinate amount of classroom time on children whose learning styles require special attention."[1] In truth, though, with a new name, some restructuring, and less publicity, the Parallel Program evolved into a more rigorous and equally successful effort under a less distinctive title, "small group instruction." Assisted by school psychologist Rosemary Hanley, selection in Lower School admissions became more refined, and students with lags in their language proficiency continued to receive individualized attention and for the most part made a smooth transition into their respective grades.

With a similar objective, the year following the inception of the Parallel Program, Barbara Mills launched and directed the Independent Studies Laboratory (ISL) in 1974, a program for intellectually gifted third- and fourth-graders to work in groups where their educational needs could be better addressed. Like the Parallel Program, ISL expanded over several years to include first and second grade and within five years, both were recognized locally and at national conferences.[2]

Man on the Arcade
Dubbed the "Penny Arcade"
for the School's head librarian
Ethel "Penny" Hardee, this arcade
bridged the James H. Ratcliffe
Hall, built in 1964, and the Grover
Hermann Library, built in 1966. To
accommodate the larger Upper
School, the arcade was demolished
in the summer of 1997, covered,
and replaced by classrooms and
offices during an extensive renovation. Because the area was so often
filled with those trying to relax,
meet, or arrive at the next class on
time, a column, "Man on the
Arcade," featuring student and faculty views, appeared in the student
newspaper, *The Page,* soon after the
paper began in 1976. Sitting here
is Allen R. Shutt '86.

Academics were in better shape. The 1971 Middle States evaluation found a "highly
structured academic schedule with well-defined sequence and requirements." It noted
that almost 100 percent of its students were matriculating in college and that St. Paul's
seemed "to be meeting the students' needs … The School is indeed very fortunate to
have in these difficult days, with so many independent schools in such serious trouble, the loyal support of a fine board of trustees, an interested parent group, and an
active and grateful alumni." A 1971 campaign brochure noted among other things the
additions of a creative writing program in the Lower School, ballet classes under Anne
Roman, advanced placement courses in the Upper School, and an art studio.[33]

The '70s ushered in creative offerings and incipient ideas: in the Lower School,
Ann Stellmann began the Parallel Program for students with special learning needs;
Barbara Mills developed the Independent Studies Laboratory (ISL) for gifted children;
Cathie Ives created the Interlingua program for studying foreign languages and cul-
ture; Joy Whiteley introduced the pre-first program (1970), the first of its kind in the
Baltimore area. In the older grades, teaching pioneer James Andrew taught Middle
School math courses without using traditional grades; J. Anthony Tyler '60 and Sam
Williams explored methods of self-guided learning using videotaped lessons directed
by Nelson Sweglar; and head librarian Penelope Partlow added the first micro-com-
puters to the library. By the end of the decade, students were taking personal finance,
philosophy, psychology, oceanography, and art history.

A decentralized administration with Upper, Middle, and Lower Schools operating in three different buildings, however, created new operational puzzles to solve.

Each division head managed everything from admissions to counseling, budgets to faculty development. In Ordeman's second year, administrators began to meet regularly in an attempt to coordinate. But the expansion made communication challenging, and ultimately fractured the intimate wholeness of earlier years. The Middle School, proudly developing its own identity, operated more or less autonomously, with its own student government and honor council, awards ceremony, field trips to Williamsburg, yearbook, and literary magazine. And the Lower School now had its own student council, electives, the *Little Crusader* magazine, commencement program, a math and computer lab, a "full instructional media center" under Carol Pieper in the library, and myriad afternoon offerings such as the Extended School Program (ESP), which grew substantially in the '90s under Mary Pfrommer and Winnie Flattery in sciences, arts, computers, and the humanities. At times, divisions quarreled among themselves as faculty in the upper grades expected students to be proficient in many areas, while those in the lower grades felt unreasonably pressured in trying to train students in every basic skill in just four years. The internal "Headmaster's Newsletter," appearing in 1982, was but one of Ordeman's continued attempts to unify divisions and to disseminate news about the School. Teacher mentoring began early in Ordeman's tenure. And faculty parties—some apparently quite notable—given by Mary Ordeman, Farnham Warriner and others certainly helped as well. Still, more than ever, St. Paul's was becoming three schools under one name.[34]

These management challenges required new business-oriented practices of organizational flow charts, job descriptions, and policy manuals. Delegation of much of the administrative work to its three heads freed Ordeman to focus on other important issues, but in doing so inadvertently distanced him from close regular contact with students and faculty. Over the course of the '70s—as with many independent schools—the headmaster had become less an academic figure and more an administrative leader with significant decision-making power. "Now a great deal of time is spent in the business of running a school and fundraising," noted Ordeman. "I'm back in the headquarters, not in the trenches."[35]

Ordeman also inherited Middleton's frustration of having too few resources to provide competitive pay and benefits for quality teachers, a consequence of a weak endowment eroded over time by capital purchases since the School's first move to Mt. Washington.[36] Historically, about 80 percent of the School's expenses came from salaries and benefits, so even a small increase for each individual had a significant impact on the bottom line. Ordeman often cited to the trustees lost opportunities due to teachers who had left or rejected positions, as well as the unfortunate bind of not having the funds to invest in order to raise more money; and tuition was already increasing at a steady rate, sometimes by as much as 10 percent. In fact, tuition had doubled every ten years from $425 in 1951 to $1,500 in 1971, making it as expensive as other private schools in the area. In 1955-56, for instance, St. Paul's was clearly a

Upper School history teacher Mitch Tullai (left), head librarian Penelope Partlow, and headmaster Jack Ordeman, sitting as the judges in a spin-off of "The Gong Show," one of many productions in the School's television studio.

good alternative for parents watching their wallets, with a day school tuition of $550 compared to Friends ($675), Park School ($740), McDonogh ($895), and Gilman ($910). Twenty years later, however, St. Paul's charged $1,800, fractionally less than some of the highest, such as Gilman ($1,950) and McDonogh ($2,175).[37]

Additionally, the St. Paul's $66,000 endowment in 1973 ranked as one of the lowest among area independent schools. (In fact, the School had less money in its endowment in 1966 than it had 50 years earlier.) The smaller Girls' School, with even lower faculty salaries than the Boys' School, had a higher endowment of $95,000, while other schools were in better shape: Friends ($235,000) and Park ($275,000), or in great shape, like Gilman ($2.26 million) and McDonogh ($4.89 million). With this data in mind, trustees W. James Price IV '42 and J. M. Dryden Hall, Jr. '50 led a $3 million campaign for the two Schools in 1974, with about half to be set aside for the endowment.[38]

Despite this success, Ordeman acknowledged once again in 1980 that faculty compensation was even worse in relative terms than it had been ten years earlier, in part a consequence of the inflated '70s dollar. As the capital campaign concluded, numbers did improve; a teacher with ten years of experience who earned $11,700 in 1980 earned $17,000 four years later, $1,000 more than the average salary of a secondary school teacher in AIMS. But compared to public school salaries, all of these numbers were low, "hardly a wage on which a man can support a family," said Ordeman.

Traditionally, and like most independent schools, salaries of Lower School faculty—composed almost entirely of women—fell well below those in the Middle and Upper Schools, but untraditionally, this no longer remained acceptable. In 1983-84, the average Lower School salary was $15,255, compared with $19,000 for faculty in higher grades. One obstacle was perception: women were mostly considered sec-

Diamonds Are Forever

In the din of choir voices, baseball was the Saints' most popular sport in the 1910s in their five-game seasons against Friends, the Country School, and the Jefferson School Midgets. But little happened when the School moved to Mt. Washington, especially with mostly track fanatics for headmasters. Faculty member Lewis Tignor '25 coached baseball in the early '30s but both it and track soon were suffocated by lacrosse for the next half century. Ironically, the one who suffocated it was also a chief patron: Howard Myers, Jr., known for "pitching the old pill" on his Boys' Latin baseball team, fell fast for lacrosse—as did the rest of the School.[1]

Some 50 years later, after a year of prodding by athletic director Rick Collins and others, eight students rallied for a jayvee baseball team in the winter of 1978-79, and 17 joined that spring, coached by William Durden and Tony Tyler '60, with a closing record of 7-5. After two years, jayvee graduated to 'C' Conference varsity in the spring of 1981, competing and practicing on playing fields off Seminary Avenue until a winless 1983 season.

Craig Pfeifer '80 at bat, perhaps prepping for the first varsity baseball team William Durden and Tony Tyler '60 began in the spring of 1981. For three years, varsity practiced and played games on a nearby field off of Seminary Road.

Lacrosse fans breathed down their necks as the sport grew in popularity, perhaps worried when the baseball team found a diamond they could call their own behind the Kinsolving Gym—the School's first—inaugurated on April 10, 1984. Headmaster Jack Ordeman threw out the first ball for an eventual loss against defending champions Mt. Carmel, though varsity scored its first victory in two years against Eastern the next day for a total of three wins that season.

From 1982 until 1990 and for a year in 1993, Tom Longstreth led the team, accruing 'C' Conference championships in 1989 and 1990. Eventually 'C' turned 'B' in 1991 and finally to 'A' in 1997, in part due to the formal institution of a new crusading jayvee team in 1992, inspired by faculty member Edward Brown; this addition filled the gap between Middle and Upper School and prepped younger students for varsity play. In 1995 and 1996, baseball acquired a second set of championships, bringing the total to four. Crusie baseball thus found its field of dreams by reversing the strategy: if you come, they will build it.[2]

Making St. Paul's Tick

(From left) Print shop manager Larry Smith; maintenance staff Mary and Jim Young;

and the 1978 cafeteria staff, Lynda Mills, Isabel Verzi, Emma Walz, and Ruth Petit.

DOUBLE DOWN

Larry Smith and his brother Will arrived in 1976, and they have been accommodating a growing school ever since, Will in the maintenance department, Larry in the print shop. In fact, when Larry arrived, St. Paul's owned one Royal Bond Copier II that printed about 100 copies each day. With their mimeograph and ditto machines, the School made, in rough estimates, some 35,000 copies that year. Today, the School owns almost a dozen modern copiers, situated around the three divisions, which churn out a good million duplicates. One footnote: when he started, Larry Smith used the A. B. Dick 360 offset printing press for more complicated jobs, a piece of equipment he still relies on today.

HANDYMEN

The move to the quiet world of Brooklandville was likely not as well-received for the maintenance staff as it was for the students and faculty. In the early '60s heads of maintenance John Bacon, Sam Williams, and then Jervis Spindler, assisted by people like Pete O'Connell, assumed responsibilities for everything from bus driving to snow removal, including a campus fire engine they had in the late '60s. And the rise of buildings compounded the number of things that could break. In 1952, the entire school totaled some 28,000 square feet, a number which in the past decade jumped from 150,000 square feet in 1989 to what will be 250,000 square feet with The Ward Center and coming Athletic Center. One truck and a staff of six has grown to six trucks and a highly skilled full-time staff of 24, including a licensed plumber, a journeyman electrician, and a former general contractor, supervised by business manager Kirk Evans and maintenance head Charles Ackermann, who oversees a plant budget of $1.2 million. For accounting types, St. Paul's is one of the few schools (or nonprofits for that matter) in the entire country to use full depreciation accounting and to totally fund that charge, which means that money is set aside every year to replace aging capital equipment. The net: a strong guarantee that buildings will not crumble and equipment will not become obsolete.

CHEZ SP

In 1954, the trustees budgeted $28,369 for a food service contract with the A. L. Mathias Company to feed 100 day students, 67 boarders, and staff at a daily price of $.40 per day student and $1.50 per boarder. Now, in 1999, in the same contract (under a different name), The Ward Center serves roughly 1,150 people from the two Schools each day, with operation revenues of $475,000 at a cost of $3.50 per meal. Ruth Petit, who still works at St. Paul's, has served the School for over 30 years.

"St. Paul's is in the best position geographically of all independent boys' schools to serve northern Baltimore County ... The prediction that by 1990 more students will come south to St. Paul's than those who will come north may well prove to be true."

John T. Ordeman, *St. Paul's News, Special Alumni Edition,* 1977

ondary income providers and not treated as professional equals. Reinforcing these stereotypes was the fact that, at this time, close to 60 percent of the Upper School faculty, made up of 14 men and five women, had masters degrees, compared to only 37 percent in the Lower School, made up of 39 women and three men. Morale began falling in the lower grades. A less expensive tuition for these lower grades, combined with the fact that the Upper School generally received more attention, made the Lower School feel under valued, a discovery articulated through surveys administered by faculty member Bill Bassett just after finishing a Klingenstein Fellowship at Columbia University. In truth, however, many perceived the Lower School as the "Golden Egg" of St. Paul's, a place that truly succeeded in its progressive educational aims. Serious debates followed and committees were assembled. Salary scales using criteria of experience and qualification appeared. Still, not until the late '80s would Lower School teachers, particularly women, approach equal compensation to that of their peers who taught higher grades.[39]

Through all of these changes during the '70s, Ordeman managed exceptionally well and the numbers worked in his favor. The School had paid off its land and building mortgages and no longer borrowed for operations; the endowment had grown from $137,000 to $1.2 million; annual giving increased from $24,000 to $105,000; the value of its buildings and land rose from about $2 million to over $3 million; a faculty of 52 full- and part-time teachers, 17 with masters degrees and one with a doctorate, had grown to 90 faculty, 50 with masters degrees and four with doctorates (22 of whom had earned degrees while teaching with the help of the School's new tuition subsidies); and enrollment had climbed by 100 to 704, particularly promising since the Lower School had made the greatest surge (184 to 287). These numbers were all good news. And Ordeman projected that the disappointment with public schools signified an optimistic future financially and in enrollment figures for independent schools like St. Paul's. Indeed, by the early '80s, acceptance to St. Paul's had become far more competitive and attractive; the School now fielded over 1000 admissions inquiries annually, and accepted less than two thirds of the applicants for the Upper School and just over half for the Lower School.[40]

Mad Scientist

Science never proved dull with Penny Miller, who helped found the Lower School science program beginning in 1971. Just as one example: the number and variety of guinea pigs under her and her students' care gave the "Pig Pack" recognition in the *National Geographic World Magazine* in 1983. Looking on (from left) are G. L. Fronk '90, Stefan P. Beittel '90, and James Lears. In recent years, science has come alive under Lower School faculty members like Mary Pfrommer.

SPLIT PATH

"Essentially for all the changes that have been wrought," Ordeman wrote as he summarized his ten years as headmaster in the first requested report to the trustees in 1977, "St. Paul's is—in its character, style, and goals—unchanged." In reports like these, Ordeman portended with startling accuracy what would eventually take shape by the '90s: "a chapel, a theater, and perhaps an indoor sports complex. These facilities could all be shared with the Girls' School, and they could be built as joint ventures." Ordeman had laid the groundwork for much that would come in the next 20 years, and the review of the Lower School by the Pennsylvania Association of Private Academic Schools (1981), as well as the Middle States review of the Upper School (1982) and finally of the Middle School (1983), provided solid testimony for Ordeman's successful tenure thus far. These reports and others found a strong commitment and willingness on the part of the School and the teachers to "take the kids who really needed the help and where you really make a difference." One evaluation found an "impressively talented, dedicated and hard-working faculty which has good rapport with its students," and that "student achievement has been high over the years as shown by standardized testing results. St. Paul's enjoys a good reputation in the area." Students, as measured in these evaluations, seemed satisfied with their education. These positive reports overall, with an endowment one thousand times its size in

Pinned Down

Bent finger and all, Lewis Tignor '25 brought 30 boys to the wrestling mats for the first time in the winter season of 1932, but just as the mat-men were gaining experience, basketball had displaced it by the 1935–36 season.

Wrestling fans had to wait another two decades before enough grapplers assembled to form a wrestling team in 1952-53, participated in the MSA in 1954-55, and achieved varsity status in 1957-58 under coach Donald Hughes. In the team's first season as such, athletic prodigy and post-grad co-captain Will Verco '58 won the MSA wrestling tournament of both public and private school students. Peter R. Keeler '60 won the MSA championship the following year, and after continued success, Hughes added a junior wrestling program in 1965-66 for the Middle School. By the last year of the decade, Hughes claimed that his last season was his best team in 12 years, including the young junior league with a 9-3 season.

This looked promising for the coming decade of wrestling at St. Paul's: the '70s. Coach James Andrew, who had been helping Hughes since 1966, would lead varsity beginning in 1969-70, and soon captured a Division II 'B' Conference championship in 1972-73. During the following year, the team boasted a 9-1 record, and wrestling had become, according to *The Crusader,* "one of the most exciting activities at St. Paul's." Indeed, parties thrown by the wrestlers' parents were apparently as memorable as the matches themselves. In 1975, after moving up to the 'A' Conference, seniors referred to the "end of a great era" in the wrestling program under Andrew, Kent W. Darrell '60, and Mark Curtis, yet the 1978-79 varsity team had only a single loss against powerhouse Mt. St. Joe. By the end of the decade, student participation under Andrew was so high that it required two distinct varsity teams and one jayvee team; 18 out of 30 wrestlers in the Upper School were awarded letters and 115 Middle School students participated. To culminate the era, the varsity team won a dual-meet tournament in an undefeated 1979-80 season, and were co-champs in the MSA 'A' tournament in 1980-81, Andrew's last season (12-2) and arguably one of the best teams in the School's history.

Desi McNelis, who had assisted Andrew for two years, then became head coach, and in the next 16 years earned 123 victories. In 1990-91, varsity went 10-3 and then 9-4 the following year, both in the 'A' Conference; and the 1997-98 varsity squad won the Maryland Independent School 'B' Division state championship, including one state champion, Keith Helman '98, the School's first.[1]

Dennis L. Childs '77 offering his opponent help as headmaster Jack Ordeman and his wife Mary (upper left) watch from the stands.

The Long Haul
The common path up the Brook-landville hill from the Girls' School to the Boys' School before The Ward Center opened in 1992. Headmaster Jack Ordeman taught the first coordinated class with three Maryvale girls in 1972, the year before coordination with the Girls' School began. By the time Ordeman left in 1985, there were four coed classes with over 60 students; and by 1998, all 33 Upper School foreign language classes, nine arts classes, and 15 others in history and science were coordinated. (Boys from left) Baker Koppelman '86, Greg Sekercan '86, B. Sanders Nice '86, and Paul Betz '86.

1966, suggested to Ordeman and others that St. Paul's was indeed on the right track.[41]

Some trustees, however, many of them newly-appointed, felt that the School was heading down a fast track to mediocrity, that the long-range plans being developed were to maintain, and not to design, a more competitive and efficient school. At the heart of this emerging tension was a disagreement over the fundamental premise of what St. Paul's should be. Ordeman, many trustees, and most faculty asserted their position that the School should set a student up for success, not failure—a habit of some competitive independent schools. In short, an institution that attended to the individual—both Ordeman's and the School's published philosophy—was not necessarily one that would send students to the most prominent colleges—a view which other trustees found unacceptable. Additionally, some board members had become ever more cognizant of parents' complaints about instances of weak teaching, and subsequently demanded that more drastic action be taken, advice which Ordeman heeded in part but did not act upon as swiftly as they wanted.

"The Page would like to heartily thank Mr. John T. Ordeman for his absolute support of press freedom during his tenure as headmaster. The School has become increasingly image conscious in recent years and there have always been those who have questioned the need for this type of frank, open coverage of news and free exchange of ideas."

The Page, May, 1985

Moreover, a major shift in power had changed the relationship between the trustees and the School in 1978, when the positions of chairman and the president of the board, originally both held jointly by the rector, were split. Halsey Cook now held the titular seat as chairman, and William N. Clements II '46 became the first term trustee president, followed by George Wills. The change seemed logical both in the short and long runs. But for Ordeman, the shift in power made it harder for him to get his positions heard, especially since Cook, who faced significant challenges elsewhere, had always been Ordeman's key supporter. And when Cook left altogether in 1981, Ordeman had far less insight into what was going on within the board politic, and did not have the proxy strong-arm during executive sessions to make his appeals and to defend his actions. Ordeman found himself with little protection from what became far-reaching decisions, mostly by the executive committee, which as one report later pointed out "really has no limitations on its power … You've got some verbiage that says the board can rescind anything … Well, that's like saying, the board can make any decision at any time and the board can later rescind it. Sure it can … So you sign a contract—do you go back and re-do it? Heck no."[42]

This change set the stage for a quick cascade of events that led to Ordeman's dismissal. At its center was an extremely critical review of the School in 1983 by an independent evaluator associated with the National Association of Independent Schools (NAIS). Now convinced that the School needed a new leader and approach, more compelling strategies, and mechanisms to improve quality, the executive committee of the trustees soon took quick action to solve what they felt was becoming a crisis.

Eighteen months after this report, Ordeman learned that his contract was not going to be renewed when he read a newsletter which mentioned a headmaster's position opening at St. Paul's and called to correct the mistake. A board meeting was hastily scheduled at which Ordeman was given the opportunity to resign. He quickly declined, angered by how it was handled, surprised at the decision, and upset at what

Graphic by John Baker '91

That *Page* in Time

The Monitor bore its first and only precocious child on October 15, 1976. It would begin as an insert, a page, or rather *The Page*, to provide students with more periodic news and to serve as "a voice for debate and comment on controversial matters," though not a "gripe sheet" with "destructive or derogatory purposes."

The first issue of *The Page* was in fact three pages, edited by Andrew Cohen '77 and advised by Michal Makarovich; it contained a debate between faculty member Tom Longstreth and Marcus Partlow '78 over junior off-campus privileges. Topically innocuous, the debate was still important as a precedent for a new level of journalistic freedom and credibility, and the first sign of *The Page's* thumb on the pulse of the whole School. *The Page* appeared once again that March, established with permanence by editor-in-chief Edward Weber '78, who developed a more news-oriented paper featuring sports articles, campus events, and music and film reviews. Within the year, *The Page* contained sections, by-lines, more in-depth reporting, and photography. Over the first year, it also published editorial responses from Headmaster

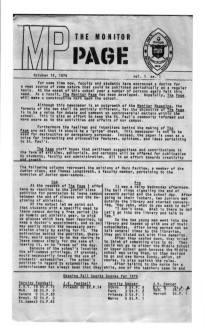

Ordeman and bold articles on topics like underage drinking, "bribery and pressure tactics" reportedly used by some students to get elected into the Student Council, and the mainstay, "Man On The Arcade," which posed a poll question to students and teachers.

From the outset, the administration supported Makarovich and *The Page* and placed an unusual trust in students' judgment to present news fairly, which would lead to the paper's long-standing, often subversive, tradition of illuminating the holes in the School's administrative policies, the truths and secrets of student life, as well as achievements of faculty and students. In 1988 the *St. Paul's Magazine* reprinted an article by Makarovich, syndicated to several national presses including *The Evening Sun,* which discussed censorship in student publications and described the trustees' support of *The Page.* With articles on abortion, homophobia, and racism, *The Page* today still administers a heavy dose of reality to those in the community who prefer to see the School as a sheltered campus on a hill.

By 1985 *The Page*, with a circulation of 1,000, had won awards for six of its first nine years. Since then, *The Page* won its highest award yet, the Pacemaker, from the National Scholastic Press Association (University of Minnesota) in 1991; the highest award from Quill and Scroll (Iowa University), the George Gallup Award; and the Medalist Award from Columbia University for being the best newspaper among the top five percent of all U.S. schools. Under the guidance of Penelope Partlow, Aerie Treska, and J. J. Cromer, the paper continued to accrue at least five major awards annually over the past five years. In total: some 150 state, regional, and national awards in 15 years.[1]

he felt was a betrayal of trust. Despite heated arguments, Ordeman refused to make the decision anything other than the board's. In perhaps his most forthright act as headmaster, he publicly announced the news to the disappointment and shock of the school community. "As the Upper School sat in chapel during assembly last year," said the lead article in *The Page* in 1985, "Headmaster John Talbot Ordeman, after all the routine business had been taken care of, rose to speak: '… the next year will be my last for me as headmaster.' As he continued on to a background of silence, there was no movement save that of a few backbenchers stirring themselves, sitting up straight to see what was going on."[43]

Ordeman agreed to stay a final year, 1984–85, his nineteenth. By that winter, tension had mounted enough to make interactions between the board president and the headmaster decidedly strained. The trustees extended their reach into the daily administration of the School and had begun to set policy without him. "In my opinion, the promise that I was made that I should have the authority of headmaster this year has been broken," wrote Ordeman, "and I hereby register my objection to actions which are in violation of the School's by-laws … I believe, furthermore, that it would be advisable, as well as courteous, at least to make the headmaster aware of the fact that an assignment of his responsibilities by the board to others was to be considered by the executive committee and to invite him to comment upon the matter, rather than to discuss the matter without his knowledge and announce to him a decision which usurps his authority as a *fait accompli.*"[44]

Many would come to say that the trustees had gone too far and executed too quickly, and that most of the events during Ordeman's last three years were ones he and they would rather forget. But in the life of a school that strives to grow stronger, regardless of whether the decisions were inappropriate or to some irresponsible, what happened was important. Boundaries had certainly been overstepped. But unlike the rest of the School, which tested each move and slowly adapted to changing times, the role of the trustees—still in fact functioning under the 1853 incorporation papers to educate poor boys—had by-laws and a relationship with the administration that had not fully accommodated a more complex, emotional, and ambitious St. Paul's School.

A NEW ERA

Ordeman's dismissal and departure rattled the School community. His successor, Robert Ward Hallett, entered into an atmosphere shadowed by a latent anger about the trustees' actions which were both remote and immediate, and which, to many, seemed sudden, inexplicable, and in that sense inappropriate. Shifts in personnel and new leadership further sensitized the community to what would become the most dominant themes for the next 15 years: change, accountability, professionalism, and rigorous coordination as an institution. Faculty, for one, missed the former camaraderie among them, a day when their dogs could roam free, when the status quo—rough around the edges, perhaps, but with substance, character, and integrity—seemed perfectly fine. And while change brought opportunity, many were comfortable—some would say too comfortable—with the way the School had been running.

As dramatic as it was, Ordeman's departure became an accepted fact over time, and many grew to believe that the School, in a much different place from 20 years before, could benefit from a new kind of leader. Hallett, a newcomer to Baltimore and to St. Paul's, arrived ready to concentrate on those issues that Ordeman often resisted—operations, fundraising, staffing—as well as to consider more systematically the School's large constituency. In general, things worked when he arrived, but much appeared disorganized and outdated. Though the School had, for instance, on aver-

Home for the Arts

Designed by James Grieves '51, who also designed the new Lower School in 1990, The Ward Center for the Arts, which opened in 1992, was named in memory of Virginia P. and William F. Ward, Sr., the parents of William F. Ward, Jr. '63, who gave $1.25 million for construction. At 29,000 square feet, The Center includes a 325-seat theater, an art gallery and reception area, painting and sculpture studios, a student publication office, and separate rooms for music and performance rehearsals.

age 170 square feet per student (a metric schools keep to assess the efficiency with which they use their facilities)—40 square feet more than the average school of its size—many classrooms were extremely cramped, particularly in the old horse stables of the Lower School. Trivial problems had piled up. The phone system was archaic; parents had become aggravated over an extended list of minor expenses; morning traffic and scheduling were nightmares; the mansion bore the atmosphere of a home, not the center of a prep school. Here was a place made up of some 850 people, whose basic character and spirit had been well cultivated, which rallied around a long history of success in sports, but which also needed improvement, in particular in the operational infrastructure, in college guidance and admissions, in its cultural offerings, and in maintaining consistent high academic standards. While St. Paul's had been competing well with its neighboring schools, it would need to be more focused—and more aggressively so—if it were going to continue to rank as one of the highest among them.

In the context of this lingering resentment about so much change, Hallett's primary strategy was to concentrate on the School's future as well as its distant past. "As one of my first jobs," he said when he began, "I wanted to unify the School in a day of celebration and spirit by looking back to our roots in Baltimore." With great effort and expense, and 20 bus-loads of students, the School launched the first "St. Paul's Day" on October 11, 1985, complete with Mayor Schaefer's proclamation, a school-wide parade downtown, and a service at Old St. Paul's, marked by an affirming cheer Hallett made official: "We Are St. Paul's!" Some people, particularly those who found these changes disconcerting, believed such activities and slogans contrived, but few had alternative ideas that could rally a community reinventing itself. St. Paul's was a place, in the minds of some of the newer administrators, that had not quite figured itself out. If "We Are St. Paul's" fell flat for some, it may have been because it somehow struck a nerve.[45]

Mostly, though, Hallett and the trustees needed a plan. The School seemed to operate with "vested interests and fiefdoms" as one 1986 report described, and "passed a life in many different directions." And while there seemed to be "strong and uniform support of a mission and a basic understanding of what the mission is," as an outside consultant claimed, "when you get down to the specifics, it's not clear." Thus, with the trustees, Hallett assembled a committee of students, faculty, alumni, and staff to chart the future, a process they completed in late 1987. In place of the personable and intuitive methods of Ordeman came a more scientific, business-oriented, and in that sense, sturdy architecture to accommodate a swelling St. Paul's in a new era of identity formation, ambition, and spirit. "Seventeen characteristics of the ideal St. Paul's School were developed and ranked by the 65 people at the Crusade for Excellence in September," Hallett wrote in 1986. "Each characteristic was examined critically by five sub-committees … with 460 solutions in these 17 areas. Of this num-

The Actor, the Businessman, and the Woodworker

In the modest suburb of Drexel Hill, west of Philadelphia, Robert W. Hallett grew up doing things. Tangible things. In fine arts (woodworking, crochet, needle point). In music (piano, *a cappella,* opera). In dance (ballet, swing). And in theater (*Guys and Dolls, Carousel*). Performer and producer, Hallett would conduct his life thinking about art (his mother was a master craftsman, her sister was an established actress), creating and executing ideas, and pitching them when necessary (his father was a traveling salesman).

In the spring of 1984, after seven months and 75 candidates, the search committee named Hallett as headmaster of St. Paul's. His experience fit: graduate of Episcopal Academy in Philadelphia and Gettysburg College; a Masters in Education from University of Pennsylvania; and two years at Wittenberg University's Hamma School of Theology. The step to St. Paul's seemed sensible to him too; as assistant headmaster and Upper School principal at Friends' Central School in Philadelphia, a K-12 Quaker school of 640, he had started its Middle School and had acted as college admissions counselor, headmaster, coach and Lower School teacher over the course of his 14 years there.

Robert Hallett at the annual pancake breakfast for young alumni, begun in 1993 and held in the mansion.

In July, 1985, at age 38, bringing with him six-year-old Timothy and four-year-old Sarah, Hallett took the helm of a school he sensed had character, caring people, and a heart, and stayed long enough to see his son graduate in 1997, to teach woodworking (his avocation), and to help celebrate the School's 150th anniversary and his 14th—an unusual number on both counts in a day when school leaders change much faster than students matriculate.

Hallett's conversion of the mansion's second floor from bedrooms to offices marked the beginning of significant change and emphasized his operational credo: the most important office was admissions, and the most important phone was at the reception desk. With that, he quickly learned the skills of a businessman; built, re-built or renovated almost everything on campus; and found new ways to raise, spend, and save money.

In an ever-daunting set of tasks—and more people to consider—Hallett continues to pray that he makes the right decisions. If he has set an anchor at St. Paul's, it is the Chapel, which he asserts without hesitation is the most important addition to the campus. And if he gets tired? He'll leave. But no one, himself included, sees any signs of the wood beginning to splinter.[1]

ber, 58 percent are perceived as solutions requiring little or no cost with immediate opportunity for implementation." While the long-range plan generally articulated seemingly obvious needs, it also revealed just how divided the School and its constituency were in prioritizing the larger projects. In terms of facilities, for instance, many saw a gym as the obvious first step; others, a facility for the arts; still others, a new Lower School.[46]

At the same time, Hallett also needed to re-staff. During the 1985-86 year alone, 12 new faculty members were hired, seven departed, and seven new trustees were elected. Although St. Paul's had many strong and dynamic teachers, the administration also had few mechanisms for evaluating performance and holding staff and instructors accountable for their work. Furthermore, while student-teacher ratios were small, well below the averages for NAIS, personnel were not being used most efficiently.[47] To help, Hallett, ably assisted by Catherine McAuliffe, appointed as a new admissions director (and three years later as assistant headmaster) Christopher Dorrance, a former colleague of his at Friends' Central, and then added a new and experienced business manager, Kirk Evans. And the three—Evans, Hallett and Dorrance, who often sat as chief administrator—defined expectations and coordinated goals and policies into a far more efficient system than before.

That the School could be treated like a business was an idea that not everyone appreciated. The gap between academic and corporate became more clearly established as Evans delegated department budgets and financial accountability and Hallett spoke in the rhetoric of finance and fundraising, molding a development team that could more systematically raise money and reach more alumni. If treating the School like a company promised financial security, and thus opportunities to make a more dynamic institution, Hallett unconditionally succeeded. After 14 years, the endowment had grown from $2 million in 1985—an impressive number in its own right—to almost $19 million in 1999; roughly 30 percent of alumni contributed only $40,000 to annual giving in 1985, a number which neared 50 percent participation and $220,000 in 1999; and gifts now represent 5.6 percent of the operating income, nearly twice what it once did. In the pool of these and other positive numbers, the headmaster's job had become one characterized by business. At the same time, in less than a decade these numbers translated to, among a series of small additions and upgrades, the construction of an arts center with the Girls' School, a free-standing chapel, a renovated Upper School, and a new athletic center.[48]

Amidst these adjustments, the community also needed reassurance that the trustees were there to support the headmaster and to govern solely in the best interest of the School and each student. With 24 term trustees in 12 committees meeting five times annually, their role was as critical as it was distanced from the everyday. "When the board meets behind closed doors," said an interview with board president Joe Burgin in the 1986 St. Paul's Magazine. "A lot more goes on than approving the operating budget." A change in the image of the board did not take long, especially under the strength of a talented board and their presidents, including Burgin; J. M. Dryden Hall, Jr. '50 (a chorister, former parent, and former trustee of both Schools); Gary DiCamillo; and the first woman to serve in the office, Lynn Homeier Rauch. Indeed, the board could take a large percentage of the credit for these successful years.[49]

ARTS FOR ARTS' SAKE

Why the conversation about building an arts center had stalled for over a decade before the symbolic golden spade broke ground in 1990 was partly because the dialogue, within and between each School, was far more about identity and complicated issues of governance than about outfitting art programs. Today, however, few can imagine how the Schools existed without what soon became The Ward Center for the Arts; what seemed like an improbable step 20 years ago appears a natural one at the turn of the millennium.

For the Boys' School, at least, advocates of an arts center in the '70s and '80s felt that the School's image still relied too heavily upon its emotional, spiritual, and half-century-old bedrock of athletics; meanwhile, opponents worried that an entire building for the arts would draw students away from playing sports, and that despite a growing enrollment, students only had so much time. Some arguments became a thin disguise, too, for a rumbling anxiety that this new emphasis would somehow make the School "artsy," a term as loaded, uninformed, and potentially destructive as the word "jock." In many ways, St. Paul's needed this decade simply to untangle misperceptions, change attitudes, and seek ways to provide a balanced education.

Certainly by the end of the '80s, with over a dozen faculty members teaching arts in the crowded space of every which corner, the need for a proper facility was no longer in question.[50] Talent and potential warranted a home. Department chair Sally Fronk and her Lower School artists; Robbin Schaffer's inspired young musicians; Jodi Beeler's Middle School art classes; Mark Wilson's handbell choirs and his structured Middle School singing program; Sue Gibbons's new Upper School humanities course; George Johnson's reinvented Upper School choral instruction; Michal Makarovich's film studies; John Thorpe and Bruce Latta's Jazz Ensemble—all were strong efforts before a center had opened. Still, a truly cohesive arts program, especially in the Upper School, was basically nonexistent.[51]

Despite the debates of whether to construct an athletic center—well-embedded in the plans and high on the list of priorities—or an arts center, the trustees had already made their choice when they hired Hallett, who had made it clear to them that the arts would become a top priority with him at the helm. As the Boys' School jostled the issue internally, building a center also required the receptive and approving ear of the Girls' School before doing anything. The campaign slogan "Two Schools: A Shared Vision" was a token phrase best illustrating, even historically, how

Bricks and Blueprints

Headmaster Robert Hallett, business manager Kirk Evans, and assistant headmaster Chris Dorrance during the construction of The Ward Center for the Arts in 1991.

the two Schools could most docilely come to terms with one another ("Shared"), and yet remain autonomous ("Two Schools"). Together they could explore the evolving, vague, yet no less central idea of the extra-curricular and the creative—as well as, of course, the benign (lunch, for example). The problem of ill-equipped cafeterias and no central place to assemble the student body was as much a problem for both Schools as the lack of a decent theater and rooms for the fine arts. Uniting resources for these expensive facilities seemed sensible enough, whereas the idea to build a combined chapel, for instance, somehow was less compelling. Perched halfway up the hill, an arts center would thus serve as a strong and functional compromise that coordinated and solidified once and for all a relationship that dated back to the founding of the Boys' School.[52]

While never easy or without obstacle, the speed at which The Center materialized was a hallmark for all that was built during the decade. The School launched the joint capital campaign for The Center in January 1990, chaired by Francis X. Knott; broke ground before a crowd of 1,000 in September; raised $5.5 million almost within a year (quickened by a $1.25 million anonymous matching gift); and opened its doors as scheduled on January 27, 1992.[53] Of course, the challenges of a joint venture in some ways began after The Center opened. With a budget based on the number of students from each School, decision-making on everything from trivial to significant issues was time-consuming and a source of strain; to help, many issues soon were relegated to the Schools' respective business managers.

Mum's the Word

For Donald Pierpont, starting the School's first Dramatics Club, "The Mummers," in 1933—with its first president Oscar Moritz '34 and first production, *Wappin' Wharf*—was probably just another early morning brainstorm of his. In the life of a small school such as St. Paul's, the longevity of individual organizations was often tied to a single leader, and such was the case with Pierpont and his Mummers; in 1942, when he entered the Navy, his ten-year, some 25-show era came to a close. The club made a few cameos in the mid-'40s and staged *Billie the Kid*, its last drama production before disbanding entirely in 1953.

Searching for space in Brooklandville, a new Dramatics Club (a.k.a. "St. Paul's Masquers") began under the direction of G. Robert Brengal, and again under Robert French, who created two productions with the Girls' School in the early '60s. But it was not until 1963, under Albert Cauffman, that the drama program would finally hold on to its costumes. Slowly, through the '70s, Cauffman produced more coed shows, directed plays like *Oliver!, Mousetrap,* and *The Wizard of Oz*, and started the annual spring musical, featuring *Man of La Mancha* in 1970. With the technical expertise of faculty members like Clifford Low '65 and often assisted by choirmaster Donald

McDorman '33 and later Rodney Hansen, plays like *Guys and Dolls* in the mid-'70s improved steadily, and joint productions fell under the guidance of Margie Farmer of SPSG. On March 9, 1984, the first faculty and staff production, *Oils Well That Ends Well*, with 63 performers and directed by Linda Knox, was successful enough that it led to a follow-up five years later called *Faculty Night Live*.

But when The Ward Center for the Arts opened in 1991 and provided facilities and seating for the two Schools, director Paul Tines took drama to a higher stage than ever. His sell-out shows—their subjects ranging from the grave (AIDS, the Holocaust) to the light (*Peter Pan*) to the classic (Shakespeare)—proved to the greater community the quantum leap students were ready to take with the arts.

TOP: (From left) Michael Furr '98, A. Hugh Williams '97, Rafael Guroian '97, Gregory Randolph '97, Joshua Freemire '97, and Colin Eagan '00 during William Shakespeare's *Midsummer Night's Dream*, The Ward Center director Paul Tines's last play and the School's first to be performed on the outside terrace of the LaMotte Gardens behind the Upper School. As an aside, the Frank LaMotte Garden was named in 1986 by the friends and colleagues of Frank LaMotte, Jr. '38. LaMotte's father served as a trustee from 1937-57.

OPPOSITE: Front and center stands Lee Ordeman '80 in the 1974 production of *Oliver!*, one of many plays Albert Cauffman directed. Science teacher Clifford Low '65 handled the sets, lighting and stage work for shows both in the Kelly Gym and later in The Center.

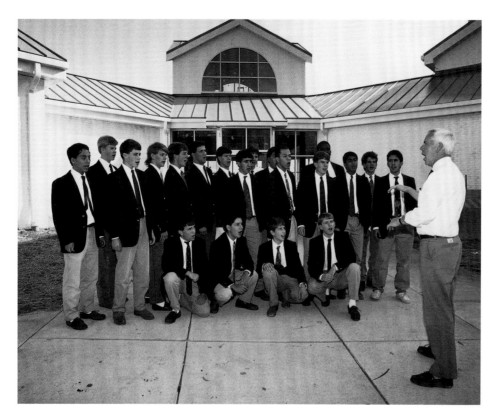

Musical Tastes

Upper School choral instructor
George Johnson directs the
St. Paul's Singers, standing here
in 1991 in the front of the newly-
constructed Ward Center. Today,
under Johnson, Mark Wilson in
the Middle School, and Robbin
D. Schaffer in the Lower School,
St. Paul's has over eight choral
groups and ensembles composed
of over 150 students. The first glee
club actually formed in 1945, with
four groups and 35 boys, under
Gatewood Segar, and later under
Donald McDorman '33 from 1948
until 1972. Two early musical
moments at St. Paul's: a jazz club
under W. C. Burris Young '51 in
1961 and the ethnic folk music
club, formed in 1962. The latter
grew from "three guitars to seven"
and became the folk-rock music
club with 27 boys, soon under
Clifford Low '65.

Together the Schools hired and paid the salary of the first director, Paul Tines, formerly the Choate-Rosemary Hall theater director and chairman. Tines would lead
The Center—immediately active with people and a packed calendar of shows—to
such success over the next five years that some even seemed wary of the growth and
the accompanying publicity. In his first year, he began a new drama club and a Summer Theater School, hosted Maryland Institute art classes, promoted exhibits, and
advertised to the greater Baltimore audience for shows and performances. In the fall
of 1997, when Tines returned to Choate, Darryl Harper became director of The Center, and Peter King joined the staff as director of drama.

As the Schools searched for common ground between their very different cultures, sometimes clashing over policy issues, scheduling, or even which shows to
produce, some would find that the joint venture actually increased the tension
between them. But few, if any, would later complain that coordination was not at its
highest, and in time these growing pains would subside. The Center, surely the riski-
est venture either School had undertaken since its move to Brooklandville, was an
experiment that no other local independent school had tried—nor any other in the
nation, for that matter—and, more importantly, was an experiment that worked. It
created a more dynamic institution, demonstrating repeatedly to skeptics a surprising
truth: MSA champions and actors in four-star drama productions could break bread
under the same roof, or even coexist in the same student.

The Other Football

"The St. Paul's boys are not allowed to enter into contests in the Rugby football games," wrote Dr. Arthur Kinsolving in 1912, a year before the School joined its first soccer league, "but they are finding the soccer foot-ball game quite as interesting and beneficial. A generous gift from Miss Marian Wyatt has provided the boys with suits and balls for this game."

Despite Kinsolving's blessed endorsement, soccer took another half century to appear in numbers on the fields of St. Paul's; in the '50s, players and coaches began to take an intermittent intramural program seriously. Eleven players soon appeared in the 1959 *Crusader*, and that year over 30 players entered at the jayvee level with five games under teachers Bill Marlow, Europhile Carel Beernink, and William Polk. By 1964, with "Little Crusies" kicking in the Middle School, jayvee became varsity and a legitimate fall alternative.

Just three years later, St. Paul's proved its athletic versatility when varsity finished with an 8-1 record under Howard A. Emsley, Jr. in 1966, and when it earned its first championship in 1970. Ten years later, under Tony Tyler '60 and Peter DiMarco, the soccer team won its second championship, particularly impressive after moving up from the 'B' to the 'A' Conference (one shy of the elite 'Double A'). Certainly the all-time scorer, striker Larry LeDoyen '81 (108 career goals), helped, tagging the only goal—and a "banana kick" at that—in the championship win over McDonogh in 1980.

Rick Canfield, Jr. followed for four years as coach with a 'B' Conference championship in 1983 against Severn. Since 1986, Howard Schindler led the varsity in the 'A' Conference for four years (1990-93) and to four championship games and two titles in the 'B' Conference. Certainly, if there has ever been a time of strong soccer, it has come recently, when Schindler and the varsity team won their second MIAA 'B' Conference championship in three years in the fall of 1997, just missing a championship victory the following year.[1]

ABOVE: Players surround Kevin Knox '86 after scoring the winning goal in an overtime game against Arlington Baptist in 1986.

On Belay!

While "phys-ed,"under the direction of Mitch Tullai and then Steven Fertig, was available in some shape or form largely as an alternative to intramurals during the Brooklandville era, St. Paul's later implemented a more structured Outdoor Education program, which uniquely emphasized character development, interpersonal skills, self-reliance, and courage. Close in concept to James Andrew's Middle School after-school "Exposure Courses," which began in 1979 and included activities in music appreciation, library skills, electronics, photography, and public speaking, the Outdoor Education officially took off in 1981 under Mitch Whiteley (who also started the popular and much-praised eighth- and tenth-grade bike trips). Over the '80s, Doug Dickey expanded the program, including "initiatives training" and monthly outings for parents, faculty, and students. By the end of the decade, the outdoors was another classroom for the Middle School, especially with a large ropes course in the nearby woods, including the climbing wall seen in this picture.

Hole in One

C. Phillip "Fairway" Bundy III '84, MSA individual golf champion in 1984 when varsity golf went 14-1-1. The sport actually managed to stay on course as a spring alternative for a short three-year stint starting in 1939, but a club would not re-emerge until 1965 under Middleton, one of his last initiatives as headmaster. The sport continued with a pocket of zealots, but finally took hold as an official varsity sport in the spring of 1983 through the leadership of Bundy, who found seven others and solicited the help of business manager Wayne Porter to be the coach; the team placed third in the MSA the following year. Porter went on to advise the team for another five years, followed by Randolph Woods. The team would not win another championship until 1994 in the 'B' Conference under Rick Collins, continuing a streak with MIAA 'B' Conference championships in the spring of 1996 and 1997. Varsity reentered the MIAA 'A' Conference in 1998, and, due to its popularity, Collins added Middle School and jayvee programs. In 1999, there were some 14 varsity members of about 50 golfers total, playing at Pine Ridge and competing at the Baltimore Country Club.

THE REIGN OF THE SAINTLY CRUSADERS

As arts took front and center, to almost unanimous delight an extraordinary era in sports had indeed emerged. Championships and winning streaks aside, some athletic records are particularly noteworthy. At St. Paul's, the string of Independent School Sportsmanship Awards was an MSA precedent, gaining its first in 1976 and five in a row beginning in 1982. In similar fashion, St. Paul's captured the first of three straight A. Paul Menton Sportsmanship Awards in 1983, which rector William McKeachie preached about at the Blue/Gold Sunday service: that St. Paul's could secure the most democratically elected of awards—and records—was something to feel proud of.[54]

And as buildings opened and enrollment grew, many more crusading Saints now populated the campus. Athletic options diversified. Tennis and baseball soon became alternatives for lacrosse; wrestling for basketball; soccer and cross-country for football. As the Upper School enrollment surged in the late '70s and '80s, the coming athletic expansion was a natural evolution formalized in a decision made by Ordeman and athletic director Mitch Tullai in 1978. Together they determined that the position of athletic director was a full-time job, especially with six varsity sports and

"The only serious conflict ever aroused by the golf club came when it was suggested that golf be made a sport at school and that a small practice course be laid out on the large hill south of the campus proper ...
All members cling to the hope, however, that from their number will issue a great hero and that golf will be vindicated and achieve its rightful status."

The Crusader, 1967

Two Faces of Lacrosse

LEFT: Robert W. Downes '81 feeling the spirit of victory. The 1980 varsity team shared an MSA 'A' Conference championship and a year later were champions. Above, another player feels the infrequent agony of defeat: after 65 years of the sport, St. Paul's has won nearly 75 percent of its games, with a cumulative record of 649-224-8.

90 percent of Upper School boys participating in athletics, more complicated Middle School scholastic schedules, a lagging Lower School physical education program, and isolated but sensitive coaching issues to manage. Tullai, who took over the Upper School admissions office and chaired the history department, ended his 25-year tenure in the position, and the first full-time athletic director, Richard Collins, took over in the fall of 1978.[55]

Besides assuming this significant and largely uncharacterized responsibility, Collins, with basketball his primary suit, faced another unusual challenge as the School questioned this single truth: St. Paul's was a lacrosse school. Through Collins's foresight, the addition of varsity cross-country (1980), baseball (1981), and golf (1983), and the increasing turnouts for soccer all potentially challenged anchors football and lacrosse, arousing sometimes hotly-argued debates about the problems of a school spreading itself too thin. Others, however, believed the School had more than one bench to warm and far more turf to cover as the alternative sports, now legitimate and competitive, became socially acceptable options.[56]

Mitch Whiteley's 1991 varsity lacrosse championship and his team's winning streak were critical evidence that neither an arts center nor other sports were going to dismantle the School's existing traditions. In fact, the 1990s were arguably equal in success—and certainly superior in range of sports—to the triumphant 1940s. A "Double Three-peat"—seven consecutive MSA varsity championships (1990-92) in basketball, and lacrosse, and five straight titles in football—either marked or were marked by The Center's opening. And championships in golf, soccer, and cross-country proved to the skeptics that alternative sports could and should have a home in the same locker room. These early victories also proved to the local athletic world that, even after the league adjustments in 1993, from a heavily competitive and unbalanced public-independent school Maryland Scholastic Association (MSA) to a newly-formed independent Maryland Interscholastic Athletic Association (MIAA), St. Paul's had competed against the big boys.[57]

Through the '90s, the Crusaders tallied even longer strings of victories in all nine sports. "Each time I'm asked why the Class of '96 has been so successful on the athletic field, I pause and search for the perfect response, but it doesn't exist," said Chris Horich '96 during his graduation speech. "My classmates and I have heard many times how remarkable it is for a school of so few students to go to six varsity championship games in one year, and bring the title home five times." Argued by some to be the "best in history," 1995-96 alone witnessed four fall MIAA 'B' Conference championships (jayvee and varsity soccer, and jayvee and varsity football), seven total by year's end (just missing an eighth in the lacrosse finals), and a continued unbroken football record and championship in the fall of 1996.[58]

Thus, the time had come for a new athletic center. When the School announced the $10 million capital campaign, co-chaired by Andie and Jack Laporte, in the fall of 1998, nearly half had already been raised by fewer than 100 people, most of whom were parents. The sesquicentennial anniversary was as good a reason as any to celebrate and to solidify funding for the next—and most obvious—addition to the School. Built as an extension to the Kinsolving Gym, whose paint had been chipping and insides gutted and replaced several times, the Athletic Center would be one of the largest of any school in the Baltimore area. With the existing space, it would accommodate three simultaneous basketball games and two wrestling meets; two batting cages; a 13,000-square-foot performance space; a fitness center; and new training and weight rooms. Hallett, the trustees, and the School broke ground on May 22, 1998, some 60 years after the construction of the first Kinsolving Gym at Mt. Washington, and over 40 years since the second at Brooklandville.

Ye Olde Dewey Decimal
Laura Taber using a now-obsolete card catalog before the Lower School library became fully automated in 1991 after the Lower School fire.

THE WORLD VIEW

As with his emphasis on the arts, Hallett would become recognized for a new focus on internationalism—interesting since he had never been overseas until taking a year-long sabbatical to live and study in England shortly before he arrived as headmaster. Part of the new emphasis on the world and culture began in 1977 with faculty member Dr. William Durden, who became a spokesperson for the growing anxiety that America needed to educate its students in a global context. "A tremendous talent shortage is in the making," he wrote in the *St. Paul's Magazine*, "and dramatically underscoring the situation are the results of a United Nations survey of what students in nine countries know about foreign cultures. The U.S. comes next to last."

It went without saying that St. Paul's always had a strong background in Latin, French, Spanish, and later German, and for years it had hosted people from other countries and refining its foreign language curriculum under teachers like Angelo Gentile, Woodruff Marston, and European native Carel Beernink, who headed the department for 21 years and who opened up the first language lab in 1962. In the early '80s, Margot Reiling, the first woman to head either a Middle or Upper School department, took a significant step in defining the relationship between learning languages and understanding culture: she argued for an increased attention to the language curriculum specifically, and to cultural awareness generally, spanning kindergarten through twelfth in a more seamless design.[59]

Across Country

Christopher A. Johnston '95.

A 1.5-mile spring stride at Mt. Washington was the cross-country alternative in the mid-'30s and intermittently through the '40s, but it was coach C. Wilfred Heller who was the grandfather of cross-country and brought it officially to the School in 1952. Heller's team, who had "finally won the battle" to keep the sport as a spring option, dominated the late '50s after the harriers first competed as a MSA varsity sport in 1954, and jumped from a dozen runners to nearly 40. The sport was soon orphaned for the next two decades once Heller left in 1959. If he was the sport's grandfather, marathoner Desi McNelis was its father, inheriting a small jayvee team under Bill Bassett and William Anthony in 1979. Once McNelis took the team, the jayvee won five straight 'B' Conference championships (1983-87) and one in the 'A' Conference in 1989 while varsity won championships in 1983 and then three straight (1985-87). Since 1988, the team has remained in the 'A' Conference with eight competing teams, garnering one of its best seasons in 1997 and earning a jayvee state championship a year later.

Hallett reinforced these efforts by introducing topics of internationalism into faculty discussions and by featuring them prominently in the School's publications. The matriculation of Taiwanese violinists Du Ming-Shi '91 and Yu Tao-Chang '91, who both joined the student body through a partnership with the Peabody Conservatory; third-grader Sheila Ravendhran in native Indian dress performing for Human Rights Day; the meteoric rise of the Model United Nations Club in the '90s under John Patterson, an influential advocate of increasing global awareness; and the brief appearance of a director of international studies—all shaped the effort and broadened students' exposure to, and definition of, culture and internationalism.[60]

In 1989, an unusual exchange program with Japan, spawned in part by Hallett, William Durden, and lacrosse, would become an integral component of the foreign language program over eight years, as well as an important, decidedly non-Western addition. Innovative and publicly admired, the exchange also activated an internal debate about how the School should teach languages. A school-wide approach in teaching either Spanish or Japanese stabilized the program as German, Latin, and French would appear, disappear, and reappear through the '90s. Nevertheless, Dr. Elke Durden, who became chair of the department upon Reiling's retirement in 1996, found through surveys that the School's offerings exceeded most other Baltimore schools. With languages integrated in other parts of the curriculum, and with regular student exchanges in France, Germany, and Spain as well as numerous teacher exchanges with Japan, St. Paul's could now legitimately point to its foreign language program as an entry point for students into an international world.[61]

IN SEARCH OF DIVERSITY

The focus on internationalism was perhaps implicitly inspired by a tireless reminder of homogeneity at St. Paul's and by a similarly tireless effort to improve it over the course of the '80s and '90s. Since the first black student arrived in 1966, minority enrollment at St. Paul's was often among the lowest compared to area private schools. In 1978, for instance, just 2.5 percent of the enrollment was listed as belonging to a minority group, compared to other independent schools, which hovered around ten percent. "Our goal is to be able to claim that we have an integrated school," Jack Ordeman said that year. Students in *The Page* noted that the problem stemmed from the School's location and its all-white image, reasons which did "not include prejudice." Successful black students like brothers Kevin '76 and Kermit Billups '79 (the School's first black student council president), both of whom received the prestigious Kinsolving Fellowship Award, gave the School more confidence, and their father, a prominent black trustee, provided a strong voice. Nevertheless, significant improvement in minority enrollment required focus and time, a fact equally true for both NAIS and AIMS. In its 1980 newsletter discussing enrollment trends, for instance, NAIS categorized minorities as a "new market," a group "historically neglected as potential providers of large numbers of applicants." That year, roughly 13 percent of the total enrollment among 900 NAIS-affiliated schools was classified as belonging to a minority; this number was only slightly above the 11 percent of total enrollment reported by AIMS-affiliated schools.[62]

Through the '80s, the School tried targeted efforts to increase diversity, such as hiring a part-time director of minority recruitment, Beulah Maxwell; joining the Baltimore Project for Black Students (a coalition of 12 area independent schools); and offering minorities scholarships, some funded through grants.[63] At the policy level, the School recognized that enrolling more minority students would not happen by accident or without added expense, and that students of color would be more successful if they began in the Lower School. Organizations, all-school conferences, and discussions ensued. Students formed the Black Awareness Club and later the Multicultural

Awareness Club to include Hispanic, Asian, and Muslim students. And the first annual Race Relations Summit of all area independent schools took place in 1992. One significant hurdle in recruiting minority students at St. Paul's was purely a result of its suburban location; in 1985, the School had one privately-owned bus for about a dozen students, and not until the early '90s was public transportation to the area even available from the city.

Nevertheless, at St. Paul's, integration was still only a single generation old, and the School endured unfortunate, but nonetheless periodic, incidents of racism and anti-Semitism, long a struggle: "Seven hundred students and 120 employees bring a variety of prejudices with them," wrote Ordeman in the early '80s. "St. Paul's, as a Christian school, must accept the obligation to help members of the community recognize the worth and dignity of every person, judging him on his own merits, and not pre-judging him on the basis of his membership in what is seen as a particular class or group or community of people." No doubt, students of color often faced cultural adjustments, social pressures, and stereotypes that their peers did not. Generalized assumptions of some students and faculty that all black students received financial aid, as one example, were common but wrong, and tacitly prejudiced.[64]

The challenge of increasing diversity, however, still mostly has to do with defini-

Come Labor On

Upper School teacher Kent W. "Skip" Darrell '60 conferring with a city resident about rehabbing a house on North Avenue, part of a project for the People's Homesteading Group. Darrell helped institute a 40-hour community service graduation requirement for all Upper School students in 1985, which inspired such efforts as the Green Grass tutoring program for underprivileged children, begun by the Class of 1989, and set the foundation for the Coldstream Project, a month-long summer program for over 60 young students coming from five urban schools, begun by Judd Anderson in 1992.

Konichiwa

The first appearance of Gakushuin—or Japanese for that matter—at St. Paul's was during trustee Dr. William Durden's trip to Japan in 1989, a year before the Crusaders became one of the first high schools to play lacrosse in Japan during the first International Friendship Games. But the idea for a possible exchange with Gakushuin, a school and university founded for the royal family in Tokyo (emblem above), did not occur until headmaster Robert Hallett, John Thorpe, and Bill Bassett went in 1990, prompting a Japanese course piloted by native speaker Kimiko Lupfer for a small group of pre-firsters and seniors. By 1991, St. Paul's was hosting a summer lacrosse camp for 40 Japanese students, though ultimately the curricular bond with Japan outlasted its athletic one, as faculty member John Patterson took charge of the exchange from 1991-95, and as Japanese educators visited St. Paul's to study its Western approach to educating. By 1995, the study of Japanese spanned the gap between the Upper and Lower Schools, a curriculum developed by Carolynn Bell, and teacher hosting programs continued as St. Paul's joined 50 other schools in the Japanese Exchange Program (JALEX).

tion. If diversity referred to a range of attitudes, skills, and interests, then the School had in fact broadened itself by orders of magnitude; St. Paul's was a place now flourishing in the fine arts, publications, clubs, music, and drama. If diversity referred to a range in social class or income, the School had made substantial progress, allocating more money to more students; while parents on the whole were wealthier, "one group receiving more and more of our concern," said admissions director Randolph Woods in 1989, "is the middle income family."[65] If diversity referred to a range of religious faiths, the School no longer collected the data or felt it compelling or appropriate to ask the question; that there were Jewish and Muslim members on the student vestry seemed evidence enough.

If diversity referred to a range of racial and ethnic groups, the School had slowly and with great effort improved at a steady rate. In 1987, 8.6 percent of the enrollment (50.7 percent of these students African American) were listed as minorities, whereas ten years later in 1998-99, this number had risen to 11 percent or 93 students (50.5 percent African American). After the School hired the first black faculty member in

A School in Flames

In the cold, wet and windy daybreak of January 30, 1990, a six-alarm fire enveloped the Lower School and what were once stables, and in under four hours had gutted most of its interior. Saddened faculty and students, dumbfounded administrators, trustees, and the curious watched 100 firefighters finally bring it under control.

No history is without its tragedy, but this event—though tragic enough—seemed too fortunate to be anything less than the quick, powerful hand of God; fortunate because of its timing, and powerful in how it unified. Insurance covered the entire building, an estimated $1 million in damage; no one was injured; many important records were saved; and the library, a newly-renovated chapel, and the multi-purpose room were partially spared. Even the astonishing swiftness with which the community rallied and headmaster Robert Hallett, board president J. M. Dryden Hall, Jr. '50, and Lower School principal Barbara Mills handled the tragedy seemed in part due to divine guidance. "In our own microcosmic way," said Hallett, "we've gone through our own Hurricane Hugo." On the front lawn of Brooklandwood, which a century before had seen summer parties for the steeplechase, 12 office trailers were erected in just over a week to house the entire Lower School.

Ten months later, a 350-pound bell—tuned to the note of E—was lowered into the central tower, a prelude to the November 26 dedication of a new Lower School in front of a crowd of 1,500. Under the leadership and hard work of trustees like Kim Strutt '67, John Wilson, Jr. '64, and Spaulding Goetze, the new building—fully equipped and architecturally beautiful—had in its stock the long wish list that teachers had shelved for years. And as the grief passed, most would soon say that it was a miracle, a symbolic emblem of recovery, and perhaps a gift disguised in a tragedy. It was, in more than one way, providential.[1]

T·H·E P·A·G·E

St. Paul's School   Brooklandville, Md. 21022   Thursday, February 8, 1990   Vol. 14, No. 5

"The light was the life of men... and the light shines in the darkness; and the darkness grasped it not."

see page 12 for related article

John 1: 4-5

Firefighters tackle a six-alarm blaze that ravaged the Lower School on January 30, causing an estimated $1,000,000 of damage.

TOP: The gutted Lower School, though the fire partially spared the Chapel, the multi-purpose room, and a few classrooms. In the background is the Upper School.

BOTTOM: On the Brooklandville lawn rose a near-instant home for the Lower School. Despite many offers to locate temporarily in area schools and churches, Lower School faculty and the administration insisted they stay on campus together.

1982, through the '80s it employed on average about two full-time teachers who were listed as minorities; by 1998 this number had risen to eight. In truth, while the 1993 AIMS evaluation pointed to the School's numbers in this area as a weakness, independent schools overall were not significantly more diverse. In 1994, AIMS reported that 15.7 percent of all independent school students fell into minority groups, compared to Baltimore County public schools (26.1 percent) and, by heavy contrast, Baltimore City schools (82.9 percent).[66]

No matter how diversity is defined, nothing could really improve until attention turned to where the issue truly arose: the admissions office. Enrolling the right students has always been a sensitive issue, as constituents often placed new kinds of pressures and unwarranted expectations on admissions officers to have their children admitted. Centralizing the office and its systems in the mid-'80s under Chris Dorrance improved the rigor and rationality with which the School could make informed decisions about whom to enroll, how to provide for them, and how best to ensure their success. The new 1991 mission statement also helped provide a framework with which to base these decisions in the School's search for "bright, determined, curious, and motivated" students who would "buy into the mission of the School," have "their character developed," and be good decision-makers when they left.

On the whole, as the School improved, expanded, and became more competitive over the course of 20 years, selecting students who were the right fit for St. Paul's was ever tougher, more emotional, and intellectually vexing. Consider that in the 1991-92 academic year, the office (now under the direction of George L. Mitchell, Jr. '78) fielded 1173 inquiries and 479 applications and handed out 287 acceptance letters. In 1997–

"At St. Paul's School, the headmaster oversees a $9.5

million institution that has 150 employees, 800 students,

64 acres of prime real estate, eight school buildings, 11

faculty homes, a physical plant valued at just over

$10 million and a $10 million investment portfolio.

In addition, the head needs to be keenly aware that the

School's constituency extends beyond its students, parents,

faculty, and alumni. The School shares special ties with

Old St. Paul's Church, the St. Paul's Choir of Men

and Boys, and St. Paul's School for Girls."

Chris Dorrance in 1995, while serving as acting headmaster

98, it fielded about the same volume (1119 inquiries, 498 applications) but accepted significantly fewer students, 221. Moreover, in 1991-92, of those students who were accepted, 50 percent chose St. Paul's; by 1997-98, this number had steadily climbed to 60 percent, as high as 67 percent in the Upper School (where it generally remained higher than the other divisions). Finally, while fourth and eighth grades were ideal moments for parents to transition their children to other schools, at St. Paul's attrition fell and its enrollment swelled. In short, over the course of the late '80s and '90s, admission had become more selective and the School more attractive to those students deciding among several schools.

Financial aid was, by necessity, tied to admissions, and therefore to diversity. The 1986 long-range plan included improving financial aid as a priority, for the School was well aware of its weakness in the area, especially when it gauged itself against reports provided by NAIS, AIMS, and the Baltimore Educational Scholarship Trust (BEST). Additionally, St. Paul's had few strategies and organized policies about how this issue should be handled. An arbitrary cap, as one example, limited the total amount given to one student to half the tuition, an exclusive measure for parents who simply could not afford the balance. Over time, the system improved. In ten years, beginning with the 1988-89 academic year, 14 percent of the student body receiving financial aid jumped to about 20 percent. Additionally, $330,000 in aid climbed to $920,000, a figure based on a fixed 10 percent of net tuition revenue (a policy established in 1992), with 25 percent coming from restricted endowment funds; the caps in aid were also eliminated.[67] With a comparable tuition of about $12,000, St. Paul's had become competitive with area schools in terms of its financial aid budget, slightly less than Gilman and McDonogh, but higher than that of Boys' Latin. St. Paul's continues its policy of giving to more students (22 percent of the student body, compared to an AIMS average of 18.9 percent in 1996) but slightly smaller amounts (about $4,400, compared to an average of $5,612), and remained true to the unusual program of giving aid to Lower School students, a potential 13-year expense. Additionally, St. Paul's made a somewhat risky—now enviable—move to create a single fee for tuition, a schedule which in most schools grew incrementally each grade and which had been in place at St. Paul's for about 50 years.

Armed with more experience, and ever cognizant of its imperative both to educate itself and to make the School a more diverse place, St. Paul's has in these past 20 years proven at the very least an earnest interest in rising to and meeting what continues to be the very real challenge of ensuring meaningful diversity.

Forty-Love

Although Louis Clark would forever be memorialized as a tennis aficionado, headmaster Appy Middleton took the first group of tennis players to task in 1946, helped by a second clay tennis court added in the spring of 1947. The move to Brooklandville stalled things until 1954, when students complained for better courts, a wish granted by 1960. National tournament contender Farnham Warriner was the swing behind the racquet for the tennis team beginning in 1955, with an undefeated record in 1957. Poor facilities, however, detained its varsity status, but it finally debuted in the MSA 'A' Conference in 1972 with singles champion Braxton D. Mitchell, Jr. '74. Tennis courts ultimately came out of Jack Ordeman's proposed sports complex, and in 1982, the School negotiated use of courts with the Homeland Racquet Club, an independent entity. The 1984 construction of 12 additional courts launched the program as a definitive member of the athletic program; in 1986, the team won its first and only MSA championship. Pictured here is Middle School faculty member Alexander Trivas '92 while a varsity player in 1992.

SEX, DRUGS, AND ROCK 'N ROLL

One cannot forget that the School's primarily suburban students operated within a media-rich, morally ambiguous, and trend-crazed society. The bold and unprecedented move in 1986 to add the School's first full-time on-campus psychologist for all three divisions, Rosemary Hanley, was the clearest indication that life was not getting any simpler.[68] As the threat of drugs, sex, and alcohol persisted—popularized and exculpated by weeknight sitcoms and by provocative movies—St. Paul's struggled to define its educational responsibilities in teaching morals and ethics. Life skills and values courses added to the curriculum in the mid-'80s were one of many such tactics, as were actions by the Parents' Club and others to support programs like alcohol and drug education. But substance abuse, escalated by the periodic and tragic instances of teenage drunk driving, was but one of many brutal reminders of the students' and community's vulnerability.

The School shared the challenges of an era occupied by topics of homosexuality, teenage pregnancy, and AIDS. "In this age of two working parents, single parents, latchkey children, 'the hurried child,'" wrote Upper School head Chris Dorrance to parents in 1999, "today's teenager feels the angst we did, but the rules are less clear and the opportunities (stakes) are much greater."[69] While drugs and alcohol had always been a looming menace, in the '90s St. Paul's had become a smart and highly visible school, a place of heightened peer pressure and competition. More kids, from more affluent families overall and with diamond-sharp social acumen, paid closer attention to the future, to college and personal achievement, to acceptance. Parents demanded more from the administration and teachers; students arrived at School earlier and stayed later, worked through weekends, practiced longer, played in games with apparently higher stakes, considered positions on more prestigious recreation league teams; and coaches endured the double-edged sword to make sports fun but never to lose. The School witnessed its unfortunate share of loneliness, anger, and even the tragic affair of suicide.

While in the Lower School an integrated values program existed, in the Upper School the advent of the health and wellness committee, the respect committee, supervised by Dr. Rich Krohn, or the peer leadership program, advised by Bill Bassett and begun by seniors Ryan P. Hanley '92 and Todd M. Simkin '92, were indications of a school attending to these needs. With the encouragement of Middle School principal Alexander Harvey IV '72, teachers Michael Schuler '76 and Rick Brocato revamped the Middle School advisor system in 1988 to work more systematically with younger students on a range of such topics as social skills, single-parent homes, and prejudice. Parent-student roundtable discussions on drugs, sex, and alcohol became a necessary step for eighth-graders growing up. And in recent years, Judd Anderson, with initiatives like the leadership council, and James Andrew, who designed entire curriculum on these issues for the Middle School, became critical advocates for students and for designing programs to provide stability and help.[70]

Shaping this landscape was the fact that the School was within eyesight and earshot of many more people than in the past, not only with student publications like *The Page*, but with its own magazines and newsletters, which came in their highest quality with the *St. Paul's Magazine* in 1986 under the future director of development Joan Abelson. Sharper and more beautiful than ever, these publications set a high standard for how the School was to be portrayed, offsetting a reality which was never so calm, clever, and organized. But the School used these publications as a vehicle to increase pride and to change image, to fundraise, and to relay news through a maze of communication channels which included Old St. Paul's, the Girls' School, and later The Center. Nor were publications exclusively for the constituents: hiring the best teachers and staff meant attracting them to St. Paul's, to the idea and its spirit, to a strong, progressive place where one could have an impact.[71]

A Place to Worship

These and other pressures—this hurried pace of life—all signaled to Hallett and the trustees that St. Paul's lacked a true center of spiritual stability and, specifically, that the School's religious faith had nowhere to ground. But how to address this dimension was neither obvious nor easy. Other than a quick weekly chapel service and the community-oriented activities of the student vestry, the role and presence of the Church had long been neglected in the life of students in the '70s and '80s. Efforts had been made, however. Chaplain Herman diBrandi and his successor, a key advisor and outspoken proponent of a renewed church connection later, the Reverend Frank Strasburger, furthered the School's religious instruction. Both Ordeman, himself a loyal Old St. Paul's parishioner, and the rector, Halsey Cook, who championed the "Greater St. Paul's Community," tried with mixed success to reinforce the relationship and its importance.[72]

More often than not, though, the commitment to and from the Church was verbal and conceptual, and rarely central to the School's daily life. Single events stand out, perhaps, such as the 125th anniversary celebration in 1974, when the School traveled down to Old St. Paul's, or the first All-School Ascension Day service in the Kinsolving Gym in 1979, both of which had meaningful intention but were unfortunately short-lived. While rector William McKeachie, Cook's successor, would later spark new life into the relationship, and loved the School as did every other rector, he arrived in 1983 with his own work cut out for him rebuilding the Church's congregation, image, and constituency base. McKeachie found the Episcopal Diocese and the order as a whole weakened in numbers and flighty in conviction. His role in the Baltimore Declaration, a document which argued for a closer reading of the Scriptures and a more conservative approach to worship and doctrine, was part of his extended effort to assert that the Church hold more firmly to its beliefs and policies. And, lastly, McK-

eachie only had so much influence as chairman of a board now composed of few regular parishioners and who, as a group, were not going to make quick commitments either financially or on the policy level. In sum, he and the Parish were not well-positioned to strengthen the church-school connection.[73]

The argument for being a church school was in many ways so fragmented by the early '80s that the very rationale almost had to begin from a *tabula rasa*. "It may come as a surprise to some," said Strasburger on the topic in 1987, "that as a former chaplain of the School, I particularly welcomed scrutiny of the status of St. Paul's as a church school. I have long felt that there is no reason for St. Paul's to be a church school simply because it has always been one." Truth be told, building a free-standing chapel was the easiest item to bury in the extensive 1987 long-range plan, especially with a facility in the Lower School. Some people also grew uncomfortable when religion and the School's Episcopal heritage entered into admissions conversations and publicity material. Nevertheless, while most schools across the nation had either de-emphasized or eliminated their religious affiliations, many at St. Paul's, especially Hallett, felt compelled to do otherwise. St. Paul's School, he and others asserted, could in fact strengthen its Episcopal and Christian grounding in a non-exclusionary way by focusing on the fundamental virtues it promised: namely, an education that valued questioning and affirming one's faith and understanding the relevance of religion in society. In Strasburger's words, the School could "remain sufficiently broad to inspire all, while remaining sufficiently particular to retain the inspiration."[74]

McKeachie, Hallett, the trustees, and many of the faculty spent the latter half of the '80s and early '90s defining the role of the Church. The era as a whole—locally and generally—biased this process. A larger, more complex, and to some, morally vapid world compelled parents to look much more carefully beyond the pure acade-

Spiritual Center

The School's first free-standing Chapel, consecrated in April 1997, seats 340. Built in Neo-Georgian architecture with a medieval-style interior, collegiate seating, a green-slate roof, and a cross-topped cupola, the Chapel features the names of all alumni, headmasters, and rectors, inscribed on panels on the wainscoting. Names of alumni who died in war are etched in marble memorial plaques flanking the altar, and a stained-glass window of the emblem behind the altar, donated by trustee Spaulding Goetze, symbolizes the spiritual anchor for the School. The rendition pictured above was drawn by Jason Owen Robertson '00.

mic curriculum and to the teaching of ethics and values. That St. Paul's was Episcopal meant that it could offer something other schools could not: a vehicle to confront sensitive and difficult issues of spirituality. St. Paul's could uniquely foster this ethos, indescribable and to many wonderfully unquantifiable. Being an Episcopal school was indeed an asset.[75]

Two critical events shaped the entire conversation and fueled a call to action in the span of just over a year: the Lower School building fell to a devastating fire in January 1990, and the mission statement, which placed the Church and its faith at the top of its list, was rewritten in 1991 under the direction of trustees Dr. William Durden and Capt. John Nicholas Brown (USN Ret.), grandson of the late Dr. Arthur Kinsolving. Whether the latter (a new mission statement with an Episcopal center) and its manifestation (a free-standing chapel) would have happened without the former (the fire) is difficult to say. Not only did the fire lead to a remarkable and inspirational display of community, but also it consigned the spiritual future of the School. Under the guiding hands of trustees like Kim Strutt '67, Spaulding Goetze, John W. Wilson, Jr. '64, and particularly J. M. Dryden Hall, Jr. '50, a commitment to a free-standing chapel was now both possible and obvious.[76]

But strengthening the Episcopal tradition was not instantaneous. Since the fire had greatly damaged the newly-renovated Helen Linthicum Chapel, weekly services moved to the Lower School multi-purpose room, a location that served as gym, theater, assembly room, and cafeteria, perfumed by the scents of cleaning agents and athletic gear. The informal setting and a progressive breed of chapel services then run by Judd Anderson prompted praise by those—mostly students—who felt that spirituality was more accessible when it had little liturgy and structure, and plenty of music, humor, and open discussion, but also serious criticism by others who felt that the services were abandoning the Episcopalian ritual and threatening this rejuvenated interest in the religious component of the School's mission. The debate, perhaps, was a modern private school version of the High Church/Low Church tension. And, ultimately, the High Church would win.

While the Lower School had an active chapel committee, headed by Ricka Peterson, as well as a strong religious program, the School as a whole first needed a more centered approach. After a series of failures to fill the chaplaincy role in the '80s, St. Paul's finally selected the Reverend Donald Roberts in 1991 who arrived feeling that the School had lost a church presence almost entirely. The chapel services, which had moved to The Center, were often hard to distinguish from assemblies.[77]

A free-standing chapel thus remained a priority to physically embody and solidify this linkage between school and church. Even five years after the fire, support from the trustees was strong; in fact, of their two main spending goals in 1995—a technology upgrade and the Chapel—authorizing the expenditure of $200,000 for a state-of-the-art computer network required as much debate and time as did autho-

The Heart of St. Paul's

Without doubt, the life of a school is its faculty. The men and women who have for 150 years taught, worried, planned, coached, mentored, and otherwise arrived on time—through days that run like educational clockwork and other days that seem to run backwards—are the makers of this School's history. They are the ones who leave chalk dust on the blackboard, who fill cleats with mud, who bring art, music, history, literature, lan- guages, and mathematics to life again and again. Each year, each day, they must start over, testing, adding, revising, learning, building trust, and shaping character. Of course, for any good school this all holds true. But one unique quality of the St. Paul's faculty has been the diverse mix of people who share a common goal about educating the individual. This page is a tribute not only to those here, but *to all* who have been a part of the School, who have marked it and the students in some timeless way.

JAMES ANDREW
Middle School
(1966-)

JOY WHITELEY
Lower School (1970-1996)
MICHAEL RENTKO
Middle School (1955-96)

ARLENE BERKOW
Middle School
(1975-97)

JUDD ANDERSON
Upper School
(1988-)

CAREL BEERNINK
Upper School
(1956-77)

JEANNE SHREEVE
Lower School
(1960-84)

WILLIAM S. POLK, JR.
Middle School
(1961-76)

CHARLES "DADDY EM" EMIG
Price Manual Arts Center
(1972-80)

BILL BASSETT
Upper School (1974-)
PENELOPE PARTLOW
Head Librarian (1971-98)

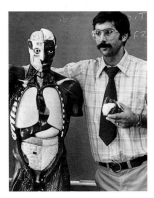

HOWARD SCHINDLER
Upper School
(1976-)

MARGOT REILING
Upper School
(1965-94)

SAMUEL WILLIAMS
Upper School
(1957-85)

MITCH WHITELEY
Upper School
(1981-)

CAROL PIEPER
Lower School Librarian
(1967-86)

CLIFFORD LOW '65
Upper School
(1969-)

JOHN THORPE
Upper School
(1983-)

FARNHAM WARRINER
Middle School
(1956-85)

BARBARA TROTTER
Lower School
(1954-82)

rizing the construction of a chapel with a price more than ten times that. Soon, the campaign began; fund-raising literature, with the theme "Building on Faith and Tradition," leveraged the School's early history and promised a "focal point of spiritual growth and moral strength." In a critical moment of support, McKeachie demonstrated the Church's commitment when he used the tercentennial celebration of Old St. Paul's in 1992 to direct the interest of $500,000 of the Church's endowment to support the newly-envisioned chapel, "connecting us ever more deeply," he said, "with the educational and spiritual needs of young people now and in the future." Under the leadership of trustee Rick Rockwell, by August 1995 the School had quietly raised $2.4 million of its $2.5 million goal, aided by a $500,000 gift from a single trustee and another of the same amount by bequest.[78]

And so, on a rainy but no less significant November 1, All Saints' Day, in 1995, the trustees laid the cornerstone, a ceremony presided over by the new Episcopal Bishop of Maryland, the Right Reverend Robert W. Ihloff. McKeachie's speech that day, making reference to the first enrolled Jewish student, James H. Tuvin '52, set the tone for a building and an idea that would soon receive almost unanimous praise. "The Chapel," McKeachie said, "should reflect all that is best in the Christian and St. Paul's tradition, even as it opens its doors to the greater number of those who, as students today, enable St. Paul's School to affirm its own heritage and honor the diversity within the School's now much-expanded constituency … The Chapel will honor the God who creates and who redeems out of love by upholding the Two Great Commandments of the heritage shared by the vast majority of our School families (and applicable to all)—that we should love God and love one's neighbor as oneself. We shall look across the central aisle of our 'collegiate' Chapel and discover who we are in face-to-face relationship with one another." Such claims found a reality. "I am Jewish, and I attend St. Paul's School," opened an article by student vestry member Ben Roman '97 in the *St. Paul's Magazine*. "Contrary to what some might believe, I have been subjected to very few situations in our predominantly Christian school where I have felt uncomfortable with my religion."[79]

The Chapel would in fact surpass most expectations of what it could do to steer the School. While Hallett and the trustees would continue to monitor a potential backlash from accusations that they were promoting the Christian faith too strongly, few ever objected. A true moment of significance was the memorial service for beloved Jewish teacher, Arlene Berkow, held not in a temple, but in the Chapel, a request she had earlier made. The Chapel did indeed serve as the center of campus and as a long-needed place of worship and introspection. With a new rector, the Reverend David Cobb; a new chaplain, the Reverend Michael Wallens; the Lower School chaplain, the Reverend Beverly Braine; and a new choirmaster, Daniel Fortune, St. Paul's now has an almost entirely re-staffed church connection and a solid base from which to grow stronger.[80]

Michael Watson '93, a key guard for the two back-to-back championship 'B' Conference varsity teams (1990-92).

TEACHING AND LEARNING

Jack Ordeman had concluded his tenure in 1985 having significantly improved academics, including honors and advanced placement courses, progressive Lower School curricula, greater coordination with the Girls' School, and a strong library system under Penelope Partlow, Carol Pieper, and Linda Knox. But the School's educational program still needed work. That a 100-plus faculty might agree on a set of methodologies, on criteria for success, or on a single curriculum was in many respects incongruous with the School's central objective—almost unconditionally understood—of adapting to an individual student's needs. Thus, efforts to streamline the educational program and raise standards potentially jeopardized what made St. Paul's unique.

As the School swung into the '80s, its size and growth had splintered much of the former unity. To make coordination of goals more challenging, the faculty in the '70s and '80s was a combination of new teachers with fresh—in some cases bold—ideas, who also had a high turnover, and legacy faculty members who had centered themselves around what some believed were antiquated practices of administering, teaching, and working together. As disagreements mounted, little was resolved. When Sam Williams left as Upper School head in 1982, Bill Bassett, who brought new approaches to personnel management, spearheaded an effort to ease a growing tension in the Upper School where this disagreement was most prevalent. Challenging presumed notions about how the Upper School might run, Bassett faced a daunting task, caught between those who had served the School well for years and those who insisted on change. In one early attempt to address the situation, Bassett invited faculty to take the Myers-Briggs personality test, a meeting which many claim was a turning point for the Upper School. Over time, these and other attempts to cultivate group consensus provided teachers with a process by which they could resolve conflict, voice their opinions, and better understand other perspectives.

A self-study chaired by John Thorpe, an integral part of the 1993 AIMS accreditation process, also brought faculty to a higher level of introspection and unity about its purpose and academic goals. Organizing the entire educational effort, most agreed, had become too complex a task to be handled informally. As department chairs enjoyed greater authority, Thorpe became the first academic dean in 1995, charged with coordinating the curriculum in all disciplines and among the three divisions, and Bassett now focused exclusively on faculty development and on hiring teachers in a more systematic way. These changes, and the creation of a school-wide academic council to help track the scope and sequence of its offerings, helped the School fine-tune its educational system and better anticipate problems.

While traditional courses in English and history expanded in content and scope, over the course of several decades the science and math programs were substantially overhauled. Mary Pfrommer, Howard Schindler, Bassett, and Cliff Low '65 all explored new combinations of traditional lectures and inquiry-based techniques in science, especially with the addition of better labs and equipment in the '80s. Soon, teachers like Ed Brady, who explored DNA sequencing in partnership with the Human Genome Project, and Schindler, who led packed national conferences on integrating forensic science into the study of biology, were increasingly bringing the real world into the classroom.

As the concept of interdisciplinary learning became more palatable in the late '80s and '90s, math and science proved easiest to interconnect. Teachers like James Andrew in the Middle School readily adapted problem solving and critical thinking into the classroom, and mathematics faculty like Bruce Latta and Penny Forbes Witter in the Lower School, with Brady in science, institutionalized concepts of technology-based curricula, students teaching students, and project-based work. Like the School itself, math and science stressed the process and the approach, not the answer.

Progressively minded, the Lower School was wholly interdisciplinary. Lower School principal Barbara Mills continued with yearly themes that molded a broad curriculum around such topics as flight, architecture, and the Olympics. Teachers like Lenora Olsen, Anne Carroll, Ellen Uhlfelder, and Jennifer O'Hearn used sophisticated strategies for teaching the humanities, social studies, language arts, and mathematics, focusing on the needs of each student and creating teaching models for other schools to follow.

Even with these improvements, the measures of learning—to the chagrin of most educators—have of course been more often than not associated with numbers. And the '90s have become even more a decade of statistics, metrics, and quantification. For students, this has meant academic awards, athletic trophies, and titles; for faculty, scores and professional recognition; for the administration, enrollment, admissions, and fundraising. St. Paul's was and is both a victim and proponent of the elusive game of numbers around which key decisions are made.

The college placement list, for one, has become a predominant measure of accomplishment. As tuition keeps climbing, parents keep expecting more from faculty, including on occasion the impossible guarantee of a college acceptance letter. In response, Chris Dorrance and Mitch Whiteley, with the mission-critical organizational skills of Betty Jean Tyler, had begun reconstructing the college admissions process in the '80s. Seniors soon had a college counselor, a clear college search and application process to follow, and methods for themselves and the School to define and showcase their unique abilities. Students were still applying to, on average, about five schools each, but were now doing so more intelligently, with research, targeted essays, and visits. With some element of chance, the help of established networks among admissions officers, coaches, and college counselors, and better applications, now students at St. Paul's seem to be entering schools more closely aligned to their interests and abilities.[81]

That said, the critical decision of a college admissions officer often depended not

High-Tech Beginnings

Academic computer chair Mona Miller in the Lower School lab in the early '80s working with Mark McLaughlin on the School's first Apple IIs, as Brenna MacDonald and Ryan Hanley '92 look on. At that time, students spent 15 minutes once a week on the machines, two to a computer. Seventeen years later in 1999, St. Paul's has over 275 computers on an eight-building fiber-optic backbone with a direct T1 connection to the Internet. Faculty, staff, and Upper School students have dial-up access to a central server and their own e-mail accounts.

only on the application itself, but on the abbreviated columns of figures in hand-outs like the "St. Paul's School Profile." These numbers are therefore worth some interpretation. In 1975 (650 students, 200 in the Upper School), 1985 (718 students, 209 in the Upper School), and 1995 (808 students, 249 in the Upper School), the average SAT scores were 1064, 1096, and 1110 respectively. And in 1975, 12 students took 21 advanced placement (AP) tests, 80 percent scoring a three or higher; in 1985 about 25 students took 32 AP exams, 65 percent scoring over three; and in 1995, 38 students took 67 AP exams, 59 percent scoring a three or higher. Finally, in 1998, the average SAT rose to 1200, and 80 percent of the students, taking 103 AP exams total, scored a three or higher, and 29 percent scored a perfect five.[82]

In some ways, these figures make interesting statements, but also tell us very little. It should first be noted that, over the past 25 years, as enrollment has increased by some 20 percent, the addition of more teachers has kept class size smaller on the whole. Secondly, while SAT scores show slight gains—and significant ones in the past few years—the test itself was re-written and re-normalized in 1996. Lastly, the number of students taking AP exams and the number of exams taken actually surged by over 300 percent, and the average score, which dipped, has in recent years shown strong improvement. Because of a poor overall performance on AP tests in 1993, concern grew that students were taking too many tests in too concentrated a time; with some adjustments in logistics, the average number of AP tests fell slightly from about two per student to 1.5, and scores have since moved higher.[83]

If there exists an underlying conclusion, it is that numbers in general terms will hardly ever describe what their advocates might hope they describe. Certainly these numbers tell us that, in this race to be a great school, St. Paul's competes well, particularly in the depth of its curriculum. But even in their glory, numbers never do much more than disappoint, for there is always a better score. There is, however, a more important truth: St. Paul's continues to focus on the student, not the score. And this truth, among the flood of digits and averages, will be critical to remember as the School seeks a healthy future.

WIRED

When St. Paul's introduced computers to students in 1967 as a science—a first for any independent school in Maryland—rather than as the educational palliative most saw it as, it steadfastly positioned them as a tool not a prescription, following need rather than novelty. After a DEC gift of a central processor and three video terminals in 1978, teachers like Nelson Sweglar, who used the tool to teach statistics, and the first director of computer studies, Mark Curtis, firmly established the idea of computing in the classroom. All of this made for a program, as headmaster Jack Ordeman said, "second to that of no other Maryland school."

With support from key trustees like Anne Reinhoff, faculty members Ilene Cohen, Curtis, and Mona Miller, now director of academic computing, led conferences and kept the School close to the cutting edge despite some resistance by those who felt computers were a fad. Curtis began to crunch admissions data and computerize the administration as operations became partly automated on the business office's machines. Meanwhile, by 1982, Miller had already begun "grooming technowizards" out of Lower School students with ten Apple II computers and created the first documented computer curriculum with scope and sequence. As Miller's young technically-inclined students grew older, the School upgraded again with the help of Cliff Low '65 and Cohen, boosted in 1988 with a $35,000 gift to wire an Upper School writing center, containing "some of the most advanced equipment available: 18 Macintosh Pluses with external floppy drives; three Apple IIs; one Apple IIgs with a color monitor; two IBM compatibles; six dot matrix printers; one laser printer; one Macintosh II file server; and one modem."

As Miller remained a catalyst for continued improvements in all divisions, others took important steps. Head librarian Penelope Partlow would supervise the automation and computerization of all three libraries, while people like Lower School librarian Winnie Flattery, who with money made available after the devastating fire in 1990 and with the help of parent Cathy Dell, automated the Lower School library entirely (and made St. Paul's one of the first private schools in Baltimore to do so).

After a year of technology planning meetings in 1994, Miller soon proposed to the trustees a campus-wide academic network, "SPnet" to share data, access the libraries, handle e-mail, and browse a young World Wide Web with the first Internet browser, Mosaic. As schools like Gilman, Boys' Latin, and Roland Park were making advances, St. Paul's became the first school in the area to lay a fiber-optic cable (at a cost of $100,000) and put in place a system that at the time was more advanced than those of many colleges. In July, 1995, Miller and the first full-time network manager, Susan Kearney, steered the School onto the information superhighway, with a web site and a fully-integrated K-12 technology curriculum within the year. With 50 new computers in 1998 alone, and stringent "Acceptable Use" policies, results of the investment "as a tool to enhance, not drive the curriculum" have led to participation in extensive on-line discussions, projects, and research. But when it comes to technology, history can hardly predict the kinds of possibilities, as some teachers speculate about earning college credit on-line, taking classes offered in other schools, and learning at home—all within a mouse click.[84]

SESQUICENTENNIAL

Now the School concludes its 150th year and reflects on its many faces: an orphanage, a choir school, a home for boarders, a place to play lacrosse, a competitive suburban college preparatory school. Parades and parties, plays and books, might make for a cozy and neat conclusion to a cozy and neat history. But such a flavor of history would surely offend its thousands of participants. The tidiest materials are the facts, and they sit like lifeless shells without motive, inspiration, hope, or faith—subjective, interconnected, and no less real. Truth therefore will always be a doorstep away. No matter. It is never what happened when, or even why, but who we are while we get there. "There," of course, is a very distant place, but in our approach, we can look to our history for guidance. We might consider what has happened over 150 years. Consider the risks, those leaps of faith, those men who looked at poor boys and thought they could sing, for God, at Sunday service; who took wiry young kids and handed them a lacrosse stick; who bought an old summer home and called it a school. What it means that out of a fire arose a chapel. These things are the designs not of chance, not of reason, but of faith. For if you look carefully—at and between these lines of history—you may see why we, the collective we, for this last year of this millennium, have kept the faith.

Center of a Lower School Spirit

by Barbara Mills

O God, give me clean hands, clean words, and clean thoughts,
Help me to stand for the hard right against the easy wrong,
Save me from habits that harm,
Teach me to work as hard and play as fair in
*   thy sight alone as if the whole world saw,*
Forgive me when I am unkind, and help me to forgive
*   those who are unkind to me,*
Help me to do some good every day,
And so grow more like thy Son, our Savior, Jesus Christ.
*   Amen.*

—St Paul's Lower School Prayer

For me, this simple prayer captures the spirit of the Lower School, a spirit I sensed when I entered the building for the first time in the spring of 1971. Age and hard use showed in the asphalt tile floors of this former stable, and the scuffed walls had been covered with many coats of paint. Then, when I looked directly into the open doors of the Chapel—the heart of the institution—and when I heard the voices of children coming from the classroom doors, I knew that the spirit of the School was housed here. Before I saw either student or faculty member I felt as if I had found the school of my dreams.

The students in one of the older groups I taught were truly interested in all areas of finance and business, and they decided to start the St. Paul's Worm Farm. The Lower School science teacher was technical adviser and the School's business manager answered financial questions. The students prepared carefully, according to

numerous books from the Getting Started In Your Own Business section of the public library. Each child had a supervisory position of some kind, although some had only worms to manage.

Students in the Lower School are valued as unique children of God, worthy of dignity and respect. When a student enters St. Paul's at age five, the Lower School has only five years to ready that child for all future school experiences, during which time the School fosters in students the positive qualities of personality—intellectual curiosity, an orientation toward learning, self-discipline, and sensitivity to others—in an atmosphere of acceptance, while at the same time holding them to standards commensurate with their academic talents.

The worm bed was a sandbox, borrowed from the pre-first, and had to be kept damp with regular nourishment (compost in varying stages of decomposition) and covered with a sheet of plywood, to keep both

Sean McAuliffe '91 greets Hara Rubin as Lower School principal
Barbara Mills offers a comforting smile. Of the variety of Mills's contributions, one of particular note is her registering the Brooklandville
campus as a Wildlife Sanctuary with the Maryland Ornithological
Society in 1971.

worms—and odors—inside. Because we could not seem to collect enough night crawlers or worms from the pavement after a rainy night, we still had to order 100 earth worms from a commercial supplier. It was an exciting day in the annals of the business when those new worms were added to the paltry number we had collected.

The Lower School faculty and administration have been prompt to respond to the students' needs with programs and the ongoing development of curriculum, using their own and the students' intellectual curiosity to take learning down many paths.

Despite publicity efforts, we made only two worm sales, one for a woman's flower bed, the other for a birthday gift. Disappointed by the lack of business, and in the face of complaints about the smell, the entrepreneurs reluctantly released the remaining worms in the woods.

Under the inspired and courageous leadership of Lower School principal Jeanne Shreeve and headmaster Jack Ordeman, two programs for children with distinct learning requirements were inaugurated early in the 1970s. The Parallel Program was created for bright students who had specific language needs; the Independent Studies Laboratory (ISL) was instituted for highly able students in a fast-paced program. By affirming that children learn best in groups geared to their style and pace of learning, the Lower School embarked on an honest and forthright educational path, one which has brought recognition to the School and success to hundreds of students.

One of our all-school yearly themes, "Westward Ho," traced the emigration of settlers across the Atlantic Ocean and beyond to the American West. Students constructed a massive Statue of Liberty which welcomed all visitors to the Lower School; the fourth-grade wing became a western town; and the second-graders turned

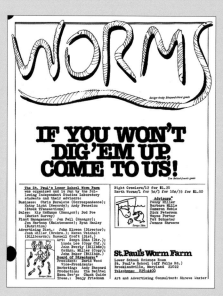

Advertisement by fourth-grader Tim Beittel '88 in a 1980 St. Paul's *Currents*.

their classrooms into a river trail featuring the missionaries and voyageurs who traveled the Mississippi.

The religious program, an integral part of Lower School life, includes community service and instruction in values. Our fourth-grade student vestry members serve as acolytes and assist the chaplain for each chapel service. For years, Lower Schoolers have packed extra lunches each week for an agency serving the homeless, decorating the lunch bags with colorful drawings and good wishes. During the Persian Gulf War, students wrote letters to "any member of the armed services" as well as to alumni who were serving there. Each class adopts a needy family for whom to provide Thanksgiving dinner and Christmas gifts. Fourth-graders serve as big buddies to the pre-firsters, meeting with them weekly to work on joint projects and to help them adjust to school.

Elected by their peers, officers of the Lower School student council, as well as the other students, learn to conduct meetings according to parliamentary order, and many of them organize family meetings in their homes using stringent guidelines of Robert's Rules of Order. A pre-firster may insist that it is not proper to say, "I make a motion."

Using literature, the Church's teachings, and events of the day, teachers help students develop sound ethical standards, moral courage, and self-reliance. When students leave the Lower School at the end of fourth grade, it is important for them to have developed respect for the heritages of both self and others; to possess a realistic and purposeful approach to life; to desire to realize their talents to the fullest; to take appropriate risks; and to be open-minded to the spiritual dimensions of life.

Human Rights Day, celebrated each year, focuses on respecting differences of religion, race, national origin, physical capabilities, and talents. Lower School students were the proud sponsors of a wheel chair athlete in the most recent Olympic games. For over ten years, they have held the record among Baltimore area schools for reading the greatest number of books and for raising the most funds during the annual March of Dimes Reading Champions Program. Grandparents' Day each year celebrates the ties of family, and gives opportunities for classmates to share the lives and heritage of their friends.

One third-grade class constructed and sent aloft a hot-air balloon during the year with the theme "Flight." When the Lower School fire destroyed their creation, the students built another one, which flew over the Lower School commencement and stole the show. First-graders fabricated nests using authentic materials of the birds they had chosen to study. The faculty transformed the loggia into the cabin of an airliner, and classes took transcontinental flights complete with multilingual flight attendants, refreshments, and an in-flight movie about Wilbur and Orville Wright. Several classes explored space, and one group built a child-sized plane to deliver air mail daily to classrooms.

A great portion of the Lower School building was destroyed by fire on January 30, 1990. Reflections of the Lower School would be incomplete without a few words about this significant and tragic event. As the fire raged, a faculty member ran inside to save important student files and medical records, while hundreds of firefighters tried to save as much of the building as possible.

The sight was horrific as the wind blew flames across the roof of the building, taking the cupola in a fiery slide. My dearest hope was that the facade would stand. Colleagues nearby tried to prepare me for its loss, but as the sun rose that morning we could see that it stood, symbolizing what the Lower School has meant for so many for so long: strength, steadfastness, and beauty.

As the fire took our School, we remembered when the student body was small enough to fit everyone into the attic for a play, how so many children could squeeze into the small classrooms, how one teacher even built a loft in the corner of her room to help. We re-dedicated ourselves to doing what we have always done best: nurturing and teaching.

The St. Paul's community and many others rallied to our aid. A radio reporter asked me early that morning if we would be able to recover. Without hesitation, I replied yes, that we would all see to it. On the day after the fire, we had already completed plans for temporary quarters in office trailers, and opened school in just over a week, greeted by the banners and balloons of students and faculty from all divisions. The fire itself was devastating, but the aftermath—with the love and support of so many people—was truly remarkable. Because of the community's determination and drive, we were able to dedicate the beautiful new building on November 26, 1990, just 10 months after the fire.

My predecessor and mentor, Jeanne Shreeve, frequently noted, "The end is inherent in the beginning." The School had come full circle from the loss of our first chapel seven years ago, and I had come full circle from the day 26 years past when I had looked into the old chapel and found the center, the spirit of St. Paul's. After the glorious consecration of the new Chapel in 1997, the heart of the School had once again been restored.

Barbara Mills was a Lower School faculty member from 1971-97 and served as Lower School principal during her last 13 years.

Notes: 1952–1999

1 The first four women appointed to the board of trustees were representatives of the Benevolent Society, listed in the trustee roster, 1 January 1953: Mrs. John T. Howard, Mrs. John A. Johnston, Mrs. J. A. Dushane Penniman, and Miss Rebecca Penniman.

2 The first two students to go through all 12 years were Shaun A. Connacher '62 and Donald D. O'Connell '62.

3 Letter from Paul Long to the author, 18 January 1999; *1951 Minute Book*, 24 September 1953.

4 Clark, *The Maturing Years*, 211; *The Monitor* (13 May 1960): 2.

5 *The Monitor* (22 November 1950): 1; *Minutes of the Meetings of The Boys' School of St. Paul's Parish, October, 1961-June, 1971*, 8 February 1965.

6 *The Monitor* (January, 1958); *Minute Book, 1961-1971*, 15 June 1964.

7 "St. Paul's Looks to the Future," 1961.

8 *The Monitor* (20 December 1956): 2; *Minute Book, 1961-1971*, 18 October 1962; A resolution of the board increased the number of term trustees from 15 to 18, and amended it so that a majority of the trustees—not exclusively voting trustees—should consist of members of St. Paul's Parish. The change in makeup of the board began under rector Harry Lee Doll, when the number of trustees who were communicants of Old St. Paul's dropped from two-thirds to half by the time Headmaster Ordeman left in 1985. Doll intentionally aimed to diversify the board and make it more representative of the broader Baltimore community. As of 1998, only one trustee was required to be a communicant of Old St. Paul's, and specifically to be a part of the Church's vestry; combined with the presence of the rector as chairman, many believe this to be a more intentional and stronger arrangement.

9 "St. Paul's Looks to the Future," 1961.

10 *The Monitor* (11 February 1955): 2; (12 October 1956): 2; (20 December 1956): 2.

11 *Minute Book, 1961-1971*, 14 October 1963; Letter from S. Atherton Middleton to Ruth W. Land, 20 June 1963; Letter from Halsey Cook to the Trustees of The Boys' School of St. Paul's Parish, 23 October 1963; Minutes of the Board of Trustees, St. Paul's School for Girls, 19 March 1964; "2 On St. Paul's Girls School Board Quit Over Race Issue," *The Sun*, 24 March 1964.

12 Letter from John Talbot Ordeman to John Walton, 4 August 1966.

13 *The Monitor* (8 January 1958): 3; (Summer, 1961): 2; (Summer, 1964): 4-5.

14 *Minute Book, 1961-1971*, 23 February 1954; 24 May 1954; 27 September 1954; 28 March 1955.

15 *News from St. Paul's School* (Winter, 1964).

16 The science building would later be named Ratcliffe Hall for chief disciplinarian, head of the Upper School, assistant headmaster, and science teacher James Ratcliffe, who also began a popular Science Club. Rules of the building's use were so heavily enforced by the ardent disciplinarian that students still occasionally mocked its "boasted features."

17 *Minute Book, 1961-1971*, 16 January 1967.

18 *News from St. Paul's School, Brooklandville* (Fall, 1966); *News* was in fact the School's first periodic newsletter begun by Appy Middleton in fall, 1963. *Minute Book, 1961-1971*, 8 June 1967; Until 1972, Elizabeth Kressler (and her successor, Virginia Heath) had for 24 years been the School's bookkeeper and assistant to George O'Connell '35. *St. Paul's School News* (Fall, 1972): 3; Lowenthal actually followed another business manager who left after a year. Soon, Lowenthal helped restructure the business office, and opened up the School's first print shop, which has been run for more than two decades by Larry Smith, whom he hired and trained.

19 "St. Paul's School Master Plan," 1966. *The Monitor* (Winter, 1965): 7; The decision to continue with boarding had been considered ten years prior, in 1955, when the trustees had given the issue serious thought. Almost all believed that boarding should remain. In 1961, the trustees had already solicited $70,000 to expand the dormitory and add "a dining hall appropriate in both space and dignity." The new dormitory was to be behind the mansion, connected to what is currently known as Ordeman Hall, which then served as the primary dorm facility. Better dining facilities and additional faculty houses were planned to accommodate the increase in students.

20 *The Crusader* (1967), 138; *Minute Book, 1961-1971*, 14 December 1970.

21 Hermann's contribution had to be matched by the School, of which the board raised 40 percent themselves, and 60 percent came from parents, friends, and alumni—which ultimately broke down to seven alumni, nine parents, and some 30 friends. The new building also included what became the Hamilton Audio-Visual room in the basement, dedicated with a gift from Marshall Austin '39 at the School's homecoming weekend in 1968. *St. Paul's Alumni News* (Winter, 1966); *The Monitor* (Summer, 1966): 6; The expansion in the library's circulation was helped by a 3,000 volume gift from Mrs. Gordon Johnson.

22 *St. Paul's News, Special Alumni Edition* (Spring, 1977): 6.

23 John T. Ordeman, "A Decade of Achievement/A Decade of Challenge," 1978; As an aside, the outside firm Ketchum, Inc., which helped organize the capital campaign, recommended in its January, 1966 proposal a joint development and alumni office to act on behalf of both Schools. The campaign itself was actually run with the Girls' School with a combined goal of $800,000. The West Wing of the Girls' School was also dedicated the same day as the Middle School (Middleton Hall), May 9, 1970, by bishop

Harry Lee Doll. The Middle School included a choir room given by former choirmaster Edmund S. Ender. The Ensign C. Markland Kelly, Jr. Memorial Foundation provided a $35,000 matching gift to St. Paul's and was created by the parents of C. Markland Kelly, Jr., who died in the WW II. *St. Paul's School News* (June, 1969): 2; The grant for the renovation of the mansion was secured through trustee William B. Bergen, former president of the Martin division of Martin-Marietta Corporation. Hermann was chairman of the board of Martin-Marietta when Bergen worked there. The $400,000 grant followed an initial gift of $50,000 to ascertain the cost of renovation, eventually completed by restoration specialist and architect Orin M. Bullock, Jr. in 1971. See Helen Henry's feature "On the Hill is Full of History. The Brooklandwood Mansion: How the Upper Half Lived" (*The Sun Magazine*, 12 December 1971) for background and details regarding the mansion's restoration, including interviews with the Ordemans and very good photos by Paul Hutchins. *News American*, June 27, 1971; *Minute Book, 1961-1971*; As Halsey Cook was a woodworker himself, he and Ordeman had already planned a woodshop, which greatly speeded the design and construction of the manual arts building. The building was named after the father of W. James Price IV '42. Price first announced to the board the $50,000 gift of John Engalitcheff, Jr., the founder and chairman of the board of Baltimore Aircoil, Inc., on June 14, 1971.

24 *Minute Book, 1961-1971*, 23 November 1965; 14 February 1966; At $3,250 an acre, the Girls' School purchased 36.5 acres on the condition that the Boys' School expand its campus by 17.5 adjoining acres. Others on the land committee with William Marbury were Richard R. Harwood, Jr. and John Walton. The merged corporation was to have a joint board and a president who would be an elected board member; the proposal also stipulated that after five years, by a two-thirds vote of trustees, the president could be a member *ex-officio*.

25 "St. Paul's School for Girls, Report of Girls' School Committee of the Dissolution of Benevolent Society," 2 June 1972; Every girl pupil in the Lower School after 50 would add $90 to the Society's annual payment of $4,500 to the Boys' School. Eventually, under the direction of Halsey Cook, the Benevolent Society officially dissolved in 1972, removing once and for all a formal financial link between the Girls' School and the Church. The Society distributed its funds of about $300,000 to the Girls School, $125,000 to the Boys' School, and $25,000 for scholarships for children of the clergy.

26 *The Monitor* (1970): 4; The editor-in-chief of *The Monitor* conducted the interview with the headmistress referred to here.

27 *The Monitor* (1974).

28 Release from the St. Paul's School for Girls Public Relations Office, "St. Paul's School for Girls Names New Headmistress," 14 February 1995.

29 *Minute Book, 1961-1971*, April 13, 1970; Letter from the Upper School students to John T. Ordeman, "Petition," n.d.

30 *The Monitor* (Spring, 1962); (Winter, 1964): 5; (Summer, 1966): 4; (1969); (1972): 3; (1974): 12; *The Page* (December, 1977): 3; *The Crusader* (1964), 83.

31 *The Monitor* (1972): 20

32 *The Page* 6.2 (March, 1978): 1.

33 *St. Paul's School Currents* (Fall, 1980): 8; Report of the Visiting Committee, Middle States Association Commission on Secondary Schools, 11-13 October 1971.

34 Robert Hallett, "From the Headmaster," *St. Paul's Magazine* 2.1 (Winter 1986): 2; John T. Ordeman, "Headmaster's Report," 13 December 1982.

35 Joan Abelson, "The Headmaster: Building on Tradition," *St. Paul's Magazine* 1.1 (Winter, 1985), 8-11.

36 *St. Paul's News Alumni Edition* (Spring, 1979): 20.

37 Letter from John T. Ordeman to Roger K. Eve, 20 February 1984. Comparing tuition fees is often problematic; some schools, for instance, include transportation and meals in their fees, while others exclude certain "incidental" expenses which actually can turn out to be quite substantial. While comparisons here are used to make generalized statements, the figures should not be taken entirely at face value.

38 The $3 million campaign was divided among the endowment ($1.6 million), scholarship funds ($500,000), and facilities ($850,000), reaching a Phase I goal of $2 million in three years. Phase II of the "Campaign for St. Paul's," launched in 1980, had raised the balance from $1 million to $1.6 million, setting aside an additional $500,000 for the endowment, and the rest for necessary improvements: a new roof for the mansion, maintenance work, storm windows throughout the campus, better heating, as well as a Lower School multi-purpose room. Some money also went toward computer education and faculty development. In April 1986, the full $3.6 million had been raised, concluding a long 12-year campaign.

39 Bill Bassett was the School's second recipient of the Joseph Klingenstein Fellowship at the Teachers College of Columbia University, following the School's first, William Durden, who completed his a year earlier. Most recently, Derek Stikeleather received a Klingenstein Fellowship for the summer of 1998.

40 "A Decade of Achievement/A Decade of Challenge," 1980; Letter from John T. Ordeman to former trustees, 29 September 1983.

41 John T. Ordeman, *St. Paul's News Special Alumni Edition* (Spring, 1977): 7-8. Evaluation reports referred to here can be found in the St. Paul's School archives. The Pennsylvania Association of Private Academic Schools (PAPAS) evaluated one private Maryland elementary school each year until the Association of Independent Maryland Schools (AIMS) developed its own evaluation program. Report by Alexander M. MacColl, Chairman of the Middle States Association of Colleges and Schools Commission on Secondary Schools, 1-2 March 1982, 2; Report by Rodman Snelling to the trustees of St. Paul's School, 27 November 1985, 5-11; This report surveyed students and found that only

between five and seven percent of them said they would rather be somewhere else (the norm, according to Snelling, was ten percent). Evaluation by the Middle States Visiting Committee of St. Paul's Middle School, April 1983, 4-15.

42 John T. Ordeman, interview by author, 26 November 1997, Baltimore, Maryland; 25 November 1998.

43 *The Page* 9.7 (18 April 1985): 1.

44 Letter from John T. Ordeman to the trustees, 16 January 1985.

45 *St. Paul's Magazine* 2.1 (Fall, 1986): 12.

46 Snelling, 14-16, 72; Robert Hallett, "From the Headmaster," *St. Paul's Magazine* 3.2 (Winter, 1987): 2.

47 Report by Alexander M. MacColl, 2-4; *The Page* 10.8 (22 May 1986): 4.

48 *Columns* 8.3 (1994): 1.

49 Barbara Bozzuto, "De-mystifying the Board of Trustees," *St. Paul's Magazine* 2.2 (Spring, 1986): 4-6.

50 Report by Alexander M. MacColl, 1-2.

51 Linda Knox, "The Arts Are Coming of Age," *St. Paul's Magazine* 5.1 (Winter, 1989): 1, 6.

52 Beth Smith, "Lila's Legacy," *Maryland Family Magazine* (Summer, 1995), 22-23; Robert Hallett, "From the Headmaster," *St. Paul's Magazine* 2.2 (Spring, 1986): 2.

53 Trustee Francis X. Knott led the capital campaign for The Ward Center, helped by a $1.25 million matching gift from what was at the time an anonymous donor. Groundbreaking occurred on September 27, 1990.

54 *The Page* 9.1 (27 September 1984): 1; Twenty-two coaches from independent schools selected the winner of the Independent School Sportsmanship Award. The A. Paul Menton Sportsmanship Award, named after the former commissioner of officials and established in 1969 by the MSA, is awarded by vote of 44 coaches from public, independent, and Catholic schools and presented by the president of the MSA. In fact, Jack Ordeman, a member of the MSA governing board, was the one who pressed for the establishment of a sportsmanship award.

55 Mitch Tullai, interview by author, 4 December 1998, Brooklandville, Maryland; Mitch Whiteley, interview by author, 3 March 1999, Brooklandville, Maryland.

56 Snelling, 17.

57 Tom Longstreth and Chris Horich '96, "That Championship Season," *St. Paul's Magazine* 11.1 (Fall, 1996): 3-6; During this "three-peat" reign, varsity football under Mitch Tullai won the championship for five straight years from 1989-93, regaining the St. Paul's-Boys' Latin Challenge Cup. Varsity lacrosse won its second straight 'A' Conference title in 1992, after its 1991 championship maintained the more obscure record for a championship in "the second spring of every decade" since 1940.

58 *Columns* 10.2 (1986): 4.

59 Elke Durden, interview by author, 7 January 1999, Brooklandville, Maryland; Margot Reiling, phone interview by author, 15 September 1998, Brooklandville, Maryland; William G. Durden, "Emerging Internationalism" *St. Paul's Magazine* 3.2 (Spring, 1987): 6.

60 Robert Hallett, "From the Headmaster," *St. Paul's Magazine* 4.2 (Spring, 1988): 2.

61 Robert Hallett, interview by author, 10 December 1998, Brooklandville, Maryland; William and Elke Durden, interview by author, Baltimore, Maryland, 18 February 1998.

62 *The Page* 2.7 (April, 1978): 2; "Enrollment Trends in Private Independent Schools," National Association of Independent Schools, Boston, Massachusetts, October, 1980.

63 Report by the St. Paul's School Administration, 1983.

64 Letter from John T. Ordeman to the parents, n.d.

65 Lee Kennedy, "A Picture of Dollars and Sense," *St. Paul's Magazine* 5.1 (Winter, 1989): 4-5.

66 Report by Christopher A. Dorrance, "Case Statement on Diversity," June, 1994. Other figures referenced here were gathered from annual reports submitted to the Association of Independent Maryland Schools which tracks minority students, teachers, trustees, and staff.

67 Kennedy, "A Picture of Dollars and Sense," 4; Figures here were also collected from the St. Paul's School admissions office and the School's archives. Area independent schools represented: Boys' Latin, Bryn Mawr, Calvert School, Friends' School, Garrison Forest, Gilman School, McDonogh, Park, Roland Park Country School, St. Paul's School, and St. Paul's School for Girls.

68 Rosemary Hanley, interview by author, 26 January 1999, Brooklandville, Maryland; Jane Lyons, "Psychologist On Board," *St. Paul's Magazine* 3.2 (Spring, 1987): 4-5.

69 Letter from Christopher Dorrance to parents, 11 January 1999.

70 Tom Longstreth, "The Advisor System: Another Link in Complete Education," *St. Paul's Magazine* 5.1 (Winter, 1989): 3; *Columns* (Spring, 1997).

71 *St. Paul's Magazine* 1.1 (Winter, 1985): 2.

72 James Tuvin '52, interview by author, Brooklandville, Maryland, 15 March 1998; Donald Roberts, interview by author, Brooklandville, Maryland, 21 August 1998; William McKeachie and James Cantler '43, interview by author, Charleston, South Carolina, 3 September 1998.

73 The All-School Ascension Day service was held on the feast day of St. Paul, January 25, 1974; Herman diBrandi, *Introduction to Christian Doctrine,* St. Paul's School, 1976; Frank C. Strasburger, "The Church Connection," *St. Paul's Magazine* 3.1 (Winter, 1987): 4-5; Frank C. Strasburger, "Keeping the Faith: the Challenge of the Church School," Episcopal Divinity School, Cambridge, MA, May, 1979.

74 Robert W. Hallett, "Reaching Beyond Brooklandville," 9.1 *St. Paul's Magazine* (Fall, 1994): 17; Strasburger, "The Church Connection," 5.

75 Strasburger, "Keeping the Faith," 11-12.

76 Robert Hallett, "From the Headmaster," 7.1 *St. Paul's Magazine* (Winter, 1991): 2.

77 Jane Lyons, "New Chaplain at St. Paul's," *St. Paul's Magazine* 7.2 (Fall, 1991): 14-15.

78 "St. Paul's Parish: Three Hundred Years in Witness, Worship and

Service" (St. Paul's Parish: Baltimore, MD, 1992), 5.

79 *Columns* 9.3 (1995): 7; Ben Roman, "Religious Diversity," *St. Paul's Magazine* 11.1 (Fall, 1996): 18-19.

80 One recent policy change: the Church now pays the entire salary of the choirmaster and the School pays the entire salary of the chaplain, which in the past they had split.

81 This data provided by Betty Jean Tyler and Christopher Dorrance from St. Paul's Upper School.

82 "School Profiles," 1975-98. Numbers have been presented in different formats over the years. Beginning in 1985, for instance, advanced placement (AP) scores were totaled over four and five-years periods, so the figures in this text are averages. Furthermore, revisions and mean adjustments to the SATs over the course of the 1990s makes it hard to draw anything more than modest conclusions about them.

83 Christopher Dorrance, interview by author, Brooklandville, Maryland, 10 December 1998.

84 *St. Paul's Currents* (Summer, 1984); John T. Ordeman, "Headmaster's Letter" (Spring, 1983); Joshua Swift, "Writing Center Opens Doors to Friendly Users," *St. Paul's Magazine* 5.2 (1989): 2; "Report of the Technology Committee," October, 1994; "SPnet: Proposal for Development of a Campus-Wide Academic Computer Network," 16 January 1995; Geordie Mitchell '78, "Grooming Technowizards," *St. Paul's Magazine*, 12.1 (Fall, 1997): 18-9; Mona Miller, interview by author, Brooklandville, Maryland, 13 January 1999.

White House on the Hill

1 Robert Erskine Lewis, "Brooklandwood, Baltimore County," *Maryland Historical Magazine* 37 (1948): 280-293; This article contains the most complete and interesting historical account of Brooklandwood. To the best estimate, Charles Carroll, Jr. built the mansion in 1793, but the date cannot be confirmed. As an aside, within various archives, records of the estate have "Brooklandwood" written as two words as well as "Brooklynwood." Interestingly enough, close similarities exist with the Homewood building of Johns Hopkins University, which Charles Carroll built for his son Charles Carroll, Jr. Most sources indicate that the mansion had always been painted white. Fannie Brown rebuilt the porch, added the wings and a northern porch, remodeled the interior in the spirit of a less elaborate Georgian revival era, enlarged the central block, and imported marble mantels from Europe. Restoration specialist Orin M. Bullock, Jr.'s 1969 proposal "Brooklandwood" contains very interesting architectural drawings using the earliest available data as well as research that confirms Lewis's own interpretations and findings.

2 According to Orin Bullock, Caton never owned Brooklandwood, was bankrupt by 1800, and would never again achieve economic independence, given perpetual financial security by his father-in-law. He also suggests that because Charles Carroll often used Caton as an agent in his financial affairs, the ownership of Brooklandwood is mistakenly credited to Caton. References to Mary Caton's beauty are common, and well-documented in a biography of her in an article by George C. Keidel, "Catonsville Biographies," *Maryland Historical Magazine* 17 (1922): 74-89.

3 Susan Stiles Dowell and Lisa Keir, "Brooklandwood," *St. Paul's Magazine* 7.1 (Winter, 1991): 10-12; "Historic Houses: 'Castle Thunder,'" Catonsville, Baltimore, 14 January 1907.

4 Louis Dorsey Clark, unpublished speech, "Brooklandwood," 1968; This manuscript also contains unique information gathered from interviews and primary sources. According to Clark's research, the Cockey family graveyard, a grave for George Brown (whose body was later moved), and a graveyard for servants are all somewhere on the estate, though they have not been found.

5 D. Sterett Gittings, "Recollections of Brooklandwood Tournaments," *Maryland Historical Magazine* 36 (1941): 278-280. "Here [at the foot of the hill] the orator of the day made his address," wrote Gittings, "couched in the lofty language of the period, and besought the knights to conduct themselves gallantly, to be *sans peur et sans reproche*, and to emulate the deeds of derring do, characteristic of Richard Coeur de Lion, Ivanhoe, and the Crusaders."

6 Erskine's article also makes these references and cites *The Sun*, Baltimore, March 15, 1935 for the note here about the Grand National races; See also Stuart Rose, *The Maryland Hunt Cup* (New York: Huntington Press, 1931).

7 "'Brooklandwood' Once Home of the Carrolls," *The Jeffersonian*, 11 July 1931. As an interesting aside, this article mentions "Brooklandwood spring water" which had a "country-wide distribution." Additionally, Emerson's fire engine and fire department were said to be among the best in the country. It is important to note, however, that in this same article it erroneously states that Carroll's land once spanned 14,000 acres in 1760 when it was in fact owned by the Cockeys. A detailed bibliography on the history of Brooklandwood, the Carrolls, and the estate's subsequent residents and owners can also be found in the St. Paul's School archives.

The Craft of Leadership

1 Helen Henry, "Old St. Paul's Rectory Is a Home Again," *The Sun*, 15 November 1964; *The Page* 9.7 (18 April 1985): 1; *St. Paul's School Currents* (Summer, 1981): 6.

The Fellow in Fellowship

1 Joan Abelson, "The Many Hats of Jim Price," *St. Paul's Magazine* 5.1 (Winter, 1989): 9-11; Phyllis K. DuVal, "Leaving a Legacy," *St. Paul's Magazine* 11.1 (Fall, 1996): 16-17; Linda Knox, "Kinsolving: A Legacy of Care," *St. Paul's Magazine* 1.2 (1985): 11-13; James W. Price IV '42 served as a trustee from 1968-82 and again from 1984-present; since then he has served as an honorary trustee. The first recipient of the Price Chair in English was Tom Longstreth.

2 Letter from John T. Ordeman to former trustees, 23 September 1983. The first Ordeman fellows were Upper School teacher Clifford Low '65, Middle School teacher Richard Peterson, and Lower School teacher Diane Pierce; John T. Ordeman, "Headmaster's Report," 8 April 1985; 17 June 1985.

Parallel and Independent Minds

1   Jeanne Shreeve and Ann Stellmann, interview, video recording, "Recollections: An Oral History of St. Paul's School," Ocean Pines, Maryland, 14 March 1998; *St. Paul's School News* (Fall, 1972): 1; *St. Paul's Magazine* 1.1 (Winter, 1985): 5-6; *St. Paul's School Currents* (Fall, 1981): 3; (Winter, 1979-80): 2; Letter by Jack Ordeman, "The Parallel Program of St. Paul's Lower School: an Explanation for Parents, Alumni and Friends of St. Paul's," January, 1974.

2   Barbara Mills's Independent Studies Lab became a model for a similar program in the Upper School designed by William Durden, the first director of independent studies.

The Other Football

1   *Triakonta* (Commencement, 1914): 2-3; *Parish Notes* (November, 1912): 6. LeDoyen's 108 career goals was a record for St. Paul's and for the area when he graduated, and he twice made All-Metro in soccer with 27 goals and ten assists. Championships were won under Howard Emsley, Jr. (1970), Tony Tyler (1980), Richard Canfield, Jr. (1983), and Howard Schindler (1995, 1997). Schindler's team was co-champion with St. Mary's in the 'B' Conference in 1995 (also a championship season for jayvee) and champion in 1997. Other championship games under Schindler were against McDonogh in 1986 and St. Mary's in 1998.

Diamonds Are Forever

1   The 1928 *Maroon and White*, Boys Latin School, 23; *1910 Minute Book*, 291.

2   Championships were won under: Tom Longstreth (1989, 1990) in the 'C' Conference, and Bruce Latta (1995) and Paul Bernstorf (1996) in the 'B' Conference.

A School in Flames

1   *Columns*, 4.1 (March, 1990): 1.

That Page in Time

1   *The Page*, (15 October 1976): 1; David Felton '85, "The Making of an Award-Winning Newspaper," *St. Paul's Magazine* 1.1 (Winter, 1985): 12-13; Angelo Otterbein '91, "Here at The Page," *St. Paul's Magazine* 7.2 (Fall, 1991): 4-5. Interestingly enough, editor-in-chief John D. Steuart '80 and Steve Lietman '80, in a history project with Mitch Tullai, published an article in the *New York Times* titled "Carter's Unkept Promises." Also of note was that for ten years beginning in 1980, Michal Makarovich organized the St. Paul's/*Baltimore Sun* annual Saturday workshop which provided guidance from both the *Sun* and *Page* editors to ten area private schools on how to improve their newspapers.

Pinned Down

1   James Andrew, interview by author, Brooklandville, Maryland, 15 January 1998; *Crusader* (1953), 54; (1958), 77; (1959), 55. Individuals could still compete in MSA tournaments prior to 1957-58. *The Monitor* (2 April 1954); (1974); (March, 1975).

The Actor, the Businessman, and the Woodworker

1   Robert Ward Hallett, interview by author, Brooklandville, Maryland, 10 December 1998; 17 December 1998; Laura Lippman, "Labors of Love," *Baltimore Magazine* (Summer, 1996): 10-15.

Quantum Leaps at the *Fin de Siècle*

by Michal Makarovich

"I am a camera with its shutter open,
quite passive, recording, not thinking …
Someday all of this will have to be developed,
carefully printed, fixed."

Christopher Isherwood, "A Berlin Diary"

Long hair, computers, critical thinking, cooperative
learning, a chapel, Japanese language, an arts center,
tell-it-like-it-is journalism …

Some dramatically new ideas slam-danced their way onto campus at the opening of the '70s. The explosive force of the '60s—civil rights, women's lib, the sexual revolution, recreational drug use, political upheavals, protests—made its controversial mark on the little private, and some would say, sheltered world of St. Paul's School. The changes did not evolve but burst ahead forcefully, exponentially.

… environmentalism, community service, filmmaking,
black student council president, Jewish vestry officers,
rock 'n roll, jazz band …

A look through *The Monitor* from 1932 to the late '60s shows little news that would jolt a parent or an administrator like its newer publications soon would. Once the Supreme Court guaranteed First Amendment rights to public school students in 1969, even small publications like *The Page* at St. Paul's could, and would, take a quantum leap in scope of coverage. In place of the late-breaking news on homecoming and Miss Sally's summer trip to France, came articles on uncomfortable and personal topics like drug abuse, teen pregnancy, and racism. Pushing boundaries may always have been a strain in the

School's history but in the last one-fifth of its 150 years, we were going 90 in a 25-mph zone.

Scene: AP English class may have ended at 3:00 but John has miles to go before he sleeps. Miles to go before he sleeps. Before conducting a meeting as president of the student council, he has to skip steps up to the Page room to see that most editors (those who have not already left for a 2:00 away-game) are screeching up to their keyboards to do last-minute edits and designs for the flats to go to press the next morning for another hot issue of The Page. *A coffee-revved editor screams: "How in hell are we going to get this ready for the printer to pick up by noon? Yes, we'll cut chapel tomorrow if we need to. And leave that door locked if anybody comes searching!" No one—not other students, teachers, or even administrators—knows like a late-working* Page *staff member the feeling of a deserted campus at 4 a.m. looking out over Greenspring Valley.*

OPPOSITE: Third- and fourth-graders in the Lower School Independent Studies Laboratory class preparing a film for the first "Night of the Arts" in 1979. As student Stuart Rosenberg listens to faculty member Michal Makarovich, Timothy M. Beittel '88 peers into the camera. Standing closest in the foreground is Benjamin B. Friedman '88, and on the left is Yvette Radwick.

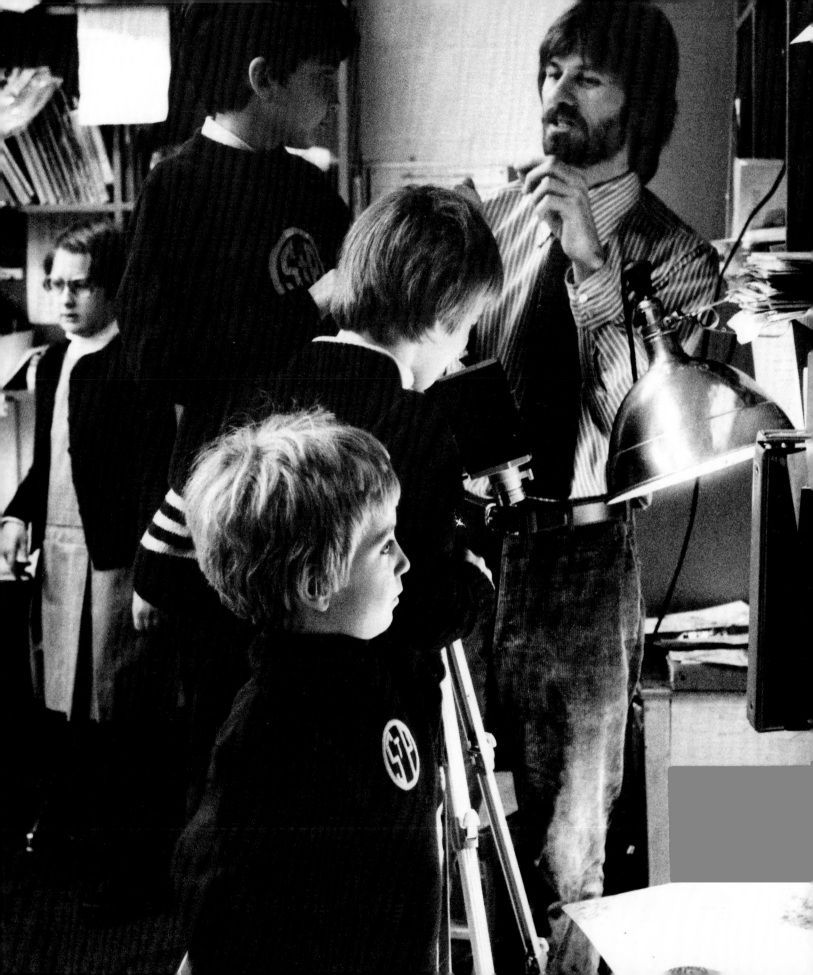

Not any or all of the late-century changes injected into the School have steered it off course. St. Paul's still has a mostly traditional atmosphere and for many board members, administrators, faculty, parents, and students, it remains desirably so.

… competitive faculty salaries, policy to support gay students, ponytails, earrings, tattoos, school psychologist, Islamic students, African American trustees, female board president, study skills, ice hockey, Asian students, sex-ed …

Like seldom before, barriers between jocks, artists, rebels, and intellects seemed to dissolve.

Scene: History classroom for a meeting of the Black Awareness Club. Close-up of the club president earnestly suggesting a change in a decades-old policy at St. Paul's: "How come we call the bookstore lady Mrs. Mueller and the admissions director Mr. Mitchell, but we call maintenance men by their first names? Is it because many of them are black?" The club motions to change uniform nametags, but complications arise when one maintenance man says he prefers being addressed as "Alvin."

Twenty-five years since I arrived, I try to find some perspective on how the community and I finally did connect. Not having ever *heard* of St. Paul's (even as a native Baltimorean), somehow I found myself sitting in the Brooklandwood Mansion in the early '70s on an oppressively hot summer day in my only suit (wool) being interviewed by headmaster Jack Ordeman for a teaching position.

On my first day of teaching, I arrived in gray velour bell bottoms, platform shoes, and a shirt decorated with a wide, flowered tie. In a class with seemingly $40,000 worth of orthodontia before me, I saw for my first time netted sticks used to catch and throw a ball. Students looked at me strangely. I thought, "On what planet have I *landed*?" Still, St. Paul's was, and still is, a place where you can make an impact, a place where all of us have in some way *nudged this world a bit.*

Scene: The Ward Center. Theatre rehearsal. Approximately 40 students are on stage listening to The Center director Paul Tines: "People. Peeee-ple. Are you going to look at each other if somebody flubs a line during a performance—out of your character's personality!? Can we be professional here?"

In the early '90s, theatre productions, especially with the erection of The Ward Center for the Arts, ceased being merely light comedies, overdone musicals, and tired mysteries, but instead began to handle topics such as AIDS, the holocaust, and date rape. In addition to staging our first Shakespeare (*Midsummer Night's Dream*), musicals shifted from Rodgers and Hammerstein to little known works such as Studs Terkel's *Working,* which encouraged rock music on stage. Productions soon regularly sold out; it became "cool" to take a date to one or go with your friends. Students became even neurotic about their commitment to theatre, either as an actor or as part of the increasingly professional technical crews. Theatre was a place for serious experimentation and professionalism. And no censorship took place.

… canoeing, ropes course, foreign exchanges, Athletic Center, new Lower School, artists, hippies, punks, burn-outs, Deadheads, brains …

The vestry began to realize that students were also composed of Lutherans, Baptists, Jews, Muslims, even atheists and agnostics. Student leadership explored areas of spiritual development that touched most students and faculty. Stealing, cheating, lying—living by principles—were investigated in skits, discussions, and "sermons" by individual students, faculty, and invited guests. Services became happenings that students actually looked forward to attending. Their voices and concerns were heard.

… female department chairs, e-mail, honors courses, coordinated classes with St. Paul's School for Girls …

Spiritual growth occurred in the area of community service, most notably since the 1960s when the School ran food and clothing drives to assist the poor in an east Baltimore project, Claremont. The '80s brought a 40-hour service requirement for many initially-resistant Upper School students who soon were working at soup kitchens, homeless shelters, and later in the Coldstream summer program as tutors and mentors of disadvantaged kids from northeast Baltimore.

Scene: December 20. Office of the chaplain. Medium shot through doorway. An altar obscured by a mound of canned and boxed food, and about 100 turkeys to deliver to the poor. At the entrance is a holiday tree covered with hats and mittens for the Claremont children.

Not everything goes smoothly. Some still buck the system and violate rules. No one has the belief that St. Paul's students are all angels dressed as choirboys with high lacy collars who do no wrong. Handing over any kind of leadership requires great faith on the part of the administration, faculty, and parents—but the track record is there. The principle: whatever you do for a student that he can do himself robs him of that much education.

Even as many students from other schools felt that St. Paul's had its guys who loved their parties and sports, others knew that there were students serious about achievement in the classroom, on the stage, in leadership activities. Our boys have been *bold in their thinking*. And this bold thinking has not only been *tolerated*; it has been *encouraged*. Former trustee president J. M. Dryden "Dutch" Hall, Jr. '50 had difficulty understanding the brazenness of *The Page* staff and their readers who appreciated total openness and controversy at the expense of bad publicity for the School. But soon won over, Hall took copies of *The Page* (teen pregnancy was the topic on the cover) to a meeting of area school trustee presidents. They seemed horrified that the board would allow such coverage in their school paper. He told them that the community valued freedom of expression. "What you say we allow," he said, "we really encourage."

Michal Makarovich taught in the Upper School from 1973 to 1994.

Epilogue

In no way could the Reverend William E. Wyatt have foreseen what 150 years would do to and for his new school chartered for "the maintenance and education of poor boys" at St. Paul's Parish. His world had not yet heard from the lawyer from Illinois who in turn had not yet heard of Gettysburg. Darwin's *Origin of the Species* could not have been banned from the school library, if there was one, since it had not been written yet. To Baltimore's trans-oceanic east, Europe was a confusion of revolutionaries and reactionaries; to its trans-montane west, John Brown's body was not yet a-mould-ring in the grave and Sutter's gold was not chardonnay.

But there is no need to re-construct Dr. Wyatt's horizon of knowledge to know that our School's beginnings were in a very different world. The ensuing sesquicent that has brought forth 2,430 alumni has seen the most dramatic developments in the history of mankind. (Only hubris would tempt us to think that in the year 2149 a reconstruction of our present horizon will not be seen as equally pre-developmental.)

The changes in the world at large have not, however, destroyed the continuity of the human race. Human nature, by definition, remains the same. So also the myriad changes by, at, and of St. Paul's have been driven, paradoxically enough, by a unique changelessness. From Saratoga Street to Mt. Washington to Brooklandville, the more things changed, the more they remained the same. For the constant that directs the history of St. Paul's and is its foundational strength—far from causing ossification—has been the living adaptation of those guiding principles that constitute our very life-blood. If St. Paul's remains faithful to its immutable principles, things will change but remain the same through the next 150 years and beyond *ad infinitum*.

What a sadly triumphalistic epilogue it would be to stop here.

God knows, and alumni know as well, that many things at St. Paul's are not so pridefully to be recalled. St. Paul's was not exempt from the pervasion of those human and American shortcomings that are today indisputably to be acknowledged and are largely, but certainly not entirely, overcome. Unexpressed *nostra culpas*, once the breast is silently beaten, must lead today to a higher degree of academic, social, and spiritual enlightenment. Nowhere and by no one has the enlightenment that will illumine and guide St. Paul's into the future been better set forth than by the trustees on June 10, 1991. In revising and reconfirming the School's aims, the board did not simply approve a "policy," but mandated a *mission*. St. Paul's, just as its onamastic, has been sent into the world where "there is neither Jew nor Greek, neither male nor female, neither slave nor freeman" (Gal. 3:28).

What are the dangers for St. Paul's, and what are its opportunities as the new Gregorian millennium opens upon us? The ultimate danger is the loss of our soul: in the one extreme, through narrow denominationalism, intransigence of spirit, and smug elitism; in the other extreme, through unprincipled pragmatism, rushed adoption of each new fad, a false egalitarianism, and emulation—albeit subtle—of public school exigencies. In the life of St. Paul's Aristotle's golden mean cannot be the resolution of extremes. To stand *in medio* will at best produce *mediocritas*. Rather, the dynamic implied by our mission requires extreme fidelity to its unambiguous terms and conditions. How can St. Paul's ensure that its graduates will "confront successfully the moral and intellectual challenges that lie before them" and "imbue each student with a sense of self which distinguishes right from wrong, reality from pretense, and which adheres to the universal truths of faith, charity, justice, hope, and forgiveness"? If such purpose is truly attained then the next millennium of alumni would also boast to their Timothy that they have fought the good fight, run the good race, kept the faith.

How to accomplish such lofty purpose? The mission statement provides the answer with pellucidity: it is chaste, elegant, and simple. The first engagement is traditional church affiliation; to gainsay this affiliation as quaint but worth naught is to re-rig our house on sand. Where else can so close by be found the unflagging "belief in the inestimable self-worth and dignity of each individual" and the anchor of our outreach, understanding, and inclusion of "those of other beliefs and backgrounds"?

Ironically enough, the second and third engagements of the mission are perhaps the easiest in which to confidently expect success. Academics and athletics are the common denominator of schools, the most basic of human inventions once nature has opened life. St. Paul's established record precludes any fears that these strengths will be compromised.

The full arts program, both fine and performing, is a natural outgrowth of our historical emphasis on music and choir. Our interaction with St. Paul's School for Girls in this and other academic and social dimensions augur an ever greater dimension in achieving this purpose.

The sixth and seventh engagements of our mission confront students squarely with their immediate responsibilities to the school community through honor code and council, to the greater Baltimore community through required service projects, and to the global community through cultural and linguistic fluency.

Alumni and parental support and involvement, the eighth and ninth fonts of engagement, have always been emblematic of St. Paul's. It can never be said to be enough and will always be essential to the purpose.

The final way St. Paul's engages its mission is the awesome province of the board of trustees. Members must by definition be "active participants in local, state, national, and international affairs" and be totally committed not only to the School's financial and educational vitality but also to a "diverse student and faculty population." This alone endows St. Paul's with the breadth of "fiduciary and policy guidance" to overcome the dangers of any extremes that may threaten it and to perceive the opportunities that will enhance it.

What an optimistic prologue it would be to stop here.

God knows, and alumni know as well, what the road to ruination is paved with, even if it is called a mission statement.

There is but one valedictorian way, then, to make it all come true. The ancient Greeks had a word for it, *Kairos*. It meant not just any point in time, but a decisive point in time. A point that comes into the life of a person or a people that can be rejected, unnoticed, neglected, passed by and be forever sterile, or that can be recognized for what it is, seized upon and used mightily for the good and glory of the person or people. To discern *Kairos* and seize the critical opportunity is the work of ultimate wisdom and the effect of special grace. *Kairos* has no less currency today than ever in the past.

Since we at St. Paul's in 1999 can no more foresee or predict the future with specificity than pastor Wyatt could in 1849, we and our successors are left with the challenge of *Kairos*: each day, and with each new developing situation, to divine the moment of our St. Paul's mission … to change, and to remain the same. Thus shall we live, prosper, and never grow less.

Brendon Hunt '92

Appendix

FOUNDERS

(February 9, 1849)

John Montgomery Gordon
Samuel Owings Hoffman
Cecilius C. Jamison
Reverdy Johnson, Jr.
Gustav W. Lurman
Thomas Hollingsworth
Morris

George Somerville Norris
Samuel W. Smith
Thomas Swann
Robert A. Taylor
John Hanson Thomas
Rev. William E. Wyatt
William Wyatt, Jr.

INCORPORATORS

(March 28, 1953)

E. Wyatt Blanchard
Frederick W. Brune, Jr.
Benjamin M. Hodges, Jr.
Reverdy Johnson, Jr.
George Somerville Norris

Thomas Swann
William R. Travers
Rev. William E. Wyatt
Edward W. Wyatt

RECTORS

St. Paul's Parish began in 1692, but for the purposes of this book, only those rectors whose tenure overlaps the School's history are listed here. The complete list of early rectors can be found in Francis Beirne's history, *St. Paul's Parish Baltimore: A Chronicle of the Mother Church* (Baltimore: St. Paul's Parish, 1967).

Rev. William E. Wyatt
(1827-64)
Rev. Milo Mahan
(1864-70)
Rev. John Sebastian
Bach Hodges
(1870-1905)
Rector Emeritus
(1905-15)
Rev. Arthur Barksdale
Kinsolving
(1906-42)
Rector Emeritus
(1942-51)

Rev. Harry Lee Doll
(1942-55)
Rev. Frederick Ward Kates
(1956-60)
Rev. Halsey Moon Cook
(1961-81)
Rev. William Noble
McKeachie
(1981-96)
Rev. David C. Cobb
(1997-)

HEADMASTERS

Sources for this list: *Parish Notes* (1888-1942); Dr. John S. B. Hodges, *Sketch of History of the Boys' School of St. Paul's Parish* (1906); Dr. Arthur B. Kinsolving, *A Short History of the Boys' School of St. Paul's Parish, Maryland, 1849-1945* (1945); Louis Dorsey Clark, *St. Paul's School: The Maturing Years, 1920-1960* (1972); and St. Paul's School minute books and archival records. In the early years, the "Headmaster" actually was referred to as "Head Master." This was merged into one word, as far as the author can tell, during the 1917-18 academic year.

Rev. William E. Wyatt
(1849-64)
Rev. Milo Mahan
(1864-70)
Rev. Henry T. Lee
(1869)
R. D. Whittle
(1870-78)
Rev. John Sebastian
Bach Hodges
(1878-1902)
Rev. E. L. Buckey
(1883-85)
Rev. M. L. Poffenherger
(1886)
Rev. Thomas H. Gordon
(1887)
Dr. C. L. C. Minor
(1888-91)
E. G. Comegys
(1891-96)
Rev. Edward S. Juny
(1896-1901)
Rev. R. S. W. Wood
(1902-05)
Miles Farrow
(1905-09)
Rev. J. Wilson Sutton
(1909)
Irving G. McGreev
(1910)
William T. Elmer
(1910-17)

Thomas DeCourcey Ruth
(1917-18)
Ernest H. Forster
(1918)
Dr. Henry Converse
(1918-19)
Harold Hastings
(1919-20)
Rev. T. J. M. VanDuyne
(1920-21)
Rev. Percy Coulthurst
(1921-24)
William Anderson
(1924-27)
Rev. Wyllys Rede
(1927)
Rev. Samuel Janney
Hutton '10
(1927-28)
Walter B. Lawrence
(1929-30)
Henry Thompson Holladay
(1930-32)
George S. Hamilton
(1932-44)
S. Atherton Middleton
(1944-66)
John Talbot Ordeman
(1966-85)
Robert W. Hallett
(1985-)

ORGANISTS AND CHOIRMASTERS

While records of organists and choirmasters go as far back as 1814, only those whose tenure overlaps the founding of the Choir of Men and Boys in 1873 are listed here. The complete list can be found in *St. Paul's Parish Choir of Men and Boys Historical Record*, compiled by Ethel Hardee in 1991 and available in the St. Paul's School archives.

Robert J. Winterbottom
(1872-81)
Arthur E. Crook
(1882)
W. H. Whittingham
(1890-92)
Miles Farrow
(1895-1909)
A. Madeley Richardson
(1909-10)
Charles Ford Wilson
(1910-13)

Alfred R. Willard
(1913-21)
Edmund Sereno Ender
(1921-53)
R. Donald McDorman '33
(1953-72)
Rodney K. Hansen
(1972-91)
David R. Riley
(1991-97)
Daniel J. Fortune
(1998-)

TRUSTEES (1849-1906)

Records prior to when Dr. Arthur B. Kinsolving became rector of St. Paul's Parish in 1906 are very incomplete; for this reason, years of the following trustees have been omitted. Sources for these names came from early publications of *Parish Notes* (1887-1906), *Parish Work* (1893-98), reports of the Parish Parochial Charities, and Dr. John S. B. Hodges's *Sketch of History of The Boys' School of St. Paul's Parish* (1906).

E. Wyatt Blanchard
G. Herbert Boehm
Leigh Bonsal
Stephen Bonsal
David S. Briscoe
Herbert M. Brune
Bernard Carter
George W. Dobbin
W. H. Ellicott
R. Lee France
S. L. France
T. Buckler Ghequier
W. W. Glenn
Rev. C. C. Grafton
R. Hazlehurst
B. M. Hodges
Alfred Hoffman

J. Latimer Hoffman
J. Harry Lee
Dr. Robert T. Maccoun
Rev. Milo Mahan
Allan McLane, Jr.
Dr. William A. Moale, Jr.
George Somerville Norris
E. Glenn Perine
Walter DeC. Poultney
John E. Semmes
C. Morton Stewart
J. Shaaf Stockett
J. Marshall Thomas
J. Hanson Thomas, Jr.
George Hawkins Williams
Charles Hanfield Wyatt
J. B. Noel Wyatt

TRUSTEES (1906-1999)

The following list of trustees and dates was generated from rosters in the School's minute books, archival records, *Parish Notes* (1906-42), and rosters from the development office (1980-99). This list includes term trustees, trustees *ex-officio*, and trustees *emeriti*. Names are printed *as they appeared* in these recorded lists.

Alice Arena
(1985-88)

Miss Doris Armstrong
(1964-66)

Charles A. Bacigalupo
(1987-93)

Daniel R. Baker
(1993-)

Mrs. Sondra Banfield
(1992-)

Janet Watson Barnhill
(1993-98)

Fernand Baruch, Jr.
(1991-92)

John Baylor
(1928-44)

Charles E. Beach, Jr. '56
(1971-73)

William A. Beale '63
(1975-77)

Gerald R. Bennett
(1964-65)

William B. Bergen
(1963-78)

Edward C. Bernard
(1995-)

William E. Berndt
(1980-84)

Samuel R. Billups, Jr.
(1980-88)

G. Herbert Boehm
(1906-16)

T. Talbot Bond
(1977-85)

Leigh Bonsal
(1906-40)

W. Graham Bowdoin, Jr.
(1906-33)

Edgar M. Boyd '36
(1978-86)

David S. Briscoe
(1906-14)

Jerrold A. Brotman '57
(1986-90)

J. Dorsey Brown III
(1981-94)

Capt. Nicholas Brown
(USN Ret.)
(1987-95)

Herbert M. Brune
(1906-48)

C. Phillip Bundy III '84
(1994-97)

George L. Bunting, Jr.
(1980-90)

Joe C. Burgin, Jr.
(1977-89)

Thomas F. Cadwalader
(1920-65)

Harry T. Campbell, Jr.
(1956-61)

Bernard Carter
(1906-12)

William B. Chambers '72
(1989-92)

Bedford Chapin '42
(1991-95)

James W. Chapman III
(1956-59)

William N. Clements II '46
(1962-63, 1975-84)

Phillip A. Clough
(1998-)

Rev. David C. Cobb
(1996-)

Antoinette A.
Coleman, Ph.D.
(1991-92)

Randall C. Coleman, Jr. '39
(1953-62)

Hugh A. Collie '80
(1992-95)

George J. Collins
(1986-91)

Mrs. William H.
Conkling III
(1961-64, 1968-74)

Rev. Halsey Moon Cook
(1961-81)

Bruce D. Cornbrooks '67
(1982-84)

Kent G. Croft '81
(1998-)

Douglas V. Croker III '66
(1987-95)

C. Carey Deeley, Jr. '69
(1984-86, 1994-)

Gary T. DiCamillo
(1989-96)

Rt. Rev. Harry Lee Doll
(1942-65, 1969-84)

Harold C. Donofrio
(1972-80)

Robert C. Douglas '69
(1990-93)

David D. Downes
(1976-87)

Harry A. Dundore
(1953-98)

Harry R. Dundore '53
(1980-83)

William G. Durden, Ph.D.
(1985-96)

William A. Edgerton '68
(1985-87)

Fred H. Eisenbrandt III '70
(1987-89, 1995-97)

Kirk Evans
(1989-)

Howell Fisher
(1928-37)

Evelyn A. Flory, Ph.D.
(1995-)

Mrs. Albert G. Folcher
(1964-65)

Dr. H. Wetherbee Fort '10
(1948-65)

Richard L. Franyo
(1988-96)

Edward B. Freeman
(1962-74, 1985-)

Frank Frick, Jr.
(1906-14)

Donald T. Fritz '45
(1970-71)

Miss Helen Garvin
(1961-64)

James H. Glenn
(1971-81)

Philip Goelet, Ph.D.
(1997-)

Spaulding A. Goetze
(1983-92)

Michael P. Goodrich
(1973-77)

Walter F. Gray, Jr.
(1970-77)

Dr. John D. Griswold
(1997-)

Marcia Hall
(1998-)

J. M. Dryden Hall, Jr. '50
(1962-81, 1986-93)

Robert W. Hallett
(1985-)

Mrs. James A. Hamilton
(1962-65)

George S. Hamilton
(1932-44, 1962-85)

Douglas S. Harrington '66
(1986-87)

George T. Harrison
(1969-82, 1985-)

Mrs. Robert S. Hart
(1958-61)

Richard R. Harwood, Jr.
(1967-70)

Melanie M. Heacock
(1994-)

David Hein '72, Ph.D.
(1996-)

Louis Horst
(1954-57)

Mrs. John T. Howard
(1952-58)

H. W. Hunter
(1922-23)

Alan W. Insley
(1976-81)

Deborah E. Jennings
(1998-)

Dr. Robert W. Johnson III
(1956-65, 1967-76)

William Fell Johnson
(1915-63)

Mrs. John A. Johnston
(1952-54, 1957-63)

John A. Johnston
(1944-52, 1956-57)

Mrs. Harry E. Karr, Jr.
(1981-83)

Rev. Frederick W. Kates
(1956-61)

Mrs. Francis E. Kennedy
(1972-81)

Dr. Langford Kidd
(1978-87)

Rev. Arthur Lee Kinsolving
(1969-76)

Rev. Arthur B. Kinsolving
(1906-51)

Herbert L Kinsolving
(1953-68)

H. Franklin Knipp, Jr. '40
(1953-58)

Francis X. Knott
(1981-89, 1998-)

William H. A. Kommalan
(1967-69)

John S. Lalley
(1970-73)

Frank L. LaMotte
(1937-65, 1969-76)

Andrea B. Laporte
(1988-99)

Fred Lazarus IV
(1988-96)

Charles L. Lea, Jr. '46
(1997-)

J. Harry Lee
(1906-11)

Edwin W. Levering III
(1962-70)

Mrs. Wilson K. Levering
(1959-66)

Mrs. Sherry Lietman
(1983-87)

Mrs. Morgan E. Loane, Jr.
(1977-86)

Lila B. Lohr
(1986-95)

Paul Lowenthal
(1973-78)

Ann Shaeffer MacKenzie
(1984-91)

Thomas H. Maddux III
(1974-78)

Thomas H. Maddux IV '78
(1997-)

Rand Mason
(1997-)

Dr. Leslie S. Mathews '69
(1982-92)

Joseph F. Matthai, Jr.
(1958-62)

Howard May
(1914-41)

Henry G. McBurney
(1967-73)

Very Rev. William
N. McKeachie
(1981-96)

E. H. McKeon
(1915-35)

W. Carroll Mead '19
(1933-42, 1945-76)

Frank D. Mead '21
(1940-42, 1948-70)

Allan J. Mead '53
(1967-80)

Mrs. Frank H. Merrill
(1958-61)

S. Atherton Middleton
(1944-66, 1969-1982)

C. Wilbur Miller
(1911-33)

Dr. Mitchell H. Miller
(1948-54, 1957-58)

Richard A. Moore '53
(1973-86)

William R. Mueller, Ph.D.
(1979-81)

Mrs. Amy L. Newhall
(1988-97)

George C. O'Connell '35
(1951-87)

John T. Ordeman
(1966-85)

James Ortega
(1989-94)

R. Wilson Oster
(1951-78)

Mrs. J. A. Dushane Penniman
(1952-65)

Miss Rebecca Penniman
(1952-53)

C. Henry Peterson
(1967-71)

Henry B. Peterson '57
(1994-98)

Mrs. Joan Beaumont
Cobb Pettit
(1995-)

Edgar Allen Poe
(1915-28, 1930-33)

Edwin W. Poe
(1906-7)

Harry E. Pollock III '67
(1987-95)

Robert Pollock
(1994-)

Wayne R. Porter
(1978-88)

Walter DeC. Poultney
(1906-29)

Robert E. Powell '52
(1967-70)

W. James Price IV '42
(1968-82, 1984-)

J. Hurst Purnell, Jr.
(1962-71)

Robert L. Randolph '44
(1974-81)

Mrs. Chloe Rankin
(1992-95)

Mrs. Lynn Homeier Rauch
(1990-)

Walter R. Richardson '36
(1974-76)

James H. Ridgely
(1974-78)

Mrs. Anne W. Rienhoff
(1982-90)

John R. Rockwell
(1987-96)

Dr. Ignacio Rodriguez
(1995-)

George E. Sanner
(1965-66)

William B. Sawyers, Jr. '55
(1973-75, 1981-87)

David P. Scheffenacker '54
(1985-88)

Ralph M. Schley '32
(1952-53)

John E. Semmes
(1906-22)

Mrs. Elizabeth Sexton
(1998-)

Stephen D. Seymour
(1983-91)

Stewart T. Shettle '79
(1997-)

M. Beach Shultz '42
(1977-78)

Robert W. Smith, Jr.
(1993-)

A. Neale Smith '58
(1978-82)

George A. Solter
(1911-14)

Henry Hodges Stansbury '57
(1996-)

Robert L. Steele III
(1996-)

H. Vernon Stehl
(1951-64)

William F. Stone, Jr.
(1949-65)

Kimberly B. Strutt '67
(1988-98)

Paul P. Swett, Jr.
(1952-55, 1957-58)

J. Fife Symington
(1962-64)

Edward A. Taber III
(1995-)

Robert M. Tarola
(1997-)

J. Marshall Thomas
(1906-11)

Robert E. Thomas
(1991-97)

Mary Ellen Thomsen
(1978-86)

T. Craig Toland '80
(1992-94)

Dennis W. Townsend
(1982-88)

Mrs. J. W. Townsend III
(1955-57)

Samuel M. Trivas
(1989-93)

Douglas C. Turnbull, Jr.
(1958-66)

Alfred Tyler
(1934-45)

Mary Frances Wagley
(1966-78)

Robert V. Walsh
(1967-72)

John Walton, Ph.D
(1956-65, 1967-80)

William F. Ward '63
(1989-97)

Charles E. Wehland
(1978-85)

Bowen P. Weisheit
(1964-82)

Bowen P. Weisheit, Jr. '67
(1981-89)

James F. Welsh
(1971-77)

Mrs. Horatio L. Whitridge
(1954-59)

William C. Whitridge
(1967-80)

John H. Wight
(1971-77)

Mrs. E. F. Shaw Wilgis
(1976-84)

Albert H. Williams
(1992-)

George S. Wills
(1977-86)

John H. Wilson, Jr. '64
(1987-94)

E. H. Worthington
(1928)

J. B. Noel Wyatt
(1909-25)

Kinloch N. Yellott, Jr. '46
(1959-62)

Thomas G. Young
(1933-53, 1957-58)

Sidney S. Zell
(1949-58)

FACULTY

With deep regret, the author cannot include years each faculty member has taught at St. Paul's. Official records have been either lost or purged, or were otherwise nonexistent. Those records which have lists are generally good, but not entirely accurate. The student yearbook, for example, began in 1941, but as the faculty and school expanded, names and pictures were omitted with growing frequency—particularly in the Lower School. School catalogues were first printed in 1931, but were not updated every year; oftentimes, these also did not include dates or complete lists. All-school rosters and internal directories of faculty and staff were not kept until the late '70s, though they have proven to be the most reliable source for the past two decades. Certainly an exhaustive effort to contact each individual would yield cleaner results, but for the purposes of this book, the lists here represent the best data available in existing sources, and have been closely reviewed by numerous people over the course of 18 months.

With this in mind, the author made one significant editorial decision—that since he felt it critical to list the faculty, the data was in fact good enough to list in broader strokes how long each faculty member taught. Approximate dates of tenure can be found in the School's development office, as well as the source document for the names here.

FACULTY MEMBERS FROM 1849-1932

Because of significant gaps in these early years, names of those who taught before 1932 and did not continue later have been placed into a separate list. The source for these names came primarily from the Parish's Parish Notes *(1888-1932).*

Edward T. Ashman
Melvin Winfrey Aylor
Suzanne Baldwin
Carlyle Barton
Rev. Carl L. F. Berhardt
John H. Brinton
J. Carrington Brown
Walter Lorrin Carrington
Ira Fulton Catlin
William E. Chamberlin
J. Peyton Clark
Albert Cottier Cooley
G. Cochran Doub
H. Graham Dubois
Joseph DuPuy Eggleston
William C. Finch
Ernest Forster

Thomas Marshall Forsyth
J. H. Gardiner
George A. Griffiths
Frederick Brown Harrison
James Higgins
Lewis Holladay, Jr.
J. P. Jacobs
Benjamin Johnson
Rev. Arthur L. Kinsolving
A. Carroll Long
John Lovett
Nannie Lynn
Danner Mahood
Alphonse A. McBee
W. H. McMeen
W. Carroll Mead '19
H. Augustus Miller
Herbert C. Moore
Arthur C. Morgan
Robert Overall
Robert W. Pearman
James D. Pinkerton
S. L. Powell
William R. Reynolds
Harry P. Rhett, Jr.
Francis B. Roseboro
Horace M. Smith
Thomas Stearns
William Stone
Benjamin P. Thomas
Harry Percy Veazie
Oliver Wolcott

FACULTY MEMBERS FROM 1932-1999

Faculty members have been grouped to help organize this list. Names are not printed twice.

Faculty who have taught for 30 years or more

James B. Andrew
Louis D. Clark
Thomas N. Longstreth
Clifford O. Low '65
George L. Mitchell '44
Michael A. Rentko
Martin D. Tullai

Faculty who have taught for 20 years or more

William A. Bassett
Carel P. Beernink
Arlene Berkow
Anne Carroll
Albert J. Cauffman
Anna C. Chambers
Helen Gambrill Clark
Richard E. Collins
Kent W. Darrell '60
Emilie Middleton Durham
Edmund Sereno Ender
Winnie Flattery
Terry A. Kelly
Linda D. Knox
Michal R. Makarovich
William Woodruff Marston
Jane B. Matthews
R. Donald McDorman '33
S. Atherton Middleton
Barbara Mills
John S. Morton III '68
Elizabeth C. Mulhern
Penelope W. Partlow
James H. Ratcliffe
Margot V. Reiling
Anne M. Roman
Howard Schindler
Jeanne W. Shreeve
Katherine L. Smith
Ann G. Stellmann
Patricia A. Talbott
Sara Anne Thompson
Barbara D. Trotter
Farnham Warriner
Joy M. Whiteley
Albert R. Wilkerson, Jr.
Samuel C. Williams
Mary Forbes Witter
Gertrude Wolf

Faculty who have taught for ten years or more

Judd P. Anderson
John B. Arrowood
Margaret Bailey
Jodi Beeler
Lynn Beittel
Mabel Bennett
George S. Blackburn
Jay Bond

James M. Boyer
Diane H. Boynton
Edward J. Brady
Richard E. Brocato
Rev. James E. Cantler '43
Ilene Cohen
Mark S. Curtis
Francis R. Dice
Peter DiMarco
Barbara G. Donick
Christopher A. Dorrance
Elke C. Durden, Ph.D.
Howard A. Emsley, Jr.
Elizabeth Smith Forbes
Frida Fraiman
Rosemary Francis
Sally Fronk
Harriet H. Garfink
Jeanne Georgelakos
Susan C. Gibbons
Peggy W. Gray
Daisy R. Gutberlet
Robert W. Hallett
George S. Hamilton
O. Kenneth Hankins
Rosemary Hanley
Rodney K. Hansen
Ethel Hardee
Alexander Harvey, IV '72
Charles Wilfred Heller
John E. Henschen
Ellen M. Hook
Donald K. Hughes
George F. Johnson
Frank W. Kimmel, Jr.
Catherine W. Knapp
Frederick Leist, Jr.
Paul M. Long
Vilma Lonsdale
Carol McCadden
Sue W. McDowell
Cecilia C. McGrain
Desmond P. McNelis
Patience McPherson
Mona Miller
Dorothy E. Moore
Howard Myers, Jr.
Jennifer O'Hearn
Lenora Olsen
John T. Ordeman
Edith M. Patterson
John G. Patterson
Ricka Peterson
Richard Peterson '61
Mary Pfrommer
Carol H. Pieper
Donald W. Pierpont
William S. Polk, Jr.
Mark. R. Reuss
Rebecca B. Reynolds
Beverly R. L. Rhett '21
James H. Rowland, Jr.
Robbin L. Daigle Schaffer
Michael G. Schuler '76
Karen Shepard
Dee Shugert
Katherine W. Smith
Patricia Smith-Verde
Steven T. Song
Martha B. Stevens
Nelson E. Sweglar
John Thorpe

John Anthony Tyler '60
Ellen Uhlfelder
Jane Walker
Lynn M. Walser
Mitchell Whiteley
Elizabeth W. Wilson
Mark Wilson

Faculty who have taught from one to nine years

Brian K. Abbott '85
Virginia M. Abraham
Winifred S. Acheson
Donna K. Adams
James Frederick
    Adams IV '46
Eric S. Adler
Cindy L. Alderman
John Alnutt '35
Rev. Jack E. Altman
Ann Darlington Andrews
Laura E. Andrews
Ruth J. Annan
William W. Anthony III
Starr B. Arbaugh
Gail C. Archer
Lloyd L. Arnold
Jacquelyn E. Bader
Vincent T. Bagli
Cameron D. Baird
Sarah P. Baird
Deborah V. Baker
O. Rowley Baker
Leroy Bald
Rev. C. Sturges Ball
Jeremy C. Barnes
Allen M. Barrett
Rachael E. Basch
Rev. Robert Lee Bast
Ted R. Baumgardner
Devere Beard
Carolynn C. Bell
Mabel Ruth Bennett
Bayard S. Berghaus '36
John P. Bernatavitz
Paul S. Bernstorf
Kimberley A. Bertozzi
Leon Bielinski
Rev. John H. Blackridge
Keith Blades
Ellen Rider Blake
Gary D. Blankenburg
Arthur Blythe
Steven A. Boardman
Frank A. Bonsal
Margaret R. Borkon
Kenneth F. Bosley
John Boynton, Jr.
Robert A. Bracken
Rev. Beverly Braine
G. Robert Brengle
Mary S. Brennan
Karen I. Brinton
Charlotte Brooks
Edward L. Brown
Victoria F. Brown
Frona Brown
J. Marshall Bruce, Jr.
Marlene Brull
Harry E. Brunett
Alice E. Buck

Paul F. Buck II
Ann Burgwyn
Patricia M. Callard
Richard D. Canfield, Jr.
Kathleen N. Caputo
Elizabeth K. Carrow
Stephanie T. Cave
Catherine Charlier
Frank E. Charlton
Dorothy S. Childs
Joseph J. Christy
Joseph P. Ciattei
Cheikh M. Cisse
Jeanne G. Clapp
Mary Ann Clark
Joan J. Clark
Cecelia M. Coleman
John W. Collinson
Scott R. Conklin
Eva Connelius
Odessa A. Conrad
Anne Cook
John Cook '40
Linda S. Cooke
William W. Cooper
Barbara E. Cornes
Eugene F. Corrigan
Jean C. Corson
Erin A. Courtney
Frances Wilder Creedon
James J. Cromer
Kevin J. Cronin
Sandra C. Cumbaa
Anne J. Dalton
Rev. Charles E. Danner, Jr.
Virginia W. Darlington
Betse Davidson
Patricia F. Davis
Elizabeth M. Davis
Andrew Davis
Rev. Paul S. Dawson
John W. deRussy '65
Rev. Herman A. diBrandi
Douglas A. Dickey, Jr.
Ross A. Dierdorff, Jr.
James E. Dillon, Jr.
Mary Doetzer
Gordon L. Donnelly
Leif A. Dormsjo
Lewis Drew
Jeffrey Dudley
Patricia F. Dudley
John F. Dunn
Helene C. Durbrow
William G. Durden, Ph.D.
Elizabeth S. Duvall
Annette Duvall
Catherine Eiff
Otto L. Elias
William P. Ellis
Charles Emig
Lois A. Emsley
Lena K. Ender
Katheryn E. English
Rev. Willard M. Entwisle
Ada E. Epting
Emily E. Estrada
Whiting Farinholt, Jr.
Jean T. Farley
Michael Fay
Rev. James C. Fenhagen '47

Steven W. Fertig '55
Bunny Fewster
Donald L. Fitzhugh, Jr.
Rev. Samuel C.W. Fleming
Daniel Fortune
Marguerite P. Fox
Helana M. Fraser
John Robert French '50
Barbara S. Frey
Walter A. Frey III
Yoko Fujita
Robert P. Fuller '39
Bonnie Gaffney
Katherine Stieff Gaines
Christopher G. Garcelon
Rev. Mark Gatza
John C. Gautreau
Jeffrey S. Gemmell
Angelo A. Gentile
Natalie W. Gilmore
Dean Gould
M. Raymore Greene, Jr. '41
Carl Grubbs
Lief C. Gustavson
Peter M. Guzy
Marcia C. Hall
G. B. Hall
Mark M. Haller
Valerie W. Hamilton
Michele Hamod
Martha Ellen Hanley
Jennifer Harbold
Darryl V. Harper
Esta Hart
Ann R. Harter
Bruce Hawkins
Charles P. Hawley
Mel Heath
Garabed W. Heghinian
Kimberley A. Heidelbach
Joleyn Hetrick
Mark S. Hilgendorf
Leila B. Hill
Erin E. Hill
Elizabeth D. Hoatson
Roseanne O. Hodgdon
Leon M. Holley, Jr.
Barbara W. Hopkins
Stephen K. Hornish
Lauri A. Hubbard
Coleen S. Hughes
Brendon M. Hunt '92
Elizabeth I. Hunter
Patricia Huntley
Joan M. Hurley
Edmondson Hussey
Mary Catherine Ives
Pamela A. Jaske
David J. Jeffery
Randolph L. Jividen
Richard Johnson
Rev. David K. Johnston
Julie Jones
Rev. Andrew B. Jones
Guy Kagey
Carol L. Kakel
Cornelius E. Keenan
Adine C. Kelly
Hazel Kidd
Kaoru Kimura

Richard D. King
Peter C. King
Robert F. Kinnaird
Rev. Arthur Lee Kinsolving
Brooke A. Knight '84
Howard Knipp
Alexander Koch
Katsura Kokubo
Richard D. Krohn, Ph.D.
Allan DeG. Lamprell
Bruce J. Latta
Theodore M. LeCarpentier
Rev. Edward C.
　LeCarpentier, Jr.
Valentine Lentz
Karen B. Levin
Molly J. Levis
Rodney Lindenmayer
Stewart Lindsay
James A. Louzan
Harry A. Love
Patricia Lowry
Blain L. Lucas, Jr.
Rev. Richard M. Lundberg
Kimiko K. Lupfer
Carville Mace, Jr.
John F. MacMullan
Nancy Macnab
Mabel S. Magill
Josephine W. Marbury
Ronald L. Marr
Robin L. Marshall
Jane Martin
Beulah Maxwell
Laurie J. May
Michael C. May
Benjamin M. May, Jr.
Verna S. Mayhorne
Carl W. McEntire
Elaine S. McGuire
Peter J. McIntosh '61
Margaret M. McLean
Rev. W. Bruce
　McPherson '58
Francis D. Mead '21
Catherine S. Meisel-Valdez
Anthony A. Meyers
Carlos E. Millan '86
Lorenzo Millan '88
Penny Miller
James P. Miller
John E. Molesworth
William A. Montgomery
Brooks T. Moore
Rebecca C. Moore
Malke L. Morris
Brenda Moses-Allen
Robert C. Mosher
Ronald Mraz
Katherine Muldoon
Margaret C. Muller
Heslett K. Murray
Susan S. Myers
Julie B. Myers
Dawson Nash
Patricia N. Naylor
John Neely
Christine Neese
A. Scott Neese
Lisa Newark

Cameron V. Noble
Howard G. Norton
Nancy C. Oates
George C. O'Connell, Jr. '61
Thomas E. Oden
Kayoko Oishi
Heather C. O'Neill
Mary E. Ordeman
Ann Oster
Andrea Panzarino
Ann Patterson
Priscilla Patterson
Richard L. D. Pearce
Nathaniel W. Peirce
Shirley A. Pentz
Marcus Pettman
Diane Pierce
Christopher B. Pierce
Pamela A. Pierce
Pamela Pitts
Sean Poland
Michael V. Pollock
Brett T. Porter
Sara J. Porter
Morgan H. Pritchett
Robert Jackson Progin
Helen K. Reed
Douglas Reinhart
Robert Reitz
Rodney V. Rice
Katherine G. Rich
David R. Riley
Julianne R. Roberts
Rev. Donald P. Roberts
Alice Robertson
Linda Robertson
Carolyn Rogers
Christopher P. Rokous
Judith S. Rokous
Voldemer Rolle
C. G. Rollins
Marcus J. Romani
Helaine Rombro
Judith B. Rosenfeld
Rev. Edward C. Rosenzweig
Bryan G. Rowe
MIchael Ryan
David E. Ryer '47
Stanley A. Sach
Martha M. Sadler
Jeannie Sawers
Honora Scheck
Denise C. Schilte
Susan B. Schindler
Gayle McK. Schmidt
Madeline P. Schmidt
Jessica Schuler
Patricia Schuster
Edward R. Seth
Betty M. Shaffer
Colburn Shindell '88
William Simmons
Kenrick P. Skerritt
Emily S. Slaughter
Albert Neale Smith, Jr. '58
Rex G. Snyder
Carter Middleton Sollers
Lori M. Song
William D. Soud
June F. Soad

Edward H. Sparrow
Betty S. Spear
Donna K. Speer
Beverly Stewart
Derek M. Stikeleather
Barbara Stone
Larry Story
Rev. Frank C. Strasburger
Jane Strickland
Rev. Robert H. Stucky
Gayle Sullivan
Joshua Swift
Robyn Talbott
Guy H. Talbott, Jr.
E. C. Nicole Talley
Kenneth Taylor
John Walker Taylor, Jr.
Priscilla Thut
Rev. William E. Ticknor
Lewis Lunsford Tignor '25
Paul J. Tines
Thomas Turner Tongue '46
Aerie A. Treska
Alexander Trivas '92
Rev. William G. Truitt
Helen P. Trumbull
James S. Tsouvalos
Melissa R. Turnage
Kristine B. Turner
Marshall S. Turner, Jr.
Rev. John W. Tuton
Roger C. Tyler
Dietrich E.O. von
　Schwerdtner
Deborah vonKelsch
Roger A. Walke, Jr.
Rev. Michael G. Wallens
Ruth Breckinridge Warfield
David T. Warfield '71
Mary A. L. Warner
Curtis G. Way
Col. A. Norman Webb
David C. Weeks
Margaret Wells
Stephen A. Wildfeuer
Jeffrey D. Wilhelm
Howard E. Wooden
Lisa Woodings
Randolph J. Woods
Rev. William G. Workman
Alan C. Wright
H. Russell Wright, Jr.
W. C. Burris Young '51
Lois M. Younkin

ALUMNI

This list was assembled and edited by Drew Ford '80 for a scroll in celebration of the School's sesquicentennial. Spellings and formats of names referred to in this history are based on how they appear here. Interestingly enough, the School did not officially give out graduation certificates until 1915 or high school diplomas until 1927, yet the first alumni association of "Old Boys" formed in 1895.

1876
Adrian Hughes
T. E. Morris

1877
Charles A. Jessup

1884
John W. Beard

1890
William H. Stone

1891
John C. Fairfax

1893
Douglas T.D. Beall

1894
Hugh W.S. Powers

1898
Irving M. Grey

1899
Horace O. Ashton
Andrew K. Murray
Pinkney L. Sothoron

1901
Walter E. Gregg
Crosdale Witts

1903
William H.B. Evans
Theodore C. Heyward
William M. McGill

1904
Wilson Haywood

1906
William Everton
Maurice McK. Hill
Daniel Hooper
J. Houston
Walter Hughson
Henry P.Veazie

1907
Henry Barrett
Bretherd Berkerly
Wallace Everton
Horace Fort
William Glines
Robert. B. Hill
James Johnson
Arthur Snyder
Alfred L. Thorp

1908
Tunis A. Craven
Alfred Fort
Winthrop Heyer
Harold C. King
R. S. Liebeg
Charles A. Lucas
Russell Ryan

1909
Thomas A. Craven
Pinkney W. Holmes, Jr.
Charles Jervis

1910
Bernard Carpenter
H. Wetherbee Fort
George M. Hatton
S. Janney Hutton
Silas McBee
Eugene W. Milby
Robert W. Nelson
Whetton Norris
George C. Thomas

1911
William T. Anderson
Thomas P. Banatt
Freeman Cross
George Forman
Channing W. Lefebvre
G. Ross Rede
William W. Rideout

1912
W. Lorrin Carrington
Leonard Clark
Edward P. Magill
S. Page Nelson
John C. Page

1913
Charles French
E. Abbott Holmes

1914
P. Naylor Isreal
Paul R. Jackin
J. P. Jackson
William J. Maddox
Avery McBee
John S. Milby
Kenneth Rede
Robert I. Slater
J. Geoffrey Strugnell

1915
Ralph E. Buxton
C. A. Clark
J. Carroll Johns
Charles R. Kloman
Charles A. Wilson
Jere M. Wilson

1916
Douglas V. Croker
Anthony Hankey
George R. Moore
Charles S. Wilson

1917
John G. Fisher
Henry M. Haberle
Thomas E. Hogben
A. Laurence Kloman
John T. Marley
Gordon Murray
F. W. Nicholas
H. K. Smoot
C. M. Vick
C. M. Wilson

1918
William B. Crane
James B. Higgins
John R. Mead

1919
George Marley
W. Carroll Mead
Paul Van Valkenburgh

1920
Thomas K. Mount

1921
A. Aubrey Bodine
Robert L. Bull, Jr.
Peyton Hundley
Frank D. Mead
Beverly R. L. Rhett
Leeds K. Riely

1922
Kendall R. Allen
James E. Baker
Reynolds Mead

1923
Robert V. Elliott
John B. Keene
Charles O. Mount
Oliver Swallow

1924
James W. Chapman III
James Valliant

1925
Seeber K. Bodine
A. C. Woodfin Booker
Lewis L. Tignor

1926
Donnell W. Baker
John E. Gallup
William L. Gould
Hugh K. Higgins

1927
James Hundley
Arthur Musgrave
Charles Stokes

1928
Clyde B. James
Richard H. Pembroke, Jr.
L. Parker Temple
Louis M. Wheary, Jr.

1929
William H. Atwell
Robert V. McQuilkin
T. Benson Musgrave
Gerard P. Nelson
Miles R. Patterson
J. Dean Tasker

1930
Wm. Dunbar Gould
Lemuel C. Hastings

1931
Webster C. Johnson
Joseph W. Parker
E. Allen Russell, Jr.
J. Cleveland White

1932
Joshua H. Cockey
Robert W. Holland
Ralph M. Schley
David Scott
Robert B. Sharpe

1933
Jason M. Austin, Jr.
James D. Beck
Bruce J. Franz
William B. Hutchison
R. Donald McDorman
John Oliver Rich
Michael L. Rodemeyer

1934
C. Morgan Blakeslee
Ralph Hain
Henry Hastings
Francis C. Kennedy
Milton Meador
Oscar L. Moritz
Theodore Poole

1935
John G. Alnutt
Miles R. Carroll, Jr.
A. Merriman Casey
Jack K. Clifford
Philip W. Cromwell
John P. Gwyer
Clark V. Hoshall
Donald W. Kalkman
Thomas L. Lee
W. Berkeley Mann
Robert Mowell
George C. O'Connell
Arthur J. Russell
Wm. C.R. Sheridan
Russell Zeigler

1936
John H. Beck
Bayard Berghaus
Edgar M. Boyd
John E. Brandau
Dabney H. M. Cruikshank
James Gulick
Howard R. Harr
Richard W. Higgins
Robert D. Maccubbin
Camille S. Marie
Walter R. Richardson
Robert N. Turner
John G. Wilson

1937
William N. Beale, Jr.
Hunter Cole
James H. Cupit
William Dew, Jr.
Donald H. Frye
William H. Gaskill, Jr.
Sherman Henderson
Russell M. Juckes
T. Wilson Scarborough
Louis Shroyer
Robert C. Stirling
John M. Tucker
G. Summerfield Whiteley III

1938
Roland H. Brady, Jr.
Clifford H. Campen
J. Julian Chisolm, Jr.
Francis B. Christopher
Peter T. Gault
Henry P. Hopkins
George V. Kelly, Jr.
Frank L. LaMotte, Jr.
Edward C. Lindsay
Guy A. Luttrell
Edward F. Morse
Clifton Phipps
John H. Poehlman
Calvin C. Smith
David M. Warren

1939
Marshall M. Austin
Randall C. Coleman, Jr.
Francis D. D'Anthony
Robert P. Fuller
Lawrence W. Galloway
Walter R. Harris
Charles W. Moxley
William B. Norman
M. Dudley Phillips
William Poole
Bosley O. Waters
Eugene L. Wolfe
Bryson Wood, Jr.

1940
W. Sydnor Chichester
J. Donald Connor
John R. Cook
Newell T. Cox, Jr.
William Driscoll
Dennis M. Hoffman
George H. Kastendike III
H. Franklin Knipp, Jr.
F. Joseph McDonald
E. Tileston Mudge, Jr.
J. Lyon Rogers, Jr.
Robert N. Schmidt Sr.
Herbert J. Smith, Jr.
Joseph S. Smith, Jr.
Norman M. Torrence
Arthur G. Turner
Willis Williams
John W. Wyatt

1941
Robert F. Beasley
Charles A Becker, Jr.
Ernest Bowersox
G. Leiper Carey III
Carroll P. Cole
Edward H. Crook
Francis Gerland
M. Raymore Greene

T. Clay Groton, Jr.
John A. Hitchcock
Thomas S. Hook
James M. Jordan III
Bernard B. Michaux
L. Hollingsworth Pittman
David W. Pohmer
George O. Purcell, Jr.
John L. Robertson III
Howard W. Smedley
Morton H. Smith
Harvey Thomas
Frank B. Williams
Welby Carter Wood

1942
T. Talbott Anderson
William DuB. Bien
William C. Briscoe, Jr.
Joshua H. Brooks
Robert Carter
Bedford Chapin
Edwin N. Chapman
Key Compton
H. Bradley Davidson
C. Donald Galloway
Frank M. Hammond
R. Morton Hayes
Seth W. Heartfield, Jr.
G. Brown Hill
William C. Hill
Francis E. Kennedy
Charles A. Mann
Edwin H. McFeely
R. Bland Mitchell
John A. Pierson
Jack B. Porterfield, Jr.
W. James Price IV
James P. Robertson
Richard W. Russell
M. Beach Schultz
Donald B. Stewart

1943
James E. Cantler
Claudius Smith Coleman
Lawrence J. Cooper, Jr.
Reginald J. Crockett
Herbert A. Davidson
Richard C. Donohue, Jr.
Grafton Eliason
Phillips L. Goldsborough III
Alexander R. Hill
John J. Hoffman, Jr.
Ralph U. Hooper
Donald M. Hopkins
George Jessop III
Peter C. Johnson
H. Lawrence Jones
Owens Hance Jones
Roland L. Jones
Goodwin S. Jordan
Don Kindler
Charles V.B. LaMotte
Robert MacDermott
Ivan M. Marty, Jr.
Keith McBee
Thomas G. Metcalf
F. Stanley Porter, Jr.
Thomas G. Proutt
George D. Rowe, Jr.
H. Arnold Schultz
Rockwell M. Smith
W. Wardlaw Thompson, Jr.
Philip H. Turner
Malbon R. Wood

1944
A. Hamilton Bishop III
Edward F. Blake, Jr.
Raymond M. Brown, Jr.
Gerald K. Chapin
Otis G. Clements
William F. Crockett
John F. Duke
Raymond A. Gore
John A. Hatfield, Jr.
Walter F. Herman
Walter R. Hitchcock
William P. Jencks
Charles Kemp
Stewart McLean
George L. Mitchell
Clifford McL. Near
Pinkney L. Near
Robert L. Randolph
Tilghman H. Sharp
Lawrence S. Sheets
Macduff Symington
Harry C. Thompson, Jr.
John A. Turner
Allen F. Voshell, Jr.

1945
Francis G. Bartlett, Jr.
Lowe H. Bibby III
F. Hooper Bond
Stuart L. Brown, Jr.
Allen Case
Jonathan W. Clausen, Jr.
Charles W. Deakyne
Gordon D. Dobbins
James H. Downs
Donald T. Fritz
J. McHenry Gillet
John E. Harrington
Carter O. Hoffman
David W. Kennedy
John M. Lescure, Jr.
C. Tilghman Levering
Henry F. G. Linthicum
Lowndes P. Linthicum
Douglas C. Lovell
Thomas Campbell Murray
Walter C. Pohlhaus, Jr.
G. Harvey Porter III
C. Herbert Sadtler
William C. Sadtler
Robert E. Sandell, Jr.
Joseph S Sollers, Jr.
C. MacNair Speed
Edward B. Stellmann, Jr.
Austin B. Taliaferro

1946
James F. Adams
Robert McV. Austin
R. Robinson Baker
Richard G. Ballard
Charles M. Buchanan
Gaylord L. Clark, Jr.
William N. Clements II
Charles B. Compton
William T. Conklin III
Thomas G. Cranwell
Thomas W. Gough, Jr.
Edward A. Hartman
B. Merryman Kemp
Charles L. Lea, Jr.
Richard E. Lewis
John R. Mann
R. Taylor McLean

Robert G. Proutt
F. Barry Robertson, Jr.
Douglas M. Stegner
Thomas T. Tongue
Friend L. Wells, Jr.
Stephen T. Whittier II
F. Kenneth Wittelsberger
Lawrence V. Woodworth
Kinloch N. Yellott, Jr.

1947
C. Norman Andreae, Jr.
T. Gordon Bautz, Jr.
David D. Bien
Godfrey Birckhead
William B. Bishop
Frederick P. Bonan
C. Prevost Boyce, Jr.
R. Frank Collins
Robert Coughlan
Douglas V. Croker, Jr.
Eric G. Curry
E. William Digges, Jr.
B. Dixon Evander
James C. Fenhagen
Theodore Gould III
Sloan Griswold
Robert C. Hall, Jr.
Ian N. Hemming
Hayward L. Heubeck
G. Russell Hicks
Edmund Hill
G. Donald Hillary
William U. Hooper, Jr.
Jacob W. Hughes
William S. Keigler
Edward Leonard, Jr.
Peter Moriarty
David E. Ryer
James H. Seeley, Jr.
Charles S. Taylor
William R. Walton III
G. Calvin Whiteley, Jr.
John A. Woodfield

1948
Arunah S. Abell
F. Mather Archer
Donald L. Baney
Joseph L. Booze
John E. Calvert
William T. Clendaniel
Thomas S. Compton
Edgar G. Cumor, Jr.
James B. Diggs, Jr.
Lindsay D. Dryden, Jr.
John S. Fulton
Richard L. Godine
Arthur S. Hamilton
David E. Henderson
Guy T. Hollyday
John Horner, Jr.
Jerrold R. Humphrey
Gordon R. Jones
James D. King, Jr.
David H. LaMotte
Laurance A. Leonard
T. Bryan McIntire, Jr.
Richard C. McShane
Warren R. Mitchell, Jr.
Randolph D. Near
Elwyn D. Northam
Roy D. Pippen
John C. Pohlhaus
James J. Richardson

Thomas N. Ruth
W. Tilghman Scott, Jr.
Edward D. Smith
William N. Stellmann
Gerald D. Sylvester
John Traband
Elliott K. Verner
George E. Weber, Jr.
William M. Wood
Glenn R. Yarbrough
Fred Zeigler

1949
Frank B. Adams, Jr.
Charles K. Bibby
Basil B. Bradford
Paul B. Burdon, Jr.
Philip F. Dice
Joseph E. Fox
Joseph F. Garver, Jr.
G. Gordon Gatchell, Jr.
Herbert L. Grymes, Jr.
Russell G. Henderson
Thomas C. B. Howard
William J. Hunter
Jerome T. Kelley, Jr.
John L. Kelly
John W. Kniffin
Robert L. Lewis
Daniel C. MacLea, Jr.
Robertson B. Magruder, Jr.
Richard M. Marcroft
Edward A. McGinity, Jr.
S. Kirk Millspaugh
Paul T. Morgan, Jr.
Stuart G. Morris
Frank P. Nasco
J. Richard Newkirk
Malcolm Parker
H. Emslie Parks
Frank M. Prince
Douglas H. Rose
Charles R. Sharretts III
J. Gainor Stehl
G. William Tanton
E. Ross Wagner, Jr.
Harold M. Warrington, Jr.
Robert C. Wentworth
Robert J. Wigton, Jr.
E. Waller Wilson
John S. Wilson, Jr.
John B. Yellott

1950
H. Eugene Agerton III
William G Anderson III
J.M. Perry Archer
Ronald L. Bray
Walter R. Carroll, Jr.
William P. Corbin
Elonzo P. Dann
E. William Davis III
Carl C. Dean
W.H. Thomas Dell
Frank N. Doughty
John A. Eilers
William V. Elder III
Frederic D. Estes
George M. Eyler
Thomas M. Fischer
J. Robert French
Lowry B. Furst, Jr.
J.M. Dryden Hall, Jr.
Robert H. Hammond
Robert M. Harper
G. Justice Jenkins

Royal F. Jewett
Donald W. Kraus
Anthony M. Leigh
Robert W. Mairs, Jr.
John McKenzie IV
Richard R. McLaughlin
John F. Miller
J. Michael Moriarty
Ronald W. Phillips
Robert T. Phipps
Sydney W. Porter, Jr.
August W. Schell, Jr.
R. VanLeer Snouffer, Jr.
Robert T. Staples
Randall J. Thompson
Frank Z. White
William T. Whiteley III
Edward H. Wisch

1951
William P. Baxter
Richard C. Burt
William L. Dols
Richard E. Doub
John D. Gassaway
James R. Grieves
R. Cyrus Griffith
Edward F. Heath, Jr.
Peter A.B. Hoblitzell, Jr.
W. Lars Hviding
Brooks T. Keller
J. Stanley Lenox, Jr.
James C. Lindsay
Stewart Lindsay, Jr.
Walton T. Loevy
Sidney C. Lusby
J. Murray Miller
Walter B. Mitchell
Francis R. Niner
Samuel M. Oberholtzer
Charles E. Pforr, Jr.
Jerome M. Proutt
Milton J. Schul
Donald Scott
Thomas B. Silcott
Frank R. Smith
Ronald R. Smith
Donald B Steynen
William H. Stone
John L. Swarm
John L. Taylor
Hanley Tom
George M. Trautman
Nelson T. Turner, Jr.
W. C. B. Young

1952
Richard L. Bland
Richard W. Britt
John T. Davenport
David P. Deland
Isaac Dixon III
Douglas M. Godine
Uly H. Gooch
Thomas Halley
Lewis P. Heck
Evans L. Hedges
Robert H. Kenney
Donald P. Malkemus
Frank N. Mayonado
Lawrence Menefee
James J. Mulligan, Jr.
David R. Nelson
John G. O'Leary
Nathan S. Pendleton III
Robert E. Powell

James E. Rutledge
Michael P. Ryer
Albert C. Sencindiver
John V. Staples
Charles D. Steuart
James H. Tuvin
Lee E. Wilhide

1953
Gerald R. Bennett
Dudley Brownell
Courtland F. Buell, Jr.
Benjamin Chambers, Jr.
Richard S. Colonell
George B. Donaldson
Harry R. Dundore
Frank O. Groesser
M. Thomas Horner
Samuel J. Hutton
Edward C. LeCarpentier, Jr.
James W. Lewis
Thomas V. Litzenburg, Jr.
Robert D. Loevy
Joseph P. Martin, Jr.
Allan J. Mead
Richard A. Moore
Thomas O. Moore
Carl A. Muly
Richard M. Nelson
Zadoe T. Parks III
Lloyd E. Sample III
Theodore K. Sanderson, Jr.
Thomas C. Tanton
William C. Traband
William K. Verner
Michael H. Weinman
Gordon H. Wentworth
James H. White
Joseph J. Woodward III

1954
Robert D. Alexander
William H. Bagby, Jr.
C. David Barnes
Richard S. Barroll
Ernest J. Betz
Stuart N. Carlisle
George R. Charles, Jr.
William Clendaniel, Jr.
Fred Crebbin IV
Burnell T. Driscoll
William G. Duvall, Jr.
James M. Fowke
William H. French
Rigby H. Graham
Wigby H. Granruth
Bruce D. Greenawalt
John C. Halliday
Frank W. Houck
George H. Jenkins
Nelson R. Kerr, Jr.
Charles G. Knoch
James Kressler
E. James Lewis
Read Madary
Gerald E. Mathison
Walter McCoy
Gordon L. Miller
Edmund S. Pendleton
Richard S. Ridenour
David P. Scheffenacker
David B. Sharretts
Paul C. Shearer
Thomas B. Shettle
James M. Travis, Jr.

Basil Wadkovsky
Neil C. Wagner
Harry B. Walker
William H. Winstead III

1955
Donald D. Bates
Orville T. Beachley, Jr.
Lawrence B. Chambers
Michael D. Clark
Thomas S. Elder
J. Timothy Fagan
Stephen W. Fertig
Howard S. Garrett, Jr.
Thomas F. Griffith, Jr.
T. Brien Haigley
Charles M. Jankey
Alan D. Jones
Brian D. Jones
Charles E. Mahaffey III
William Meglitz
Harry W. Nice III
Ronald G. Noble
William G. Patterson, Jr.
William S. Powell
Wylie L. Ritchey, Jr.
W. Edward Rose
William B. Sawers, Jr.
J. Michael Sheehan
Jeffrey Z. Slutkin
M.A.H. Smith, Jr.
A. John Southall
Richard B. Surrick
Arthur V. Teagarden
Carl R. Tuvin
Roger B. Williams

1956
Hilary E. Bacon III
Robert T. Barclay
Charles E. Beach, Jr.
Osborne P. Beall, Jr.
C. Lincoln Bogart
Upton P. Bonner
Adrian M. Bronk
George W. Campbell
Robert D. Cheel, Jr.
Thomas J. Crum
Gerald M. David
L. Brooke Davies
Charles E. Farr
Wayne E. Flanagan
Jonathan T. Ford Sr.
Douglass B. Forsyth
James D. Francies
Roger B. Goss
J. Michael Hayner
Carl G. Hilgenberg
Allan J. Hirshey
Louis Horst, Jr.
Joseph W. Huey
Peter S. Jones
Alphonse J. Kelz, Jr.
Michael G. Marsh
Frederick L. Miller
Joseph A. Nollmeyer
Richard W. Owen III
Donald C. Pace
John E. Pforr
Alan L. Powdermaker
Mark Powdermaker
Nicholas M. Ratcliffe
Charles E. Rodgers
R. Ford Verdery
Robert L. Walker
Francis W. Welch III

1957
Laurence S. Barringer, Jr.
Robert M. Barroll
Joseph M. Braden, Jr.
Jerrold L. Brotman
Brent F. Buchheister
Whitner L. Church
Robert H. Cullen
Robert E. Diehl
David Downs
Edmund P. Duvall
John S. Duvall
Albert G. Folcher, Jr.
Leonard I. Frenkil Sr.
Steven F. Giberson
Carroll T. Giese, Jr.
R. Hutchins Hodgson, Jr.
Parker J. Leimbach
Thomas R. Love
M. Gordon Lyons
John Mitzelfelt
Roger P. Mooney
Henry B. Peterson
William N. S. Pugh
Charles W. Shaeffer, Jr.
J. Clyde Simons
Reginald M. Smith, Jr.
S. Barron Smith, Jr.
Randall T. Sollenberger
Henry H. Stansbury
Edward W. Warren
R. Streett Whitefoord
C. Lynn Wickwire
J. Donald Willoughby, Jr.
Robert F. Wolf

1958
Allan B. Ashbury
David M. Barney
George S. Bayley, Jr.
James C. Burch
Paul R. Burch
Henry L. Cabell III
Joseph L. Carter, Jr.
J.M. Rowland Clarke
C. Evans Clough
Ronald W. Cox
Charles C. Darrell
P. Kittridge Donaldson
Alexander M. Fisher, Jr.
Armstrong H. Forman II
Edward B. Freeman, Jr.
Conrad M. Goodwin
J. Evans Goodwin
James D.C. Gouldin, Jr.
Robert S. Hachtel
Jay Holloway
P. David Jackins
Earl P. Johnson
George I. Jones
William F. Kalb
Douglas Korschgen
James A. Ludwig
Kent W. Marbury
Roy D. Mayne
W. Bruce McPherson III
Harry B. Mecaslin III
E. Warner Minetree
W. Laurence Nielson
Ross D. Parham
Laurence C. Post, Jr.
Alan S. Rutherford
Austin F. Schmidt III
Peter C. Sheehan
A. Neale Smith, Jr.
William R. Vercoe

Robert J. Vetters
G. Randolph Walker
Fred T. Walrath
Richard White
Frederick A. Whiting
John S. Wolf
Thomas G. Young III

1959
William M. Annan (Ret.)
Frederick E. Blenckstone
John T. Bossert
W. George Bowles, Jr.
David C. Cain
Howard E. Cann, Jr.
John B. Carr, Jr.
Raymond B. Chism
Thomas C. Cover III
James A. Crum
Van N. Fochios
Cornelius O'B. Gibson
Robert A. Gore
Preston W. Hartman
David F. Heron
F. Grant Hill
Frederick A. Holden
Thomas F. Johnson, Jr.
William J. Kerr
William H. Kommalan
Edward J. Lang
Wilson K. Levering III
Thomas W. Lewis
Thomas L. Lilly
Arnold McCoy
J. Stevens McCulloch III
Arnold B. McKay
Thomas E. Meade
August V.B. Millard
C. Parker Parsons
John S. Pearson
James W. Ruth, Jr.
Richard L. Sher
John A. Sherwood
Charles Smith III
John A. Tompkins III
Walter L. Toy
John G. Turnbull
K. Rodney Turner
Douglas G. Walker
William W. White III

1960
Wilson K. Barnes, Jr.
Stephen A. Barney
R. Russell Beers
Frederick R. Betz
Barry E. Birch
John R. Bland
John W. Brigstocke
Ridgely G. Britton
John G. Carroll
Garnett Y. Clark, Jr.
William R. Clark
Carl D. Clarke, Jr.
John B. Clough
Thomas M. Cook
R. Brinton Crocker
John S. Darrell
Kent W. Darrell
John F. Davies II
W. Cary deRussy
Charles E. Gunnoe
Henry D. Hammond, Jr.
Samuel J. Hornsby IV
Edward L. Jordan
Peter R. Keeler

Albert J. Kelley II
James Kelly II
Lawrence H. Lack
William B. Love
Bruce H. Low
William O. MacArthur, Jr.
W. David MacCool
W. Bruce Michael
H. Drew Morgan
James L. Murrill III
Robert E. Robertson III
John S. Rutherford
G. Stephen Ryer
Lauren T. Scheffenacker
James L. Shreeve
J. Anthony Tyler
Charles S. Verdery
Elmon L. Vernier, Jr.
George Wofford, Jr.

1961
Ralph A. Ashton, Jr.
Thomas C. C. Bond, Jr.
LeRoy A. Brandt
Eben J. Bray
Paul Brookes
Ralph M. Burnett
Robert D. Campbell
Thomas E. Carson V
George F. Carter, Jr.
Marion H. Chambers III
Johnson Couch, Jr.
Cary M. Cullen
C. Jeffrey Dickinson
Louis H. Diven
William B. Dobson III
David W. Fisher
Ronald D. Gart
Frederick L. Gates
Samuel P. Glover
Richard J. Gunkel
James R. Hammersla
Joshua S. Horner
Jack K. Hoskins
Robert S. Hoyt, Jr.
Kurt H. Kaltreider
John Orr Kenny
Michael A. Leahy
Gary Lewis
David L. Maulsby, Jr.
Peter J. McIntosh
George C. O'Connell, Jr.
Richard D. Peterson
Ronald O. Post
Charles L. Potter
Robert S. Purvis
James A. Richardson
Dermott Rigg
Robert H. Riley III
Howland S. Roberts
Robert A. Ruth
Melvin J. Schultz, Jr.
Charles C. Shafer, Jr.
Lester S. Smyth, Jr.
Donald R. Snyder
Charles H. Tompkins III
Charles J. Turner
Frederick O. Viele II
John W. von Briesen
Jon M. Wickwire
John H. Wight
Richard Williams

1962
W. Gary Almond
Nathaniel D. Arnot
John A. Baden III
Winston R. Blenckstone
Bradley N. Bowers
John C.G. Boyce, Jr.
R. Bruce Bremner
H. Meredith Bryant, Jr.
H. Bruce Campbell
Joseph M. Coale III
Shaun A. Connacher
James R. Dykins
Robert T. Greenland
Philip A. Hickman
Robert V. Jones
J. David Kommalan
P. Donald Mallonee, Jr.
William F.C. Marlow, Jr.
Peter D. McManus
William W. Miley
Robert D. Minnix
Thomas F. Murrill
Cary H. Neblett
Donald D. O'Connell
William H. Parsons
David B. Patterson
Charles F. Peace IV
Carl H. Schultheis, Jr.
Murrell E. Smith, Jr.
John B. Toy, Jr.
J. Dennis Turner
C. Ridgely Warfield

1963
John F. Beaird, Jr.
William A. Beale
Steven L. Beccio
William S. Boykin, Jr.
Lawrence T. Brown
Jerrold R. Cann
James G. Chalfant
Thomas H. Clark
Robert F. Cockey
T. Coleman duPont
Robley L. Feland
Henry E. Flanagan, Jr.
Charles J. Froehlich III
Howard L. Gilbert III
John W. Gore
Bryan H.M. Griffin
Paul W. Harrison III
Byron D. Huffman, Jr.
John S. Hyde
Thomas G. Lacher
William S. Lyon-Vaiden
William J. Maloney III
A. Lawrence Marston, Jr.
J. Edward Martin
William B. Matthews
James M. Moore
Paul Muller III
Carl Ortman
Cortland R. Pusey
William B. Reed, Jr.
Thomas G. Scully
Dudley Shoemaker III
Talbot T. Speer, Jr.
James R. Stone
William Forrest Ward, Jr.
Chelsea C. White III
C. Dennis Wile
Michael P. Wise
John D. Young III

1964
E. Alexander Adams
Robert Archer III
George T. Benbow III
Thomas L. Bien, Jr.
Nelson M. Bolton
David C. Bramble
Gerald F. Bresce
Marty Cain
Pete L. Caples
Richard J. Chambliss, Jr.
John R. Chapman, Jr.
James Cheston
Robert R. Davis
Edward K. Dickinson
Charles J. Fleury IV
Stephen H. Folcher
David M. Funnell
Thomas C. Hasson
Dana H. Hodgdon
Stephen W. Jones
James M. Jordan IV
Frank Kaltreider
Richard A. McClary
Bradford R. McCormick
John Merryman III
G. Allen Moulton
Robert W. Muldoon, Jr.
J. Todd Mulvenny, Jr.
Lindsay C. Passano
Chesley H. Prince
Terry L. Purvis
Walter Sanders
James G. Sasscer
Thomas L. Shreeve
Robert L. Tarring, Jr.
William H. C. Ticknor
Ronald W. Voss
Robert L. Walker
John H. Wilson, Jr.

1965
A. Bryce Anderson
Frederick McD. Anderson
Carel Peter Beernink
Christopher H. Bready
John R. Brown, Jr.
R. Sherwood Brumfield
Frederick S. Carroll
H. LeRoy Carter III
Peter C. Chambliss
John P. Coale
Randall C. Coleman III
Bruce Van Cott
Charles N. Curlett
Paul T. Day
John W. deRussy
Lindsay D. Dryden III
Blaine duPont
Ward Everhart
Ray R. Forseille, Jr.
Richard W. Funnell
John R. Gimbel
John M. Grove
Arthur J. Hand
A.G. Henry Hanssen III
William R. Harlan
J. Russell Hodgdon
Michael P. Horner
Carroll P. Kakel III
Clifford O. Low
Robert F. Luers
Paul T. Mackie III
Joseph F. Matthai III
J. Alexander McCosh

Robert D. McDorman, Jr.
J. David Morris, Jr.
Robert R. S. Parks
Walter Y. Pindell, Jr.
James A. Pine
Earl G. Roberts
Stephen E. Sanford
Jack E. Steil
George F. Strutt, Jr.
James P. Wagner
W. Byron Waltham
Alexander D. Webb
William E. Webster III
John J. Williar
Robert S. Zeman

1966
S. Hamilton Adams
T. Delano Ames
William E. Barr, Jr.
G. Michael Borkovic
Stephen P. Boykin
Gregory D. Brown
Michael A. Buck
James W. Cooper
Douglas V. Croker III
Clifford L. Cryer
Meril-Lee Dunn, Jr.
Peter R. Eldridge
John C. Emery III
William S. Gordon
Thomas C. Groton III
H. Russell Hanna, Jr.
Philip E. Hardee
Douglas S. Harrington
John E. Hayward, Jr.
Scott D. Hello
Gordon T. Hill
Kent C. Hoffman
Robin J. Holt
Jeffrey D. Hooper
Dode A. Hoskins
Nelson P. Janz
Richard J. Johnson
Aubrey E. King III
J. Todd Laudeman
David K. Leighton
David H. Luther
Robert A. MacCool
Robert L. McDowell, Jr.
Peter E. Muller
William V. Nardiello
Stephen L. Nason
Wayne L. Nield II
Roy M. Norris
James C. Paynter
Thomas R. Pentz
Paul Phillips
Jeter C. Pritchard III
M. James Roeder, Jr.
William J. Schwindt
James O. Souders, Jr.
Thomas C. Swiss
H. Kirk Unruh, Jr.
Robert H. Williams
S. Clayton Williams, Jr.
Richard E. Yellott III
Peter G. Zouck, Jr.
Robert L. Zouck, Jr.

1967
O. Bowie Arnot
Richard L. Beard
Benjamin A. Bosher, Jr.
Sandford C. Boyce
Joshua S. Brumfield

Steven W. Buck
Richard J. Caples
Thomas K. Carey, Jr.
William H. Conkling, Jr.
Bruce D. Cornbrooks
George W. Croker
H. Russell Dischinger
Edward C. Dukehart, Jr.
D. Bruce Eason
Charles F. Ellinger
John B. Ellinger
John F. Gaines
Daniel F. Hall
M. Wiley Hawks
Rodger C. Henning
Gary L. Kelly
D. Randolph Lewis
Maynard G. Lewis
Warren Liddell
Steven J. Littleton
Richard M. Marie
Thomas Massey III
Andrew W. McCosh
John B. Mitchell
Thomas Parran III
James H. Peace
Michael P. Pearce
Louis B. Pieper
Harry E. Pollock III
John N. Ridgely
John E. Rossell III
Glen A. Ruzicka
Raymond H. Seipp
Howard W. Smedley
C. Henry Smith III
R. Bruce Smith
Thomas W. Speed
John R. Starr
David J. Stavers
Christopher S. Stinebert
Kimberly B. Strutt
William S. Warner, Jr.
Bowen P. Weisheit, Jr.
Christopher C. Wilson
Richard L. Wolfinger
Chesley W. Yellott

1968
Daniel B. Brooks II
David R. Brown
Gene W. Brown
Robert W. Clark, Jr.
William W. Cooper
Joseph F. Dalton, Jr.
Richard C. Darrell
Stephen F. Edelen
William B. Edelen II
William A. Edgerton
Daniel Eidman
James M. Gaskill
C. Gordon Gilbert, Jr.
Kenneth N. Gilpin III
F. Bryant Gould
David N.W. Grant
Stephen H. Greenston
David R. Hanna
Christopher R. Hardee
Gordon K. Harden, Jr.
Frank M. Harrison
Hartwell Harrison
William H. Hatter
D. DeVries Holland
G. Jarrell Jobson
R. Brooke Kaine
Robert D. Kearney

Geoffrey L. Kotzen
Edwin W. Levering IV
Theodore J. Low
Robert E. Lundvall
Robert G. Maier
William J. McFeely III
Melvin E. Minter, Jr.
Richard C. Mollett
Mark D. Morris
John S. Morton III
Stuart M. Pearman
R. Nicholas Perryclear
John G. Power
Ben W. Price, Jr.
George B. Rasin III
Michael L. Rodemeyer, Jr.
Leonard H. Rosenberg, Jr.
Frederick V.W. Slagle
W. Christopher Spencer
Roger W. Stenersen, Jr.
William Stump, Jr.
J. Frank Supplee IV
Douglas R. Tarring
Eric W. Walsh
Winston S. Wood

1969
Gary A. Bailey
William B. Bergen, Jr.
Michael Joseph Bershad
Thomas W. Binns
Christian E. Blom
William W. Bond
Edwin N. Chapman, Jr.
Robert W. Coleman
Kevin A. Cook
C. Carey Deeley, Jr.
David B. Dempsey
Stephen F. Dennis
Robert C. Douglas
Ivan R. Drechsler III
Colin M. Duer
Victor C. duPont
Norman C. Durham
Robert W. Hayward
G. Robert Heaps
Scott R. Hopkins
Charles Thomas Kemp IV
Michael P. Kirby
A. Mitchell Koppelman
Matthew B. LaMotte
David C. Leithauser
Joseph T. Loane
W. Peter Marie
Leslie S. Matthews
David Lee Maulsby
Jay R. Myers IV
Robert H. Pritchard
John V. Raser III
Frank B. Robertson III
Allison Malvern Rossell
Barry Douglas Roysdon
Alfred E. Sharp III
J. Dean Tasker, Jr.
John S. Tilghman
Craig R. Unruh
Elwood L Wadsworth, Jr.
Edward O. Weant III
Justin White III
John J. Wolf IV
Ellis Woodward
Kinloch N. Yellott III
Paul F. Zeller

1970
W. Peter Allen
William T. Bartgis
Bradford E. Blake III
Bryant Boucher
Thomas M. Bruggman
Francis H. Chapelle
Robert F. Chapman
George V. Clokey, Jr.
Charles T. Conkling
Robert D'Antonio
A. Laurence Dee
David L. deLorenzo
David H. deVilliers, Jr.
Peter Dischinger
Fred H. Eisenbrandt III
Kurt G. Everhart
David G. Fidler
R. Hooper Goldsborough
John H. Hessey V
Robert E. Horton III
Dave D. Kelly
John S. Lalley, Jr.
Blair F. Laughlin
Frederick A. Leist
James V. Lobell
P. Marshall Long, Jr.
R. Gordon Long, Jr.
Keith W. McBee, Jr.
A. Lee McCardell III
William H. Milnor
Daniel T. Moulton
Richard A. Norris
Andrew B. Pollock
Mark C. Remington
William K. Renner
Edward B. Rogers
Noel Rush II
John B. Seal III
Webster E. Shipley III
Stephen M. Smith
David M. Speed
John N. Stack, Jr.
Guy H. Talbott III
Gary Tegler
W. Frank Thomas II
Victor A. Traub III
D. Boone Wayson
Rexford L. Wheeler III
Daniel S. Wilson
Steven R.D. Wyman

1971
Allen M. Barr
Larry D. Bennett
Hank P. Bonk
Davis E. Burgess
Joe C. Burgin III
Peter S. Chapelle
William N. Clements III
Taylor Cook
Anthony B. Court
Geoffrey C. di Brandi
Kirk Dugdale
Page Edmunds III
R. Wayne Eisenhut
Geoffrey A. Feiss
Stephen H. Friend
Ellwood L. Hall, Jr.
Eric W. Hardee
Thomas A. Hays VI
Grant E.G. Healey
Eugene N. Helms, Jr.
Fred J. Hodges IV

Carter O. Hoffman, Jr.
Philip B. Hopkins
W. Eric Loch
Charles M. Maddox, Jr.
William Marshall
Gary J. Martin
Neil R. Massey
Douglas T. Mayne
Calvert C. McCabe
Carter N. McDowell
S. Eyre McKenrick, Jr.
David S. Mudd
Frederick W. Ohrenschall
Chadwick J. Pfeiffer
Allen Rude
Alfred B. Sadtler
G. Bradley Sanner
Thomas W. Schultz
Kerry C. Sewell
W. Joseph Smith, Jr.
Harry B. Turner
James B. Walker
Bailey B. Walten
David T. Warfield
Charles S. Williams
Benjamin H. Wilson
Donald J. Zimmerman

1972
Barry G.M. Bledsoe
William B. Chambers
William F. Childs IV
Barton M. Cockey
Gary S. Cornbrooks
John Cox
Richard G. D'Antonio
David R. Dalbke
Kenneth L. DeGarmo
Robert W. Ecton, Jr.
David W. Forbes, Jr.
Jeffrey M. Gleason
James S. Grant
David B. Gumm
Alexander Harvey IV
Christopher T. Heald
C. David Hein
Jonathan R. Heptinstall
Jon C. Hughes
G. Brock Johnson
A. Preston Kelly, Jr.
Andrew A.D. McBee
E. Dawson Nash
Mark D. Ostroff
William M. Owen, Jr.
Walter L. Patton III
Laurence H. Pieper
Robert L. Platt
J. Michael Recher
John T. Sadler III
John J. Salley, Jr.
Thomas M. Searles III
Joel B. Sewell
H. James Smith III
Robert A. Snyder
Stephen H. Stoelting
J. Michael Strickland
Brooks A. Tegler
Luke A. Tennis
Mark L. Walsh
John M. Will
Benjamin R.
   Winneberger, Jr.

1973
Charles N. Andreae III
J. Bradley Barnhart
R. Steven Blizzard
Timothy K. Cockey
William P. Cook IV
G. Kirk Culbertson
M. Kevin deLorenzo
H. Charles Donofrio, Jr.
David G. Donovan
Thomas E. Doriety
Richard M. Feete
W. Scott Franklin
J. Ben Funk
Walter Granruth III
John J. Grasmick
Charles E. Gucker
James D. Haugh
Amos F. Hutchins III
Randolph T. Kohler
David J. Marble
Neville R. Martin
Myles R. McComas
Charles W. Mitchell
Timothy M. Moulton
Gary P. Norris
Warren B. Powell
Roark D. Raker
Hamilton Rowan II
Jeffrey S. Seal
John F. Seets
Joseph S. Sollers III
Richard L. Staples, Jr.
Earl C. Stauffer
J. Edgar Steigerwald III
James L. Thomas
William W. Walker
Jonathan W. Weisheit
J. Stevens Wilson

1974
William F. Andrews III
Steven A. Bacharach
Robinson S. Baker
Aaron Barchowsky
Charles E. Bauer
J. Bruce Boucher
William A. Boykin IV
Gerald L. Bray
Christopher C. Burgin
Joel P. Byrd
Gregory S. Callanan
Conrad P. Carter
James S. Carter
W. Bosley Davis
Michael C. Dubin
James E. Dunn III
Randolph B. Ecton
David G. Franklin
Mark D. Fritz
H. Bruce Funk
Richard Gochnauer, Jr.
Patrick Harrigan
William B. Hartman
J. Whitaker Hauprich
James N. Heptinstall
Thomas R. Hodges
Charles F. Hoot
David M. Hughes
Mark A. Hughes
J. Edward Johnston III
Ridgely C. Kelly
Alexander Kennedy
Alexis B. LaMotte
Bradford R. Lewis

Wilbur M.L. Maurath III
John McQueen
Braxton D. Mitchell, Jr.
Matthew A. Morris
Christopher A. Pistell
Walter C. Pohlhaus III
Jonathan R. Price
Christopher H. Randall
Stephen B. Recher
David Redding
Chase Ridgely III
Michael J. Seets
Peter B. Sparks
David I. Spear
William T. Sunderland
Mark V. Thomas
Michael F. Wood

1975
Harold G. Albert, Jr.
Stockton T. Baker
Samuel C.P. Baldwin, Jr.
John M. Black
William E. Carlson
Robert B. Carroll
Harvey S. Childs
Christopher S. Cockey
Michael M. Collie
Joseph B. Coster III
Franklin G. Dawson
Paris P. di Brandi
Henry A.B. Dunning III
Frederick S. Fischer III
Brian K. Gabriel
Stephen T. Galloway
J. Patrick Gayhardt
Peter C. Gentry
John E. Gerber III
Michael A. Gettier
David J. Glenn
Davis G. Groth
Richard C. Johns
Kenneth M. Keverian
Thomas E. Koch
John F. Kohler IV
Donald H. Mays, Jr.
Michael C. McComas
Stuart H. McFeely
Richard C. McShane, Jr.
Brian R. Millhouser
Walter B. Mitchell
Donald B. Nippard, Jr.
Richard F. Obrecht
John C. Ohrenschall
Peter Parker, Jr.
Ralph V. Partlow III
Dirk R. Pieper
Leland D. Powell
James F. Ridgely
John T. Shehan, Jr.
Stephen R. Smith
Robert D. Teasdall
Charles W. Wagner, Jr.
Thomas S. Warner
Dana M. Weant
John S. Westerlund

1976
Bruce D. Armstrong
John Bacon III
Kevin L. Billups
A. Stoney Cantler
Brett M. Chambers
Robert S. Clements
Stanley R. Clinton
Thomas H. Cover

Roger E. Drechsler
Peter W. Eisenbrandt
Peter C. Elfert
Bruce J. Fiske
William P. Geary, Jr.
Stephen P.W. Gilbert
Robert B. Giovanelli
William H. Hall
Mark D. Halpern
William P. Harrison
Stephen H. Hartman
William G. Holden
Henry P. Hopkins III
Robert L. Huether
Edward A. Kitlowski II
C. Bayard Kohlhepp
Edward G.S. Leist
John R. Leist
Gustave E. L. McManus
Donald L. McQueen
D. Cameron Miller
William H. Neumann
Geoffrey A. Peters
John H. Riehl IV
Michael G. Schuler
David S. Schwartz
Peter D. Smith
Jonathan W. Stevens
Damon A. Trazzi
Stuart L. Vogel
Gregory W. Wareheim
Andrew E. Wells

1977
William E. Berndt, Jr.
Ronald O. Binetti
James E. Blake
Jonathon K. Braase
Henry L. Cabell IV
Charles vK. Carlson
Dennis L. Childs
Andrew B. Cohen
Brook H. Cumor
Cornelius H. Darcy
John S. Davis
S. Gregory Eierman
Peter G. English, Jr.
Hunter K. Fedderman
Eric M. Flesher
Craig A. Flinner
Jeffrey C. Fountain
Richard A. Froehlinger
Lloyd V. George
J. Ross Germano
Ralph W. Kettell II
Douglas P. Kingston III
Paul R. Lewis
William W. Magruder IV
John R. Marshall
Timothy K. Michels
Eric J. Mills
Thomas N. Mitchell
Streett E. Moore
M. Andrew Norman
Lawrence P. Park
Thomas J. Park
William M. Pellington
Manfred H. E. Pfeil
William J. Price V
F. Jeffress Ramsay, Jr.
Perry C. Reith
William H. Rhodes, Jr.
Hunter R. Rich
David P. Scheffenacker, Jr.
William S. Spicer III

Robert C. Stephens
Donald W. Thorup III
W. Edouard Trumbull
William T. Whiteley IV
Marcus E. Whitman
Peter Wight, Jr.
Samuel F. Zeller

1978
Nader Anvari
Kurt M. Boren
Robert B. Brinkley
Scott Buckler
Thomas W. Cammack
Jeffrey G. Cook
Thomas A. Downes
Michael X. Dugan
Bruce L. Elliott
Davis C. Emory
Stephen W. Frey
Hamid Golpira
M. Brett Goodrich
Kenneth B. Gore, Jr.
S. Alexander Green
Jeffrey P. Harvey
Geoffrey D. Holland
John Hollis
Gordon B. Jones
Christopher N. Kandel
Eric T. King III
Bernard J. Land
Clifford B. Lull III
Thomas H. Maddux IV
Harvey E. Marshall
Kevin N. Masland
George L. Mitchell, Jr.
Donald F. Obrecht
Marcus W. Partlow
Michael J. Riehl
K. Lee Riley, Jr.
Stephen B. Schuler
Jason C. Seal USMC
Daniel W. Shirley
William J.D. Somerville III
Peter B. Stellmann
Steven B. Stenersen
Oliver C. Von Muehlen
Edward J. Weber, Jr.
John O'D. White, Jr.
Bruce H. Winand
John Z. Windsor, Jr.
Jonathan B. Zengerle

1979
Vernon J. Bankard
Kermit S. Billups
Trevor P. Bond
Harry C. Dundore
Kirk P. Eidson
Charles P. English
James B. Ensor
John R.S. FauntLeRoy
Thomas M. Galvin
Timothy E. Grey
H. Bart Halpern
Frederick K. Handley III
Robert G.T. Hinton
John H. Horine
Todd F. Hunter
Jay E. Johnson
R. Scott Johnston
William L. Kamberger, Jr.
John S. Kerns III
Thomas B. Lalley
J. Mitchell Lambros

Stuart A. McHenry
Christopher P. McShane
Louis G. Merryman
Robert J. Murphy
J. Howard Murray
William E. Ness
Jeffrey R. Park
D. Guy Parsons
Christopher M. Patterson
Douglas A. I. Pippin
E. Curtis Rountree
Herbert Sadtler II
J. Ketchum Secor
T. Michael Shera
Stewart T. Shettle
Dennis M. Troy II
Thomas R. Vuicich
E. Richard Watts III
Charles T. Wehland
Eric W. Weinstein
David B. Westerlund
Robert C. Weyrich

1980
L. Maxwell Anastopulos
Lars J. Belin
Edward L. Blanton III
Craig L. Boynton
T. Sean Brooks
Hugh A. Collie
John B. Coulson
Andrew J. Darcy
David C. Darrell
John R. Davis
Paul W. DeLaski
Michael F. Delea III
Darren A. Foreman
Dean C. Foreman
Robert S. Gaines, Jr.
Michael E. Glenn
Gregory H. Green
Joshua M. D. Hall III
Brinton H. Hoover
Jeff L. Johnson
Robert G. Kaestner
Peter T. Kandel
Mark S. Kapiloff
Henry A. Lederer IV
Steven A. Lietman
Ronald L. Maher, Jr.
Thomas Mainolfi
John S. McCleary, Jr.
Guy M. McKhann II
Michael A. McShane
Andrew C. Miller
Lawrence F. Naughton
D. Lee Ordeman
Gregory A. Panayis
J. David Patterson
Mark J. Pellington
Craig W. Pfeifer
Brooks H. Pierce
Steven R. Pohlhaus
Robert P. Schlenger, Jr.
Donald G. Slaughter
James E. Smart
Martin D. Smith
Jonathan M. Staber
John D. Steuart
T. Craig Toland
Scott F. Vogel
David B. Wells
William F. Wendler II
Stuart E. Williams
Charles H. Wineholt III
Daniel L. Workman

1981
Robert M. Berndt
Henry M. Bond
William M. Brewster, Jr.
Daniel C. Burton
Dean J. Catanzaro
Louis L. Chodoff
Charles C. Cobb
Daniel W. Colhoun III
Halsey M. Cook, Jr.
Kent G. Croft
Douglas R. Dawson
Fredrick S. Dawson
Michael J. Demos
Bruce E. Doub
Todd R. Douglas
Robert W. Downes
Paul A. Dundore
Steven A. Farmer
T. Brandon Fewster
J. Drew Ford
Michael B. Gilland
James C. Godey, Jr.
F. Gillis Green
S. Scott Haigley
C.F. Claflin Hall
John M. Hebeka
Stewart P. Hoover
Andrew M. Kidd
Jeffrey S. Knight
Christopher P. Kreeger
Andrew E.L. LaMotte
Bryan H. Loane
Anthony J. Lotman
Paul F. McKean, Jr.
James G. Miller
Brooks T. Moore
William K. Morrill III
William D. Naughton, Jr.
Allan F. Park
Jonathan N. Portner
Keith R. Prem
Wayne T. Prem
Julio O. Purcell
Walter A. Reiter III
Thomas G. Riehl
Richard Christian Riley
Jeffrey Scott Roberts
Henry A.H. Rosenzweig
William B. Sawers III
Wm. Scott Schneidereith
Michael J. Shuehler
Benjamin O. Tayloe VI
Stephen M. Van Besien
Todd N. Wareheim
J. David Wetzel
Gregory S. Weyrich
David A. Wineholt
L. Edward Wolf III

1982
John A. Addy
James G. Blair, Jr.
Shane A. Braganza
William R. Davis III
Paul A. Denoncourt
Edward M. Dolby
George C. Doub III
Scott D. Evander
Andrew L. Faulkner
Christopher S. Fewster
Kevin P. Fitzgerald
Michael H. Green
Stephen R. Green
William T. Greenbaum

Cameron M. Huey
Robert B. Irving
James G. Joyner
Jason E. Knight
John B. Kostmayer
Stefan N. Kozlowski
Larry L. LeDoyen, Jr.
Stewart C. Lee
James R. LeFaivre
George E. Linthicum IV
Howard P. Louthan
Peter B. Lull
E. Brent Matthews
John D. McDonough
Mark M. Menendez
Walter E. Miller III
Jeffrey P. Natterman
Marc R. Panayis
Keith A. Plasse
Paul H. Powell
William N. Pugh III
Michael E. Reiriz
John D. Ridgely, Jr.
Philip T. Ruxton
David A. Schuler
Robert S. Stevens
William B. Thomas
James F. Turner IV
Robert E. Ukkelberg
Glen W. Wagner
Robert B. Wagner III
Richard S. Wills

1983
John E. Adams, Jr.
Brent H. Antrim
Thomas M. Bacigalupo
John D. Baker
George D. Carroll
Thomas W. Cole IV
D. Alexander Darcy
Kent W. Darrell, Jr.
Austin X. Dopman, Jr.
William R. Fauntleroy II
Henry D. Felton V
Tyler H. Haynes III
Jack K. Hoskins, Jr.
Joseph I. Huesman, Jr.
Thomas J. Kenneally
Robert J. Kenner
Andrew C. Kohn
Mark F. Longstreth
Alfred P. Marano
Ian B. McCausland
William T. McPherson
Steven C. Mitchell
Joseph F. Morrison
Jeffrey B. Muneses
Antonio Olmedo
Patrick L. Ousborne
Ronald E. Patterson
Robert C. Pohlhaus
Michael L. Ponsi
Craig A. Prem
Robert J. Reier
John B. Rich
Robert A. Roman, Jr.
C. William Schneidereith III
Charles D. Sergeant III
Peter C. Sheehan, Jr.
Guy S. Shipley III
Matthew J. Smith
Gordon E. Snider
Eric D. Strine

Stuart M. Sutley
J. Preston Turner
Michael B. Watriss
Patrick T. Williams
W. Scott Wood

1984
Gregory W. Ayers
Basil B. Bradford, Jr.
Thomas W. Bramble
C. Phillip Bundy III
Dean R. Bushmiller
Austin B. Childs
Peter J. Clark
C. Mark Dees III
Andrew L. DeLaski
L. James Derrickson III
A. Damian Dhar
David P. Dodge
Timothy D. Downes
Eben C. Eck
Donald J. Gilmore
F. Nelson Gilmore
Lawrence M. Gleason, Jr.
Philip J.D. Green
Reynaldo P. Guzman
A. Erik Hestvik
Karl A. Hilbert
Robert A. Johnson
Brooke A. Knight
Christopher E. Kosmides
Federico D. Laffan
Eric M. Levitt
Nicholas J. Mantis
J. Christopher McGrath
Allan F. Mead
L. Jordan Millan V
T. Christopher Mitchell
Gregory N. Mix
Michael N. Morrill
Richard B. Mosher
Timothy C. Naughton
Barry P. Oxford, Jr.
Timothy S. Parker
Benjamin S. Riley
George F. Ritchie
Thomas L. Samuel, Jr.
Alexander C. Sapir
Scott M. Seymour
Steven D. Silverman
Carl P. Smith, Jr.
Steve S. Suskind
Alexander M. Taliaferro
Edward F. Wilgis
Bradford C.D. Wills
David D. Wood

1985
Brian K. Abbott
Robert M. Barroll, Jr.
William P. Bartholomay IV
Paul A. Berry
Richard J. Cross III
Mark A. Daffer
David Brian Daily
David O. Felton
Carlos F. Fernandez
R. Riggs Griffith VI
Andrew M. Hameroff
Samuel M. Hoff
Peter A. Hrehorovich
Seth A. Hurwitz
Robert M. Johnston
Paul W. Kase III
Fremont J. Knittle III

Carter Meade Mason
Peter S. McCleary
Thomas R. Moore
Thomas J. Myers, Jr.
J. Timothy Reiter
Mark D. Riley
J. Kemp Sawers
Paul P. Schafer
Erik J. Scheps
Patrick N. Schlag
Joseph H. Seipp III
Peter J. Sfondilis
Lucas P. Siple
M. Russel Tadder
Jason F. Trumpbour
Thomas R. Tuttle, Jr.
Christopher J. Vaka
Brian A. Villmoore
David B. Walcher
Timothy S. Welsh
Robert I. White III

1986
Ethan E. Alsruhe
Eugene A. Arbaugh II
Paul L. Betz, Jr.
Steven M. Blair
David F. Blenckstone
Richard A. Brull
Jeffrey A. Budnitz
Robert A. Burgin
John J. Campanella
H. Christopher Carroll, Jr.
Gregory Derogatis
Brian C. Doak
Mark Albert Dugan
Sarath H. Fernando
Gregory K. Finkelstein
A. John Frankian
David K. Gildea
Christopher Gunst
William R. Harman, Jr.
Lee Hendler
John R. Hornady IV
Shawn E. Hoshall
David M. Huether
Dawayne M. Judd
Francis X. Knott II
Baker R. Koppelman
Andrew P. Kreeger
John Linsenmeyer
William C. Luttrell
Carlos E. Millan
Douglas H. Miller
Charles R. Morrison
Edward L. Morton
James R. Murphy
B. Sanders Nice
Trent W. Nichols III
Hensie D. Page
R. Scott Pierce
S. Gerard Reid
David Scott Richardson
D. Stewart Ridgely III
A. VanVleck Robinson
Todd A. Sapre
Thomas B. Scheffenacker
Derek T. Seipp
Gregory A. Sekercan
Allen R. Shutt
John L. Sindler
Gregg R. Sobeck
E. Harrison Stone, Jr.
Hammond W. Swam
Pierre R. Theodore

Christian A. Tittel
Brandon J.L. Welch
Matthew A. Welsh
Thomas Wilby
A. Russell Wilkerson III
Johnathan L. Zipp

1987
Rayman I. Ally
John C.R. Archer, Jr.
Brian K. Bartholomay
Sami A. Brahim II
Christian M. Brandjes
Clayton D. Chilcoat
Mark A. Clements
A. Raj Dhar
Scott G. Dietz
Jeffery M. Finke
C. Todd B. Garliss, Jr.
Scott M. Gibbons
Spaulding A. Goetze, Jr.
James R. Hedeman III
Robert A. Herbert
Lee H. Hine
Kenton R. Holden, Jr.
Mark A. Horney
Louis Horst III
Kevin K. Knox
M. Alexander Koch
Charles J. Kresslein
Michael J. Kresslein
Mark F. Leister
Stephen W. Mason
Gary S. Maxa
Serrick A. McNeill
Juan A. Millan
Alvaro A. Montoya
George B. Morris, Jr.
Gregory C. Naughton
Troy Evan Oden
Christopher B. Peterson
Gary O. Prem
John C. Rienhoff
William D. Rowe II
Mitchell G. Schmale
Jeffrey K. Schultz
William S. Scott III
Alfie P. Shird
Carter W.W. Smith
Benjamin C. Sutley
Michael S. Swanenburg
David H. Tambling
James S. Tokarz
Charles A.P. Turner
Paul A. Villmoore
Wilson Yan

1988
DeVere S. Beard
Timothy M. Beittel
E. Gillet Boyce II
Brian M. Brown
Timothy W. Burdette
Jonathan A. Collins
Matthew E. Costa
Charles T. Cummings
Bernard Francis D'Aleo
Jordon Keith Davies
John P. Demos
Sherif Elias
Reinaldo A. Fernandez
Benjamin B. Friedman
Keith M. Gatchalian
Mark David Groth
Ryan Hamilos

Daniel E. Hoff
Allan D. House
J. Michael House
Robert P. Howard
Steven J. Howard
W. Matthew Hyman
Darren M. Jones
F. Stuart Knott
Joshua L. Kogan
Joseph W. La Seta
Frank B. Martien
Matt T. Marx
Robert W. McCoy
Lance J. Miceli
Lorenzo Millan
Jonathan R. Mitchell
Clayton L. Moravec III
Mark W. Mueller
Christopher A. Pierce
Michael V. Piercy
Charles H. Platt
Vincent L. Reese
Brandt M. Rider
Dudley G. Riggs
Joseph W. Robinson
Christopher P. Rogers
J. Zachary Samios
Steven Schwartz
Paul R. Semon
Cregg R. Seymour
James S. C. Shindell
Jeffrey L. Simkin
David S. Stockbridge III
Thomas M. Stone
Joseph L. Sutton
James F. Thomas
John M. Townsend III
Bryan D. Tracey
Jason R. Trader
John G. Turnbull III
Justin H. Woelper
Bradley R. Wright

1989
Ryon H. Acey
Wilson K. Barnes III
Christopher L. Bunting
Andrew L. Coale
Frank D. Corto
Charles N. Curlett, Jr.
Evan P. Deane
Michael A. Dent
Timothy E. Eaton
C. Ian Fusting
Nicholas V. Giardina
Michael A. Giudice
Mitchell T. Goetze
Brian H. Heidelbach
David S. Kelly
Charles A. Lonsdale
Tommy S. Macris
John F. Menchey
Daniel H. Millender, Jr.
James P. Mitcherling
Kirk L. Olsen
Erik R. Ortel
Jeffrey S. Ousborne
Clifton G.M. Presser
Marshall L. Reid
Jason C. Rose
Michael T. Rumsey
James E. Samuel, Jr.
Robert A. Schauble
Scott G. Schuebel
Mark G. Senula

M. Alexander Shipley
Eric R. Smith
Patrick Neil Smith
John T. Tapscott
Scott C. Tognocchi
David B.W. Townsend
Nicholas B. Truitt
David A. Wagner
Jeffrey A. Wallace
John Wang
John J. Webster
Colin R. White

1990
Scott S. Bacigalupo
E. Collin Back
Stefan P. Beittel
Friederich J. Boetzelen
Eric D. Brotman
William R. Buttram, Jr.
Andrew T. Carter III
Mark Frederic Chase
E. Charles Covahey III
John F. Davies III
F. James Brown DeRose
Charles C. Emmons III
Michael I. Feinglass
Carroll D. Ford II
Gordon L. Fronk
Michael S. Fuller
C. Scott Garliss
Todd A. Goetze
Peter W. Greene
Robert Summer W. Haines
John B. Harrington
Robert W. Horst
Evan J. Klein
Todd P. Lamonia
Samuel E. Lee, Jr.
Geoffrey G. Leech
William G. Love
Charles W.S. MacKenzie
Zeke M. Marshall
Jan D. Maslack II
David E. Mattingly
Gregory A. McHale
Marmaduke S. Miles, Jr.
Paul E. Murray
Scott E. Reid
H. Charles Rienhoff
J. Andrew Robinson
Alexander L. Shreeve
Bryce J. Smith
D. Graham Smith
Samuel J. Spriggs, Jr.
Charles F. Stein IV
Christopher F. Trail
Robert S. Uhlfelder
R. Craig Walters
Brett M. Wells
Trevor W. Wells
Eric A. White
Matthew H. Woodworth
Patrick F. Worrall

1991
Nicholas M. Abbott
Jose Alonso
John F. Baker III
G. Graham Boyce
James D. Brown IV
Jeremy T. Bryant
Ross P. Charkatz
Wade H. Chilcoat
Albert L. Chung
John F. Cougle

Ming-Shi Du
Kyle S. Durkee
I. William Fannin III
Ian P. Faria
Michael H. Fronk
Christian Winter Fusting
Gary C. Geating
William P. Gibson
John J. Griggs III
Douglas E. Horelick
Richard H. Hubbard
Daniel G. Kelly
Nicholas Kennedy
Mark Paul Kohout
Nathaniel K. Low
Shawn M. Mahoney
Sean T. McAuliffe
Robert P. McDavid
J. Raul Molina
Angelo F. Otterbein
Jonas C. Packer
M. Mostafa A. Razzak
John M. Reazer
Brian D. Riley
N. Alexander Samios
Jeffrey A. Springer
Shane P. Tanzymore
W. Bradley Wallace, Jr.
G. Trevor Wilby
D. Seward Woelper
Tao-Chang Yu

1992
Theron O. Alexander
Harry Axelrad
Aaron G. Bean
Jamie W. Bell
Vipin Bhalla
Andrew M. Borst
Robert H. Bouse III
Derrell J. Bradford
Jeremy C. Brashear
Bradley K. Byrnes
Kevin M. Cooper
G. Russell Croft
Jeffrey Derogatis
Gregory C. Durham
Jeremy D. Eaton
Stephen W. Eggleston
Sean B. Frey
Benjamin D. Gannon
Joseph C. Gelbard
Dimitri A. Georgelakos
Craig R. Gift
Ryan P. Hanley
Jon C. Hartman
Jonathan S. Hemphill
John A. Hovanec
Jack C. Hubbard
Brendon M. Hunt
G. Simms Jenkins
Timothy D. Johns
Larry P. Katsafanas
Thomas R. Keratzes
John J. Kim
Brandon S. Levine
Shannon W. Locke
Alexis G. Lyons
Niels K. Maumenee
Anthony P. McCord
Karl F. Mech III
John B. Menzies
Darrin H. Millender
Thomas Kevin Morgan
Marc S. Nasrallah
T. Brett Naylor

John P. O'Hearn
Jeffrey R. Pacy
William J. Peeples
D. Sage Platt, Jr.
Oscar Ramirez
Scott R. Rockwell
Renato Rotondo
Randolph B.D. Roulette
Joshua A. Scheinker
Andrew C. Schnydman
Jason A. Schuyler
Anthony W. Schweizer
Craig P. Scornavacca
Benjamin J. Seigel
Todd M. Simkin
Matheau J.W. Stout
Mark A. Sutton
Troy A. Thingelstad
David C. Thompson, Jr.
Travis H. Trader
Alexander Trivas
Brian J. Tsai
John D. Uhlig
Miguel G. Vilar
Timothy C. Whiteley
G. Robert Wilson
Christopher M. Wimer

1993
Brant K. Bandiere
Nicholas O. Bent
Thomas R. Chilcoat
Adam H. Confer
Matthew A. Curtis
Joshua P. Dansicker
Jason B. Dorshow
Patrick M. Doyle
Sinclair Eaddy
Walid F. Gellad
Ziad F. Gellad
Peter A. Georgelakos
Bart A. Gerstenblith
A. Martin Gibbs
Timothy K. Gibson
Robert C. Gillis
Matthew C. Gilner
Eric D. Gregory
Ryan C. Grimes
Matthew K. Hankins
Steve H. Karvounis
Bryan G. Kernan
Carim V. Khouzami
Stephen B. Leggin
Allen S. Lloyd III
Todd C. Lowe
Joseph S. McCulloch IV
Jeremy A. Medeiros
Robert A.L. Meyer
Graham J.E. Miller
Christopher H. Nauta
Paul F. O'Hearn
Thomas M. O'Hearn
Charles E. Offutt
Jonathan K. Patton
Jorge A. Ramirez
Bradley C. Read
Haroon A. Rehman
Jeffrey B. Saxton
Ian R.K. Seletzky
Hugh M. Smallwood
Albert N. Smith III
Benjamin B. Strutt
Sean G. Tadaki
Joseph N. Tambling
James S. Thompson
Andrew S. Truitt

Jonathan G. Tsucalas
F. Joseph Unitas
Michael O. Watson
Joseph T. Willett
Jason R. Woods
Jason D. Woodward

1994
Ted R. Andersson
Lawrence J. Baird
Robert A. Ballentine
W. Parker Baxter III
Christian J. Beach
Shawn C. Bean
Thaddeus B. Bower
Damien Christea
Nathaniel F. Coughlin
A. Tolson DeSa
Jonathan J. Eckley
Matthew A.S. Esworthy
R. Grayson Frain II
Joseph B. Garliss
John W. Greene, Jr.
Joseph M. Grimm III
Daniel J. Hadley
Charles R. Harlan
Marshall W. Hawks
Scott J. Hendrick
Brian N. Hershfeld
Mitchell W. Hook
Jason S. Horich
Peter H. Karvounis
Sean J. Keenan
D. Scott Keir
J. Alexander Kelly
Jin Su Kim
James D. Love
Brett T. Lutz
Charles P. Merrick IV
Keith S. Miceli
Matthew B. Mueller
C. Ashton Newhall
J. Dawson Nolley
David J. Notarangelo
Laurence F. Oster
Frederick M. Peightal III
Chad J. Pfrommer
Matthew W. Pilachowski
Timothy A.V. Pollard
James A. Pollock
Eric G. Prior
Brian M. Reese
Jason M. Rockwell
William R. Ruhl
Adam Z. Salihi
Jeremy A. Scheinker
John R. Solter, Jr.
Matthew G. Springer
Michael E. Summerfield
Steven F. Truitt
R. Addison vonLunz
Christopher B. Walcutt
E. Justin Weigold
Mark A. Woodall
J. Ryan Woods
J. Todd Yuhanick
David B. Zienty
A. Brandt Zipp

1995
Alexander B. Bartlett
Gregory Bassmann
James R. Bendos
Nathaniel J. Bent
Clarke T. Bessent
T. Erich Black

Peter J. Boscas
David G. Cameron
Matthew F. Celentano
Neal M. Charkatz
Craig C. Ciekot
Robert S. Coleman
Andy H. Cooper
Matthew F. Crafton
Craig D'Alessio
Nicholas DeLeonardis
Matthew A. Emmons
Padraic J. Fahey
Eric G. Finke
Owen D. Fitter
Michael J. Franks
R. Alexander Franyo
D. Jefferson Freedenburg
Sean R. Gamber
J. Esteban Garcia
Joel A. Gellar
Patrick J. Giardina
Douglas L. Hickman
Ryan J Hilliard
James F. Hillier
Joey J. Hipolito
George H. Hocker III
Joshua C. Hooper
W. Preston Jacobs
Alan Janofsky
Christopher A. Johnston
Gordon L. Kaufman, Jr.
Edward W. Kissinger
Yuri Konetspolskaya
Christopher F. Laporte
Jarrod B. Lippy
David K. McCarter
G. William McCulloch
Thomas A. McInnes, Jr.
Stephen J. Miller
E. Tileston Mudge V
John D. Nesbitt
Robert M. O'Shaughnessy
Scott R. Paymer
Gokul G. Prabhu
Thomas H. Pritchard
J. Tucker Radebaugh
Hasan A. Rehman
Christopher N. Rockwell
Sean O. Shafik
Thomas S. Sheldon
Christopher J. Singletary
Kevin B. Stevenson
Timothy C. Swiss
Steven M. Taylor
John S. Thrash
Garth A.L. Timoll
Jason M. Turner
Robert D. Uhlig
Alejandro J. Vilar
Bruce D. Wallace
Gregory P. Yin

1996
David I. Ally
Peter J. Belitsos
Christopher A. Berrier
William O. Bond
Brandon J. Bortner
Carl B. Boucher
Cornell A. Brown
Tiano M. Brown
William G. Burdt
Ray J. Chang
Woo S. Choe
Robert B. Coale

Index

Photo Sources and Credits: